A. PHILIP RANDOLPH

Jervis Anderson

A. PHILIP RANDOLPH
A Biographical Portrait

Harcourt Brace Jovanovich, Inc.
New York

B
Randolph,
A. P.

First edition
ISBN 0–15–107830–0
Library of Congress Catalog Card Number: 72–88790
Printed in the United States of America
B C D E

Most of the material in this book appeared originally in *The New Yorker,* in slightly different form.

The poem "If We Must Die," by Claude McKay, is from *Selected Poems of Claude McKay,* copyright 1953 by Bookman Associates, and is reprinted by permission of Twayne Publishers, Inc. The Carnegie Corporation of New York granted permission to quote extensively from Ralph Bunche's unpublished research memorandum "The Programs, Ideologies, Tactics, and Achievements of Negro Betterment and Interracial Organizations," prepared for the Carnegie Foundation–Gunnar Myrdal Study, June, 1940. The excerpts from *Eleanor and Franklin,* by Joseph P. Lash, are reprinted by permission of W. W. Norton & Company, Inc., New York, and André Deutsch Limited, London, copyright © 1971 by Joseph P. Lash.

To the memory
of my mother and father

Salvation for a race, nation, or class must come from within. Freedom is never granted; it is won. Justice is never given; it is exacted. Freedom and justice must be struggled for by the oppressed of all lands and races, and the struggle must be continuous, for freedom is never a final fact, but a continuing evolving process to higher and higher levels of human, social, economic, political and religious relationships.

—A. PHILIP RANDOLPH

They say that he [Randolph] is absolutely to be trusted, that he cannot be influenced unduly. He stands four-square to all the winds, he stoops to no wiles or artifices to attain his goals. He is steeped in principle, and he has the complete certainty of a true reformer in the eventual triumph of his cause. He adopts none until he is certain it is morally right and that it will result in advantage to the entire community. Like the Abolitionists this makes it impossible for him to be discouraged or to be lacking in patience; he can wait indefinitely—certain of the righteous ending of the battle in which he fights.

—OSWALD GARRISON VILLARD

Contents

Illustrations

Preface

When I came to the United States, in the fall of 1958, I had no idea who A. Philip Randolph was. In Jamaica, where I was raised, I had never seen or heard his name. This, I later thought, was strange. By the time I left the island, I was in my early twenties. And though I had not been in close touch with the course of the black struggle in America, the names of some of the prominent participants were familiar to me.

Through the *Gleaner,* our only morning newspaper, where I got my first job after high school, I had learned of Walter White, the NAACP, Roy Wilkins, the Reverend Adam Clayton Powell, Jr., the Reverend Martin Luther King, Jr., Marian Anderson, Paul Robeson. C. L. R. James and W. A. Domingo were supposed to be prominent West Indian radicals in the United States. The *Gleaner*'s editor, Theodore Sealy, was fond of recalling Claude McKay, whom he had known before McKay migrated to America to become an important poet and left-wing intellectual. One of my uncles in Kingston liked to read to me from his old, dog-eared copy of Marcus Garvey's *Philosophy and Opinions.* He had lived briefly in Cuba as a young man, in the 1920's, and had joined Garvey's Universal Negro Improvement Association. In the late 1950's, when he was past sixty—and when, as it seemed to me, he had lost almost all interest in public controversy—Garvey was the only political memory that occasionally brought the spark back into his eyes. For a year before leaving Jamaica, I worked for a weekly newspaper, *Public Opinion,* the voice of the island's Socialist and independence movement, which was then led with uncommon brilliance by the late N. W. Manley. There I met Peter Abrahams, the South African novelist and Pan-African intellectual, who had recently come to live in Jamaica. Abrahams told me of the profound influence of W. E. B. Du Bois upon the development of his racial consciousness as well as upon the Pan-African movement. But nowhere had I ever seen or heard a word about A. Philip Randolph.

I was therefore surprised, on coming to the United States, to find that Randolph was a figure of enormous distinction in American life, and one of the major protagonists, in this century, of the struggle for black freedom and social justice. If I had not discovered that even then, it would soon become clear, as I heard and read more about him, and as the civil rights movement—over which he diffused a lifetime's fund of moral prestige—swelled to its crest in August of 1963.

It would not be true to say that I have been thinking, ever since the early 1960's, of writing a book about Randolph. In fact, it was hardly the kind of enterprise that would have enticed me. This was not, obviously, because there was nothing to write about him, but, on the contrary, because there appeared to be so much, and because he himself was already installed so monumentally in the public mind that there seemed no point in attempting further memorials. It is true, though, that since the early sixties I have been greatly absorbed with Randolph's history, and, especially since 1967, when I met him, with the connections between—and the contradictions of—his public career and personal character.

What I have written—in preparation since April, 1969, when Randolph turned eighty—is not, and was not intended to be, a biography. It seeks not to portray Randolph's life in exhaustive detail, to appraise his stature as a black figure, or to assess his place in American history. I call what I have done a biographical portrait, and it bears the marks of my own selective interest and curiosity—as well as the irrevocable loss of some of the most important biographical sources in Randolph's life. While Randolph co-operated generously with my efforts to obtain material, he asked nothing in return, not even a chance to see the manuscript.

In retracing the main outlines of his life—lingering here and there over my absorption with his character—I have simply wanted to see for myself the road he has traveled, how he handled himself along the way, and, more clearly, the kind of man he has become.

I / Prologue

His old-fashioned office is situated in an ancient building overlooking the main street of Harlem, USA. Yet it is a command post looked to for tactical consultation and strategic advice by leaders of mass movements from Montgomery, Ala., to the Sahara and elsewhere. Visitors from Asian and African nations beat a path to his door. He has lived most of his 70 years in this city; yet he is perhaps better known abroad than he is on the street where he lives.

—WILLIAM DUFTY, in the *New York Post*,
December 28, 1959

1 / Native Grounds

These were the poorest people of the South, who poured into New York City during the decade following the Great Depression. These migrants were told that unlimited opportunities for prosperity existed in New York and that there was no "color problem" there. They were told that Negroes lived in houses with bathrooms, electricity, running water, and indoor toilets. To them this was the "promised land" that Mammy had been singing about in the cotton fields for many years.

        —CLAUDE BROWN, in *Manchild in the Promised Land*

Blacks had started coming to New York City long before the Great Depression. One was Asa Philip Randolph, who lived in Harlem throughout most of its history as a black community, having arrived there in 1911, at the end of the first modern wave of black migration to the North. During the years of World War I, there had been an even greater flow—the one that furnished the Northern reservoir for Marcus Garvey's great black nationalist movement. Then, as Brown says, there had been the swell after the Great Depression. The migrants, especially the ones before the Great Depression, did not come only from the South. Thousands came from the West Indies. Nor were all the Southerners from the cotton fields. Some were businessmen and aspiring politicians; and some, like the young Asa Randolph, were budding intellectuals filled with dreams of careers in art, education, entertainment, or the arenas of political protest and radicalism. But Brown was absolutely right: to all of them New York City—Harlem—was the promised land.

It did not, as we know, turn out quite that way. A few people found what had chiefly drawn them there. Aspiring black Republican politicians, men like Charles Anderson and Edward A. Johnson, achieved great power and prestige in Harlem during the first two and a half decades of the century. Real-estate men and speculators did so well for themselves that they are to be credited with having opened up Harlem as a black residential community. And those who came merely in search of "houses with bathrooms, electricity, running water, and indoor toilets" cannot have been disappointed. The essence of what New York City, or Harlem, promised, however, was freedom from the "color problem"—an equal opportunity for the pursuit of racial and political happiness—and this freedom, if it is not as elusive today as it once was, is yet to be fully achieved.

Yet the early Harlem experience was not a total loss. The migrants, especially during and after World War I, established the most important black cultural and political community in America. By the mid-1920's, the community's drive for self-definition and self-expression would generate one of the most spectacular bursts of black creative activity—the literary and cultural Harlem, or Negro, Renaissance—the country has ever witnessed. Politically, Harlem was also, for all its limits, for all the aspirations it imprisoned, a somewhat freer place in which to operate, to articulate the demand for black freedom, than any other oppressed or colonized black community or country in the world. Thus Harlem became, even before the Renaissance, the international center of black nationalist and black radical agitation, giving an enormous impetus to the awakening of black mass consciousness in other parts of America and the world.

The "heresies" that young black radicals and nationalists—migrants like Hubert Harrison, W. A. Domingo, Marcus Garvey, Chandler Owen, and A. Philip Randolph—could preach in the halls and on the street corners of Harlem during World War I, the magazines they could write, edit, and circulate, would, at the time, have earned them imprisonment in the West Indies, probably banishment from colonial Africa, and, quite likely, murder in the South. But as an example of the inspiration these "heresies" gave to other black freedom movements, Kwame Nkrumah, who led Ghana to independence, said years later that the most influential book he read as a young student in the United States was Marcus Garvey's collection of speeches and newspaper writings, *Philosophy and Opinions*. Another example is Jamaica, West Indies, whose independence movement—the People's National party—emerged out of a small group that Jamaican W. A. Domingo, once one of Randolph's closest radical collaborators, organized in Harlem in the late 1930's.

The two most important main streets in the history of black Harlem have been 135th and 125th. One Hundred Thirty-fifth, between Fifth and Seventh avenues, gave blacks their first taste of fine tenement dwelling in the community. It was from those immediate environs that black residency pushed outward, steadily darkening once all-white Harlem. It was at the intersection of 135th Street and Lenox Avenue, spawning ground of the first generation of Harlem radicals, that the young A. Philip Randolph, a native of Jacksonville, Florida, made his first appearance as a street-corner agitator. And it was in that general area that the headquarters, the magazines, and the newspapers of all the black radical and nationalist organizations of World War I—notably Randolph's *Messenger* and Marcus Garvey's Universal Negro Improvement Association—were based.

By the late 1920's, nationalism and radicalism no longer in vogue, and black Harlem having spread rapidly outward, 125th Street—formerly an all-white preserve—had become the new center. It was a different kind of center, though, lacking the distinctly black historical and intellectual flavors that once clung to 135th. It was brasher, gaudier, and saucier, given more to the arts of pleasure, entertainment, business, and consumption. But, in a way that 135th had never been, it became, and would remain, a paradigm of the total life of Harlem, a crucible of its various styles, flavors, politics, and warring business interests. In 1925—when Harlem lost the moderate interest it had once taken in radicals of his stripe—A. Philip Randolph organized a union of sleeping car porters; and, joining the migration of action from 135th Street, he and the porters' union also came to 125th Street, where, during the 1940's, the Brotherhood of Sleeping Car Porters would become perhaps the most important black political institution in America.

Until it was torn down in 1969, to make way for an ultramodern concrete-and-glass structure, 217 West 125th Street—a few doors east of the Apollo Theater—was perhaps the most widely known office building in Harlem. Around the turn of the century, it had been an exclusive, all-white apartment dwelling, adjoining the Harlem Opera House—built by Oscar Hammerstein I in 1889. In 1937, some ten years after it had been converted into an office building, 217 received its most prestigious tenant, the nationally known Brotherhood of Sleeping Car Porters—which, after a heroic twelve-year struggle, had recently won recognition from the Pullman Company. Randolph's union was still the most renowned tenant there when, in 1968, it moved to new headquarters, at 103 East 125th Street.

By then the Brotherhood had seen its best days. It had never been one of the larger unions (at the height of its power and influence, in 1941, it had 15,000 members), and, in 1968, the membership had dropped to about 2,000. What remained of its prestige rested upon the important role it had played between 1940 and 1950—when it had been the spearhead and the principal sustenance of black mass politics in America—and upon the even greater reputation of its head, A. Philip Randolph, whom it had catapulted into a position of national leadership in the labor and civil rights struggles.

During the March on Washington movement of the 1940's, when Randolph became the leading black public figure in the country, 217 West 125th Street had been the political headquarters of black America; and though, during the 1950's—when the modern civil rights movement began to emerge—it was superseded in importance by other black headquarters, it still remained, until 1968, one of the country's essential political addresses. It was where political figures of different colors, nationalities, and outlooks came to confer with Randolph. Because of Randolph's presence, it was one of the few places in Harlem where community groups of diverse political persuasions could meet over common grievances. And it was perhaps the only place in America where the younger civil rights chieftains of the 1950's and 1960's occasionally forgot their personal and organizational rivalries.

The most prominent of these younger leaders in 1958 were Roy Wilkins, of the NAACP; Lester Granger (soon to be succeeded by Whitney Young), of the National Urban League; James Farmer, of the Congress of Racial Equality; Dr. Martin Luther King, Jr., of the Southern Christian Leadership Conference; and Bayard Rustin, an eclectic pacifist, Socialist, and black radical. When a spokesman was required for the entire civil rights movement, and the younger leaders could not agree upon a candidate among themselves, they agreed on Randolph—both because of his age and because he had the longest and most consistent record of service in the freedom movement.

After a White House meeting with President Eisenhower, in June of 1958, Roy Wilkins explained why Randolph had been designated spokesman: "We felt that he was the best qualified by long experience,

knowledge of the problems . . . and because he was so articulate."
Granger said he deferred because Randolph "was the senior among us
not only in terms of age but in national prestige. He was known on the
national scene before any of us in that delegation, and before Martin
Luther King, Jr., was born." As always, however, the primary reason had
been because they could not bring themselves to elevate one of their
number into the leadership of the civil rights movement. Though they all
respected Randolph, their ambitions were such that some of them were
not too keen to have him around, and would have preferred if his prestige did not intrude itself so frequently upon their own sovereignty.

Randolph's office at the Brotherhood's headquarters looked out over
125th Street. It was a long rectangular room, covered with a pale green
wall-to-wall carpet, and sparsely furnished. At the eastern end was his
desk, and at the other end was an old wine-colored leather couch, soft
and well broken from long use. An American flag and an ensign of the
Brotherhood stood at either end of the couch. There was a large book-
case, against a wood-paneled partition, halfway between the couch and
Randolph's desk. And all four walls were hung with large photographs of
the founding officers of the union: Randolph himself; Milton Webster, of
Chicago; Bennie Smith, of Detroit; Ashley Totten and Thomas T. Patterson, of New York; E. J. Bradley, of St. Louis; and C. L. Dellums, of
Oakland.
A visitor's first impression of Randolph's office was one of serenity,
especially when he was there working quietly, his horn-rimmed glasses in
place, and looking—despite his splendid presence—somewhat lonely in
the large, slightly darkened room. The first impression of his office would
endure, but that glimpse of him was usually fleeting. No sooner did a
visitor enter than Randolph laid aside his work, took off his glasses, and
left his desk to meet his guest in the middle of the room. Tall, and smiling cordially yet correctly, he always looked tastefully dressed. This appearance, together with the gracefulness of his movement and the slightly
studied fluency of his gestures, suggested some past attachment to matters of fashion and an enduring one to the idea of style.
In the summer, he usually had on a blue serge suit, complete with a
black vest—or a beige sweater buttoned down the front—a knitted black
tie on white shirt, and a white handkerchief seeming sometimes to flower
rakishly out of his breast pocket. At other times of the year, he showed a
preference for heavy tweeds. By the early 1960's, when his health began

to worsen, he presented a fragile, sensitive, and often grave face, which looked striking under his soft white hair. Now he no longer carried the large heavyweight's body he had developed in the 1940's, but was returning to the willowy one of his younger years, when, as a young radical in Harlem, during World War I, he had been referred to by a detractor as "string-bean Randolph."

In 1960, however, at the age of seventy-one, he was still erect of bearing, as if it were a stance he was no more ready or able to surrender than his nature. There was, yes, a slight drop in the shoulders, but on him it did not seem an omen of the advancing years so much as an extra element of his elegance. He walked briskly—partly a willed defiance of age and partly out of habit—looking, with the lively swing of his arms, like a cross between a soldier and an esthete of lithe, smart movement. As one would hear from him, a good deal of this style was rooted in the earliest memories and commands of his father. Overall, he recalled the spirit of Arthur Schlesinger, Jr.'s description of Andrew Mellon: "Slight and frail, with prominent features in a grave face, he had a gentle Edwardian formality of manner and dress." But since Randolph was a tall, smooth, and cool black, and since his view of his life—or its early commands— had required him to assert a formal dignity that the aristocratic Mellon might have been able to take for granted, his features and aspects of his bearing recalled more appropriately those of Juano Hernandez, as one remembers him playing Lucas Beauchamp in the film of William Faulkner's *Intruder in the Dust*. In any event, it was no wonder—as Murray Kempton once remarked—that the old sleeping car porters called him "chief," and handled him as delicately as they would "a piece of old china."

On the afternoons when he had no visitors in his office, Randolph took off his jacket, unbuttoned his vest, loosened his tie, and stretched out on the old wine-colored couch for a nap—like a country lawyer, someone said. This was not just a way of nursing his strength; it was also his only way of relaxing. C. L. Dellums, of the Brotherhood, who has known and worked with him since 1926, says that "Randolph learned to sit erect and walk erect. You almost never saw him leaning back, reclining. No matter how enjoyable the occasion, you look around and there's Randolph just as straight as if there was a board in his back. He can't relax the way you and I do when we're sitting around talking. The only time he does is when he puts on his pajamas and props himself up in bed."

"The man had so much dignity," Dellums says, mentioning one of the characteristics of Randolph most widely remarked upon, "it was as much a part of him as his limbs." Nothing so confirms this as an incident that took place the night of March 26, 1965. It was at the end of the civil rights march from Selma to Montgomery. Randolph, who had joined the final leg of the journey, was standing in the Montgomery airport, awaiting a flight to New York, when—suffering one of the spells of dizziness sometimes caused by his heart ailment—he collapsed. "I've never seen anything like that in my life," recalls Rachelle Horowitz, Bayard Rustin's secretary, who, with Rustin—head of the A. Philip Randolph Institute—was waiting to accompany Randolph back to New York. "He complained that he was feeling tired, and before we could do anything, he was falling backwards. But no one ever fell backwards like that. His eyes were wide open, and he was still bolt upright—going down with absolute dignity."

Those of Randolph's admirers who are inspired by his dignity protect it with as much zealousness as he does. After Randolph collapsed, Rachelle Horowitz says, "Photographers, thinking he was going to die, rushed forward, with flash bulbs poised. But Bayard held them off with his fists. He said nobody was going to get a shot of Randolph flat on his back." Nor would Rustin risk leaving Randolph in a Jim Crow hospital in the South. He placed Randolph on Dick Gregory's chartered jet, and flew with him to New York.

Joseph L. Rauh, a Washington attorney and a long-time partisan of liberal, labor, and civil rights causes, recalls:

In 1950 Mr. Randolph asked me to help get the Brotherhood of Sleeping Car Porters into the Railway Labor Executives Association. The Labor Executives had a nice lily-white organization of all the presidents of all the railway labor unions, and they excluded Mr. Randolph. So we filed suit saying that they had no right to keep us out. When they saw we were winning they decided to discuss a settlement. They invited Mr. Randolph and me to come to the Hamilton Hotel [Washington, D.C.] to talk the matter over with them. They did not even offer us a seat when we entered the room. This made me sick, but I didn't say anything. Nor did Mr. Randolph. George Harrison, president of the Railway Clerks, who is seated, says, "Randolph, I understand you want to be a member of the Railway Labor Executives." Mr. Randolph said, "Yes, I believe we are entitled to membership." George Harrison says, "It'll cost you," and named a fabulous figure—several thousand dollars. I didn't see what the hell was worth it. I looked over to Mr. Randolph and he never blinked an eye. He said, "We will meet our obligations." And Harrison said, "Well, you're a member of the Railway Labor Executives," and sort of dismissed us.

This was late in the evening, and I remember something else. We went out and he thanked me, and he was so nice in thanking me for having won that fight. We were standing on the northeast corner of Fourteenth and K streets, and I said, after he thanked me, "Well, Mr. Randolph, we ought to have a drink to celebrate this." Now, this is 1950 in Washington, D.C. In that period you couldn't go to a restaurant with a Negro, you couldn't go to a movie with a Negro, they still had restrictive covenants. In other words, this was a Southern Jim Crow town. "Well, Mr. Rauh," Mr. Randolph said, "of course we should have a drink to celebrate this. Where do you suggest we go?" Boy, this was a loaded question. I said, "Mr. Randolph, you have two choices." He said, "What are they?" I said, "Well, there's my house, where my wife would love to give us a drink—and she knows of my real reverence for you—or we can go to the railroad station, because there is no bar or restaurant where you and I would be accepted." I'll never forget this if I live to be a thousand: he looked at me and he said, "Mr. Rauh, I think it would be preferable if you and I had a symbolic drink here on the corner." Then he paused just a fraction of a second and said, "I bid you good night," and turned on his heel and walked away. It's something I'll never forget, because I've never seen such magnificent dignity.

Though his health was failing, Randolph's voice retained the power and attractiveness of his younger years. After hearing him speak at the March on Washington, a reporter from the *New York Times* observed that Randolph's voice was "soft and deep, almost like an organ," and that his language, "biblical in its eloquence, never seems directed to his immediate audience, but somewhere out beyond, perhaps to the whole human race." Also remarkable was his accent, suggesting a cultivated mating of the Bostonian and the West Indian. People have been as curious about the influences upon his "cawn't," "enhawnce," and "mawsses"—not to mention the antique words he uses, like "verily" and "vouchsafe"—as they have been about the sources of his dignity. How did *he* come to talk like that? "He pronounces his words so grandly," a black woman said, after hearing him for the first time, "that you'd swear he was putting on an act. It's only when you look at him and listen a little longer that you know he's a real sincere man."

Throughout his life, it was the people who wondered about his accent who were responsible for spreading the idea all over America that he was educated at Harvard. He had never received anything from Harvard—at least, not until June, 1971, when it gave him an honorary Doctor of Laws for being "a wise and courageous leader of labor, pioneer champion of civil rights, whose early and unflagging struggle for justice and widened economic opportunity made a signal contribution to our nation's life." He had never even earned an academic degree, though he had been an evening student at the City College of New York. Randolph himself has confessed to three major formative influences upon his speech: listening to his father, a self-trained preacher of the African Methodist Episcopal church in Jacksonville, whose sense of language had been shaped by the Bible and the black Reconstruction oratory of the Reverend Henry Mc-Neal Turner; studying Shakespeare and elocution, when he had thought, as a young man, of becoming an actor; and reading the abolitionist speeches of Frederick Douglass and Wendell Phillips.

One of the paradoxes of Randolph's character, considered so, at least, by many who are frustrated in their attempts to know him more intimately, is the contradiction between the generosity of his public emotions and the wall he has erected around his private self and feelings—having, not unlike the Amherst poetess, selected his own personal society and closed the door. The wall seems to have been there for so long, and Randolph has grown so accustomed to the privacy it encloses, that he accepts it as a matter of course, and has little or no sense of what "strangers" suffer when they collide against it—or that they should suffer. He eludes inquiry into his personal world either by changing the subject—though always deftly and gracefully—or, to deflect a question, by giving a quite different answer from the one sought. He is a man of enormous good manners and good taste, and, at this point of a conversation, relies upon similar qualities in a questioner. But, as such men are, he is often disappointed. Still, pressed again on his point of reticence, he retains his manners and himself. He suggests, with a disarming smile, that "perhaps we could talk about that at some other time"—hoping, usually, that there will not be another time, or, if there will be, that the curiosity of the moment will dissolve in the interim.

Perhaps he is a surviving exemplar of the values of reticence that civilized personal conduct at an earlier time—for there cannot now be many people who are at a greater polar remove from the current vogues of exposé and the personal confessional. Or perhaps there is nothing more to say than simply that Randolph is a certain version of the gentleman. According to a character in Faulkner's *Sartoris,* "To be a gentleman, you must have secrets." Faulkner might well have liked Randolph, if, as Jean-Paul Sartre once observed, "the men Faulkner likes . . . are men who have secrets and keep quiet." And yet one is tempted to wonder about Randolph—as Sartre wondered about Faulkner—"What does he do when he's alone? Does he put up with the endless prattle of his all too human consciousness?"

As far as can be ascertained, only a handful of people have shared Randolph's inmost thoughts: his parents; his brother, James; his wife, Lucille; his radical comrade of World War I and the early twenties, Chandler Owen; the man with whom he built the Brotherhood of Sleeping Car Porters, Milton Webster; and, possibly, Bayard Rustin—all, except the last, now deceased. Thus people who cannot think of him without paying tribute to his graciousness, courteousness, politeness, and compassion for social causes also cannot avoid commenting upon his apparent aloofness.

The late Gertrude Elise Ayer, a former Harlem school principal, and one of Randolph's political associates in the twenties, once said of him, "He is full of lovely greeting, but greeting is enough. As long as he has known me, he sometimes looks at me with his sweet smile, and says, 'Do I know you?' I refuse to tell him my name. He's a very cordial man, but what a strange sort of cordiality! I don't think he's really a social person." A Harlem journalist—another former colleague who has known Randolph since the latter first came to New York—says today, "Randolph is not a colorful character privately. Publicly he is. I don't think he'd have many insights to give."

Other acquaintances have been puzzled and hurt by his "strange sort of cordiality." One day in 1943, Randolph and his friend Milton Webster were having lunch in the Palm Café, on Chicago's South Side, when Willard Townsend and the United Electrical Workers' James Carey came in. Randolph had never met Carey, but knew Willard Townsend, who was black, very well. He had helped Townsend organize the redcaps —porters who worked in train stations and terminals—into the United Transport Service Employees of America. Seeing his old pals in the café, Townsend, said to be one of the most gregarious men in the country, took Carey over to their table to introduce him. "Townsend," according to an observer, "expected to be received warmly as one of the boys fighting discrimination in the labor movement. Instead, Randolph was stiff and cordial, and Webster was so frosty that Townsend wanted to sock him. Carey considered the reception 'positively insulting.' "

Yet Randolph's formal cordiality at other times could be quite winning. Every Christmas, before his wife died, he used to have baskets of fruit and flowers sent over to his neighbors—in the Dunbar Apartments, at 150th Street and Seventh Avenue. Along with the baskets, he sent little notes extending "felicitations of the season from my dear, beautiful wife and myself to you, my good neighbors, without which the good life is unattainable." One day in 1948, while leading the campaign to desegregate the armed forces, he learned that one of his assistants had sent a mimeographed letter to President Truman. Though he was not excessively fond of Truman at the time, he considered it a breach of etiquette to send a mimeographed letter to the President of the United States. He wrote Truman, expressing his personal apology.

But underlying all this graciousness, however formal and stiff at times, was a surprising toughness and resiliency. Murray Kempton once wrote, "His only vanity is his manners. . . . He carries a courtesy so old-fashioned that the white men with whom he negotiates are sometimes driven to outsized rages by the shock that anyone so polite could cling so stubbornly to what he believes."

Another important section of the Brotherhood's headquarters, on West 125th Street, was the porters' recreation room. Old porters came there every day to play card games and exchange memories. On occasion, the room, also called the union's auditorium, was used for community meetings or press conferences. The community meetings, convened around Randolph's prestige, brought together a number of transient and warring coalitions, including even, sometimes, the Black Muslims. The latter were there only because of the personal regard that Randolph and Malcolm X—despite their differences—had for each other during the early 1960's. "All civil rights leaders are confused," Malcolm X was once quoted as saying, "but Randolph is less confused than the rest." And Randolph, who then considered himself "a friend and admirer of Malcolm," was the only one of the major civil rights figures who invited the Muslim minister to meetings of common interest to blacks in New York. Malcolm did not always want to come. He said he didn't believe black people were going to get anything from such meetings, that whatever they got they would have to take. Randolph would reply that he agreed, but that "blacks are not going to take anything without organization." He once recited to Malcolm a passage that often recurs in his public speeches: "At the banquet table of nature there are no reserved seats. You get what you can take, and you keep what you can hold. If you can't take anything, you won't get anything; and if you can't hold anything you won't keep anything. And you can't take anything without organization." But, of course, as both men well understood, organization was not the main issue between them—what chiefly stood between them was their different perceptions of what they wanted to take.

One of the meetings Malcolm agreed to attend in the Brotherhood's auditorium, in 1962, had been organized by a group called the Committee on Social and Economic Unity—comprising representatives of labor, civil rights, religious, and civic organizations from the black and Puerto Rican communities. Randolph invited Malcolm to represent the black nationalist and Muslim points of view, since, he felt, they were legitimate parts of the total community sentiment. When Malcolm arrived, however, a number of Harlem ministers, objecting to his presence, threatened to walk out. Malcolm X's philosophy, they said, did not reflect the broad interests of the committee. Randolph replied that if Malcolm was not allowed to sit, then he himself would have to withdraw. When any group sent an emissary to a community meeting, he argued, that emissary was entitled to be recognized. This attitude was probably why the Black Muslims trusted Randolph more than they did any other black leader.

One of the last important community meetings in the Brotherhood's auditorium was held in December, 1966. It was called by Randolph to protest the action of the House of Representatives in stripping Adam Clayton Powell—who held the seat in Congress that was once Randolph's for the asking—of his chairmanship of the Education and Labor Committee. Many who knew that Powell had for years disparaged "civil rights leaders" like Randolph, and who felt that Powell's conduct as a congressman was not exactly above reproach, criticized Randolph for organizing a meeting in his defense. But Randolph saw Powell as the most prominent and powerful black elected official in the country, who, because of his committee chairmanship, was in a position to influence government policies upon which millions of black Americans depended. And since, as Randolph felt, Powell was no guiltier of misconduct than several other congressmen, his demotion not only was a display of moral hypocrisy on the part of the House, but also reflected contempt for black citizens. "The community has to support Powell," Randolph explained, "because it may be a generation before another Negro can attain the power the Congressman now has."

Still, those whose feelings about Powell were not moderated by any such sense of his political importance continued to believe that Randolph, in defending the Congressman, was squandering valuable prestige. No doubt, it was decisions of this kind that had led one journalist to remark that "Randolph has never betrayed anyone except in some of his political endorsements." It may also have been why Murray Kempton observed that "as always, when the cold wind blows upon a sinner in Harlem there's no cloak for him but Mr. Randolph's." This was probably true, for, according to Livingston Wingate, one of Powell's more ardent supporters, Randolph was the only figure in the community who could have organized an effective protest meeting in the Congressman's behalf. "With me alone," Wingate told a reporter, "they'd have just said I'm Adam's boy. They'd have said that about any of us. But they can't say that about Randolph."

The more than 250 political, religious, and civil rights representatives at the meeting included Jesse Gray, a leader of the Harlem rent strike movement; Percy Sutton, Manhattan Borough President; Basil Patterson, New York State Senator; William Booth, New York City Commissioner of Human Rights; Bayard Rustin, executive director of the A. Philip Randolph Institute; and the Reverend Wyatt Tee Walker, pastor of Harlem's Canaan Baptist Church.

It was "a terribly disordered meeting," one observer said. "Everyone's anger kept running off onto side streets." In the *New York Times,* David Halberstam made special note of Jesse Gray, "clad in a sweater, angry in his language, serving warning to all white men on the Powell issue." Amidst all the disorder, Halberstam said, Randolph, the chairman, not only remained calm, but was also "elegant, aloof and professorial in his language"—or, as he struck the man from the *New York Post,* acting "as though he were presiding over the House of Lords."

The older residents of Harlem had grown accustomed to seeing Randolph acting that way. Not all of them shared or understood the attitudes in which such a manner was rooted, but some humored it and others respected it—in the way they would not bother to examine the ceremonial authorities of an old community bishop or an old chief. The younger Harlemites, however—young enough not to be burdened by their elders' deference—felt neither humor nor respect for Randolph or the ceremony in him. Nothing so illustrated the extremes of attitude that the older and younger generations held toward Randolph than an incident, during the meeting, which Kempton reported in the *New York Post:*

A young man by the name of Donald Washington kept interrupting with ill-founded imprecations against Percy Sutton. . . . He went on for a long time, until Randolph with immense patience said it was time for him to go home. Washington answered: "You're not my leader. I'm not a porter." The men in the hall had listened for an hour with tolerance that exists only in Harlem to an adolescent berating the Borough President. . . . But then Donald Washington said "You're not my leader. . . ." When Washington said one word to Mr. Randolph, a huge adult voice rang through the hallway: "Don't you talk to him like that," and someone slapped Washington's mouth as a man might a small boy. It was a rite of purification; everyone present, except, of course, Mr. Randolph, could forgive any excess except blasphemy.

From 1911, when he arrived from Jacksonville, at the age of twenty-two, to 1968, when, at the age of seventy-nine, he retired as president of the Brotherhood of Sleeping Car Porters, Randolph spent his entire active career in Harlem. For the last thirty-five of those years, he lived in the Dunbar Apartments, a five-acre complex of six houses, containing 511 apartments, at 150th Street and Seventh Avenue. Named after the poet Paul Laurence Dunbar, they were built by John D. Rockefeller, Jr., just before the Depression, to meet the demand by middle-class Harlemites for apartment living in keeping with their status. They are somewhat drab and run-down today—if they retain a vestige of middle-class excellence, it is only in comparison with some of the shabbier-looking tenements in the neighborhood—but in 1928, when they were completed, they were considered by architectural experts to be "the most attractive model tenement in America," and were awarded a first prize for design by the American Institute of Architects.

When they were opened, and for several years after, the Dunbar Apartments accepted only Harlem's top people. The first manager—whose name was an unnecessary ornament to the prestige of the enterprise—was Roscoe Conkling Bruce, son of the U. S. Senator from Mississippi during Reconstruction. To keep out "the lodger set," no roomers were allowed; nor were "the sporting fraternity, the daughters of joy, and the criminal element." Bruce personally interviewed every tenant, each of whom was required to present flawless references. Thus only clerks, civil servants, artists, prominent political figures, teachers, and Pullman porters—the more educated and prosperous of whom were considered "the aristocrats of Negro labor"—lived at the Dunbar. Some of the most notable residents over the years were Paul Robeson; Randolph; Layle Lane, a Socialist, schoolteacher, and pioneer in New York teacher unionism; Bill Robinson, the comedian and tap dancer; James Weldon Johnson; Leigh Whipper, once a prominent black actor; and Walter White, of the NAACP.

When Randolph moved there, in 1933, it was his standing in the community alone that qualified him; he had almost no income. Nineteen thirty-three, one of the worst years of the Depression, was also the year when his struggle—then more than seven years old—to organize the Brotherhood of Sleeping Car Porters almost collapsed. One day, he had come back from a trip to Chicago to find that his wife, Lucille, had borrowed the down payment on one of the five-room co-operative apartments, and moved in. The Randolphs' tenancy was to long outlive the Dunbar's glamour.

A midafternoon in the summer of 1968, Randolph left his office on West 125th Street to return, a bit earlier than usual, to his apartment. It was a hot day, and his physician, Dr. James Granady, had advised him on the phone to take the rest of the afternoon off. As he had done throughout his life in Harlem, he rode the bus home. He did not notice, when he got off the bus, that three young men had gotten off behind him and followed him across one of the courtyards of the Dunbar into his building.

Arriving at the door of his third-floor walk-up apartment, he was fumbling for his keys when they came up behind him. "Say, brother," one of them said, "have you got some money? I need carfare." Randolph said he had nothing but a quarter, fished it out of his pocket, and handed it over. "Oh, the old man must have more money than that, some real money," another of them said, grabbing him from behind. Locking his arm around Randolph's neck, the young man choked him while the others went through his pockets. They found a dollar. Disgusted, one of them threw the dollar to the floor. "See if he has any jewelry," the one holding Randolph said. "He must have a watch." When they found nothing on his wrist, or in his brief case, which they had snatched and rifled, they roughed him up against a wall, threw him down, and walked away —leaving him disheveled, his pockets hanging out, and his papers scattered around him. They probably had no idea who he was—though there is no way of knowing whether the knowledge would have made any difference. Of course, who they were is of no importance, except that by then they were not just the children but the grandchildren of some of the earliest arrivals in the promised land.

Randolph slowly picked himself up, collected his papers, and weakly unlocked the door of his apartment. Had he collapsed, there would have been no one at home to help. His wife, Lucille, had died on April 12, 1963, four months before the March on Washington—and three days before she turned eighty and he seventy-four. Their marriage had been childless, and he had been living by himself ever since. His housekeeper, Corrie Jones, a grandmother, living in Harlem—who had promised his wife to take care of the house as long as he or she lived—was out shopping for groceries. None of his neighbors had seen or heard the incident.

"Lucille Randolph," recalls Benjamin McLaurin, an officer of the Brotherhood, "was a beautiful and outgoing woman. She loved people. Randolph liked to be alone, but she sought people out all the time. She was a fine entertainer in her younger years; some of the best parties in Harlem were given by her. She read a lot, loved to tell stories, and once took a course in short-story writing at the New School for Social Research. She was also a woman of serious political ideas. She was once a member of the Socialist party and the American Labor party, and a good friend of Mary McLeod Bethune. And I've never known anyone more generous."

Lucille had been confined to a wheel chair for more than ten years before she died—suffering at first from arthritis and later from a broken hip, which never quite mended. Randolph, says a friend of the family, "prolonged her life by getting her the best treatment money could buy. Whenever she became very ill, he hired nurses around the clock, and if she had to go to the hospital he paid for the best care." The expenses over those years were considerable, especially for someone of Randolph's income. At no time in his life had he earned more than $15,000 a year. In 1959, an old friend wrote requesting a loan of $250. "I am sorry I cannot help you to this extent," Randolph replied. "You know Lucille has been ill for almost ten years . . . and, of course, this is quite a financial problem . . . but I am sending you $50."

Though he spent a good deal of his time out of town, traveling on Brotherhood or political business, Randolph was unstinting in his personal attentions to his ailing wife. As one of Lucille's friends in Harlem recalls, "When Mrs. Randolph was sick, A. Philip came home every evening he was in town and sat by her bedside and read her the day's newspapers, the Bible, or Shakespeare. If she was suffering during the night and couldn't sleep, he would leave his bed and go sit by hers, hold her hands and comfort her. Even after she died and he was living alone in the apartment, he went and sat in the same chair every evening by her bed and read to himself." During Lucille's illness, one of Randolph's cousins in Jacksonville came up to assist Corrie Jones. "He wouldn't allow us to feed her any cheap foods," the cousin remembers, "only the best cuts of steak. For months, at one time, the menu was nothing but steak. I ate steak until my hair started to fall out. Mrs. Jones and I used to make pancakes for ourselves, so one morning, on his way out, Mr. Randolph walked by the kitchen and stopped by the door. I guess he smelled what we were cooking. 'Please don't give her any pancakes,' he begged. Mrs. Jones and I couldn't even slip up and cook a biscuit, and everybody likes a nice biscuit. I guess a lot of things we did got across him, but he never showed it."

There was a certain justice in Lucille Randolph's total dependence upon her husband in the last years of her life, for she, early in their days together, had been not only the family's sole reliable breadwinner, but also a steady moral supporter of her husband's career in left-wing politics and labor organizing.

Deeply devoted, they were "Buddy" to each other throughout their marriage. When he was out of town, even if only for a few days, she wrote him, from her wheel chair, expressing concern for his welfare or issuing little wifely reminders "You must be careful," she once wrote to him in Los Angeles, "there is always someone on the lookout for guests whom they think have money. Don't keep your wallet in your pocket; keep it pinned to your inside shirt." And in 1954, she wrote to him in Chicago, "You know, Buddy, the 25th of this month is our 40th wedding anniversary and every one of our friends here is getting checks for their dates. Dr. G. was married 30 years, and Rose got a check. ——— Stevens, married 28 years, she got a check. Mrs. Simmons got a check. So please, Buddy, don't let me down. Please send me a check by return mail so I can show it, and put it right in the bank."

Though Randolph was one of the most handsome and attractive public figures in America, his wife entertained no jealousy over the amount of time he spent traveling or the many female admirers she knew he attracted. According to another of her female friends in Harlem, "There were always lots of women chasing Randolph. Some of them even came to the house under the guise of visiting Mrs. Randolph, but he never gave them a second look. Sometimes Lucille would have to call him out of his room where he was reading to be introduced to some of them. Of course, it never bothered her that all these women were after him. She used to say, 'Let them try.' She knew Randolph was absolutely faithful and that he had no time for them. Every excuse he got, every speech he made, he talked about his beautiful wife. Of course, that only made the bitches madder. Some of them used to say they wished Lucille would drop dead so they could have Randolph. After she died, women were calling him up from all over the United States. He had to change his telephone number and get an unlisted one."

A month after Randolph was mugged at the Dunbar, Bayard Rustin moved him downtown—into a five-room apartment in the co-operative houses built by the International Ladies' Garment Workers Union, in the Chelsea-Penn Station South district, where Rustin himself lives. "We had to move him for two reasons," Rustin says. "At his age and with his heart condition, we had to find a house where he didn't have to walk up three flights. Secondly, we had to get him into a building where there was some real protection. And there is no better place than a co-operative owned by the trade-union movement, in which he had spent so many years of his life."

Randolph himself had never been interested in owning a home. Once, when it was more prosperous, the Brotherhood of Sleeping Car Porters had offered to buy him a house, but he had refused. He had no interest in owning property, he said, and did not, in any event, like to accept gifts. All of this has elicited a strangely mixed tribute from a doctor in Harlem, who worked closely with Randolph during the March on Washington movement of the 1940's:

"Randolph's greatest weakness was his indifference to this thing called the medium of exchange. He didn't know or care a damn thing about money or personal advancement. He had this idea that money was corrupting. He was just as satisfied living in two rooms as he would, living in a mansion. He was one of the most unrealistic men I know. He was a good man, a spiritual man, but he was probably too damn spiritual. One of the men in his union once said to me, 'The difference between Randolph and you and me is that he would rather see his name in a headline in the *New York Times* than own a building. You and I would rather own the building, wouldn't we?' I said to him, 'You goddamn right.' "

II / Fathers

We are creatures of history, for every historical epoch has its roots in a preceding epoch. The black militants of today are standing upon the shoulders of the New Negro radicals of my day, the twenties, thirties, and forties. We stood upon the shoulders of the civil rights fighters of the Reconstruction era, and they stood upon the shoulders of the black abolitionists. These are the interconnections of history, and they play their role in the course of development. —A. PHILIP RANDOLPH

Proverbially, ministers' sons are grandchildren of the Devil; and, general, off-hand observation of one's neighbors does, on the whole, bear out this unflattering opinion. Yet, on the other hand, as all authorities agree, ministers' sons achieve eminence several times more frequently than the number of cleric fathers in any community entitles them to do.
—EDWIN T. BREWSTER, in *South Atlantic Quarterly*, July, 1925

2 / "Son of the Church"

One morning in March, 1956, when Randolph arrived at his office, on
125th Street, he found a book on his desk, resting on top of the day's
mail. It was a copy of *The Romance of African Methodism,* a short
history of the African Methodist Episcopal church, and it was a gift from
the author, the Reverend George A. Singleton. Though the compliments
on the inside of the front cover did not say so, the book may well have
been meant as a birthday present. Singleton had been following Randolph's life for some time, and knew, if only from reading the papers,
that in a few weeks, on April 15, he would be sixty-seven.

Randolph's physique, which had fleshed out in the late 1930's and
early '40's, was still burly. Someone described him at the time as "a huge
hulk of a man, weighing more than two hundred pounds." And his face
—which had once been thin and somewhat aquiline—was round and
cherubic. His eyes, as always, were gentle and a bit diffident—hardly the
stereotype, as some people had remarked, of a labor leader. Yet if one
forgot the eyes and the gracious manners—saw only the round face, and
the powerful frame in its three-piece suit—a labor leader's large cigar
would not have looked out of place in his mouth. Then again, as Lester
Velie, a labor writer, had observed, "a labor leader . . . could be a
superbly cultured human being with a vision—a figure like A. Philip
Randolph."

But Randolph was not as hearty as he looked. He suffered now and
then from dizzy spells, and had only recently been advised by the Mayo
Clinic, where he had spent a few days undergoing tests, to drop some of
the weight and cut down on his public activities. Nearing sixty-seven, he
was also moving down through the afternoon of his career. Though his
was still one of the most important names in America, the sound of it no

23

longer carried the magic it once did—as in mid-1941, say, when the New York *Amsterdam News* had recognized him as "the number one Negro leader in America."

The Reverend Mr. Singleton, who lived in Philadelphia, was a retired minister of the AME church. He was also a former editor of the *Christian Recorder*, the church's weekly organ. It was in the early forties, when Randolph was at the peak of his public popularity, that Singleton had met him, in Philadelphia. And, learning that Randolph not only had been raised in the AME church, but was also the son of an AME preacher, Singleton had been following his career with a special pride ever since; Randolph was a leader in the struggle for freedom, and nothing in the heritage of African Methodists was so memorable as the fact that their church was the cradle of racial protest in America.

Though Randolph did not like to accept presents from people, Singleton's was different. It was not one of those necessities of a household, which, Randolph felt, every man should rely upon himself to provide. It was nothing so much as a sentimental token of Singleton's esteem, and a most fitting one, at that. As much as anything else, Randolph liked to read the history of religious movements. None interested him more deeply than the rise of Protestantism in Europe and the spread of Methodism in America; and no aspect of Methodism in this country appealed to him quite as much as the story of the African Methodist Episcopal church.

Before putting the book aside to turn to his union's business, his eyes caught Singleton's inscription on the inside of the front cover:

The Hon. A. Philip Randolph—Distinguished son of the church which stems from Richard Allen who was born a slave Feb. 24, 1760. As he struck a telling blow for religious freedom in 1787 when he left the Methodist Church as a protest against segregation you are incessantly waging a battle for the political emancipation of our people of African descent.

Randolph recalled later that he chuckled to himself. Like most men, he enjoyed hearing himself praised, though he seldom allowed himself to take it too seriously. Part of the reason, he once said, was that throughout his career he had worked as either the head or a member of a team, and was reluctant to take credit for work he had shared with others. What he enjoyed the most about praise was the rhetoric of it. And his chuckle was partly a tribute to Singleton's. If he liked the substance of what Singleton had written, it was not for himself, but for his late father

—to whom, he felt, it would have been quite pleasing. Randolph had not become what his father had once wanted him to be—one of the leaders of the AME church—but he believed the old man would probably not consider it a total loss were he here to read what the Reverend Mr. Singleton, an AME stalwart, had written. It may have been his latest argument in one of those unresolved dialogues that go on between fathers and sons.

But more than anything else, Randolph chuckled because he was wondering how much Singleton really knew about him. To be a son of the AME church was certainly to be, in part, a political son—to carry on the tradition of black protest that the church had begun. Did Singleton know that that was as far as it went, that in matters strictly religious he had long stopped being a son of the church? When he first arrived in New York, as a young man of twenty-two, he had attended Methodist and Baptist churches in Harlem and the black section of the old Tenderloin district, in the upper West Fifties. Even then, the reasons were more intellectual than religious, because he had already started to have doubts about religion before leaving his father's house, in Jacksonville. After being drawn into the world of politics and protest, Randolph had stopped going to church altogether. Since then he had had only the most secular use for churches, mainly as platforms for his political opinions— at any rate, those churches that were not alienated by his social doctrines, but opened their doors to him.

Randolph had not, of course, thought that the church was useless. It was certainly "the most powerful and cohesive institution in Negro life." He simply had ceased to believe it had much value as a religious institution: too many preachers were "salesmen of heaven," rather than spokesmen in the struggle for social change. Nor could he see that "there was going to be any great emancipation of the Negro or anybody else because of religious beliefs." If the Reverend Mr. Singleton knew of all this, then he must not have minded it. For even he may have been troubled over the AME's dwindling reputation for political militancy in recent years. Still smiling, Randolph put the book aside and turned to the Brotherhood's business.

Ironically, almost two years after Singleton's book arrived, Randolph decided to rejoin the AME church. In December, 1957, he wrote to the Reverend Richard Allen Hildebrand, pastor of the Bethel AME Chapel, on West 132nd Street, saying he wished to become a member. Hildebrand was pleased "beyond measure to welcome so distinguished a person," and hoped that Randolph would attend services "whenever you find it possible." Somehow, Randolph seldom found it "possible." He had not explained to the Reverend Mr. Hildebrand that it was not any discovery of religious faith which had brought him back, but merely a wish to contribute to the church's survival as an important social institution. Thus, since he rejoined, Randolph has been satisfied to send Bethel an annual check for $350 to help carry on its work. In 1965, Hildebrand was succeeded at Bethel by the Reverend Henderson Randolph Hughes. "I can't say Mr. Randolph does any attending," Hughes told a visitor one day in 1970, "but he sends his check every year."

Randolph got much of his social attitude toward the church from what he remembered of his father's ministry, and what had been written and said of the AME's political history. Religious as the Reverend James William Randolph was, he brought to his congregation on Sundays a predominantly social gospel. "My father," his son was to recall, "preached a racial religion. He spoke to the social condition of his flock, and always reminded them that the AME church was the first black militant institution in America." Asa Randolph had therefore grown up "with a sense of the church as a social institution," and had become "more attached to the institutionalism than to the faith." At the turn of the century, when he was growing up in Jacksonville, the kind of preaching his father did was an urgent need among poor blacks. But such work could scarcely go on without material support. And the young Randolph knew, from watching his father's weekly struggle to make ends meet, how desperate was the poverty of his congregations.

The "first black militant institution in America" originated in Philadelphia toward the end of the eighteenth century, a few years after the struggle for American independence. In 1786, the Reverend Richard Allen, an ex-slave, returned to Philadelphia to take up a part-time preaching assignment at the predominantly white St. George's Methodist Episcopal Church and, on his own time, to minister "to my African brethren who have been a forgotten people." Allen, who had been born in the city twenty-six years before, had been sold at an early age to a planter in Delaware. As Allen grew, the planter not only encouraged him to read and study the Bible, but also was converted by his slave to Christianity and to a moral revulsion against slavery. In appreciation, Allen's master allowed him to buy his freedom in depreciated Revolutionary currency. Traveling around one of the Methodist circuits in Delaware, Allen so impressed the white ministers with his eloquence and "mastery of the scriptures" that they recommended to Bishop Francis Asbury, one of the leaders of the Methodist church in America, that he be ordained. And it was Asbury who, after hearing Allen preach, had recommended him to St. George's, in Philadelphia.

Allen proved to be such an inspiring minister at St. George's that more blacks than ever started coming to the church. To discourage the influx, the white elders decided to segregate the congregation, restricting all blacks to the back of the balcony. Not even the Reverend Richard Allen, on those Sundays he was not in the pulpit, was exempt from the humiliating arrangement.

During prayers one Sunday morning, Allen and one of his colleagues, the Reverend Absalom Jones, made the mistake of kneeling in an empty part of the balcony that had been reserved for whites. While they were praying, a trustee came up behind them, tapped them on the shoulders, and told them they were not allowed to kneel there. Allen suggested, in a whisper, that they at least be allowed to remain until prayers were over. The trustee said no, they would have to get up that very moment, and started pulling them from their knees. But before both men could be pulled to their feet, prayers ended, and Allen, turning to the rest of the blacks in the balcony, beckoned them to follow him, and walked out of St. George's. They never went back. As Allen put it later, "They were no longer plagued by us."

With their followers, Richard Allen and Absalom Jones organized a group called the Free African Society, which held prayer meetings and lived in an "ethical and beneficial brotherhood" pledged to "support one another in sickness, for the benefit of their widows and fatherless children." Evaluating the importance of the Free Society, more than a century later, W. E. B. Du Bois was to call it "the first wavering step of a people towards organized group life."

In 1794, doctrinal differences between Allen and Jones split the membership of the Free Society. Allen organized his faction into the Bethel African Methodist Episcopal Church, and, inspired by this example, other AME congregations sprang up in Baltimore; Wilmington, Delaware; Attleboro, Pennsylvania; and Salem, New Jersey. In 1816, the five groups met in Philadelphia and organized a national African Methodist Episcopal church, with Richard Allen as the first bishop. As Benjamin Tanner, one of its later bishops, described the new organization, it was

"a church of men . . . to think for themselves . . . to talk for themselves . . . to act for themselves; a church of men who support from
their own substance, however scanty, the ministrations of the word
which they receive; men who spurn to have their churches built for them
. . . men who prefer to live by the sweat of their own brow and be
free."

This philosophy of freedom and self-reliance was to permeate the
church's work and growth, to help shape the character of a large number
of the people who were raised in it—especially during the nineteenth and
early twentieth centuries—and to determine the attitude of its early
preachers and bishops toward the issue of American slavery. This attitude was, by and large, one of political militancy, with preachers urging
slaves to revolt, to seek their salvation through resistance rather than
through waiting patiently upon the Lord.

Such advocacy, which could be made with relative safety in the North,
quickly got the church in trouble in the South, where it had set up districts in 1818. By 1820, preachers and organizers—exhorters, as the
latter were called—were being dragged off platforms, horsewhipped,
jailed, or run out of towns in the South. In 1822, when the Reverend
Morris Brown's congregation in Charleston, South Carolina, was suspected of helping to foment the Denmark Vesey slave insurrection, the
AME church was banned in the South. Brown was forced to escape to
Philadelphia, where he later succeeded Richard Allen as the senior
bishop.

It was not until the end of the Civil War that African Methodism
returned to the South. It reached Florida in 1867, when a district was
established in Tallahassee, where, after "a most feeling" inaugural address, by the Reverend Alexander Wayman, the freedmen were said to
have cried with joy to have lived to see "a Bishop of their own race."

After Tallahassee, one of the first congregations organized in Florida
was at Monticello, capital of Jefferson County. Monticello, one of the
most picturesque towns in the state, had broad, shady streets, fine old
houses, and residential districts planted with camellias and Cherokee
roses. It had become, by the 1860's, the chief manufacturing center of
Florida—with shoe, cord, and wool factories, and the only textile mill in
the state. The factory hands were, in part, ex-slaves, many of whom had
migrated there over the years from other states, especially Virginia. They
were mainly Methodists. Before the War they had been welcome in the

white Methodist church—a branch of the Methodist Church, South—at the corner of Walnut and Olive streets. But after Emancipation, as had happened in other states in the South, they had been either squeezed into segregated benches or driven from the church. In Monticello, it was these people who became the founding congregation of the AME church.

One of the children who were brought to the new church was James William Randolph. Born in 1864, he was the son of John and Amelia Randolph, from Virginia. The father was descended from slaves who had worked for John Randolph, of the famous Virginia family. While young James Randolph was growing up "between the pews" of the AME church at Monticello, he attended a grade school that white Methodist missionaries from the North had opened, after the Civil War, for the children of ex-slaves. He appears to have been a bright student. In his early teens, the AME church appointed him a Sunday-school teacher, and his parents, not having the means to advance his education, apprenticed him out as a tailor. By the age of twenty, he was both a self-trained preacher and an accomplished tailor. As was the custom with self-trained preachers in those days, he informed the presiding elder of the church district that he felt "a call to preach," and was ordained into the AME ministry.

Because of the example he was to provide his children, it is worth looking at some of the influences that shaped his own character. The young minister, following what he had heard of the traditions of his church and the lives of its founding fathers, had immersed himself in whatever religious or political histories were available to him. During the Reconstruction years in which he grew up, his public attitudes had also been formed against a background of black political militancy in Monticello—a period during which black groups frequently armed themselves to defend their right to vote. An example of the political spirit among blacks in Monticello at the time was a notice that one of the armed groups nailed to the front door of the post office: "We understand that the White People in This Place Say they intend to Kill some of the Colored People in This Place. If such a thing is started Here We Would Not give much for This Place Town and People."

As a young African Methodist, he had sharpened his religious and political outlook upon the church's two major periodicals: the weekly *Christian Recorder* and the quarterly *AME Review*. They were not only outstanding church organs, but also two of the most radical black intellectual journals of the day. Before the Civil War, for instance, slave-owners, afraid of the influence of the *Recorder*—which used to be smuggled into the South—had branded it "a dangerous document."

The Reverend James Randolph—who, like the majority of blacks, was a Republican—had also grown up in a socioreligious climate in the black South that was dominated by the personality of the Reverend Henry McNeal Turner. Turner, one of the strongest and most attractive characters in the history of black America, was the bishop in charge of the Georgia and Florida districts of the AME church, the best intellect of the church in the South, a potential black nationalist—which he later became—and the leading black Republican of the Reconstruction era. One of the memorable orations of Southern political history was the speech that Turner, a member of the Georgia legislature, made to that body in 1868, when it moved to expel the black representatives:

. . . I hold that I am a member of this body. . . . I shall neither fawn nor cringe before any party nor stoop to beg them for my rights. . . . I am here to demand my rights, and to hurl thunderbolts at the men who would dare to cross the threshold of my manhood. . . . Whose legislature is this? . . . You have the elements of superiority upon your side; you have our money and your own; you have our education and your own; and you have our land and your own too. . . . The black man cannot protect a country if the country doesn't protect him; and if, tomorrow, a war should arise, I would not raise a musket to defend a country where my manhood is denied.

It was not the voice alone of black political militancy, but, above all, of African Methodist radicalism. The speech was to fix itself in the consciousness of most young African Methodists growing up in the South at the time. And the example of Bishop Turner—in his eloquence, his fearlessness, and his candor—would be one of the enduring influences upon the Reverend James Randolph, as well as upon his children—who would themselves later come to meet and admire Turner. Beyond these facts, nothing of importance is known about how the Reverend Mr. Randolph was raised.

Family friends of the Randolphs in Monticello were James and Mary Robinson and their four daughters, Mattie, Esther, Carrie, and Elizabeth —the youngest. Like John and Amelia Randolph, the elder Robinsons were descended from Virginia slaves. Just before young James Randolph was ordained, the Robinsons left Monticello to live in Baldwin, a town in the northeast of Florida, fifteen miles from Jacksonville. Mary Robinson, who had been a staunch member of the AME congregation in Monticello, transferred her devotion to the church in Baldwin, Campbell's AME Chapel. But, as she found, the quality of the ministry at Baldwin was disappointing, and when she heard that James Randolph had been ordained into the ministry, she urged her congregation to appoint him. Thus, in 1884, a few months after he was ordained, the Reverend Mr. Randolph arrived in Baldwin. The elder Robinsons welcomed him and treated him as one of their own.

Baldwin was then a small community of about 400, roughly half of them blacks. It was a lumbering town at the junction of a number of railroads, and the men there made a living chiefly from laying railroad crossties, "dipping turpentine," and cutting pulpwood and pine logs, which railroad flatcars carried to paper mills in Fernandina and Jacksonville. The dirt roads were unnamed, and Campbell's AME Chapel stood at the intersection of two of them. The chapel was a small wooden building, with wooden shutters, and lit at night by kerosene lamps and storm lanterns hanging from the rafters. The membership was small, about fifty. The Reverend Mr. Randolph preached on the first and third Sundays of the month, led prayer meetings on Wednesday evenings, and taught Sunday school on Sunday mornings.

A bachelor and a family friend, he was a frequent guest in the Robinsons' log cabin, about two miles from the church. He would end up marrying the youngest of the Robinsons' girls; and later on, his own children would spend much time in the old, rotting log cabin. One of his sons was to remember that life there was sometimes a heroic struggle against the elements. In the winter, old newspapers and rags had to be stuffed into cracks in the siding to keep out the cold wind. When it rained, water leaked through holes in the roof, and all the family's tubs and buckets had to be used to catch the rain. But on clear nights nothing was sweeter than to lie in bed and enjoy the stars twinkling through the broken places in the roof.

None of the Robinsons, except the father, ever missed a Sunday in church, if they could help it. In the morning, Mrs. Robinson, a light-skinned woman, packed her four daughters into a four-wheel wagon, drawn by a black mare, and drove to the chapel. They carried food for the day, and did not return until late at night. James Robinson, stern and aloof, and light-skinned enough to pass for white, was a man who visited no one and seldom had any visitors. He had no interest whatever in the church, or in much else besides his work. He even shunned the singing and praying that went on in the cabin every night before bedtime. *His* devotions were to raising hogs, drying and smoking bacon for sale, and stocking a woodshed from which he supplied logs to the wood-burning railroad engines.

In 1885, a year after he arrived in Baldwin, James Randolph married the youngest of the Robinsons' daughters, Elizabeth. He was then twenty-one, and she, thirteen, was one of the brighter pupils in his Sunday-school class. Two years later, in May, 1887, Elizabeth had their first son, James William, Jr. And on April 15, 1889—after they had moved to Crescent City, where the Reverend Mr. Randolph had been called to a larger congregation—their last son, Asa Philip, was born. His father named him after Asa, one of the kings of the Old Testament, who, according to the fifteenth chapter of the First Book of Kings, "took all the silver and the gold that were left in the treasures of the house of the Lord, and the treasures of the king's house, and delivered them into the hand of his servants."

Over the years, because of his lack of formal training, the Reverend Mr. Randolph was unable to rise to any position of prominence in the AME ministry. Nor, for the same reason, was he ever found attractive by the wealthier and more sophisticated middle-class congregations, in whose pulpits alone he would have been able to earn a decent income for himself and his family. Preachers of his sort, lacking the smell and the aura of the seminary, were, as the late Dean Kelly Miller of Howard University once said, "held up to ridicule by their more haughty Christian co-workers."

Yet, while he could certainly have used the money, the Reverend Mr. Randolph did not display any appetite for high churchly power, or any great desire to fill the bourgeois pulpits—though, later on, the vision of one of his sons rising among the higher echelons of the church would have a considerable appeal to him. For himself, he was strongly attached to that strain in AME tradition which held that the church's principal mission was to minister to the masses of the race—to nourish their social morale as much as to save their souls. In his own way, and in his own day, he was also something of a black nationalist. He taught, for instance, that Jesus and Moses were, if not black, men of color. And he liked sometimes to throw a quotation at his neighbors, over the fence or from the pulpit: "Ethiopia shall stretch forth her hand unto God and shall worship Him under her own vine and fig tree." Nor, as Asa, his younger son, was to remember, could he bring himself "to lick the boots of the powerful bishops" in order to get big churches and advance his career.

The Reverend Mr. Randolph never got a "big church." He was to spend his life shuttling among small and poor congregations. He cut none of the romantic figure of the circuit rider traveling among his charges with mule and pack. He went by railroad, steamboat, or dray, with his Bible wrapped in a package under his arm. His parishioners were not clerks, businessmen, and professionals, but mainly poor domestic servants and unskilled laborers. At this level of service, he barely earned enough to live, but he gained a reputation for eloquence and boldness as a preacher, and was loved and respected for his kindness and integrity.

After more than two years in Crescent City, the Reverend Mr. Randolph was invited to Jacksonville to take over a small congregation. On the surface, it was hardly an attractive assignment. The congregation— with just over thirty members—was not even as large as the one in Crescent City. Nor, unlike Crescent City, did it have its own place of worship —meeting on Sunday mornings in a rented room on Jefferson Street. But there would be compensations. He would again be able to preach in Baldwin, at least one Sunday a month, since Baldwin was only a short distance from Jacksonville. And he was also promised a chance to preach in two small rural churches, in Palatka and Green Cove Springs, also within a reasonably short distance of the city. Not the least important consideration was the opportunity, for whatever it would be worth, of working in a big town. So, toward the end of 1891, with their two young sons— James, four, and Asa, two—the Randolphs moved to Jacksonville.

3 / Getting Religion

Jacksonville, by 1901, was well on the way to becoming the business metropolis of Florida. It would become that, but the progress was interrupted on May 3 of that year, when a fire wiped out a large section of the city, burning down 150 blocks—more than 2,000 homes—and leaving some 10,000 homeless. It was the most devastating of the fires that were frequent in Jacksonville, then built largely of wood.

Where blacks were concerned, fires seem to have been the worst part of it in Jacksonville. The city was considered a good place to live, and in the late nineteenth century blacks composed about a third of the population. They not only owned some of the finer homes, but also, as the city was still relatively unsegregated, they lived wherever their money took them. Mostly, though, they lived together in neighborhoods called Oakland, Brooklyn, Burbridge Addition, La Villa, and East Jacksonville. James Weldon Johnson, who was born in La Villa, in 1871, recalled that while growing up there,

most of the city policemen were Negroes; several members of the city council were Negroes; one or two justices of the peace were Negroes. When a paid fire department was established, one station was manned by Negroes. I was in my teens when the city government was reorganized and Joseph E. Lee, a Negro, and very able man and astute politician, was made Judge of the Municipal Court. Many of the best stalls in the city were owned and operated by Negroes; Davis and Robinson, a firm of Negro commission merchants, were land stewards for the Clyde Steamship Company; and there was no such thing as a white-oriented barbershop.

Another former resident of Jacksonville, a Johnson contemporary, remembers that "a lot of the colored people used to ride around in nice carriages; they had something; they had class."

34

But that was only part of the story. Most blacks in Jacksonville were poor, and owned neither homes, high offices, nor fine carriages. They were mainly house workers, factory workers, tradesmen, and service attendants. Then, too, as James Weldon Johnson also remembered, Jacksonville later became "a one hundred percent cracker town."

When the Randolphs arrived, Jacksonville was not yet, of course, that kind of racist town, but the change must already have started. The family settled in the Oakland section, predominantly black, and, as Asa Randolph would recall, "the toughest part of town." They lived in a rented two-story house on the 600 block of Jesse Street, between Spearing and Palmetto streets. The old house had a shingle roof, weatherboard sidings, and a small front porch on the ground floor. The sidings were painted green, and the window and door facings white. A ramshackle picket fence in front had so many slats broken or missing that the chickens, cats, and dogs of the neighbors wandered in and out as they pleased. There were two oak trees at the gate, and on festive occasions, like Christmas, James Randolph whitewashed the lower trunks.

The Randolphs lived simply, even spartanly. The living quarters of the house, on the ground floor, were furnished with old, utilitarian pieces. The only thing of any ornamental or esthetic distinction—though it was scarcely something the family could do without—was a large kerosene lamp with an elaborately flowered shade, which sat on an old center table. On Saturdays, Elizabeth Randolph got down on her knees to clean and polish the floor, but at Christmas time she prevailed upon her husband to buy a straw carpet to cover it. She wanted the carpet partly for relief from routine household drudgery and partly for a change that would reflect the special Christmas mood. It was similar to changing around the furniture in the house, as some other poor families did every Christmas, to give the place a fresh look, especially for the imagination of the children. But it was necessary for Mrs. Randolph to prevail upon her husband because, with his slender income, he approved only the most essential purchases —which a straw carpet could hardly be said to be, at Christmas or any other time. By February or March, anyway, when the carpet started coming apart, it was thrown out into the back yard to be burned. During the winter, the living room was heated by a small fireplace, and the upstairs bedrooms by an old-fashioned iron stove.

Before the boys grew up and started buying their own, or bringing them home on loan from the public library, there were a few books— representing the range of the Reverend Mr. Randolph's intellectual interests and some of the sources of his self-education. His younger son remembers that there were Shakespearean dramas; the novels of Sir Walter Scott, Charles Dickens, and Jane Austen; the writings of Charles Darwin and John Calvin; poetry by Keats and Shelley; historical accounts of the AME church; and one or two things in American and African history. There were also the inevitable family Bible, back issues of the *Christian Recorder* and *AME Review,* and a radical black political journal of the period, called the *Voice of the Negro.* Before the boys could read, their father sat them down regularly, and read and explained parts of this literature to them, hoping as much to encourage the habit of reading as to arouse their interest in serious affairs. Later, when they were able to read for themselves, he would insist that they spend part of every afternoon with his books.

The family, it is remembered, was "always in debt," and had to produce as much of its own food as possible. There was a garden in the back yard which grew bananas, tomatoes, lemons, collard greens, lettuce, and potatoes. There were also chickens and a couple of hogs. And when Elizabeth Randolph's parents came in from Baldwin to visit, they brought home-cured bacon and smoked pork.

A couple of doors away lived the Hansberry family. The father, Theodore Hansberry, was a steamboat pilot, who plied up and down the St. Johns River, taking picnickers and vacationers to the resorts and medicinal spas around Palatka and Green Cove Springs. In his spare time, the Reverend Mr. Randolph taught his sons to read and write, but when he was busy he sent them over to Theodore Hansberry's younger daughter, Fanny—who was more than ten years older than the two boys—to continue the lessons. The two families became close, and Fanny sometimes came over and taught the boys in their parents' living room. The Randolphs, she recalls today, in her mid-nineties, "were fine people, poor but respectable. There was nothing fancy about their place. When you went into their house you could see from what they had and how they kept the place that they were much better than the life they could afford."

The Reverend James Randolph was a tall, black, and sparely built man with a deep and powerful voice. Asa remembers him with "a high nose, a chin beard, and a certain refinement and polish of bearing"—especially on Sunday mornings, when he put on his long frock coat, vest, and celluloid collar. Despite his Calvinist temperament, he was not entirely out of sympathy with human error. For instance, though he never drank himself —and would not permit any bottle in his house that had once contained liquor—he took no moral position against people who drank, especially if they did so in moderation. His puritanism was unyielding only in such matters as gambling and "lewd women." His relaxations were few and, in keeping with his means, rather simple: reading his books, his church magazines, and the *Times-Union* and *Metropolis;* chewing tobacco; or smoking three-for-a-nickel Virginia Cheroots. Now and then, when he was in funds, he splurged on Cremo cigars, at a nickel apiece.

One of his wife's nieces, who once lived in the home, recalls that James Randolph "was a lovely man. He loved the boys and the boys loved him. If his wife told him, 'Don't give the boys any money, you can't afford it,' he would just go behind her back and hand it to them just the same. He might give the boys a little scolding sometimes, but that was all; he could never bring himself to whip them. You couldn't eat a thing in that house without him praying first. Come dinnertime, we used to say, 'Well, it's almost time to eat and almost time to pray.' He walked graceful, just as straight as you can get, and he taught the boys to walk like him. If he caught one of them slouching, he would call out, 'Come on, now, shoulders back.' He spoke English from his heart, never got angry, and never worried about money. If the church paid him, okay; if it didn't, okay, too. His wife was the go-getter."

Elizabeth Randolph was just as tall as her husband, but lighter skinned, with high cheekbones and long, flowing hair. Asa describes her as "a beautiful woman with a radiant smile and firm eyes that could look straight through you." She was the disciplinarian of the household, and, according to Asa, supervised her sons "with the rigidity of a corporal." Like her mother, Mary Robinson, Elizabeth was an ardent churchgoer, possessing deep swells of religious emotion. Asa remembered that after testifying on communion Sundays, his mother, overcome with emotion, sometimes buried her face in her hands and burst into tears. But, like her father, she made no friends, unless they were in the church, paid no social calls—even on her neighbors—and went nowhere, except to religious affairs, funerals, weddings, or to see her parents in Baldwin.

Within a year of arriving in Jacksonville, the Reverend Mr. Randolph started raising funds to build a permanent place of worship for his new congregation. He raised enough to buy a plot, at the corner of Eighth and Davis streets, and to erect upon it a modest, roughhewn, clapboard structure, which he named the New Hope AME Chapel. Several years after his death, in 1924, the church would be modernized in concrete and renamed the Greater New Hope Chapel. A daughter of one of New Hope's first members has not forgotten some of the affairs the Reverend Mr. Randolph organized to raise money to build the church: "On Saturday nights, they used to have big sales of fried chicken and fried fish. Those days you could get a whole big fish for ten cents. Sunday nights, after the fry, the Reverend Mr. Randolph made his financial report, and accounted for every piece of chicken and fish that was fried. He was just that honest."

The salary from New Hope—even with the addition of what the Reverend Mr. Randolph got from Baldwin, for preaching there one Sunday a month—was never enough to support his family. Nor was the situation much improved when he was given the two other rural churches he had been promised, in Palatka and Green Cove Springs. Usually, when he came back from visiting those churches, he sat by the fireplace and counted up his receipts. The two boys, who often watched from a distance, "never saw anything but coins, and nothing larger than a quarter." Sometimes, instead of coins, he brought home his salary slung over his shoulder in a burlap bag containing corn, potatoes, fruit, or a side of pork. "Dollar Sunday" was his best time of year. That was the one day of the year when—as the national AME church had decreed in 1872— each member had to contribute at least a dollar toward the upkeep of the church.

"Low salaries," Harry Roberts, a student of the rural ministry, once wrote, "mean . . . that the average rural minister is hardly able to accumulate savings for a rainy day, for retirement, or for his widow and children at his death. Since the churches in general lack a pension or retirement system, the minister is often left stranded in old age or his family is often left to shift for themselves. . . . Or, as is common, the minister and/or his wife may engage in some sort of employment during the week." It was an accurate description of the Reverend James Randolph's situation.

Falling back upon the trade he had learned while growing up in Monticello, he and his wife built a shack in the back yard, and together they repaired, dyed, cleaned, and pressed clothes. Elizabeth, a seamstress, who made her own clothes and those of the boys, also took in some extra sewing. Still, James Randolph, who was a better craftsman than a businessman, made very little money. His few white customers usually paid promptly, but the bulk of his clientele, his black neighbors—knowing full well that he never pressed anyone for debts—always took back their clothes on credit. His wife had to be the "go-getter." Whenever he went out to return the clothes, she insisted on going along with him, and enforced a rigid policy with the customers of "no money, no clothes." Even so, according to Asa, "this brought in an average of ten dollars a week. And during hard times it wasn't more than three dollars."

Against the advice of his wife, who had, by now, given up on him as a businessman, Randolph plunged into two other enterprises to supplement his income. The first was a small meat market, which he bought, with a loan, from a man in the neighborhood who had gone bankrupt. The market failed within a month, leaving the minister with a substantial debt. We are not told the reason for the market's original failure, but under James Randolph it was because, once again, he had extended credit liberally and indiscriminately. There was a bittersweet consolation for his sons: while the market lasted, they "ate plenteously."

The other venture was a wood-selling business. "In those days," Asa would recall, "the Negro community burned wood for cooking and for heating the homes. A lot of enterprising Negroes ran woodyards, and my father decided to get into it. He got hold of an old nag and a dray, bought up wood wholesale, and hired a man to drive around retailing it. But he couldn't buy enough wood at low enough prices to make a profit. Besides, the man he hired was robbing him blind. In no time, the business busted. The old horse had to be returned, and my father had to scuffle for a long time to pay off the debt."

The father was the chief moral influence on his sons. When they started attending school, he made reading a mandatory daily activity for them. People who grew up on Jesse Street remember that one of the familiar sights on the block was James and Asa Randolph reading every afternoon on the family porch. Beaman Hearn, a playmate of Asa's, who lived across the street, remembers that "those boys did practically nothing but read. Matter of fact, if Asa and I were burying a cat behind the house, he wanted to read a service."

Though they "found out differently" as they grew older, James and Asa Randolph were told by their father that most of the great men in the world were men of color. Thus to be black was not to be inferior. They should consider men like Hannibal, Crispus Attucks, Nat Turner, Denmark Vesey, Toussaint L'Ouverture, Frederick Douglass, Richard Allen, and Henry McNeal Turner. They didn't even have to look that far afield, he said; if they looked right there in Jacksonville they would see a man like Joseph E. Lee, the collector of revenue for the whole of Jacksonville. "Think of that!" he would add, in one of his favorite inspirational expressions.

Clear speech, the Reverend Mr. Randolph urged his sons, was the first law of communication, and he served as their first model for clear articulation. A word like "responsibility" came out of him as "res-pon-sa-bil-itay." "It trembled with meaning," Asa has said. Their father also issued them injunctions concerning truthfulness to one's self, falseness to no one, and the unimportance of a man's purse compared with his good name. He was an admirer of the apostle Paul, after whose example he urged the boys always to "speak the whole word," whatever the cost, and to leave no task unfinished, whatever the difficulty. And for the nourishment of either his ego or theirs, wherever he took them around Jacksonville, he introduced them as "two of the finest boys in the world."

The minister did not object to his sons' visiting other churches on Sundays. In fact, he was glad that they sometimes went to the Bethel Baptist Church, where they could listen to one of his models for eloquence, the Reverend John E. Ford. He demanded, though, that they be in church every Sunday—barring illness, or similar acts of God. Nor should they forget that no church was superior to their own, and that no faith took precedence over African Methodism. As a matter of fact, despite his admiration for the Reverend Mr. Ford, he considered denominations like the Baptists to be of "a lower breed," for any church whose system required the rite of immersion "lacked a certain caste of religious culture." Besides, unlike the African Methodist church, a formal national structure, "anybody could start a Baptist church."

Wanting to introduce the boys to his experience as a circuit rider, the Reverend Mr. Randolph sometimes took them along with him to Palatka and Green Cove Springs, twenty-nine and fifty-six miles, respectively, up the St. Johns River. James, with a mind of his own, usually went with great reluctance; such trips, he felt, were intrusions upon his time and interests, which were mainly study. But Asa, who was always eager to accompany his father, would find the experiences unforgettable: getting off the steamboat and wading through streams, sometimes up to their knees, before arriving at the little churches; or being met at the wharf with an oxcart, and spending Saturday night in a member's log cabin. The services on Sunday were like revival meetings, held under a broad sheet of canvas supported in the middle and around the edges by poles.

Scenes of poor people screaming, falling to the ground, and rising later to confess that they had gotten religion—such scenes would fix themselves in his memory. But it was not the religious mystery of it all that would remain in his mind. It was his dim sense that, in the emotions and imaginations of such people, getting religion was a way of escaping their social condition. As he said years later, if that kind of emotion were translated into politics, it would represent "the awakening and even the uprising of the masses."

At an AME convention in Jacksonville, Asa finally got to meet one of the heroes of his father's boyhood, Bishop Henry McNeal Turner. The Reverend Mr. Randolph, who knew Turner by then, took his sons up to the bishop and, as usual, introduced them as "two of the finest boys in the world." Asa would recall his elation when Turner patted them on the head, and said their father was a fine man. The bishop was the most impressive-looking man Asa had ever seen—"he had a powerful body, with a large head, stern eyes, and a red, freckled, rugged, and imperious face." Turner looked "like a tyrant," everything the boy had imagined of the powerful AME bishops he had heard and read about. Asa was hardly surprised when he heard later that, at an AME conference in the South, during Reconstruction, Turner had pulled two revolvers from his pockets, slapped them down on the Bible, and declared, "My life depends on the will of God and these two guns."

Black boys do not, of course, grow up in the South—in America—without also being touched by explicit racial experiences. For the Randolph boys, however, they were the kinds of experiences that stamped their imaginations rather than scarred their lives. There were times when Asa and his brother, working as newsboys, found themselves pushed to the back of the line when they went to the *Times-Union* to pick up their papers. But those were of almost no consequence. The experiences that exerted a powerful hold on Asa's memory were mostly those of his father's own responses to racial situations. The first was probably the one that affected him the most, for he saw his father humiliated. They had gone together to return some renovated clothes to the white foreman of a sawmill. "Get the hell out of here," the man had shouted at the Reverend Mr. Randolph. "Take the clothes to my house, or I'll throw you off the property." The father had turned away in silence, understanding the futility of a reply, but not quite knowing, for the first time, how to look his son in the eye.

Then there was the afternoon at home when a group of men came up to the gate, called out the Reverend Mr. Randolph, whispered something to him, and left. James and Asa noticed that when their father returned he was exchanging sad glances with their mother. A black man had just been locked up in the Duval County jail, and the rumor was that later that night a white mob was going to break into the jail and lynch him The men who had come to the gate were passing the word and recruiting an armed group to stand guard around the jail come nightfall. James Randolph had volunteered, and at dusk the men returned for him. There were two guns in the house: a shotgun behind the chest of drawers upstairs, and a Bull Dog pistol in one of the drawers. Randolph gave the shotgun to his wife—who, trained by her father, James Robinson, was a deadly shot—and told her to keep vigil on the front porch and protect the home in his absence. He tucked the pistol under his coat and left with the men. Elizabeth Randolph sat up all night, with the shotgun across her lap, while the two boys huddled together in the living room. The Reverend Mr. Randolph returned at dawn, looking tired but happy. The men had massed around the county jail all night, and stood off the mob. Asa was about ten then, old enough to understand the reason for his father's mission, but still so young that he imagined a greater terror over his own household than over the man in the county jail. But unlike the incident at the sawmill, he was now left with a more positive image of the black situation: not one of powerlessness, but of the "possibilities of salvation," which resided in unity and organization.

There would be another positive memory of his father's response to racism. By the early 1900's, with Jim Crow statutes being passed all over the South and Jacksonville rapidly becoming "a one hundred percent cracker town," its public accommodations were segregated. The Reverend Mr. Randolph forbade his sons to read their books in the segregated reading room of the Jacksonville public library. Nor, he ordered, should they ride the Jim Crow streetcars. They should do as he did: walk to wherever they wanted to go in the city.

James Randolph was to set his sons a vivid example of cultivation, a fact somewhat surprising in one of his humble origins. Though he displayed considerable polish—in style as well as in appearance—his was a cultivation not so much of manners as of spirit. Perfect manners could scarcely be expected of a man who had trained himself in so much. Such perfection, in any case, would have been a dubious achievement in someone whose chancy income obliged him to scutter continuously in order to feed himself and his family. He was, very simply, a self-made gentleman, one who was guided by the values of civility, humility, and decency, inspired by religious and social service, and utterly devoted to the idea of dignity. He was, in these senses, a model of *gravitas*—exemplifying attitudes of the spirit and standards of conduct that seemed oddly out of joint with his social and economic circumstances, as well as with the primitive racial climate and environment in which he had shaped himself.

He is a reminder of those miracles of graceful self-creation one sometimes encounters in home-grown black patriarchs, imparting moral refinement to the poorest of families. Of course, such men—though perhaps only a generation removed from slavery—are sometimes not strangers to what is in books, and they have seen in action, somewhere, the values and standards that have captured their imaginations. So one has a glimpse into the secret of their miracle. Still, watching what they have formed of themselves and how they have raised their children, one can pay them no finer tribute than to wonder how on earth they managed to do it.

Asa and his brother, James, were close friends. They went almost everywhere together, studied at home together, and, despite the two-year difference in their ages, were in every class at school together. The success of this unusual partnership was due mainly to James. A better and more serious student than Asa, James was particularly brilliant at languages and mathematics, and it was the help he gave Asa in those subjects, while they studied at home, that enabled his younger brother to hold his own in classes that would otherwise have been too advanced for him

Though always in poor health, and more retiring in temperament than his brother, James was also, by far, the more physically aggressive. At the Oakland elementary school, where they were sent for a short time, James gained the reputation of never backing away from fights with the "street boys," as his mother called them. A severe embarrassment to the class dunces—the prize pupil who always had the answers—James paid for his brilliance after school. If he was the aristocrat of the classroom, the dunces were the aristocrats of the streets. Secure upon their own turf, they taunted him into fights. Since his bravery was far in excess of his skill, his brother, the more pacific Asa, would plead with him to ignore the physical challenges. But James would refuse, and often went home with a bruised face and swollen eyes. On such occasions, Asa sustained his bruises as well; for despite his abhorrence of physical combat, he was unable to stand idly by and watch his brother being beaten. When they arrived home, their mother, who "hated nothing so much as a coward," would want to know only one thing: had they stood up and fought? Usually, thanks to James, they had. But if she gathered that they had not, she added a few bruises of her own.

James was not himself particularly impressed with his reputation as a student, though it must have been difficult for him not to enjoy the fact that almost everyone else was. "He was the brains," says the cousin who once lived in their home. "He had a superior mind." At Edward Waters College—then an AME industrial school—which they attended after their parents finally took them away from the rougher elements of the Oakland elementary school, James's admirers showed how much more highly they regarded him than his brother. Except that Asa loved to read, there was nothing he excelled at in school; and though during class breaks he seldom left his brother's side, the other students would shunt him aside, to get to talk to James. Thus if Asa was noticed at all, it was simply as his brother's faithful appendage. It was not until both boys entered the Cookman Institute, in 1903—at the ages of sixteen and four-teen—that Asa, as he was to say, "came into my own."

The Cookman Institute, on Davis Street, in East Jacksonville, was one of the memorials to the Northern white Methodist concern for the educa-tion of black children in the South. Its academic standards were some-where between those of a high school and a junior college, and certainly higher than those at Edward Waters College—with which the Randolph parents had also become dissatisfied. The institute—which was the first high school for blacks in Florida, and, for a number of years, the only one—was founded in 1872 by the Reverend S. B. Darnell, of the Metho-dist church's Northern branch, and named after the Reverend Alfred Cookman, another white Methodist, who donated the funds for its con-struction.

When the young Randolphs arrived there, the faculty was made up equally of Southern black teachers and Methodist teacher-missionaries from the North. The missionary part of their interest was to develop "desirable" sexual and family mores among the young blacks—attitudes that the institute had considered even more urgent in the 1870's, when most of the students were the children of freed slaves. "For nearly half a century," Jay S. Stowell wrote in 1922, "[Cookman] has maintained a high moral, spiritual, and intellectual standard for the thousands of young men and women who have come under its influence. Many colored people in Florida love and honor 'Old Cookman.' . . . Many of the early pupils were ex-slaves, and their eagerness to learn was most touching. Old men and old women sat side by side with boys and girls in the class. . . . Cookman never forgets that she is a Christian school and emphasis is put upon the development of the moral and religious life."

Academically, the school taught what it called "the higher branches" —natural sciences, French, Greek, Latin, ethics, mental philosophy, law, mathematics, public speaking, literature, music. It also taught "branches" that, if not so high, were absolutely essential to the survival of some, probably most, of its graduates—shoemaking, tailoring, agriculture, printing, and home economics.

The headmaster was then the Reverend James Docking, of Boston. His most important assistants were Lillie M. Whitney, a Greek, Latin, and mathematics teacher, from New Hampshire; Arthur Grant, a black Floridian, who was the choir and music master; and Mary Neff, of Cincinnati, who taught literature, ethics, and drama.

To the academic student body at the time, the Misses Neff and Whitney were the most popular of the teachers, and—from what their surviving graduates, most of whom are octogenarians today, say—seem to have left the most lasting impression. In fact, it was Mary Neff who changed Asa Randolph's academic life and enabled him to emerge from the shadow of his brother's. A photograph of both women, taken in 1906, shows Miss Neff, apparently in her forties, with her hair swept back severely from her face, and ending in a bun at the back. Her black dress has a high collar of white lace, and her features— sensitive but solemn—give her the appearance of a stern moralist. Lillie Whitney seems to be in her fifties. Her hair is white, and is also swept back into a bun, but leaves her face in a less severe relief. Not only is her face warmer and more relaxed; there also is a hint of playfulness in her eyes and around her mouth. She appears to be disciplining it, as if to let go would be to lose something of her authority.

As one of their schoolmates has said, James and Asa Randolph "did not need any missionary work. Morally they were two of the outstanding boys at Cookman." But with Lillie Whitney's tutelage, James is said to have become one of the most brilliant Latin and mathematics scholars Cookman ever produced. And under Mary Neff, Asa suddenly displayed gifts which marked him as the school's best student in literature, public speaking, and drama. His was also the most impressive voice in the school choir, and by the time he joined the baseball team, on which he excelled as a catcher and first baseman, he had achieved a "following" among the students, independent of his brother's, and a feeling for the first time that "I was important in my own right."

James Parker, then their senior at Cookman, and now a retired physician in Red Bank, New Jersey, still remembers the young Randolphs: "The biggest crowds came out to watch baseball at Cookman when Asa Randolph was playing. I would guess he could have made a career as a baseball player, if he had wanted. With that voice of his, he could also have made a career as a singer. He was very artistic; had no interest in the trivial aspects of life. He was retiring, he spoke impeccable English, but wouldn't open his mouth unless asked. He and his brother never raised hell like some of us, who would cut class sometimes and run off with the girls. They were two of the most handsome boys at Cookman, but they weren't the kind of fellows girls would pick to go out and have a good time with. Morally, they were beyond reproach."

At his and his brother's graduation, in 1907, Asa was chosen class valedictorian—an honor he was sufficiently impressed with to prepare a speech entitled "The Man of the Hour," though today not even he remembers what the speech said. He remembers, however, that when—before leaving the house for the graduation ceremony at the Odd Fellows Hall—his father asked him why he had decided upon such a subject, he said something about his future and "what I would like to see young Negroes do."

Fifty-six years later—in September, 1963—Arthur Garvin, a resident of Brooklyn, who hadn't seen Asa since they were together at Cookman, wrote to congratulate him on his leadership of the March on Washington, and to recall their "good fortune" in having "come under the angelic influence of Miss Lillie Whitney and Miss Mary Neff." Randolph replied that they were "two of the finest teachers who ever lived," and that "the history of the New England schoolmarms who came South is yet to be written."

If a romance of Asa Randolph's career at Cookman were being written—a career that had uncovered such promise and had ended upon such a high note—it would seem amiss not to say that he stepped out of Cookman upon a higher road, at least upon the road to college. After all, boys whose greatest distinction at Cookman had been the good taste that led them to seek out his and his brother's company were, in the weeks or months after graduation, being packed off by their parents to universities like Fisk, Howard, and Lincoln—training grounds for lawyers, realtors, teachers, and dentists: what W. E. B. Du Bois called "the Talented Tenth." But a more accurate term for some of these young men might have been "the Favored Tenth"—for which of them, at Cookman, had been as talented as James and Asa Randolph? Yet how many of them had come from poorer families? Finding the money to send their boys to college was, indeed, entirely beyond the means of the Reverend James Randolph and his wife. In a sense, it might have been more profitable for the boys to have studied one of the "lower branches." At least, so it was to seem for some time.

The morning after his speech at the Odd Fellows Hall, Asa, eighteen, was hired by the Union Life Insurance Company to walk the black neighborhoods of Jacksonville collecting premiums. And, the next week, James, twenty, was hired by the post office to make special deliveries. They were the most prestigious jobs either was to hold in Jacksonville— except later on, perhaps, when James became a Pullman sleeping car porter.

After about a month, Asa tired of collecting premiums, and over the next four years he clerked in a grocery store, drove a delivery wagon for a drug company, stacked logs in a lumberyard, pushed wheelbarrows in a fertilizer factory, and carried water and shoveled dirt for an outfit laying railroad crossties.

Through this dreary, sometimes backbreaking succession of occupations, perhaps only his cultural interests, some of which he had developed at Cookman, sustained him spiritually. He was now buying his own books, and was reading more literature, history, and contemporary affairs. He was giving public readings of the Bible, Shakespeare, and the poetry of Paul Laurence Dunbar at black churches and theaters. With three of his classmates from Cookman, he had formed a barbershop quartet, and they were often invited to perform in the homes of some of the more prominent black residents. His own voice was so impressive that Sidney Whittick, a prominent tenor in Jacksonville, encouraged him to become a professional singer. And he was the leading actor in a dramatic group, which played mostly in churches and schools, and occasionally in public theaters. Asa was to remember appearing at the Crown's Theater, in downtown Jacksonville, in plays like *East Lynne* and *Way Down East*.

One of Asa's leading ladies in these productions was young Ruth Lofton, who worked part time in the "colored" section of the Jacksonville public library. She would recall that a play she and Asa once appeared in "made such a hit that they wanted to take us to perform in Orlando." But Ruth's mother had refused, saying she had no wish to see her daughter become "a stage woman."

Asa Randolph's cultural activities brought him in contact with some of Jacksonville's most beautiful young black women. Miss Lofton was only one of them—although Ruth, with her smooth, café-au-lait skin, wouldn't *think* of calling herself black. "Colored," she says today, is more appropriate, "because I have too many different strains in me." Asa formed no serious attachments among these girls. Elizabeth Randolph was "very strict about us mingling with girls and possibly getting mixed up in any condition which might reflect on the character of the home." It might have reassured Mrs. Randolph enormously to learn that mothers like Ruth Lofton's held even stronger feelings about their daughters getting mixed up with boys. Yet all the girls were impressed with Asa Randolph. Ruth Lofton herself, who later married a successful Jacksonville physician, says of Asa, "He was born with the courtesy and gentlemanliness that few Negroes are born with. When I passed him in the streets, he bowed and lifted his hat. Of course, he was a star actor. He had a wonderful voice, a fine physique, and a Christian military bearing that few men had, and he was the more handsome because of it. Asa could face any man and look him in the eye, white or black. He always had a nice answer for everybody. But he could hurt your feelings with it; he was one of the few people who could always hurt you with a soft answer. In my girlhood, I would say he was the finest man I ever met."

The time came, as it was almost sure to, when the Reverend James Randolph began regarding his younger son as a fine prospect for the AME ministry. He had given up any such thought about James, because, ever since James started going to Cookman, he had taken to challenging his father's belief in the existence of God. The issue was never settled between them, of course: the boy pressing the demands of scientific proof, and the father clinging to faith and the perceptions of the religious imagination.

Asa told his father that he had no interest in becoming a preacher, or even in ending up as a bishop of the AME church. He had not yet made up his mind, he said, whether he wanted a career in politics or one on the stage. The Reverend Mr. Randolph reluctantly abandoned his old dream of giving back one of his own to the church—joining, he may have realized, a large company of clergymen, whose sons had risen to deny such dreams.

Well, he told the boys, at the very least it was time they got religion. *Religion!* they said. Did he seriously expect them—like the saints in Palatka—to fall on the ground, "hear" voices, "see" visions, then rise and confess they had accepted the Lord? To them—if they were to be interested in it at all—religion should be more than a mere drug to dull the pain of life in a racist society. Religion would have to seize them with unmistakable authority, as it had seized Saul of Tarsus on the road to Damascus. Their father replied that, after all, they were a preacher's sons, and what kind of standing would he have in the eyes of his congregations if he couldn't even bring religion to his own offspring? Elizabeth Randolph concurred. And since her opinions, particularly upon matters of the church, were not easily set aside, the boys agreed to go ahead and get religion—and, more important, get the folks off their backs.

There were, of course, as the boys decided between themselves, at least two ways of getting religion: you could get it, or merely appear to get it. So one Sunday night when the Reverend Mr. Randolph, after a sermon, made one of his infrequent calls for witnesses—and people seized with the spirit were literally collapsing in the aisles—James and Asa winked at each other, fell out among the converts, and "passed out." When they "came to," they went to kneel at the "mourners' bench," and, along with everyone else, testified as how they were glad to have gotten religion. At home, later that night, the event was acknowledged with rejoicing, and their mother embraced them, in tears.

But where Asa was concerned, it was probably the beginning of the end of his life at home. To dissemble religious feelings day after day—or Sunday after Sunday—would present a greater challenge to his acting talents than the occasion on which he had "discovered" those feelings. And to appear to backslide would, in the end, be perhaps more painful to his parents than if he hadn't gotten religion at all. Besides, he realized that one of the professional ambitions he was turning over in his mind—going on the stage—was almost sure to bring him into a head-on collision with his parents. He certainly could not stay in Jacksonville and pursue a life on the stage, for in the opinion of his mother and father there were few occupations more worldly or disreputable. If he wanted to do that, it would be much safer to go away, and present them, from a distance, with a *fait accompli.*

At the time, Asa's social and political opinions were being formed against the background of one of the most heated ideological debates ever to take place in black America—the classic conflict between Booker T. Washington and W. E. B. Du Bois. It had started as early as 1895, when, at the Atlanta Exposition, Washington not only had virtually acquiesced in segregation and the proscription of black political rights in the South, but also—favoring industrial training—had belittled the importance of higher education as a priority for blacks. In an eloquent address, Washington assured the assembly of white Southern political and economic power that "the wisest among my race understand that the agitation of questions of social equality is the extremest folly." Washington, speaking little over thirty years after the abolition of slavery, felt that the ex-slaves' need for economic rehabilitation and self-sufficiency was the most urgent. "It is at the bottom of life we must begin," he submitted, "and not at the top."

The ensuing debate was to rage through the entire first decade of the new century. Washington's position, Du Bois replied, amounted to "a policy of submission," and "practically accepts the alleged inferiority of the Negro." Although Du Bois did not ignore the importance of industrial training, he felt "in conscience bound to ask of this nation three things: 1. The right to vote. 2. Civil equality. 3. The education of youth according to ability."

Du Bois's position, which came to be favored largely by Northern white liberals and black-protest intellectuals, represented the *avant-garde* of twentieth-century racial protest action. Washington's, which found support among a larger number of conservative black and white Republican politicians, was identified with accommodation to the white Southern *status quo.* The coalition of black intellectuals and Republicans that endorsed Washington's ideas—backed up by the readiness of the Republican party to reward his supporters and punish his detractors—was described as "the Tuskegee machine," named after Tuskegee Institute, of which Washington was president. And it was partly to counter the influence of this "machine," as well as to propound his own doctrine, that Du Bois organized the Niagara movement in 1905, which, four years later, became the National Association for the Advancement of Colored

People. Thus it was that Du Bois, who was also then a Socialist, became the first prominent "race radical" of the new century, and the NAACP the pioneer of the next half century or so of civil rights protest.

Du Bois's argument at the time, contained most notably in his collection of writings, *The Souls of Black Folk,* and in his equally famous essay, "The Talented Tenth" ("The Negro race, like all races, is going to be saved by its exceptional men"), was to shape the thinking of a significant portion of the black intelligentsia that came of age between the 1890's and 1910. As James Weldon Johnson was to say—though, as a writer for the *New York Age,* a pro-Washington paper, he was at one time identified with "the Tuskegee machine"—*The Souls of Black Folk* "had a greater effect upon and within the Negro race in America than any other single book published in this country since *Uncle Tom's Cabin.*"

The Randolph family—at least, the males, since Elizabeth Randolph took little interest in such matters—followed the course of the protest-accommodationist debate through the writings of Du Bois and Washington as well as through the political journals of the day. The Reverend Mr. Randolph was torn between the appeals of the two great advocates. He was a tradesman himself, and, if only because of the hard time he had supporting his own family, could not disagree with Washington that a dollar earned in the factory was more important than a dollar spent at the opera. And, of course, he had always been a Republican. But if James Randolph's head belonged to Washington, his heart belonged to Du Bois; for he, too, was alive not only with the dream of black political rights, but also with a love for what are called the higher things of life—or, at Cookman, the "higher branches." As said earlier, he was an interesting contradiction: a man with roots in the proletarian soil who had somehow sent out fine tendrils of middle-class manners and values. Several years later, his son Asa would present a similar contradiction to a political associate in Harlem: "He was a poor preacher's son, yet he had the virtues of the proletariat as well as the bourgeoisie. This is a hard thing to understand." In any case, Asa's father found it just as hard to make up his mind between Washington and Du Bois.

The elder son, James, was not without some interest in the question. But since his enthusiasm was reserved for scholarship—he was still studying Latin and mathematics in his spare time—he merely brushed Washington's position aside with bored disdain. It was Asa who rallied the most militantly around the Du Bois banner. He had found *The Souls of Black Folk* to be "the most influential book" he ever read. He saw Booker Washington as "a man of organization, but not a man of great social revolutionary vision for the Negro. He was down to earth, matter-of-fact, practical, looking for immediate gains, whereas Du Bois thought about the future achievement of Negroes, upon the highest level of human excellence." The overwhelming conviction Asa formed from reading Du Bois was that it would be "absolutely necessary to fight for social equality," a conviction he would retain for the rest of his life—even after, as would happen, his admiration for Du Bois's politics declined.

Asa was never more impatient with life in Jacksonville than he was after reading *The Souls of Black Folk*. It was clear to him that the climate for whatever interests he wanted to pursue—be they on the stage or in politics—would be more favorable in the North. It was in the North that the chances for a stage career were the greatest. (Two of the inspirations to ambitious black boys in Jacksonville then were the Johnson brothers—J. Rosamond and James Weldon—who had left the city for brilliant musical and literary careers in New York.) And it was in the North where ideas of racial freedom flourished.

Some years earlier, while a student at Cookman, Asa had had a taste of New York life. A cousin, who was the janitor of three apartment houses on Eighty-ninth Street, between Columbus Avenue and Central Park West, had invited him up to spend the summer vacation. Asa had earned pocket money by working as a "hall boy" for his cousin, and selling the *New York World* on the upper West Side. He had spent the money on fashionable clothes and the vaudeville shows of Bob Cole and J. Rosamond Johnson. But above all, he had found New York "big and lovely," and had had "a feeling that there was more freedom here."

In the spring of 1911, Asa told his mother that he and his friend Beaman Hearn, across the street, were going to New York for a few months, and that they would return by early fall. That was *Hearn's* plan. If Asa could help it, if he could catch on to something in New York, he was not coming back to Jacksonville. In April, both young men took their savings and sailed for New York City on the Clyde Line steamboat *Arapahoe*. To help defray the cost of the passage, the Reverend Mr. Randolph had asked the headwaiter, a friend, to give the boys jobs in the kitchen, and on the voyage up, Asa washed dishes "until I got cramps in my fingers." It was a useful introduction to some of the jobs he would soon be doing in New York City to support himself.

4 / Home to Harlem

As the turn of the century approached, segregation and disfranchisement spread across the South, and the first large wave of black migration
to Northern cities began. The exodus, which lasted until about 1910, was
nowhere near as large as the one during the years of World War I; but it
drained the region of so many of its black professionals, businessmen,
and intellectuals that it came to be known as "the migration of the Talented Tenth." They were the class that sensed most keenly the crippling
blow which the restoration of the old order of white supremacy would
deal to the hope for racial equality As Gilbert Osofsky, a Harlem historian, writes: "When T. Thomas Fortune, William Lewis Bulkley, and
North Carolina educator and politician Edward A. Johnson came north,
each emphasized he could no longer live under Jim Crow and racial violence. George Henry White said he left North Carolina because he
'couldn't live there and be a man and be treated like a man.' He believed
that thousands of others would follow him. Booker T. Washington told
the Board of Trustees of Tuskegee, in 1903, that 'for every lynching that
takes place . . . a score of colored people leave . . . for the city.'"
Many of the black leaders who remained in the South—who found
that their racial ideology could dwell peaceably enough with segregation,
or who were merely content to let their buckets down where they stood—
were disciples of Booker T. Washington's philosophy of accommodation. Though not all of Washington's believers remained in the South, by
1910 much of the hope for black freedom and equality was domiciled or
exiled in the North. Of the 60,534 blacks in Manhattan, for example,
only 14,309 were natives of the state of New York. And the majority of
black businessmen, professionals, and politicians who then resided above
the Mason-Dixon line had been raised below it. Referring to this period,

53

Carter Woodson, the black historian, remarked that Southern blacks were deprived of their potential militant leadership as the Talented Tenth fled to the North. In any event, it was on the tail end of this prewar movement that the young Asa Randolph—in search of opportunity—and his friend Beaman Hearn—in search merely of diversion—arrived in Harlem.

In addition to their place of origin, the two Floridians bore a few resemblances to each other: they were both twenty-two, and both had dark, smooth faces, and heads of thick, curly hair. Their differences were more numerous, however, and were the kinds that suggested differences in character. Randolph, over six feet tall, had the slender but durable build of a long-distance runner. His features were sharp and delicate, and his eyes mirrored an unresolved contest between diffidence and self-assurance. There was no such indecisiveness in his voice—a baritone of marvelous depth and resonance. Despite his bookishness, he dressed like a man to whom style was important, and who took a certain pleasure in how well he looked. It explained, no doubt, why, as a boy in Jacksonville, he used to take the choicer pieces of the clothes their mother sewed or bought for them, leaving the duller pickings for his brother. One of the earliest photographs taken of him in New York shows him wearing a heavy gray derby, a black overcoat with velvet Chesterfield collar, and white spats over black shoes. The hat and overcoat seem a size too large for him, but the expression on his face suggests that he is quite pleased with his appearance.

Beaman Hearn was shorter and chunkier, with a rounder and more fleshy face. His voice was higher pitched, and his eyes more decisive. Nor did he share his friend's reserved manner, interest in things of the mind, or liking for stylish dress.

When they arrived, in April, 1911—a month after the tragic Triangle fire in downtown Manhattan—black Harlem was contained between 128th and 145th streets, and bordered, east and west, by Fifth and Seventh avenues. Harlem beyond those boundaries was white; it was apprehensive as well, for the black section was pushing outward, slowly darkening new territory. The month the two young men arrived, Samuel J. Battle had just been appointed the first black policeman in Manhattan. John G. Taylor, the white president of the Harlem Property Owners Association, was complaining in the *Harlem Home News*, a white publication, that "white renegades" were "backing Negro speculators in their value destroying ventures," that ten years earlier "there were only a few Negro families in Harlem," and that "now there are thousands in the shakeup."

But no one would be able to check the outward push of black Harlem; and, in the words of James Weldon Johnson, white residents "began to flee. They took fright, they became panic-stricken, they ran amuck. Their conduct could be compared to that of a community in the Middle Ages fleeing before an epidemic of the black plague. . . ." One of the few remaining white enclaves in the black area was a row of thirteen attractive tenement houses on the north side of 135th Street, between Seventh and Lenox avenues. In 1911, the rich, all-black St. Philip's Episcopal Church, which had recently moved to Harlem from West Twenty-fifth Street, closed the largest black real-estate deal in the city's history up to that time when it bought the entire row of buildings on West 135th Street and rented them to black tenants.

It was transactions such as this that dismayed and outraged the Harlem Property Owners Association. And some of the "Negro speculators" John G. Taylor was complaining about were realty firms like Nail & Parker (owned by John E. Nail and Henry C. Parker), which had handled the St. Philip's deal; and the Afro-American Realty Company, headed by Philip A. Payton. These two enterprises were the largest and most successful of their kind in the history of black Harlem. Dedicated to buying up homes and renting or selling them to blacks, these realtors were chiefly responsible for opening up Harlem to black residency, and, ultimately, for expanding and transforming the community into the black metropolis it was to become.

Randolph and Hearn had hoped to stay with the latter's aunt, then a cook at the fashionable Theresa Hotel, at Seventh Avenue and 125th Street. She had no space for them, however, and sent them to a friend, who had recently bought a home on 132nd Street, between Seventh and Lenox. The friend liked the two young men from Jacksonville. They looked like "decent boys," after all, and she gave them a room for $1.50 a week.

The two Jacksonvillians spent the first two months or so wandering through Manhattan, sightseeing and taking in the stage shows. But Randolph's mind was never far from the purpose that had brought him to New York: to become a stage actor. In the mornings, Harlemites used to encounter the odd spectacle of the young Randolph reading aloud from one of his books as he walked from his room on 132nd Street to a restaurant at the corner of 130th and Lenox, where he had breakfast. "People used to look at him and shake their heads," recalls Beaman Hearn, "as if they were sure he was going out of his mind." Randolph's favorite haunts in the city were the New York Public Library, at Forty-second Street and Fifth Avenue, and the old Hippodrome, at Forty-fourth and Sixth, where, for twenty-five cents, he could spend an entire day watching variety and vaudeville shows. Perhaps the musical stage was part of his interest in the theater. After all, James Weldon Johnson, one of the examples of what a boy from Jacksonville could do in New York, not only was a poet, literary intellectual, and political journalist; he also was writing lyrics for vaudeville, in collaboration with his brother, J. Rosamond Johnson.

But by August, not having worked a day since they arrived, Randolph and Hearn had run out of money. They "woke up one morning to find" that "we didn't even have the dollar-fifty to pay the rent." Deciding that morning to find jobs, they combed through the employment section of the *New York World,* and answered an ad for porters at an all-white apartment building on West 148th Street. When they arrived at the building, however, they found more than a dozen men waiting to apply. This was critical. Desperately in need of funds, and having no experience in portering, they could hardly afford to face such competition. So, doing some quick thinking, Randolph walked up to the men, and, in his most confident baritone, asked, "Any of you boys know anything about typewriting?" The men were surprised at the question, but nevertheless said no. "Well, you're wasting your time," Randolph told them. "These people are looking for men who know something about typewriting." After standing around for some time, the men slowly drifted away, leaving Randolph and Hearn as the only applicants. Hearn was hired to run the elevator, and Randolph to operate the lobby switchboard. They had been saved by one of the impish twists to Randolph's personality. Fanny Hansberry, teaching him to read and write when he was a small boy in dresses and curls, had found him "full of tricks. He was a natural right-hander, but as soon as you turned your back he was trying to write with his left."

Late in October, Hearn returned to Jacksonville. Randolph asked him to stay awhile longer, but he insisted on honoring the pledge he had made to his parents, to return to Jacksonville by fall. His father—a prosperous plasterer—had promised that if he returned by then, he would be given enough money to start himself in a fruit-and-vegetable business.

Randolph, now practically alone in the city, did—in view of his background—the only natural thing: he turned to the churches. Considering the social and cultural role that churches performed at the center of black communal life, they were, he felt, the only places he could hope to meet young people with backgrounds similar to his. Most of the black churches in Manhattan were then located in the West Fifties, the upper section of what was known as the Tenderloin district. But, with Harlem opening up to blacks, the preachers were moving uptown, and the churches would soon follow.

After looking in on a few Sunday services, Randolph learned of the young people's organizations that were connected to the different churches, and soon confined his attentions to them. These were the Baptist Young People's Union of the Mount Olivet Baptist Church, on West Fifty-third Street; the Lyceum of St. Mark's Methodist Church, also on West Fifty-third Street; the Allen Christian Endeavor Society of the Bethel AME Chapel, on West 132nd Street; and the Epworth League of the Salem Methodist Church, on West 133rd Street—where the minister was the Reverend Frederick Cullen, foster father of the poet Countee Cullen.

Randolph's interest in these organizations had little to do with religion. He merely wished to meet people with whom he could pursue his own social and intellectual interests, and from whom he could gather a surer sense of life in New York. As he said later, "There was a certain standard, social standard, in the life of Negroes in Harlem then, different from today. You had a little gloss. There was a deeper sense of respectability within the Negro group. They were trying to do things, trying to achieve status for the race. You had the underworld, to be sure, but you had some good types of people. They set the tone of the community. James Weldon Johnson, for instance. He was living there. He was a man of fine dignity, artistic gifts, and literary accomplishments. A lot of these people were in the churches, and you saw them in the so-called better-class restaurants that Negroes would go to. All of these churches had great preachers, great spiritual strength. You take a man like the Reverend Reverdy C. Ransom. He was connected with the Bethel AME Chapel, and he was a powerful champion of Negro rights, a man of great culture. These churches had the understanding and the feeling that their young people's societies represented an important force for the attraction of the young."

As it turned out, Randolph did not find it so easy to pursue his social and intellectual interests in the young people's organizations. The majority of them allowed no secular interests to intrude upon their study of the Bible. Those were clearly not the ones Randolph wanted. A more promising exception was the Epworth League. True, the league's principal devotion was also to the Bible, but it permitted itself a wider range of concerns and activities—including a theater club—and therefore attracted young people who were not wholly indifferent to the questions of the day. Though his initial feelings about the Epworth League would not last, Randolph found it the most congenial of the youth groups, and went there often.

Taking no part in the Bible discussions of the league, he simply sat back and listened. But when he thought they had gone on long and safely enough, he gently provoked them onto the riskier and more controversial paths of politics and current issues—one of which, inevitably, was race. He was seldom satisfied by the outcome, however. Especially on the race question, he was full not only of the militancy he considered the dearest part of his AME heritage, but also of the new protest wine of W. E. B. Du Bois. His colleagues in the league held such gradualist opinions concerning the pace of racial progress, though, and expressed them with such reverence and circumspection, that probing inquiries into the race question were seldom, if ever, possible. Recalling his frustration, Randolph later reported that the young people in the Epworth League "seemed unable to conceive of any program for racial change that was not disciplined by religious manners or endorsed by the black Republicans."

All of this could make him despondent at times. He had come to New York not only considering himself a student of Du Bois's racial radicalism and a potential member of the Talented Tenth, but also carrying the notion that the city was a center for ideas of freedom. Yet the political quietism of the Epworth League represented a unique opportunity for him. If its boat needed rocking, then there was no one who, by ideas and impatience, was more qualified to do so. This he set out to accomplish, with such apparent success that several subsequent meetings of the league broke up over Randolph's "heretical social opinions" and "irreverent observations" upon religion. Though Asa Randolph, as they called him, made a handful of converts, the majority in the league regarded him as "a godless troublemaker"—a description he enjoyed only slightly less than the actual trouble he caused them.

A member of the league's Bible set was Theophilus Lewis, a young man with an interest in the theater, who would become a drama reviewer for the *Messenger,* the radical magazine Randolph founded and edited a few years later. Lewis, today a theater reviewer for *America* magazine, recalls that "Randolph was the outstanding member of our Epworth forums. He had us talking about everything under the sun. When the meetings broke up, sometimes late in the evenings, he still had us arguing passionately through the streets, on our way home." Some of the attractive girls in the league would have been more impressed with a little personal attention from the handsome and intelligent young Southerner. But as one of them says today, pointing to her head, "He was *all* up here."

The theater club, Randolph's other interest in the Epworth League, was not, given a choice, the kind of group he would have preferred to join. It promised neither the improvement nor the wider exposure of his talents that he desired. Its players, barely above the Sunday-school level of competence, lacked even the semblance of professional polish he had acquired while appearing in amateur productions in Jacksonville. But with his ambitions, any opportunity to keep his skills in shape was better than none at all—especially in a town like New York, where he was acquainted with no one of any importance, and certainly not in the theater. The club's chief activity was rehearsing scenes from Shakespeare and presenting them, at least one Sunday afternoon a month, before community audiences at the Salem Methodist Church. Though Randolph's appearances in these scenes brought him no attention that would be useful in furthering his career, they gave him the chance to "memorize every line from *Othello, Hamlet,* and *The Merchant of Venice.*"

A measure of attention *would* come—a while later, after his search for professional polish had taken him, quite by accident, to the City College of New York. He had been curious for some time about an impoverished-looking member of the league, a young man named John Ramsay, who, everybody said, was a student at City College. Randolph had found this hard to believe, having felt, in light of his experience after leaving Cookman, that a college education was virtually out of the reach of poor families—most of all, poor black families. In fact, he might not have been able to attend even Cookman had it not been a free educational institution. Yet here was Ramsay, who, from all he could see, did not surpass him in means—nor, for that matter, in brains—going to college.

One day he expressed his curiosity to Ramsay—more delicately than he had turned it over in his own mind—and was "astonished" to hear that you didn't need to have money to go to City, that a good high-school record was enough. Well, then, Randolph felt, he qualified eminently: his Cookman record was as nearly brilliant as it could be for someone who was no good whatsoever at mathematics; and, shifting from one menial Harlem job to another, earning barely enough to feed himself and pay his rent, he "didn't have a quarter." As he said to Ramsay, City College was, indeed, "the only kind of college *I* will ever be able to afford." In February of 1912, wanting to improve his elocution, he registered at City for two evening courses in public speaking.

The improvement must have been rapid, for at one of the Sunday afternoon performances at the Salem Church, soon after Randolph starting going to City, he caught the eye of an important man in the theater. This was Henri Strange, a black Philadelphian, then the leading tragedian on the Harlem stage. A few days after the performance at Salem, Randolph was dining in a luncheonette on Lenox Avenue when Strange entered, and, finding no other empty seats, took the one at Randolph's table. Strange introduced himself and remarked that he had caught the young man's performance at Salem the previous Sunday. "With your voice and diction, it doesn't really matter whether you can act," Strange said, and offered to sponsor Randolph into his drama group.

Ecstatic, Randolph wrote triumphantly to his parents in Jacksonville: a professional stage career was about to open for him. Thus he had no immediate plan to return to the South. Their response was shattering, though not altogether surprising. It was all right with them, his parents replied, if he felt there was a future for him in New York; but under no circumstances could they approve of a son of theirs spending his life on the stage, especially in a town like New York.

It was not a complete surprise to him because he knew very well that in the hierarchy of things his parents had always considered evil the professional stage ranked very high—somewhere below gambling and "lewd women." He had merely hoped that they would consider the stamp they had left on his character strong enough to resist whatever they regarded as evil in the life of the stage. But though he was now a man of twenty-three, and entirely responsible for—or entitled to—his own choices, he had no intention of defying his parents on an issue they considered so vital to their morality. Nor could he be indifferent to the damage his action might conceivably do to their morale, especially his father's. A preacher's failure to recruit his own offspring to the church was not necessarily fatal to his self-esteem or to his position in his neighborhood and his congregation, but the same could not be said if it turned out that his son had found the "immoral" life of the stage more enticing than the life of the church.

The theater now eliminated as a serious ambition, Randolph focused his interests upon politics. To create a climate of discussion more suitable to his tastes and his needs, he withdrew from the Epworth League, and, with some of the freer thinkers there, formed his own current-affairs group, called the Independent Political Council. At City College, he dropped public speaking, and, over the next few semesters, registered for courses in history, political science, philosophy, and economics. His racial outlook and his general political temperament were fairly well formed by then, but it was during this phase of his career at City College that he was introduced to an ideology, socialism, that would be a major influence upon the shape of his political future.

The switch in courses at City brought Randolph closer to the political life on campus, and he found the classrooms and corridors to be among "the hottest beds of radicalism in New York City." In 1912 and '13, campus radicals were championing the causes of the Industrial Workers of the World, probably the most radical labor activists then in America. These campus groups were raising funds and holding rallies in support of two great IWW campaigns in the East—the textile strikes in Lawrence, Massachusetts, and Paterson, New Jersey, in 1912 and 1913, respectively. Randolph's interest in the 1913 strike was heightened by the fact that one of the staunchest supporters of the IWW in Paterson was Hubert Harrison, a pioneer radical intellectual in Harlem, the community's leading street-corner orator, and a member of the Socialist party in New York.

Among the radical heroes to CCNY evening students were William D. ("Big Bill") Haywood and Elizabeth ("Rebel Girl") Gurley Flynn, of the IWW; and Eugene Victor Debs, of the Socialist party. Debs, a passionate spokesman for socialism, an early advocate of industrial unionism, and himself a member of the IWW, polled nearly a million votes in the 1912 presidential election, as the candidate of the Socialist party. The combination of Debs's prestige, the growing popularity of the Socialists, and the militant industrial unionism of the IWW had helped to raise hopes on the left that a Socialist millennium was at hand. A few years earlier, Julius A. Wayland, editor of the Socialist weekly *Appeal to Reason*, had announced to his readership: "Socialism is coming. It's coming like a prairie fire and nothing can stop it. . . . You can feel it in the air. You can see it in the papers. You can taste it in the price of beef. . . . The next few years will give this nation to the Socialist Party." On a campus like City College, no one felt these hopes more strongly than the evening students. In the daytime, many of them were, like Randolph, struggling to make a living. And, especially because they had to make it in New York City, they probably knew a little more about "the price of beef" than Julius Wayland, living out in Kansas, closer to the cows.

Ironically, some of the leftist movements that were now capturing Randolph's political fancy on the campus—and that would help to extend his previous views on race radicalism—had been in their infancy during the very period, following Booker T. Washington's "Atlanta Compromise" of 1895, when he was falling in love with Du Bois's ideas in Jacksonville. Only a year prior to Washington's Atlanta speech, Eugene Debs's American Railway Union, which helped to pioneer industrial unionism, had been crushed by the powerful Pullman Company. In 1901, Debs had been one of the founders of the Socialist party of America. The IWW had been organized in Chicago in 1905, two years after Du Bois published, in *The Souls of Black Folk,* his most powerful arguments against the Washington philosophy of racial accommodation. And the same year, the revolutionary events that were to overthrow czarism in Russia, and give a strong impulse to radicalism in America, had been foreshadowed in the mutiny aboard the Russian battleship *Potemkin.* Responsive to this heady current, even Du Bois had joined the Socialist party soon after its founding. He had remained a member until the fall of 1912, when, after supporting Woodrow Wilson over Eugene Debs, he had resigned from the party "to escape discipline."

It was in a course taught by J. Salwyn Shapiro, an assistant professor of history and economics at City College, that Randolph first read the socialist literature and, as he put it, "the history of European working-class movements." The "discovery" was so "exciting" that, in his spare time, he "began reading Marx as children read *Alice in Wonderland.*" It was, he would say, "like finally running into an idea which gives you your outlook on life."

Part of this outlook was a broader philosophy of the racial struggle. A believer previously in pure-and-simple racial radicalism, he now felt that if some of the conditions which victimized black Americans were endemic to the nation's economic life—thus intensifying the competitive struggle between black and white workers, exacerbating racism, and politicizing hate—then the movement for racial freedom could not proceed independently of the movement for social and economic change. "The problem of people fighting each other," Randolph said later, "was based upon the fact that they were fighting the competitive system. Hence the end result was conflict with each other. And, of course, they had the stereotypes and myths of race and people, and looked at the myths and stereotypes instead of looking at the human being or the economic situation."

But the teacher at City who impressed Randolph the most—less for his political ideas than for his Socratic style of mind—was a young liberal professor of philosophy and politics named Morris R. Cohen. Cohen, a man with "a biting tongue," had a "magnetic impact" upon his students. They were both fascinated and exasperated by his habit, during class discussions, of expressing no firm convictions upon any subject, preferring to reply to questions by posing more challenging and provocative ones of his own. Revealing the source of his attitude, Cohen wrote years later, in his *Faith of a Liberal:* "In the pride of my youth, I used to characterize myself as philosophically a stray dog, unchained to any metaphysical kennel. It seemed to me better to brave the muddy realities of the unprotected out-of-doors, the uncertain food, the attacks from the rains and winds of factual experience." In any event, Randolph says today that Cohen "stirred more intellectual restlessness and discontent" in him "than any other teacher at City College."

The political institution that then dominated the allegiance of black Americans was the Republican party. Half a century after Emancipation, Republican politicians still regarded their grateful black supporters with a smug assurance. Few attempts were made to court or retain the black vote beyond the practice of rewarding conspicuous members of the race—or black ward leaders—with important federal appointments. Black voters, who attracted little attention from the Democrats, regarded these appointments as tokens of the continuing esteem in which they were held by the political party that had presided over the abolition of slavery. In Jacksonville, the most important of these appointees had been Joseph E. Lee, one of the men whom the Reverend James Ran-

dolph, a staunch Republican himself, had held up to his sons as a model
of what black men could achieve. When Asa Randolph arrived in New
York, the man who occupied a similar position there was Charles W.
Anderson, Collector of Internal Revenue for the Second District. The
elevation of men like Lee and Anderson had to be approved by Booker
T. Washington's "Tuskegee machine," which, during Teddy Roosevelt's
administration, was the clearinghouse for all black political appointments.
When Woodrow Wilson came to office in 1912, practically all black
federal officeholders, including Anderson, lost their jobs. But especially
during the Wilson administration—distinguished for its indifference to
the problems of black citizens—Republican politicians remained confident that it would take a "sledge hammer" to drive the black vote from
"the Party of Lincoln."

Randolph—now a budding Socialist—felt "nothing but contempt"
for politicians in both parties who so cynically ignored or exploited the
black situation. So strong was his feeling about the Republicans that it
almost cost him his membership in the City College evening school's
debating society. That happened prior to the 1912 presidential election.
The society was holding a mock Republican convention, and Randolph
—quite unwisely—was selected to place the name of William Howard
Taft in nomination. Randolph advised the officers of the society that his
selection was probably an error, inasmuch as he felt no political sentiments that might be remotely helpful to the nomination of a Republican.
Well, they told him, "just make up a speech, say anything." Randolph
smiled and agreed, no one seeming to have caught the glint of mischief in
his eyes.

"Convention" night, he appeared at the podium dressed in a stovepipe
hat, black cutaway, wing collar, and black bow tie, all of which he had
picked up in a secondhand clothing store in Harlem. Before a large audience, which included Dr. Frederick Robinson, assistant director of the
college's evening division, Randolph "nominated" Taft by attacking the
Republican party and "saying everything about Taft that would get him
defeated." Needless to say, especially because of Dr. Robinson's presence, the society was acutely embarrassed. Though Randolph was not expelled, he was never again allowed to make a presentation at one of the
society's public affairs.

A year later, making his debut in serious Harlem politics, Randolph
got a chance to oppose the Republicans more legitimately. The party had
just refused to endorse John M. Royal, a Harlem realtor, as a candidate

for the Board of Aldermen (forerunner of the City Council). Having no reason to fear the loss of black electoral support, the party of Lincoln felt no need to offer the black community any gift so exorbitant as its own black candidate. This time, however, Royal defied the party. Rather than withdraw in favor of the white Republican nominee, Royal ran as an independent on the racially insurgent slogan "The black man first, the black man last, the black man all the time."

Impressed by this defiance of the Republicans—as well as by the precedent of a black Harlemite running for political office—Randolph joined Royal's campaign, and canvassed and distributed literature in his behalf throughout the black community. He also pressed into Royal's service his colleagues in the Independent Political Council, the current-affairs discussion group he had formed after withdrawing from the Epworth League. But the campaign was a disaster; Royal was soundly defeated by the regular party candidates. "Randolph worked for Royal," recalls Theophilus Lewis, then a member of the Political Council, "because Negroes had no elected positions. One of the things he was saying then was that we needed to elect our own people—aldermen, assemblymen, state senators, and so on. Well, we didn't get Royal elected. The Republicans didn't want him, and the Democrats had a foolproof machine. Election day I was watching at the polls in one of the districts where Royal was on the ballot. Women weren't voting then, only men. That election district had about 175 enrolled Democrats—almost all of them white—and that darned Tammany machine brought out 170 of them. The Republicans got about 200, mostly black, and poor Royal got about 5."

Whatever the intellectual and political excitements of City College, Randolph was having a difficult time supporting himself. One of his classmates, Oscar Rosner, today a prominent lawyer in mid-Manhattan, used to meet him "on cold evenings walking along Convent Avenue on his way to class. He was hungry sometimes, but always anxious about the state of the world. He was doing anything to make a living, down to scrubbing floors." Randolph seldom held down a job for very long. Because, as he felt, "the jobs Negroes could get weren't worth spending much time on," he made a habit of walking off them after he had earned enough to last him a few weeks. And he was fired from a number of others for, as he says, "stirring up trouble and sowing seeds of discontent among my co-workers."

Somehow, he lasted for several months at the Amsterdam Avenue office of the Consolidated Gas Company, working as a porter. All his attempts to stir activity among his fellow porters failed. "Look around you," he would say. "Is it only white men who can be bookkeepers and supervisors? Why can't Negroes do those jobs? Are we only good for sweeping floors and washing windows?" But the men, Randolph says, "had no ear for that kind of talk," and finally he "gave up and left."

In the early spring of 1914, he talked his way into a job as a waiter (he had no previous experience) on the *Paul Revere,* a Fall River Line steamboat that plied between New York and Boston. He barely lasted the first day. Receiving an order for "littlenecks" and steaks—and having no idea what "littlenecks" were—Randolph returned with the steaks first. A huge, gruff, black headwaiter, who had overheard the order—and who, in any case, did not believe Randolph's claim of previous experience —stepped in the young man's path, took the tray from him, and ordered him out of the dining room. "You don't know the first thing about waiting on tables," he told Randolph. "Where did you ever hear of anyone serving steaks before clams?" But Randolph asked for a chance, and was placed on probation for the rest of the trip.

Everything, probation and employment, expired when the *Paul Revere* returned to New York. Coming back from Boston, Randolph was caught trying to organize the waiters and kitchen help against conditions in the "glory hole"—the small, crammed, foul-smelling quarters on such steamboats, where the men slept, fought, gambled, and swore all night, while a naked bulb burned overhead. Randolph had first encountered the "glory hole" on the *Arapahoe,* on which he had worked as a kitchen hand on the journey from Jacksonville to New York. He had been so terrified that he had "promised God" never to set foot in such a place again if he was permitted to escape alive. "I never knew you had people like that," he said later. "It was like Hades to me."

Randolph was usually proud to be fired for stirring up trouble. It strengthened his sense of himself as an agitator, and raised his prestige among the members of his Independent Political Council. The council, giving lectures and conducting debates in the black churches, was by then developing a reputation in the community for political militancy. "We were having a great time," Randolph remembers. "We didn't think of the future, of establishing a home, getting ahead, or things of that sort. Those things weren't as important as creating unrest among the Negroes."

He would soon discover, however, that establishing a home could have its unexpected rewards. Marriage—which had, up to then, been practically unthinkable, especially to a young man of such slender means —was to take him almost unawares, free him from the struggle to make a living, and enable him to devote himself entirely to "creating unrest among the Negroes."

5 / Starting Out

One evening in the late spring of 1914, Randolph and his Independent Political Council appeared in a debate at Salem Methodist, and when it was over, a member of the church—one of the conservative young men he had encountered in the Epworth League—came up to congratulate him. The young man's name was Ernest T. Welcome, and complimenting Randolph was the lesser part of his intention; he really had a proposition to make. He had recently opened an employment agency in the community, he said, and he could use someone of Randolph's abilities and public interests to help him run it.

The two men had come to know each other fairly well, not because of any political kinship they had discovered in the Epworth League, but because Welcome had a musical background that appealed to one of Randolph's former interests. Welcome, a fine tenor, was a member of the Salem choir. His wife—the former Jennie Vander Zee, sister of Harlem's famous photographer James Vander Zee—was an accomplished pianist, who gave lessons to the children of black Harlem's well-to-do. James Vander Zee remembers that Welcome "had the finest tenor voice I ever heard." Randolph had been drawn to all of this, reminded of families in Jacksonville in whose homes he had once passed leisurely musical evenings. In fact, soon after he started going to the Epworth League, the Welcomes had invited him to a few such evenings in their home. Leaning against the piano while Jennie Welcome played, he had joined his baritone with Welcome's tenor in charming duets.

But beyond that, Welcome, whom Randolph found devoid of any serious progressive ideas, did not interest him. He took no one seriously "who did not spend their time thinking about Negro freedom." The men he would admire the most in his public career would be those with a

greater interest in social ideas and causes than in "making money or
getting ahead"—though the man soon to become the closest friend of his
life would barely meet that standard. Randolph felt, in any case, that the
precepts Welcome seemed to live by bore too close a resemblance to
those Fred R. Moore, editor of the conservative *New York Age,* once
recommended to his young black readers in Harlem: ". . . first, get a
wife; second, become a member of the church; and, last but not least,
join the Republican Party." But Welcome had one gift, in addition to his
fine tenor, which Randolph was obliged to acknowledge: "He could
charm himself into the good favor of almost anyone." Yielding to the
pressure of Welcome's charm, and, no doubt, to the pressure of his own
economic situation as well, Randolph agreed to join the agency.

The great wartime migration from the South and the West Indian islands was in its early stages, and Welcome had been among the first in
Harlem to open employment offices for the new arrivals—perceiving, of
course, the rewards all this promised to enterprising businessmen. But
Welcome did not wish to be known as the operator of a mere employment agency; no desirable social status having yet accrued to that sort of
enterprise, he considered it a "low terminology." He named his agency
the Brotherhood of Labor. It would not merely *sell* jobs to people, but—
in keeping with the social purpose implied in its higher-sounding name—
would also attempt to attract new migrants from the South, and educate
them in the political and social conditions of life in New York City. It
was here that Welcome needed Randolph, for he had none of the abilities necessary to achieve his higher aims. The next few months, for a
small percentage of the take, Randolph designed posters and handbills,
and wrote political pamphlets for distribution among the newly arrived
migrants as well as among potential ones in the South.

The office of the Brotherhood of Labor was in an old apartment house
near the corner of 135th Street and Lenox Avenue, looking across to the
row of apartment buildings St. Philip's Church had bought in 1911. It
was in this building that one of the most important turns in Randolph's
affairs would occur.

Down the corridor from Welcome's office, there was a beauty salon,
owned and operated by an attractive thirty-one-year-old widow named
Lucille Green. She was light-skinned, of medium height and build, and
had a head of short-cropped hair, prematurely silver. After watching her
come and go for several weeks, the twenty-five-year-old Randolph asked

Welcome who she was, and was told she was one of the "socialites" of Harlem, "a sort of upper-class person" of comfortable means. Welcome offered to introduce them, and one morning when Mrs. Green came in, he led Randolph down the corridor into her salon.

Born Lucille Campbell, in Christianburg, Virginia, in 1883, she was one of the three children of William and Josephine Campbell, and was trained as a schoolteacher at Howard University. At Howard, she had struck one of the upperclassmen, Leigh Whipper—later to become a well-known black actor—as a "smart-looking girl with a gregarious smile." "Progressive, a good dresser, sharp as a tack," she was, Whipper felt, "the kind of girl any man would fall for." The man who fell most successfully was a Howard law student, Joseph Green. They married after graduation, and moved to New York City, where Lucille taught school and her husband worked as a customs officer. Not long after they arrived, however, Joseph Green died.

In 1913, Madame C. J. Walker, the black cosmetics millionairess, arrived in Harlem from Indianapolis, where she had developed and commercialized a formula for straightening kinky hair. To help popularize her formula and extend her business in Harlem, Madame Walker—who built a town house on West 136th Street and, later, a mansion at Irvington-on-the-Hudson, north of the city, in Westchester County—opened a school to train young women in the Walker hair beauty system. Graduates of the Lelia College—named after Madame Walker's only child, A'Lelia—operated their own salons, using only Walker products and the Walker beauty system. Lucille Green, who had given up school teaching after her husband's death, was one of the first graduates of Lelia College. She not only started her own salon on 135th Street, but also became a close friend of Madame Walker and a member of the "society" that grew up around her in Harlem.

Lucille became one of the more accomplished and sought after of the Walker students. Her customers ranged from the black elite in Harlem to well-to-do crinkly-haired whites from "downtown." And one day a week she traveled out to the fashionable Marlborough Blenheim Hotel, in Atlantic City, to serve a similar white clientele. Her prices seem to have been high, and brought her a considerable income. She once made a wig for her old college mate Leigh Whipper, who, after leaving Howard, had been an athletic coach in Virginia before moving to Harlem. According to Whipper, it took him ten years to pay for the wig. But this may have been commentary less upon the size of Mrs. Green's bill than upon the state of Whipper's pocket, because for many years after coming to Harlem he was a struggling actor in the Lafayette Players, one of the important theater groups in Harlem at the time.

As Asa Randolph put it, he and Mrs. Green were immediately "taken" with each other. He considered her "beautiful, gregarious, elegant, fashionable, and socially conscious." He also found that they not only had the same birthday, April 15, but shared an interest in socialism and Shakespeare as well. Following her interests, later on, Lucille was to be a Socialist candidate for a seat on the New York City Board of Aldermen; a member, along with Randolph, of a small amateur group in Harlem, called Ye Friends of Shakespeare; organizer of a Harlem Fresh Air Fund for poor children; founder of the Harlem branch of the Howard University alumni association; and a chaperone of the Debutantes Club, founded by A'Lelia Walker, daughter of her friend Madame Walker. According to an original member, A'Lelia founded the club in 1921 "as a means of presenting her daughter in society. A'Lelia had all that money from her mother, and she had sent her own daughter to a fine school in Atlanta, but she wanted a little social background for the girl."

Though they were anything but equal in material possessions, Randolph and Lucille Green were equally generous of disposition, a mutuality that no doubt deepened their interest in each other. Two of their acquaintances at the time paid them quite similar compliments. One said "he would give you his last quarter," and the other said "she gave away even the things she needed if she felt you needed them more." Randolph himself later observed that "her greatest love was for people"; and she, in praising him to a friend, would say that one of his more admirable qualities was "heart."

Mrs. Green's first impressions of the young Randolph, however, were, as she summed them up, that he was "exotic." It is not clear what exactly she meant by that, but it may well have been her word for the combination of Randolph's handsomeness, fine and courtly manners, dignified bearing, impressive voice, private reticence, public rebelliousness, and devotion to the serious side of life. Nor is it unlikely that she detected something in his appearance which suggested that he was indifferent to, or, at any rate, lacked, money—a poverty that, to a woman of her means, and in a man so admirably endowed in other respects, may simply have enhanced his attractiveness in her eyes.

The combination of Randolph's qualities was probably uncommon among the young men of Lucille Green's acquaintance; it would have been at any time. Despite the serious aspects of her own interests, she was, as Randolph had been told, a "socialite"—and, in prewar Harlem, that meant going to lots of parties, dances, and soirees, most of them presided over by the social set of which Madame Walker had become the center. It was not a sociey of old families or possessed of old money, even as such things were measured among blacks; old families and old money were to be found mainly in Brooklyn, among blacks who had no memory of ever having lived anywhere but in New York, and who, when they examined the roots of their lineage, found no trace of Southern soil or servitude. Madame Walker's society consisted largely of successful speculators of recent vintage, community clubwomen, new urban professionals, and other parvenu varieties. The kinds of young men it attracted, moreover, were those who were drawn chiefly by the promise of a swell time in the company of beautiful, gregarious, and well-to-do women.

On a more genteel social plane, Lucille Green was an established member of St. Philip's Episcopal Church, then, and for several years after, the wealthiest and most prestigious black congregation in the world. To have been seen in a St. Philip's pew of a Sunday was to have been certified instantly as belonging to "the better element of colored people."

Randolph's courtship of Mrs. Green—or "Buddy," as they would always call each other—was brief and unspectacular. He took her to political lectures, movies, and a few stage shows. She sometimes invited him to Madame Walker's parties, but he always begged off, saying he had no time to waste with "fly-by-night people." A Harlemite who knew him at the time "never saw him at a dance or a party. He had bigger things in view."

In November, 1914, they were married at St. Philip's by the Reverend Hutchens C. Bishop, the rector, who had met Randolph through Lucille, and who was distressed that so "fine" a young man showed signs of "throwing away his talents on socialism." Bishop was scarcely Randolph's kind of preacher, anyway. He much preferred a man like Reverdy C. Ransom, of the Bethel AME, who felt, as he did, that if most blacks belonged to the working class, then the race problem would be solved only by Socialists, those holding "that the rights of men are more sacred than the rights of property."

Randolph had not wanted a church wedding, but his wife had insisted on St. Philip's—thinking, no doubt, of the social damage a civil ceremony might do to her standing in the church. She had compromised by

allowing him to choose the wedding trip, which—not entirely to her surprise—turned out to be a ride on the open streetcar from their new
apartment at 2453 Seventh Avenue to South Ferry and back. Even that
was a considerable concession to convention, for, saturated in politics as
his mind was, he would just as soon have taken her down to Union
Square to listen to Eugene Debs.

A few months later, at a party at Madame Walker's, the new Mrs.
Randolph was introduced to the man who would become her husband's
closest friend and comrade. His name was Chandler Owen, and he was a
friend of her old acquaintance at Howard, Leigh Whipper, and a student
at Columbia University. Owen was ten days older than Randolph, having
been born on April 5, 1889, in Warrenton, North Carolina. After four
years at Virginia Union University, at Richmond, he had entered Columbia in 1913 to study sociology and political science. Owen was light-
skinned, had bright, alert eyes in a round, fleshy face, and was a chunky
five feet, seven inches tall. He had gone out for football at Virginia
Union, where Leigh Whipper had coached, but, rejected as being too
short, he had become a cheerleader instead.

Owen struck Lucille Randolph as aggressive and irreverent. He
seemed to hold a critical opinion on everything, and was especially cynical on the subject of women. After listening to him for some time, she
paid Owen one of the highest compliments then in her gift. She told him
he talked just like her husband. What she chiefly had in mind, of course,
was his political irreverence, because, beyond that, Owen and her husband were as unlike in how they talked as they were unlike in personality. As George S. Schuyler would write of Owen, several years later, he
was "a man of ready wit and agile tongue, endowed with the saving grace
of cynicism. . . . Owen was gifted in hyperbole and his sarcasm was
corroding."

Despite his social iconoclasm, Randolph had no marks of cynicism;
and though, until he met his wife, he had displayed no enduring interest
in any woman, he had never been less than courtly toward them. In his
life, there was hardly a woman Randolph admired, even from a distance,
whom he did not seem to find "beautiful," however baffling the estimate
sometimes was to less generous eyes. Perhaps he simply felt, as one of
his contemporaries—Eubie Blake, the jazz pianist and composer—once
said, that "all women are flowers." In any event, he discussed them with
an appropriate delicacy; if he found that wasn't possible, he preferred to

remain silent on the subject. And while Owen frequented cabarets, played poker, and devoted an inordinate amount of time to the contemplation of money and social success, Randolph had little time for anything that did not advance his interest in radical politics. So it was merely a similarity in the energy of their dissent that Lucille Randolph had observed, and that had led her to invite Owen to come around to their apartment the following day and meet her husband.

Provided that what bound him to people—especially politically—was important enough, Randolph seldom recognized differences; and what struck him at once about Owen was the similarity of their political temperaments. Here, Randolph recognized with delight, was a "natural-born iconoclast," a man "who did not believe in anything, including the church," and who was "just as discontented as I was about the racial problem." But his refusal to be influenced by the differences between himself and Owen did not mean that he failed to see them, or that, in some respects, he did not find them surprising.

He observed, for instance, that Owen knew nothing about socialism; that his political ideas derived mainly from his reading of sociologist Lester F. Ward. But what surprised Randolph the most was Owen's absorption in the dream of getting rich. And despite nearly a decade of radical activism, Owen would never abandon his dream of "making a pile," as Randolph put it, "and living on Easy Street." Randolph, of course—strongly stamped by his father's example—"had an inner spirit against chasing money." As for the rest of Owen's habits—as partygoer, poker player, and "a sort of person about town"—Randolph felt they were his own affair.

Owen—who, for most of his life in New York, lived at the Olga, a residential hotel, at the corner of 137th Street and Lenox Avenue—was never to marry. A self-proclaimed student of marriage, he held that since romance fed upon novelty, it could not be lasting; and, without romance, there was no point to marriage. "I have frequently heard wives complain," he would write, toward the end of 1917, "that their husbands will not even caress them, kiss them, fondle them. . . . What is the matter? . . . It is the passing of novelty. It is the love of, the desire for, the longing and the yearning for variety." Nor, in Owen's view, was boredom the only subversion of marriage, for he would write again, in the early 1920's: "Marriage is not obsolete, but it is becoming so. The more leisure, the more divorce."

Yet, however closely Randolph and Owen were drawn together by the political attitudes they shared, one may still wonder how two men with such disparities of personal character could each become the best friend the other was to have. Part of the answer lies in the paramount importance Randolph attached to political comradeship and his disregard of personal differences. But there is also a possibility that he may have been secretly fascinated by some of the anomalies of Owen's character. Randolph certainly admired Owen's aggressiveness. In himself, the closest resemblance to aggressiveness was defiance—evidenced more in a determined fidelity to matters of principle than in any belligerency of personal manner. Years later, aggressiveness was something he would admire again, even need, in Milton P. Webster, the man who was to supplant Owen as a friend and political comrade.

Randolph allowed himself to be amused by the fact that Owen was "a sort of person about town," a term which, if it was not simply one of his typical euphemisms—as when, in 1928, he referred to an editor of the *Pittsburgh Courier* as "the dark person in the woodpile"—must have meant that Owen was a cut above the ordinary man about town. Perhaps it was only in so describing this facet of Owen's worldiness that he felt free to associate himself vicariously with it—the way boys whose upbringing has been somewhat sheltered admire the wildness and abandon in those of their companions whose upbringing has been so free that they seem practically to have raised themselves. And since an alliance so contradictory in its personal ingredients could scarcely have been founded except upon mutual consent, it must be presumed—in the absence of his own testimony—that Owen entertained a similar admiration for Randolph's studiousness and gentility. At the height of their political partnership in Harlem, during World War I, others would call them Lenin and Trotsky, but throughout their lives they would always address each other familiarly as "Boy."

After their meeting in 1915, Owen introduced Randolph to the writings of Lester F. Ward, and Randolph, in his words, "led Owen to Marx." Neither had a steady job. Randolph had left the Brotherhood of Labor soon after his marriage, his wife having assured him of her willingness to support him in the pursuit of his public ambitions. And Owen, who had merely done odd jobs around the Columbia campus, felt no further obligation to continue, having found that he was welcome to share in the subsidies of the Randolph household.

When not attending their classes at City College and Columbia, the two spent their spare time together—chiefly at Randolph's apartment and at the New York Public Library—studying "the theory and history of socialism and working-class politics" and "their application to the racial problem in America." In the evenings, whenever radicals like Eugene Debs, August Claessens, Elizabeth Gurley Flynn, Abraham Shiplacoff, or Morris Hillquit were appearing in Socialist and labor forums downtown, Randolph and Owen went to hear them. And whenever Hubert H. Harrison, black Harlem's own Socialist spellbinder, was speaking at the corner of Lenox Avenue and 135th Street, the young men would be there.

Randolph would confess to "the greatest admiration" for Eugene Debs, particularly "Debs's position on the Negro, his belief that the best chance for the elimination of racial injustice, which was rooted in the competitive economic system, lay in the socialization and democratization of the system." But as a Socialist, Randolph thought, Debs was "not much of an ideologue"—like Morris Hillquit, for instance, "a sophisticated and doctrinaire" intellectual. "I doubt," Randolph once said, "that Debs knew much about Marx and the consequence." What he found singularly inspiring in Debs was an "eloquent humanism." Randolph "had not met a white man with such spiritual character, such a great and warm feeling for the human mission of socialism." His own approach to socialism was to be mostly spiritual and humanist in character, though not without some evidence that he understood "Marx and the consequence."

Toward the end of 1916, Randolph and Owen joined the Socialist party. Even if they had not been spiritual converts by then, they may still, on pragmatic grounds alone, have seen no sensible alternative. As Randolph said, "The Republicans knew they had the Negroes in their pockets, and the Democrats looked down on them. Neither party thought it had to offer Negroes elective office, and neither had a program for the Negro. The Socialist party was the only party that had a philosophy and an economic program that took account of the race problem and whose economic analysis addressed itself to the solution of the Negro's problems."

Feeling, by the end of the year, that they had "discovered all truth," Randolph stopped going to City College—though in later years he went back for an occasional course—and Owen dropped his studies at Columbia. They reorganized the Independent Political Council, with Randolph as president and Owen as executive secretary; and since the members, however militantly they dissented from the conventional politics of the community, were not Socialists, the two leaders gave the council a moderately radical program: "To create and crystallize sentiment against present conditions through an organized educational campaign; to compile and distribute literature, and to conduct public lectures on the vital issues affecting the colored people's economic and political destiny; to appraise men and measures in public life; to examine, expose and condemn cunning and malicious political marplots; to criticize and denounce selfish and self-styled leaders."

Following the example of Hubert Harrison, as other young men in Harlem were doing, Randolph and Owen now became soapbox orators themselves, propagandizing on the street corners for socialism and labor unionism. Due largely to Randolph's oratorical gifts, they quickly became the most notorious street-corner radicals in Harlem, exceeding even Harrison in the boldness of their assault upon political and racial conditions in the country. Most week nights for several years to come, they were to be seen at the corner of Lenox Avenue and 135th Street, the center of the militant consciousness of black America. Less than impressed with the political character of the intersection, *Harlem Magazine,* voice of the white neighborhoods, had its own description for Lenox at 135th. Said the magazine in December, 1916· "Over on Harlem's 'bug house' corner, where the self-appointed orators hold forth nightly, he who pauses to listen for a while will hear much talk about 'the people.' From their remarks it appears that those who have gained a fortune by practising industry, and those who comprise the ruling power of corporations are not entitled to be classed as 'the people.' "

Sunday nights, "bug house" corner shifted a block westward, to 135th Street and Seventh Avenue, for a weekly open forum, where the cream of the soapbox intelligentsia shared the same platform, and took turns enlarging "upon everything," as Randolph said, "from the French Revolution, the history of slavery, to the rise of the working class. It was one of the great intellectual forums of America." To Randolph, there were few pleasures more sweet. After these forums, and sometimes after his own week-night meetings, Randolph, still savoring the nectar of the evening, rounded up a selection of the livelier young minds, and invited them over to his apartment to continue the arguments.

A survivor of the prewar soapbox era in Harlem recalls that "Randolph attracted large numbers of young people. He got us thinking in social and economic terms. Of course, most of the older people didn't think about much in the line of new political ideas. But Philip Randolph just seemed to carry the young people in his palms. His delivery was so impeccable and his culture was so attractive. Instead of rabble rousing, he just talked. I know he attracted me. I couldn't wait to hear what he had to say. And if other soapboxers wanted to hold on to their audience, they had to be careful not to hold their meeting too close to where Randolph was preaching."

As they sometimes do about radical zealots, people wondered what Randolph did for a living, for, apparently, he held down no job, and had no visible means of support. A few knew better, to be sure. A former member of the Independent Political Council "never knew him to do any work for a salary, but I never saw him without a starched collar, a carefully knotted tie, a white handkerchief in his breast pocket, and a blue serge suit that looked like he had just bought it from Brooks Brothers. It was his wife, of course. She had a good hairdressing business, and she was a sweet and motherly woman. He was lucky to have had a wife like that. Only she could have put up with all those people he used to bring home from political meetings two, three times a week to talk till one, two, three o'clock in the mornings."

Today, Randolph loves to acknowledge the debt. "We were," he recalls, almost excitedly, "on an uncharted sea. Chandler and I had no job and no plan for the next meal. But I had a good wife. She carried us."

In January, 1917, something finally fell into their laps. One day they went into an office building, at 486 Lenox Avenue, looking for larger meeting space for their Political Council. While there, they were recognized by William White, president of the Headwaiters and Sidewaiters Society of Greater New York. White, who had heard them several times on the street corners, called them into the society's headquarters, on the third floor, and told them they were just the men he wanted to see. He had an idea for a monthly magazine for the waiters, White said, and he thought they were the ideal pair to edit it. Instead of looking for office space of their own, White suggested, why didn't they just move into his society's headquarters? They could have practically half of the large room for themselves, and, beyond writing and editing the magazine, they were free to use their end of the room in whatever way they wished. Finally, White said, they could be assured of total editorial freedom, down to deciding what the magazine should be called. To the young men, White's was not just an irresistible proposition; it was a stroke of such luck that their main problem was how to accept without appearing too eager.

White gave them the sunnier end of the room, looking out through a bay window upon Lenox Avenue. It was furnished with a desk—large enough to accommodate Randolph on one side and Owen opposite him —two soft leather chairs, a typewriter, a file cabinet, and a few folding chairs. Here, for the next eight months, the two young men brought out the *Hotel Messenger,* the name they chose for the magazine. They also held daily meetings with members of the Political Council, as well as with other young radicals in the community who, having nothing better to do with their daytime hours, drifted in every now and then for political discussions.

It was then—considering it a suitably impressive by-line for a political journalist—that Randolph started referring to himself as A. Philip Randolph, rather than Asa Randolph or Philip Randolph, as most people in Harlem called him. The choice may well have been inspired by some of the most important and impressive-sounding political by-lines in Harlem at the time: Fred R. Moore, James Weldon Johnson, and T. Thomas Fortune—all writers for the *New York Age.*

Radicals in the community who dropped in at the *Hotel Messenger* were young men like Lovett Fort Whiteman, a Texan, who had graduated from McGill University; Cyril V. Briggs, a native of the Dutch West Indies, and an editorial writer for the New York *Amsterdam News;* W. A. Domingo, a Jamaican nationalist and socialist, who had migrated to Harlem a few years before; and Hubert Harrison, a native of St. Croix, in the Virgin Islands. Though Harrison had assumed the status of a father figure in Harlem radicalism, he was a young man. Six years older than Randolph, he was only thirty-four in 1917.

Randolph's favorites were Harrison and Domingo, both of whom, between the war and the early 1920's, were to figure importantly in his career. Harrison was a short and stocky black man with a reverberating voice which, according to a contemporary observer, "commanded his audience to stand still and listen." A friend, Claude McKay, the Jamaican-born poet and novelist, said that Harrison's head "resembled an African replica of Socrates," and that when he laughed "he exploded in a large, sugary black African way, which sounded like the rustling of dry bamboo leaves agitated by the wind." Other Harlemites simply called Harrison "the black Socrates," a reference mainly to the professorial manner he affected on the soapbox, his "encyclopedic knowledge" of political history, and his habit of traveling around the city with a bag of books, which he sold for a living to street-corner audiences in Harlem, Union Square, and Wall Street. Harrison, who had joined the Socialist party a few years after its formation, wrote occasionally for the New York *Call,* the party organ, and for the *International Socialist Review.* He also contributed book reviews to the *New York Times,* the *New York World,* and the *Modern Quarterly.*

By 1917, Harrison had resigned from the party, and no longer shared Randolph's and Owen's uncritical enthusiasm for socialism, but he still considered them the most impressive of the young radicals in Harlem. Later that year, when Randolph and Owen published an antiwar pamphlet, *Terms of Peace and the Darker Races,* Harrison was lavish in his praise: "These two brilliant young leaders of the Independent Political Council have given us a pamphlet that is unique. We often find Negro leaders who are radicals on the subject of their race. But frequently they know so little of anything else that they have no real attitude, no opinions worth while on anything else. . . . The authors are bold—perhaps too bold for safety's sake—but in these days of cowardly compromise and shifting surrender we cannot find it in our hearts to condemn the opposite qualities." Despite their eventual differences, Randolph would continue to revere Harrison as the "father of Harlem radicalism," and would describe Harrison's death in 1926 as "an impoverishment to the community."

What Randolph admired the most in W. A. Domingo was "a penetrating and logical mind and a thoroughgoing grasp of Marxism." Nor, as in the case of Owen, did he permit this admiration to be impaired by his discovery, later on, that Domingo, despite his radicalism, "had a rather astute business mind." In fact, Domingo was to become a successful importer and distributor of West Indian foods in New York. Visiting Randolph at the *Hotel Messenger,* one day in 1917, Domingo had revealed his business mind by proposing a scheme whereby Randolph might establish himself in a self-supporting enterprise. A considerable profit was to be made, Domingo suggested, from roasting and selling potatoes on the street corners of Harlem. (It may not have been as wild an idea as it sounded, because around that time Mrs. Mary Dean—immortalized in Harlem's social history as "Pig Foot Mary"—was accumulating a small fortune from cooking and selling pigs' feet on street corners. She later paid $42,000 for a five-story apartment house at Seventh Avenue and 135th Street, and sold it at a profit of $30,000.) Randolph laughed at Domingo's suggestion, either because he hoped that would discourage any further discussion of the subject, or because he thought Domingo was joking. But Domingo was quite serious; he insisted that both of them hop the streetcar down to the Lower East Side and shop around for a potato roaster. They were unable to find one, however, and Randolph was relieved at the collapse of "my first and last venture in private enterprise."

The *Hotel Messenger,* which circulated monthly among black waiters in the New York area, folded in August, when William White fired his two young editors. A group of disgruntled sidewaiters had come to Randolph and Owen with the story that headwaiters were selling uniforms to sidewaiters at exorbitant prices and pocketing kickbacks from the uniform dealers—a racket that the editors exposed in the *Hotel Messenger.* Since William White was indebted more to the headwaiters than to the sidewaiters for his office as president of their society, he considered the exposé a threat to his own position. He denounced the two editors as ingrates. How dared they embarrass him in his own magazine, he demanded, after he had literally taken them in off the streets? He ordered them out. And since he wanted no reminder of them around his office, he told them they were welcome to take the furniture with them.

Unrepentant—proud, in fact, of what they had done—Randolph and Owen returned a few days later, took the furniture, and set up office in a building next door, 513 Lenox Avenue, determined now to make it on their own. First, to practice some of what they had been preaching, they organized their own union, the United Brotherhood of Elevator and Switchboard Operators, of which they would later lose control. Hearing that the Socialist party wanted someone to co-ordinate Morris Hillquit's mayoralty campaign in Harlem, Randolph and Owen not only took the job, but also formed the first black Socialist political club in Harlem's Twenty-first Assembly District.

Next, all within two months, they launched their own monthly magazine, the *Messenger*—dropping the "hotel" from its masthead to indicate that the magazine was no longer an organ of the waiters, as well as to dissociate themselves from "the thought controllers in the hotel field." Though Randolph and Owen may have wanted to start their own magazine in any case—considering the importance they now attached to radical political journalism—they founded the *Messenger* in response to the "steady and numerous requests" of their "intelligent, radical, forward-looking and clear-eyed patrons." Some of the patrons were undoubtedly white Socialists and trade unionists downtown, who were aware of Randolph's and Owen's reputation as Socialist propagandists in Harlem; who were interested in supporting an organ of socialism and labor unionism in the black community; and who, in the years ahead, would help the magazine to survive through their contributions and advertising. But, at the outset, the *Messenger*'s most important patron was Randolph's wife, Lucille. Without her money, Randolph has said, "we couldn't have started the *Messenger*."

Thus, in addition to the sustaining role Lucille Randolph had been playing, and would continue to play, in her husband's private and public life, one of the important footnotes to the history of radicalism in Harlem must surely be that she was indispensable to the founding of what her husband would call "the first voice of radical, revolutionary, economic and political action among Negroes in America"; what William Dufty, of the *New York Post*, described as "one of the ornaments" of its age; what, Dufty continued, "has been called one of the most brilliantly edited magazines in the history of American Negro journalism"; and what the Justice Department, two years after the magazine's founding, would regard as "by long odds the most able and the most dangerous of all the Negro publications."

III / The Most
Dangerous Negroes in America

Our aim is to appeal to reason, to lift our pens above the cringing dema-
gogy of the times, and above the cheap peanut politics of the old reac-
tionary Negro leaders. Patriotism has no appeal to us; justice has. Party
has no weight with us; principle has. Loyalty is meaningless; it depends
on what one is loyal to. Prayer is not one of our remedies; it depends on
what one is praying for. We consider prayer as nothing more than a fer-
vent wish; consequently, the merit and worth of a prayer depend upon
what the fervent wish is.
> —A. PHILIP RANDOLPH and CHANDLER OWEN, in the *Messenger*,
> November, 1917

. . . we venture the assertion that the spirit of self-defense, and the de-
termination to respond unflinchingly when the occasion calls to fight the
battles of life, to ward off every attack, to redress every grievance, to take
reprisals upon assault, to defend one's rights at every angle, and one's life
to the utmost, is more highly to be prized than a thorough knowledge of
all that Aeschylus or Euripides ever wrote. I would rather be a crack shot
when shooting is needed than be the most finished Homeric scholar in the
land. —RANDOLPH or OWEN, in a *Messenger* editorial, 1919

Attorney General Palmer said that the most dangerous Negroes in the
United States were these two guys.
> —THEOPHILUS LEWIS, a former *Messenger* writer

6 / Against the Grain

The *Messenger* entered "the broad world of human action," as its editors put it, in November, 1917, seven months after the United States entered the war, and the same month as the Russian "October" Revolution. These two events—one in the demand it made upon the patriotism of black citizens and the other in the impulse it gave to American radicalism—would have a powerful impact upon the racial and political militancy of the magazine's tone in the first three years of its life.

The *Messenger*'s political prose was thoughtful and analytic, if powered by the inevitable verve and flourish of agitational rhetoric. Technically, the magazine was neat and attractive in appearance, suggesting something of the high standards of printing that even poorly financed journals were once able to call upon. Though its personality was reflected mainly in its editorials and political commentary, it also published fiction, poetry, and criticism of the arts, and carried photographs or line drawings on its front cover. Slightly larger than a regular-size magazine, it was printed by the Brooklyn Eagle Company, and sold for fifteen cents—apparently a mark of some distinction at the time, since Chandler Owen would boast later that the *Messenger* "was the first 15-cent publication among Negroes."

But its fifteen-cent status may have earned the *Messenger* more in prestige than in revenue. It was always in debt—seldom able to meet its rent on time, unable some months to appear at all, having occasionally to await the return of its coeditors from fund-raising lecture tours of New York and other cities, and in no position to offer anything but token payments to contributors. Its drama reviewer recalled years later that the only fee he ever received from the *Messenger* was carfare to the theater and back.

85

This uncertain state of financial affairs had its effect upon how often the magazine moved its office. After a few months at 513 Lenox Avenue, where it was born, the *Messenger* was evicted for nonpayment of rent. It found a new home at 2305 Seventh Avenue, and remained there through its best years. In 1924 it was evicted again, and moved to 2311 Seventh Avenue, where it stayed until 1928, when it folded for lack of funds.

The lifelong struggle to make ends meet was due in part to the magazine's management, its coeditors having to function also as the chief business geniuses—Randolph as president of the Messenger Publishing Company, and Owen secretary-treasurer. Of course, Randolph's particular gifts for earning and handling money—even his interest in such matters—were well known by then. But something better might have been expected of Owen. Despite his fascination with the subject of wealth and the amount of thought he gave to acquiring some for himself, he displayed no greater gift than Randolph for keeping the magazine solvent. Later on, a couple of business managers would come to the *Messenger*'s aid, but neither would be able to lift it out of the slough of red ink that always threatened to overcome it.

The *Messenger,* virtually Randolph's whole life until 1925, collected around it a number of intellectuals, who came to be known as *Messenger* radicals. These, in some instances, were merely young readers who agreed with the magazine's politics. By and large, though, *Messenger* radicals were contributing editors of the magazine. The first two were W. A. Domingo and Lovett Fort-Whiteman, young radicals from the group that had passed a good deal of time with Randolph and Owen when they were running the *Hotel Messenger*. But at different times up until 1925 —as new contributing editors were added, and as old ones broke with the magazine, or simply fell off the masthead—the list would include George Frazier Miller, a tough, plain-spoken Episcopal preacher from Brooklyn; William Colson, a veteran of World War I; Ernest Rice Mc-Kinney, a left-wing graduate of Oberlin College, whose parents, in Virginia, had been acquaintances of Frederick Douglass; Abram L. Harris, a Howard University economist; Robert Bagnall, a Detroit preacher, and the NAACP's director of branches; William Pickens, a Yale-educated professor of political science at Morgan State College, and an NAACP field organizer; George Schuyler, a self-educated Socialist and satirist from Syracuse, who had a greater admiration for Henry Mencken than

for Karl Marx; Wallace Thurman, a fictionist of the Harlem Renaissance; and Theophilus Lewis, the drama reviewer, whose acquaintance-
ship with Randolph went back to their days in the Epworth League.

Because of the shifts in political attitude and allegiance that took
place around the rise of the Garvey movement and the formation of the
Communist party in America, the *Messenger* radicals were a somewhat
inconstant fraternity. Some, like W. A. Domingo and Lovett Fort-
Whiteman, who started out with the magazine, later broke with it; and
others, like William Pickens and Robert Bagnall, who joined it later, had
at one time, especially during and immediately after the war, been cool
toward it. Pickens had even once evoked the magazine's contempt, as a
member of "the conservative Negro leadership." Nor were all of them
political radicals, although, in varying degrees, and according to their
own lights, all were progressive on the race question.

But the *Messenger* radicals were merely part of a larger group, known
as the Harlem, or New Negro, radicals. Though the latter shared the
Messenger's brand of racial and political militancy, most of them had no
formal ties with the magazine. Some even edited radical journals of their
own. The more prominent names were Richard B. Moore; Otto Huiswood; Cyril V. Briggs, who resigned from the *Amsterdam News* to start
his own magazine, the *Crusader* ("which fears only God"); Hubert Harrison, editor of the *Voice* ("journal of the new dispensation"); William
Bridges, editor of the *Challenge;* and William H. Ferris, a radical black
nationalist, and an editor of Marcus Garvey's *Negro World.* In addition
to writing for the *Messenger,* W. A. Domingo founded his own weekly
journal, the *Emancipator* ("to preach deliverance to the slaves"), and,
having once been friendly with Garvey in their native Jamaica, also
helped—until they fell out—to edit the *Negro World.*

Today, it is chiefly these men, including Randolph and Owen, to
whom the term New Negro Harlem radicals applies. With the exception
of Ferris, they were all Socialists or economic radicals—although Hubert
Harrison had evolved his own variety of radicalism, an amalgam of
pragmatic socialism and black nationalism. Not all of them would remain Socialists. In 1921, Briggs, Huiswood, Fort-Whiteman, and Moore
would break with their colleagues and become the voices in Harlem of
the newly formed American Communist party. There was one other distinguishing mark of the Harlem radicals: most of them came from the
British West Indies, the Dutch West Indies, and the Virgin Islands. It

was this that caused one of their more conservative black American critics to remark that the typical Harlem radical was "an over-educated West Indian without a job." Self-educated they may have been, but hardly overeducated, for almost none of them had graduated from a university.

Among the fourteen short editorials in the *Messenger*'s first issue were pieces titled "The Rioting of Negro Soldiers" (in Houston, Texas); "Woman Suffrage and the Negro"; "Peace"; "Who Shall Pay for the War?"; "Friends of Irish Freedom"; "Organizing the Negro Actor"; and "Making the World Safe for Democracy." There were two departments of public commentary—Randolph's "Economics and Politics" and Owen's "Education and Literature"—which would become permanent columns, and which, along with the editorials, would constitute the political heart of the magazine.

Other features included an attack upon "Business and the War," by Scott Nearing, a white Socialist; "Nemeses—a Story," by Lovett Fort-Whiteman; and four poems by Walter Everette Hawkins, one of which began: "There's too much talk of heaven / Too much talk of golden streets / When one can't be sympathetic / When a needy neighbor meets." But, of course, it was politics—not literature, obviously—that was the *Messenger*'s forte. As the editors would claim a few years later —while comparing W. E. B. Du Bois's *Crisis* unfavorably with their own magazine—"with us, economics and politics take precedence to music and art." While that would remain true for most of the *Messenger*'s life, the quality of its literary offerings would improve markedly in the early 1920's, when it sometimes published the work of Langston Hughes, Claude McKay, Countee Cullen, and Wallace Thurman.

The inaugural issue of the *Messenger* noted America's entry into the war against Germany—with predictable displeasure—but it was conspicuously silent on a political event of even greater moment in the life of radicalism: the October Revolution in Russia. Since there was hardly a radical journal at the time that failed to note and applaud the event, the silence of the *Messenger*—which considered itself to be part of the American radical mainstream—was surprising. It was not until its next issue, in January, 1918, that the reason became clear: the November issue had gone to press before the triumph of the Bolsheviks. Thus, later than its radical contemporaries, but second to none in its ardor, the *Messenger* joined the fanfare:

The Bolsheviki . . . represent the extreme radicals—not in the sense of being unreasonably extreme in their demands, but in the sense of being unwilling to take a half loaf when they were entitled to a whole loaf. . . . They demand that the land which the workers till and mine with their toil shall be owned and operated by the workers for the welfare of the workers. . . . The leaders of the Bolsheviki are Lenine and Trotsky, misrepresented here by the metropolitan press as German agents. This, of course, is simply malicious libel uttered to discredit these rulers of Russia, lest their teaching should awaken the proletariat of the world to his power and his right to a fair share of the world's goods. Lenine and Trotsky, however, are sagacious, statesmanlike and courageous leaders. They have a thorough understanding of the international situation. . . . They are calling, nevertheless, upon the people of every country to follow the lead of Russia, to throw off their exploiting rulers, to administer public utilities for public welfare, to disgorge the exploiters and the profiteers.

Since the Russian Revolution strengthened in all radicals the hope for similar victories in their own countries, the *Messenger,* together with the largely Socialist American left, continued for some time to celebrate the advent and the advance of the new order over which the Bolsheviks presided. To the *Messenger,* the Russian Revolution was "the greatest achievement of the twentieth century," and signified that the old world was passing and that a new one was being born. Heartened later by the "ceaseless step" of the Soviet government, the *Messenger* cheered, "On with the dance." But joy was not to be unconfined, or to last, for, in 1921, the steady march of Bolshevism would split the American Socialist movement, its revolutionary left wing breaking away to join the American Communist party, organized that year. The *Messenger* would suddenly lose its enthusiasm for the Russian dance. The Harlem radicals would themselves be split. Men who had spoken in the same voice since 1917 would become bitter political enemies. Randolph not only would remain with the Socialists, but also would begin a lifetime of opposition to the Communist movement.

In entering "the broad world of human action," the *Messenger*'s editors pledged themselves "to do our 'bit' in supplying light and leading." These, in Harlem and in black America, would consist not only in the advocacy of an economic solution to the racial problem, but also in a broad attack upon the following: the country's political and economic system, which, it was felt, fostered racism and social inequality; the "conservative Negro leadership," most of which urged a continued allegiance to the Republican party; the predominantly racist and craft-oriented American Federation of Labor, which, in excluding all but a handful of blacks from the working-class movement, made a mockery of the black radicals' call for working-class solidarity; protest radicals of the Du Bois and NAACP school, whom the *Messenger* and like-minded black radicals considered no longer radical enough; and Marcus Garvey's doctrines of black capitalism, black nationalism, and emigrationism, which, in the political and economic nature of American life, were seen as palliatives rather than solutions.

But the first two years of the magazine's life were devoted primarily to advocating labor unionism and socialism among blacks, and to protesting both World War I and the violence black Americans suffered in its wake.

In none of these ventures did the *Messenger* succeed. Its advocacy of labor unionism would founder not only upon the racial practices of the AFL, but also upon the antiunion attitude that the established black leadership had developed in reaction to racism within the Federation. Blacks were restrained by this leadership from joining unions, both because of the racist policies of organized labor and because, as the leadership said, it was with the property-owning class rather than with labor that their true interests—jobs and economic uplift—lay. As Horace Cayton and George Mitchell have observed, "Toward the labor movement, the Negro upper class has been generally antagonistic. . . . Their reasoning seems to have been that, if the Negro is to be exploited, it is better that he be exploited by the white employer who offers some rewards in the form of more employment and promotions than by white workers." And, in 1921, almost four years after Randolph and Owen had begun their work, W. E. B. Du Bois wrote in the *Crisis:*

Theoretically we are part of the world proletariat in the sense that we are mainly an exploited class of cheap laborers; but practically we are not part of the white proletariat and are not recognized by that proletariat to any great extent. We are the victims of their physical oppression, social ostracism, economic exclusion, and personal hatred; and when in self-defense we seek sheer subsistence we are howled down as scabs.

It must be added, however, that the advice of the leadership was hardly necessary. The majority of blacks already held similar attitudes toward business and labor, due largely to their experience of racism in the major

Courtesy Schomburg Collections, The New York Public Library, Astor, Lenox and Tilden Foundations

segments of the labor movement. Thus while a few blacks were organized, the prevailing sentiment within their community at the time was that blacks should shun unions and that unions did not want them. Even scabbing, once identified largely with black workers, was justified on similar grounds.

It was difficult, then, for black workers to understand how members of their own race could come to them preaching and promising racial solidarity in organized labor. Although, in light of the entrenched antilabor feeling, no answer to this question would suffice, Randolph and Owen had a ready-made one. It was not the racist and conservative craft unions they were advocating solidarity with, they said, but the Industrial Workers of the World. The IWW, they pointed out, organized along industrial rather than craft lines, was radical in politics, and excluded no one on the grounds of race or color. The reason this answer would not do was that most blacks saw the IWW as just another labor union, and one, therefore, that was opposed to private property—in whose camp their best chance for economic advancement lay. Besides, at the time, the majority of blacks—second to no group in their feelings of patriotism

—shared the general white conviction that the IWW was un-American. Even Du Bois—not then known for any great reverence for conventional American thinking—wrote in the *Crisis* that "we do not believe that the methods of the IWW are today feasible or advisable."

Thus the *Messenger*'s evangelizing in behalf of organized labor—specifically the IWW—would fail, despite as stirring an appeal as this:

The IWW is the only labor organization in the United States which draws no race or color line. . . . There is another reason why Negroes should join the IWW. The Negro must engage in direct action. He is forced to do this by the Government. When the whites speak of direct action, they are told to use their political power. But with the Negro it is different. He has no political power. . . . Therefore the only recourse the Negro has is industrial action, and since he must combine with those forces which draw no line against him, it is simply logical for him to throw his lot with the Industrial Workers of the World. . . . The editors of the Messenger have made a thorough study of the economic and social problems in the United States. We know the history of labor organizations. We know that the American Federation of Labor is a machine for the propagation of race prejudice. We therefore urge the Negroes to join their international brothers, the Industrial Workers of the World. . . . Old-line Negro political fossils know nothing of the labor movement, do not believe in labor unions at all, and have never taken any active steps to encourage such organizations. We make this statement calmly, cooly, and with a reasonable reserve. The very thing which they are fighting is one of the chief factors in securing for Negroes their rights. That is Bolshevism. The capitalists of this country are so afraid that Negroes will become Bolshevists that they are willing to offer them anything to hold them away from the radical movement. Nobody buys pebbles which may be picked up on the beach, but diamonds come high.

The campaign for socialism—in the end, no more successful than the one for labor unionism—was inaugurated with the *Messenger*'s endorsement of Morris Hillquit, who, in the election of November, 1917, was the Socialist candidate for mayor of New York City. What would frustrate the magazine's "educational campaign" for Hillquit and for socialism was both the reserve toward alien doctrines that most of the black community shared and the hold the Republican party retained upon the allegiance of black voters. Black Republican leaders felt so sure of Harlem's support that they hardly bothered to conduct serious election campaigns. As Owen wrote in 1918, "When we began our work in New York, most of the political leaders could be found in Mattheny's Saloon,

135th Street and 7th Avenue . . . drinking liquor and smoking cigars. No campaign except a beer and sandwich campaign was made." Thus, he also claimed, the *Messenger* and its editors were among the first to attempt a serious educational campaign in Harlem politics.

The Hillquit candidacy, one of the major Socialist candidacies in the United States at the time, provided a convenient beginning for the *Messenger* and its editors. It gave them not only an opportunity to associate themselves with the national and international issues the American Socialist movement was raising, but also a prominent platform from which to argue the superior claims of the Socialist party upon black support.

In October, 1916, Fred R. Moore's *New York Age* had submitted "Ten Reasons Why Negroes Should Support Charles Evans Hughes for President." Some of them were that "the Republican Party was conceived in the interest of the Negro and was born for his emancipation"; that it was "the only party that has ever done anything for him. It freed him, enfranchised him, educated him, and guaranteed to him civil, religious and political equality before the law"; and that it "recognized the Negro in the distribution of Federal patronage in accordance with the service rendered."

The *Messenger* adopted a similar mode of presenting the case of the Socialists. Giving, in November, 1917, twenty-five reasons why blacks should support Hillquit and the Socialist party, the magazine said, in part, ". . . the SP is the Party of the working man . . . 95% of Negroes are working people . . . the SP advocates the abolition of high rents . . . Negroes suffer more than any other people from high rents . . . the SP advocates the city ownership and operation of the subway, elevated and surface car lines, the electric, gas, and telephone companies . . . the SP advocates a more efficient police system which will use more brains than billies . . . the SP is the party of economic justice . . . the SP is for peace."

The editors were not so dispassionate in dismissing Hillquit's regular-party opponents. Mayor John Purroy Mitchel, running for re-election as a Fusion candidate, was "a menace to the Negro," a "Negro baiter, black man's hater, Woodrow Wilson's man, police Negro clubber, son of a confederate soldier." Randolph and Owen said that though they had not heard of Judge John Hylan—the Democratic candidate—before, that was not so serious a disqualification as the fact that he was the candidate of William Randolph Hearst, and, since "Hearst always knows his man," also "anti-Japanese and anti-Negro." William Bennet, they said, "heads the Republican ticket," and "that alone is unfortunate." Hillquit, of course, was the only candidate "any self-respecting Negro could vote for."

But the major part of Randolph's and Owen's campaign for Hillquit was conducted outside the pages of the *Messenger,* since only one issue of the magazine appeared before the election. Toward the end of the summer of 1917, the Socialist party had appointed Randolph and Owen to co-ordinate Hillquit's campaign in Harlem. The two editors had done this by organizing the first Socialist club in the area—the 21st A.D. Club —made up largely of their fellow radicals. This group also fanned out through the community, canvassing in Hillquit's behalf and heckling the public meetings of the regular-party candidates.

The most publicized incident of the campaign took place in late October, when Theodore Roosevelt came to the Palace Casino, in Harlem, to support the Fusion candidacy of John Purroy Mitchel. The meeting was chaired by the Reverend Adam Clayton Powell, Sr., and on the platform were some of the most important politicians and clergymen of the community—the "big Negroes" of Harlem, as Randolph called them. Deployed throughout the audience, a group of Hillquit's supporters, organized by Randolph and Owen, hissed and heckled the speakers. But the most dramatic demonstration came when Roosevelt got up to speak. The young radicals not only hissed and heckled, but also, by prearrangement, started walking out—hoping, since they were scattered throughout the hall, to create the appearance of a mass exodus.

The *New York Age,* a pro-Roosevelt paper, was furious at the "self-appointed censors—earning so much per night as soap-box orators":

These rowdies who espouse the cause of the Socialist candidate made themselves obnoxious. . . . Had not three-fourths of the audience been decidedly friendly to those talking in the interest of fusion, the disturbance-makers would have broken up the meeting. . . . Even Theodore Roosevelt . . . was insulted by these ruffians, who sought to follow out a program which had been arranged some hours before. They insulted everybody, even the prominent colored ministers who spoke. This element was made up of Negroes who are seeking to secure real democracy in this country by advocating violence and who are opposed to the right of free speech, and their anarchistic tendencies were fully emphasized during the evening, making a powerful impression on the minds of those who believe in law and order. After the meeting, a group of colored men standing on 135th Street, near Lenox Avenue, were engaged in conversation, during which they severely criticized the rowdy tactics of the Socialists. One was heard to remark: "If what that radical bunch did is a sample of what they would do if they came to power, excuse me."

Hillquit lost—John F. Hylan was elected by a plurality of 147,975—but his was the largest vote (145,332) a Socialist candidate had ever polled in New York City. An even more heartening statistic was the *Messenger*'s estimate, never disputed, that 25 per cent of the votes in Harlem had been cast for Hillquit. If true, it was a remarkable tribute to the unprecedented "educational campaign" the Harlem radicals had conducted. The *Messenger,* understandably elated at what seemed a breakthrough for the cause of economic radicalism, called the black Socialist vote "a thing which gives the Negro the greatest political respect," and which "stamps him as thinking and not blindly following the eagle—the emblem of the old hypocritical and lying Republican Party." But the future would bring nothing to sustain the elation; such a large Socialist vote would never again be approached, let alone duplicated, in Harlem.

Ironically, the Republican party, which the *Messenger* had mercilessly attacked for refusing to run black candidates in black communities, beat the Socialists to the punch in 1917 when it successfully ran Edward A. Johnson—a lawyer, who had arrived from Raleigh, North Carolina, in the early migration of the Talented Tenth—to represent one of the Harlem districts in the New York State Assembly. To regain the initiative for the Socialists, the *Messenger* editors now promised Harlem that next time around there would be not just one, but several "able colored men" on the Socialist ticket, and that "it will be difficult to prevent the ticket from receiving 75% of the Negro votes." The "election of Negro candidates is not enough," the magazine said. What was now demanded was the selection and election by blacks of their own Socialist candidates. "So long as the Negro votes for Republican or Democratic Party candidates," the *Messenger* submitted, "he will have only the right and privilege to elect but not to select his representatives. And he who selects the representative controls the representative." Developing the point more militantly, the magazine argued in another editorial:

No white man is good enough to rule black men without their consent. And it is pretty well ascertained that it is unsafe for one class to leave its fortunes, political and economic, to another class. . . . The intellectually decrepit Negro leaders have seemed to have had a vague religious reliance upon the "goodness" of all white Republicans and they have not been able to appreciate the fact that they have been mere pawns upon the political chessboards for conniving, wirepulling, unscrupulous Republican tricksters. . . . The Socialist Party is supported financially by the working men and women and since its platform is a demand for the abolition of the class struggle between employer and worker . . . the Negro should select a positive good—Socialism.

The next opportunity to select that "positive good" came in 1920, when the Socialists nominated five black candidates in Harlem: Frank Poree for the state senate; W. B. Williams, Grace Campbell, and Chandler Owen for the state assembly; and Randolph for state comptroller. The latter, according to the *Messenger,* was the highest office to which any party had nominated a black man in more than fifty years, and "the only instance in which a Negro of intelligence and principle has been nominated for such a high office." But perhaps Socialists did not demand of their candidates for comptroller any ability or experience in the management of fiscal affairs.

The magazine's prediction, two years earlier, of a 75-per-cent Socialist vote in Harlem proved to be a phantasm. Every one of the black Socialist candidates was defeated. In Randolph's case, however, "intelligence and principle" seem to have been recognized. In the most impressive showing of any of the black Socialist candidates, he polled 202,361 votes state-wide, only 1,000 fewer than Eugene Debs, running that year as the Socialist candidate for president, polled in New York. Yet while every black Socialist was defeated, four black Republicans and one black Democrat won seats in the state legislature.

Randolph, who had emerged as the most attractive black candidate the Socialists possessed in New York, would be nominated the following year for secretary of state. But he would be defeated again, and would not even match the vote he had polled for comptroller. Despite a number of appeals in the future—notably a bipartisan one from the Republicans and Democrats in 1944 to run for congressman from Harlem—he would never stand again for public office.

Nor would the Socialists ever recover the toe hold they had apparently gained in Harlem during the war. Thus what Randolph had written in the *Messenger* in 1918, while trying to break the power of the Republicans among blacks, was still true: "Future historians will marvel at the political contradiction of a race of tenants and workers accepting political leaders selected by landlords, bankers, and big capitalists."

7 / Hell, No!

In April, 1917, while Randolph and Owen were still editing the *Hotel Messenger,* President Wilson, asking for a declaration of war against Germany, told the Congress, "The world must be made safe for democracy. Its peace must be planted upon the tested foundations of political liberty. We have no selfish ends to serve. . . . We are but one of the champions of the right of mankind."

By November, when their own magazine, the *Messenger,* appeared, the war had become perhaps the number-one issue among American Socialists, to the majority of whom it was a war not for "democracy," "political liberty," or "the right of mankind," but simply for profits—or the "selfish ends" of business. At an emergency Socialist party convention, in St. Louis, a majority of the War and Militarism Committee recommended "unalterable opposition" to the war, on the grounds that "wars of contending national groups of capitalists are not the concern of the workers."

As Socialists, Randolph and Owen fully endorsed what became the official position of their party. "Who Shall Pay for the War?" they asked, in the very first issue of their magazine.

. . . obviously, those who profit from the war should pay for it. . . . How can profits be made out of the war? The answer to this question is: by selling to the government those things which are needed to keep the war going. . . . Now, Mr. Common Man, do you own any of these things? If you don't, then you cannot profit from the war. Then you ought to see to it that the government confiscates all profits made out of the war to carry on the war. Let the government take 100% and peace will come.

They gave Scott Nearing space in the same issue to accuse "the American business interests of using the world crisis as an occasion for making money" and "as an excuse for a great drive to strangle the effective part of the American labor movement." In January, 1918, the magazine declared proudly that "the Socialist Party—the only party of principle—opposes the useless sacrifice of blood and the hogfat profits which the profiteers are coining out of the sufferings of the people." And Senator Robert La Follette—"man of independence, brains, and character"—was praised for remaining in his seat "when others rose to applaud the President bearing his war message."

What evoked the strongest opposition from Randolph and Owen, and from their fellow radicals in Harlem, however, was the irony of black American soldiers being asked to risk their lives abroad in defense of freedoms denied them at home. Addressing President Wilson in their magazine, Randolph and Owen charged, "Lynching, Jim Crow, segregation, discrimination in the armed forces and out, disfranchisement of millions of black souls in the South—all these things make your cry of making the world safe for democracy a sham, a mockery, a rape on decency and a travesty on common justice." Under such circumstances, they concluded, it was unthinkable that black men should serve. The feelings of the New Negro radicals, the *Messenger* editors said in an editorial, "will not be downed by prayers of patriotism. Their gospel of obey and trust has been replaced by one of rebel and demand. The deep bitter injustices perpetrated upon their black brothers and sisters well up in their bosoms like bitter root and gall. They really mean that this world must be made safe for them. Until then it is not safe for any democracy."

But they were speaking for themselves, for the sentiment among blacks was overwhelmingly in favor of serving. Answering their country's call was, they felt, a unique opportunity to demonstrate their patriotism, enhance their claim to full freedom at home, and, in not a few cases, obtain steady work. Consequently, before the war was over, 200,-000 black soldiers would serve in army camps at home, another 200,000 would fight in France, and black civilians on the home front would help finance the war effort by purchasing some $250 million worth of war bonds and stamps.

The voices most blacks preferred to heed belonged to the established and, in many cases, conservative leadership of the race. They were the black press, the black church, and, above all, men who counseled, "First your country, then your rights"—causing Randolph and Owen to denounce them as "Old Crowd Negroes," or "hand-picked, me-too-boss, hat-in-hand, sycophant, lick-spittling Negroes."

Who were some of these men? One was Robert Russa Moton, Booker T. Washington's successor at Tuskegee Institute, who, in March, 1917, had written to assure President Wilson "that you and the nation can count absolutely on the loyalty of the mass of Negroes to our country and its people, North and South; and as in previous wars you will find the Negro people rallying almost to a man to our flag." Another was Roscoe Conkling Simmons, editor, orator, and nephew of Booker T. Washington's third wife. "I am an American, proud of it," Simmons boasted, "and jealous of both the power and the reputation of my country and my countrymen." Others were Dean Kelly Miller of Howard University; Emmett J. Scott, a former private secretary to Booker T. Washington; Robert H. Terrell, a judge of the municipal court in Washington; George Haynes, an executive of the National Urban League; Charles W. Anderson, Republican politician and former Collector of Internal Revenue in New York; W. H. Lewis, a Boston attorney; and Fred R. Moore, editor of the *New York Age,* who had been appointed by the Theodore Roosevelt administration as minister to Liberia. But the most surprising name on the *Messenger*'s list was that of W. E. B. Du Bois, the architect and acknowledged leader of the modern protest movement, and whom even his critics were obliged to recognize as the foremost black American intellectual of the twentieth century.

It had been relatively easy for Randolph and Owen to dismiss the genuine conservatives, those protectors of Booker T. Washington's accommodationist legacy, who had counseled, "First your country, then your rights." It was far more difficult—perhaps even painful—to dismiss Du Bois, the man whose thought and personal example had helped to forge the protest conscience of their generation. But, together with the Harlem radicals, they *did* dismiss him—in a controversy that announced more dramatically than any other that while black leadership would probably remain in established and trusted hands, a new and more militant strain had emerged to challenge and contest their influence.

In July, 1918, amid rumors that Woodrow Wilson had offered him a desk captaincy in the army, Du Bois published an editorial in the *Crisis,* calling upon blacks to close ranks behind the war effort. "We of the colored race," the *Crisis* argued, have no ordinary interest in the outcome. That which the German power represents spells death to the aspirations of Negroes and all darker races for equality, freedom and democracy. Let us not hesitate. Let us, while this war lasts, forget our special grievances and close our ranks shoulder to shoulder with our own white fellow citizens and the allied nations that are fighting for democracy. We make no ordinary sacrifice but we make it gladly and willingly with our eyes lifted to the hills.

The Harlem radicals were shocked. And it was Hubert Harrison, the senior among them, who made what appears now to have been the definitive indictment of the editor of the *Crisis*. In an editorial, "The Descent of Du Bois," * in his magazine, the *Voice,* Harrison wrote:

The essence of the present situation lies in the fact that the people whom our white masters have "recognized" as our leaders (without taking the trouble to consult us) and those who, by our own selection, had actually attained to leadership among us are being revaluated and, in most cases, rejected. The most striking instance from the latter class is Dr. W. E. B. Du Bois, the editor of the *Crisis*. Du Bois's case is the more significant because his former services to his race have been undoubtedly of a high and courageous sort. Moreover, the act by which he has brought upon himself the stormy outburst of disapproval from his race is one which, of itself, would seem to merit no such stern condemnation. . . . Dr. Du Bois first palpably sinned in his editorial, "Close Ranks." . . . But this offense . . . lies in a single sentence: "Let us, while this war lasts, *forget our special grievances* and close our ranks. . . . " From the latter part of the sentence, there is no dissent, so far as we know. The offense lies in that part of the sentence which ends with the italicized words. It is felt by all his critics that Du Bois, of all Negroes, knows best that our "special grievances" which the War Department Bulletin describes as justifiable consist of lynching, segregation and disfranchisement and that the Negroes of America cannot preserve either their lives, their manhood or their vote (which is their political lives and liberties) with these things in existence. The Doctor's critics feel that America cannot use the Negroes to any good effect unless they have life, liberty and manhood assured and guaranteed to them. Therefore, instead of the war for democracy making

---

* Harrison disclosed later that the statement was originally written "at the request of Major Loving of the Intelligence Department of the Army at the time when Dr. Du Bois . . . was being preened for a desk captaincy at Washington. Major Loving solicited a summary of the situation from me as one of those radicals qualified to furnish such a summary. This he incorporated in his report to his superiors in Washington, and this I published a week later in the *Voice* of July 25, 1918, as an editorial without changing a single word."

these things less necessary, it makes them more so. "But," it may be asked, "why should not these few words be taken merely as a slip of the pen or a venal error in logic? Why all this hubbub?" It is because the so-called leaders of the first mentioned class have already established an unsavory reputation by advocating this same surrender of life, liberty and manhood, masking their cowardice behind the pillars of war time sacrifice. Du Bois's statement, then, is believed to mark his entrance into that class, and is accepted as a "surrender" of the principle which brought him into prominence—and which alone kept him there. . . . For the sake of the larger usefulness of Dr. Du Bois, we hope he will be able to show he can remain as editor of the *Crisis;* but we fear that it will require a good deal of explaining. For our leaders, like Caesar's wife, must be above suspicion.

The editors of the *Messenger* were neither as measured nor as graceful in their dissent. With characteristic belligerence, they asked: close ranks around lynching, disfranchisement, and segregation? "Since when," Owen added, "has the subject race come out of a war with its rights and privileges accorded for such a participation? . . . Did not the Negro fight in the Revolutionary War, with Crispus Attucks dying first . . . and come out to be a miserable chattel slave in this country for nearly 100 years?" And, advising Du Bois, Kelly Miller, and William Pickens to "volunteer to go to France if they are so eager to fight to make the world safe for democracy," the *Messenger*'s editors concluded that "we would rather make Georgia safe for the Negro."

More than fifty years later, at the end of his political career, and with no trace of acrimony in his memory, Randolph would recall the controversy in words somewhat similar to those Hubert Harrison had used in 1918: "We couldn't see any justification for the leader of Negro thought asking Negroes to forget their grievances, and himself accepting a captaincy from Woodrow Wilson—Wilson, who was one of the greatest racists in America. We felt Du Bois was betraying the principles on which he had risen to Negro leadership; we felt he was retracting his past as the leader of the Negro *avant-garde*."

Even before the eruption over the war, Randolph had been moving away from another of the major principles on which Du Bois had risen to leadership. This was the principle of the Talented Tenth—the black intellectual aristocracy that was to save the race, and of which Randolph had imagined himself a potential member soon after arriving in New York. "The Negro race, like all races," Du Bois had written around the turn of the century, "is going to be saved by its exceptional men. The problem of education, then, among Negroes must first of all deal with the Talented Tenth; it is the problem of developing the Best of this race that may guide the Mass away from the contamination and death of the Worst in their own and other races. Can the masses of the Negro people be in any possible way more quickly raised than by the effort and example of this aristocracy of talent and character?"

As the young radicals in Harlem had seen it, before and during the war, it hadn't worked out that way. Looking around them, they saw, as they claimed, an educated professional class that was either helping to perpetuate conservative political traditions or acting more in behalf of its own cultural interests and aspirations than of the urgent practical needs of the masses. The Talented Tenth, these radicals felt, belonged on the street corners, the only places, especially in Harlem, where the masses had an opportunity of sensing and being sensed by those who claimed to be functioning in their interests. In fact, despite the limits of their own success with the masses, the radicals were also convinced that if there *was* a Talented Tenth—a class endeavoring to discharge the kind of obligation Du Bois had assigned it—then it was they, the politically belligerent young men for whom the bourgeois "aristocracy of talent and character" had nothing but contempt. Even when Randolph looked at Du Bois, the founding ideologue of this elite, he—"a rough-and-tumble soapbox Socialist," as he called himself—saw nothing but a "parlor Socialist," an "intellectual aristocrat," and a figure "whom no one in the streets could recognize as radical."

As Randolph said later, the crucial flaw in the character of the Talented Tenth—the reason it failed to provide the political grass-roots leadership that was expected of it—resided in its philosophy of "individual merit" and the idea its members held of themselves as "exceptional men." Such men—inordinately pleased with the uniqueness and advantages of their status—did not, as a rule, find it in their interest to close the gap between themselves and less fortunate men. If, then, they were in any kind of political motion, it was a motion against those conditions of American life that were affronts to their special status, and not against the pressing everyday problems of the masses. As Horace Cayton and George Mitchell later put it, they pursued their own class objectives "in the name of the masses."

This is not to say that any of them was truly opposed to the principle of racial freedom. As they claimed, all black men were radical on the race question. But that was just the point: they could conceive of radicalism in no broader terms. As Randolph has said, "I didn't feel there was the necessary racial and social and economic militancy in the Talented Tenth to give strength and force to the liberation of the black masses. The Tenth represented little more than a mere revolt against discrimination. They had no fighting force in them. So where real radicalism was concerned, they were like window dressing."

The Socialist radicals felt that the example of personal uplift and "individual merit" the Talented Tenth provided was not sufficient. Nor was it sufficient for them to champion the notion, even as aggressively as they often did, that blacks were as American as any white nativist. If progressive struggles were being waged in the society in behalf of all Americans who were politically and economically victimized, then the Tenth—ordained leaders of a group that was more seriously victimized politically and economically than any other—could scarcely stand aside from those struggles. Therefore, when Randolph dismissed the elite leadership as "Old Crowd" and "hat-in-hand," it was not in the sense that they were obsequious Uncle Toms, but because, in opposing political and economic radicalism among blacks, they were affirming their allegiance to limited modes of racial protest—thereby helping, even unwittingly, to perpetuate the political and economic values in America that had first enslaved and subsequently oppressed the race.

Later generations of black intellectuals—not known for any connection to the radical movement—would echo the Harlem radicals' critique of the Talented Tenth. Writing in 1939, Cayton and Mitchell were to observe that the idea of the Tenth "has been used as a rationalization for the development of the talented upper class rather than, and often to the detriment of, the black masses." Henry Lee Moon, one of Du Bois's successors as editor of the *Crisis*, wrote in 1948 of the leaders of the Niagara movement—the first political assembly of the Talented Tenth: "Their cause was just, their motives pure, their goals noble and practical; but they were perhaps too far removed from the masses to inspire them to action—too conscious of their own privileged position as black elite." And as late as 1970, a successful professional in Harlem, who, a few decades earlier, would himself have qualified for membership in this elite, would say that "the Talented Tenth started looking out for themselves. They were exploiters. They were saying one thing to the masses but at the same time they were feeding their own pockets."

But despite the political differences, Randolph retained a high personal regard for Du Bois—though the aristocratic and erudite editor of the *Crisis*, born in New England and educated at Harvard and Berlin, was never known in those days to have acknowledged the existence of the bold young Harlem radical. As often happens, what Randolph most admired in Du Bois's personality corresponded, in some degree, to what he admired in himself: "I liked his Chesterfieldian character—the gracefulness and circumspection of his personal deportment, his adherence to the fine manners of his background." It was another reminder of one of the enduring contradictions of Randolph's own character: that, "Chesterfieldian" himself in taste and deportment, his public passions should have selected the relatively boisterous society of mass politics. Finally, when Du Bois died in 1963, at the age of ninety-five, after having joined the Communist party—moving further to the left than the *Messenger* editor had ever been—Randolph would also praise him as "one of the great intellectual wheels of the Western world, black or white, and one of the most articulate voices for human freedom and dignity."

After Du Bois called upon black Americans in 1918 to forget their "special grievances" and close ranks behind the war, the *Messenger* became even more belligerent in its opposition. "No intelligent Negro," it declared, "is willing to lay down his life for the United States as it now exists. Intelligent Negroes have now reached the point where their support of the country is conditional." For such statements, the *Messenger*'s editorial office was visited in the dead of night by agents of the Justice Department. Several mornings, the editors arrived to find their files had been ransacked, furniture broken, and back issues of their magazine confiscated.

Dauntless, like other Socialist spokesmen they took their antiwar campaign to the public platforms. Hearing, in the summer of 1918, that Randolph and Owen were planning to tour Chicago and other cities to speak against the war and "to get colored people interested in the Socialist movement," Walter Bronstrup, a leader of the party in Cleveland, invited them to include that city in their itinerary. They were to bring along 200 copies of the July issue of the *Messenger,* to be sold during the "propaganda meetings."

It was a dangerous time for antiwar Socialists. In June, 1917, Congress had passed the Espionage Act, empowering the government to censor newspapers or ban them from the mails, and to punish, by fines of up to $10,000 and imprisonment of twenty years, anyone found guilty of obstructing conscription. And in May, 1918, the act had been amended to make even the *attempt* at obstruction a felony. In the summer of 1917, Kate Richards O'Hare had been sent to the penitentiary for an antiwar speech in North Dakota. The feeling against antiwar radicals ran so high that even the trial judge, in passing sentence upon Mrs. O'Hare, seemed to share it:

This is a nation of free speech; but this is a time of sacrifice, when mothers are sacrificing their sons, when all men and women who are not at heart traitors are sacrificing their time and their hard-earned money in defense of the flag. Is it too much to ask that for the time being men shall suppress any desire which they may have to utter words which may tend to weaken the spirit, or destroy the faith or confidence of the people?

In March, 1918, Rose Pastor Stokes had been prosecuted, and would be sentenced to ten years in prison, for saying, in a letter to the *Kansas City Star,* that "no government which is for the profiteers can also be for the people, and I am for the people while the government is for the profiteers." And three months later, on June 30, Eugene Debs had been arrested in Cleveland—and would be sentenced to ten years—for saying, in Canton, Ohio, thirteen days previously, that "the master class has always declared the wars; the subject class has always fought the battles. The master class has had all to gain and nothing to lose, while the subject class has had nothing to gain and all to lose—especially their lives." (Even Du Bois, who believed the Socialist party was "wrong in its attitude toward the war," wrote a year later in the *Crisis* that "we raise our hats silently to men like Eugene Debs who let not even the shadow of public shame close their lips when they think themselves right.")

The July, 1918, issue of the *Messenger* was also quite dangerous—would, at any rate, be deemed so by government agents. It contained an editorial, "Pro-Germanism Among Negroes," which said in part:

At the recent convention of the National Association for the Advancement of Colored People, a member of the Administration's Department of Intelligence was present. When Mr. Justin Carter of Harrisburg, Pa., was complaining of the race prejudice which American white troops had carried into France, this administration representative rose and warned the audience that the Negroes were under suspicion of having been affected by German propaganda. In keeping with the ultra-patriotism of the oldline type of Negro leaders (?) the NAACP failed to grasp its opportunity. It might have informed the Administration representative that the discontent among Negroes was not produced by propaganda, nor can it be removed by propaganda. The

causes are deep and dark—though obvious to all who care to use their mental
eyes. Peonage, disfranchisement, Jim-Crowism, segregation, rank civil discrimination, injustice of legislatures, courts and administrators—these are
the propaganda of discontent among Negroes. The only way to remove this
general unrest and widespread discontent among Negroes is to remove these
cankerous causes. The only legitimate connection between this unrest and
Germanism is the extensive government advertisment that we are fighting
"to make the world safe for democracy," to carry democracy to Germany;
that we are conscripting the Negro into the military and industrial establish-
ments to achieve this end for white democracy four thousand miles away,
while the Negro at home, though bearing the burden in every way, is denied
economic, political, educational and civil democracy. And this, despite his
loyalty and patriotism in the land of the free and the home of the brave!

On the night of August 4, while Randolph and Owen took turns addressing a mass meeting at the corner of East Ninth and Chestnut
streets, in Cleveland—advising blacks, especially, to resist conscription
and fight at home to "make America unsafe for hypocrisy"—Walter
Bronstrup and a party member, John Frenholz, moved through the
crowd selling the *Messenger*.

Stirred by the character of Randolph's and Owen's remarks, a Justice
Department agent bought a copy of the magazine from Bronstrup, and
found in it several articles—especially "Pro-Germanism Among Negroes"—that seemed to him "open to question." Breaking up the meeting, and pulling Randolph, who was then speaking, from the platform,
the agent arrested both editors and held them for investigation the following day.

It came out during the investigation that Owen had been drafted, classified 1-A, and was—according to his draft board in New York, which
was contacted by the agent—"waiting for orders to entrain." In fact, his
draft board informed the Cleveland authorities, Owen was needed for the
August quota, and should be kept under surveillance. According to the
agent's report, Randolph appears to have been more resourceful in
avoiding the draft. It claimed that when arrested he was carrying documents showing that he had been classified 4-A, on the grounds that he
was the sole support of his wife and children. The report may have been
inaccurate, however. Not only was Randolph's wife then *his* sole support, but their marriage was, and would remain, childless. Randolph was
also to deny the report. Ten years later, when the Industrial Defense
Association, of Boston, accused him of having evaded the draft, he made

a public statement saying that he "did not attempt to misrepresent the facts of my life in order to escape conscription," but that as "a pacifist so far as national wars" were concerned, he "was fundamentally opposed to the war." And, as it turned out, he was drafted after the incident in Cleveland.

At the end of the investigation, both men were held for trial, charged with violating the Espionage Act: that they did

unlawfully, knowingly and feloniously, the United States being then and there at war with the Imperial German Government, willfully print and cause to be printed, publish and cause to be published and circulated, in a certain language intended to incite, provoke and incur resistance to the United States and to promote the cause of its enemies in a certain publication known as the *Messenger*.

They were held in $1,000 bail. Randolph later reported that "a colored woman of wealth in Cleveland came down to get us out, but they turned her away." After two days in jail, they were brought to trial, and arrived in court to find Seymour Stedman of Chicago, a prominent Socialist lawyer of the time—who was soon to appear in the defense of Eugene Debs —waiting to represent them.

Randolph would humorously recall the proceedings:

The judge was astonished when he saw us and read what we had written in the *Messenger*. Chandler and I were twenty-nine at the time, but we looked much younger. The judge said, why, we were nothing but boys. He couldn't believe we were old enough, or, being black, smart enough, to write that red-hot stuff in the *Messenger*. There was no doubt, he said, that the white Socialists were using us, that they had written the stuff for us. Seymour Stedman was ready for a grand political defense, indicting the war and everything else. But the judge looked at him and said, "I don't think we are going to have a trial. I am going to release these boys in your custody, and I want you to see to it that they return to their parents' homes."

Then he turned to us: "You really wrote this magazine?" We assured him that we had. "What do you know about socialism?" he said. We told him we were students of Marx and fervent believers in the socialization of social property. "Don't you know," he said, "that you are opposing your own government and that you are subject to imprisonment for treason?" We told him we believed in the principle of human justice and that our right to express our conscience was above the law. He almost changed his mind then and there. "I *ought* to throw you in jail," he said. "But take my advice and get out of town. If we catch you here again, you won't be so lucky."

Owen and I jumped on a train and headed for Chicago, where we were to address another mass meeting, in one of the black churches. But the news of what happened to us in Cleveland got there ahead of us. When we got to the church, we found a crowd gathered outside, and the building locked; the minister had closed up and left town. He wanted no part of us. So we just got ourselves a soapbox, set it up on the steps of the church, and went right on blasting the war. We couldn't sell any *Messengers* because they had been confiscated in Cleveland.

From Chicago, they went to Milwaukee—where the immigrant German Socialists "were astonished to find black men who knew anything about socialism." From Milwaukee they headed for Washington, D.C., where government agents had threatened to arrest them if they showed up and mentioned the name of Woodrow Wilson. They attacked Wilson anyway, and left town scot free, on their way to Boston for a mass meeting at Faneuil Hall, where Harvard-trained Monroe Trotter, Boston's leading black radical, "was the only Negro who had the guts to join us on the platform." After Boston, they went back to New York. "We knew we were risking jail," Randolph told a friend later, "but we didn't give a fig. We were young, we were against everything, and we weren't going to back down from anything."

It is not clear why, except for their brush with the law in Cleveland, Randolph and Owen escaped prosecution. A possible explanation was that the Justice Department, wanting no acquittals under the Espionage Act, prosecuted only when it was reasonably certain of obtaining a conviction. Another possible explanation was that the Justice Department, though it kept them under constant surveillance, may have been more interested in going after white radicals. William Dufty, in the *New York Post* of December 30, 1959, suggested yet another reason: in 1918, "it was Wilson who bent. The Justice Department recommended prosecution of 'the most dangerous Negro in America.' But, Randolph was informed later, Wilson declined to act; he felt it would not be wise."

Apparently, less drastic measures would suffice for the editors of the *Messenger*. No sooner had they returned to New York, toward the middle of August, than they received news that Postmaster General Albert Burleson had denied second-class mailing privileges to their magazine—or, as Randolph proudly preferred to put it, "Burleson threw the *Messenger* out of the mails." A few days later, Chandler Owen was drafted and sent to an army camp in the South, where he served 120 days, till the end of the war. And, late in October, Randolph was notified that he would be drafted to fill the November quota. But where pacifist objections could no longer save him, providence did: two days after his draft-induction notice arrived, armistice was declared. Otherwise, Randolph might yet have ended up in jail, for, as he said later, he "had no intention of serving."

8 / "If We Must Die"

After the collapse of Reconstruction and the rise of Jim Crow rule in the South, with all its accompanying evils, nothing portrayed more vividly the fluctuations and the anguish of the black struggle for freedom than what happened in America while the war went on, and especially after it was over.

In 1917, with some 400,000 black soldiers in uniform—having eagerly answered the country's call to defend "the right of mankind"—a wave of violence more intense than any they had suffered so far in the twentieth century was unleashed upon large sections of the black population. Even the soldiers at home were not exempt. Not only were they segregated, and assigned the menial tasks of servants at army camps around the country; they were also insulted and harassed in public places. In Houston, Texas, in September, 1917, thirteen black soldiers were hanged and forty-one imprisoned for life, after employing arms to defend themselves against the attacks of a white mob. In 1917 and 1918 alone, some fifty-eight black civilians were lynched in the South. And, in the great wartime migration then in progress, the thousands of job-seeking blacks streaming into Northern industrial centers ran into a series of bloody clashes with white workers—the most violent of which took place in East St. Louis, in 1917, when more than forty blacks were killed.

Yet all of this was a mere prelude to what black soldiers found in 1919, when they started coming home from Europe. On the political front, large areas of American democracy were under the heel of Attorney General A. Mitchell Palmer, who, with the scantest regard for civil liberties, was waging a crusade to smash the American radical movement and suppress political dissent. But to black soldiers, most of whom were not, in any case, sympathetic to radicalism, that was not so serious as what was happening on the racial front. In what came to be known as the "red summer" of 1919, more than twenty bloody race riots broke out across the country, in which hundreds of blacks were killed, injured, and imprisoned. As with the wartime outbreaks, "the basic cause of these riots," according to historians August Meier and Elliot Rudwick, "lay in white fears of economic competition and voting power of urban black migrants. The mobs harassed and murdered black victims without hindrance because of police prejudice and ineptitude. . . . Generally all the Negroes could do was attempt to flee."

To blacks, who had believed that fighting abroad would help to usher in an era of good racial feeling, 1919 meant that the prospects for such an era had diminished rather than increased. Kelly Miller of Howard University had written, at the end of the war: "After the Negro has proved his value and worth in all of these trying ways, when after this he asks for a full measure of equal rights, what American will have the heart or the hardihood to say him nay? . . . Regarded in America as the most alien of aliens before the war he demands recognition today as the most loyal of loyalists." The failure to obtain any such recognition was one of the most severe blows black idealism had ever suffered in America. Thus whatever impact World War I and its violent aftermath made upon "the post-war crisis in American values," it could hardly have been more serious than the impact upon blacks' imagination of the country. Where others, enjoying the luxury of contemplation, could reflect upon the crisis in American values, millions of embittered blacks became alienated from much of those values—as anyone must see who considers the astonishingly rapid growth of Marcus Garvey's huge black nationalist movement after the war.

W. E. B. Du Bois, who had advised the forgetting of "our special grievances" as an investment in a postwar reconstruction, was also bitterly disillusioned. "For bleeding France," he wrote in the *Crisis,* in May, 1919,

. . . we fought gladly and to the last drop of our blood; for America and her highest ideals we fought in far-off hope; for the dominant Southern oligarchy entrenched in Washington we fought in bitter resignation. For America that represents and gloats in lynching, disfranchisement, caste, brutality, and devilish insult—for this in its hateful upturning and mixing of things we were forced by vindictive fate to fight also . . . we return—we return from fighting. We return fighting.

By the following year, say August Meier and Elliot Rudwick, Du Bois was so "embittered at the wave of racial proscription that followed the war" that he "predicted a race war in which Negroes, allied with Asians, would overwhelm the white race."

Even Randolph and Owen had themselves begun to think in terms of a postwar reconstruction. Shortly before the war ended, the *Messenger,* taking the opportunity to reiterate its Socialist program, had said:

The reconstruction program for the Negro must involve the introduction of the new social order—a democratic order in which human rights are recognized above property rights. We recognize, in sketching, in broad outline, this new order that there cannot be any separate and distinct principles for the social, political and economic emancipation of the Negro which are not applicable to all other people.

But for all the progress that was made in this direction, and with all the black blood being spilled in American streets, the *Messenger* might just as well have stuck by, or reiterated, what Owen had written earlier, while opposing the war: "Since when has the subject race come out of a war with its rights and privileges accorded for such a participation?"

If the Socialist movement was to capture the imagination of the black masses in Harlem and elsewhere, this—at the height of the postwar disillusionment—was the moment. Despite the racism within organized labor that had impaired the effectiveness of their Socialist message, it was the black radicals, after all, who had practically prophesied that their people would be betrayed after the war. For that reason alone, they would seem to have earned a place—the right to one, at least—in the front rank of black mass leadership. It was not to be, however. Hundreds of thousands of blacks, smarting from the slap in the face to their American idealism, flopped to the other extreme: not into the arms of socialism, which, now more than ever, they saw as just another white idea, but into the consoling embrace of Marcus Garvey's black nationalist movement. Good prophets but poor—or, at any rate, unattractive—suitors, the Harlem Socialist radicals were soon left with little more than their magazines. But in their magazines they still had their voice, and, throughout 1919, responding to the wave of violence against blacks, they raised it with a defiance and an irreverence that were probably unsurpassed in black American journalism until the 1960's and '70s.

Nothing better expressed the essence of this response than the sonnet "If We Must Die," by Claude McKay, which, the poet said, "exploded" out of him during the "red summer" of 1919. McKay, a friend and admirer of Hubert Harrison, then had only a marginal relationship with the Harlem Socialists, being more closely connected with the white radicals downtown. And it was in the *Liberator,* edited by Max Eastman, that "If We Must Die" first appeared. But it was immediately picked up and reprinted in Randolph's and Owen's *Messenger* and in Cyril Briggs's *Crusader:*

> If we must die, let it not be like hogs
> Hunted and penned in an inglorious spot,
> While round us bark the mad and hungry dogs,
> Making their mock at our accursed lot.
> If we must die, Oh let us nobly die,
> So that our precious blood may not be shed
> In vain; then even the monsters we defy
> Shall be constrained to honor us though dead!
> Oh, kinsmen! we must meet the common foe!
> Though far outnumbered let us show us brave,
> And for their thousand blows deal one death-blow!
> What though before us lies the open grave?
> Like men we'll face the murderous cowardly pack,
> Pressed to the wall, dying, but fighting back!

After its appearance in the Harlem magazines, the poem was run by almost every black journal of any consequence; was recited in clubs and cabarets, and at mass meetings; and, on Sundays, provided the more militant black preachers with a fighting peroration.

No journal exemplified the spirit of McKay's poem more militantly than the *Messenger.* Calling for "a patriotism which practices that 'Any man who protects the country's flag shall be protected by that flag,' " Randolph and Owen condemned America as "the land of the most criminal Huns in Christendom."

When the *Atlantic Monthly* and Du Bois's *Crisis* rejected a poem by Archibald Grimké protesting the hanging of the thirteen black soldiers in Houston, the *Messenger* ran the poem in full. Titled "Her Thirteen Black Soldiers," it ended:

She who put her uniform on them, heard their enemy
She flew at its call and hanged her brave black soldiers
She hanged them from doing for themselves what she ought to have
    done for them
She hanged them for resenting insult to her uniform
She hanged them for defending from violence her black soldiers

Rejecting the poem, Du Bois had written Grimké: "We have just been specially warned by the Justice Department that some of our articles are considered disloyal. I would not dare, therefore, to print this just now." The *Messenger* also printed Du Bois's letter, with its own comment: "Almost anyone after reading this poem would very naturally wonder why the *Crisis* magazine, supposedly published by and for Negroes, could not publish this poem, written by a scholarly man . . . it is not surprising that the *Atlantic Monthly,* a reactionary organ, could not publish it. But why would this be true of the *Crisis?* The logic of the poem is absolutely sound."

Dissociating itself from the spirit of a hallowed American tradition, the *Messenger* said, in its Thanksgiving issue of 1919:

This is the *Messenger*'s Thanksgiving Number and we wish to give thanks. We do not thank God for anything nor do our thanks include gratitude for the things for which most persons usually give thanks at this period. With us, we are thankful for different things and to a different Deity. Our Deity is the toiling masses of the world and the things for which we thank are their achievements.

Other "different things" the editors were thankful for included: "the Russian Revolution, the greatest achievement of the twentieth century . . . the world unrest which has manifested itself in titanic strikes . . . the growth of industrial unionism . . . the New Crowd Negro . . . the waning influence of the Old Crowd Negro . . . the steady oncoming of the new order of society in which Thanksgiving will be relieved of its cynicism and hypocrisy."

Maintaining, in light of the race riots, the right of blacks to self-defense, Randolph and Owen published a cartoon showing the militant "New Crowd Negro" riding an armored car through Chicago, Washington, D.C., and Longview, Texas (scenes of some of the worst race riots), with guns blazing away at white mobs. "Since the government won't stop mob violence," the New Negro declares, "I'll take a hand." The caption read: "The New Crowd Negro Makes America Safe for Himself."

Developing this point in an editorial, "How to Stop Lynching," the *Messenger* invoked "Anglo-Saxon jurisprudence," which "recognizes the law of self-defense." And, discussing "The Cause and Remedy of Race Riots," the magazine argued:

The solution will not follow the meeting of white and Negro leaders in love feasts, who pretend like the African ostrich that nothing is wrong. . . . On the economic field, industry must be socialized, and land must be nationalized. . . . Black and white workers must unite in the same unions, ask for the same wages, same hours and the same working conditions. . . . Politically all peoples must be enfranchised without regard to race, creed, sex or color. Educationally, schools must be revolutionized. . . . The people must organize, own and control their press. The church must be converted into an educational forum. The stage and screen must be controlled by the people. . . . We recognize that the preceding . . . may take years for attainment. . . . Hence, we offer this immediate program. *Physical force in self defense.* While force is to be deplored and used only as a last resort, it is indispensable at times. The lesson of force can be taught when no other will be heeded. A bullet is sometimes more convincing than a hundred prayers, editorials, sermons, protests and petitions. . . . *Larger Negro police force* in Negro districts will help to keep down riots. . . . *Lastly revolution must come.* By that we mean a complete change in the organization of society. . . . When no profits are to be made from race friction no one will longer be interested in stirring up race prejudice. . . . When you make a thing unprofitable you make it impossible.

It was during 1919 that Randolph and Owen came to be known in Harlem as "Lenin and Trotsky," and, to critics who found neither amusement in their antics nor anything worth distinguishing between Socialists and Bolshevists, as "wild-eyed Reds of the deepest dye." It was also in April of that year that Algernon Lee, director of the Rand School of Social Science, a Socialist and trade union institution on East Fifteenth Street, in New York, invited them to join his faculty as part-time instructors.

The Rand School, named after abolitionist Carrie Rand, had been founded in 1916, by the American Socialist Society, to educate organized and unorganized workers in economics, politics, and literature. Among the left-wing intellectuals on the faculty in 1919 were Max Eastman, Oswald Garrison Villard, Harry Laidler, Joseph Schlossberg, Charles A. Beard, August Claessens, H. W. L. Dana, James O'Neal, Scott Nearing, and Norman Thomas. Algernon Lee's invitation to the *Messen-*

ger's editors—to lecture on "The Economics and Sociology of the Negro Problem"—was merely a recognition of their "sound interpretation of the economic history of this country." But to those who regarded the Rand School as the academy of American Bolshevism—especially after it was denounced by the Department of Justice and the New York State legislature—its recognition of Randolph and Owen was a further sign not only that they were "Reds of the deepest dye," but that the dye was probably indelible.

The two editors now felt the postwar backlash against radicals of all stripes—anarchists, Bolshevists, Socialists, pure-and-simple black militants. And the backlash came not only from the more predictable quarters of white America, but also from die-hard conservatives within their own race. A correspondent, calling himself the son of black abolitionists, wrote the *Messenger:*

. . . I am amazed and horrified by the spirit of race hatred that [the Messenger] manifests and the evil effects upon the Negro race that it is calculated to produce. I regard you, the founders, editors and particularly friends of the Messenger as the worst enemies of the Negro race. . . . In proof of this assertion I cite the cartoon . . . entitled "The New Crowd Negro Making America Safe for Himself." That cartoon is enough to make the blood of every white man who is not a Bolshevist or a professional Negro-lover stir and quicken very perceptibly. . . . Really, it seems to be your deliberate intention to provoke armed conflict between whites and blacks of this country. I can understand why the Bolshevik white men who are supporting the Messenger should adopt that course. They believe in wreck and ruin. . . . I call upon you to come out from among the Bolshevists and have nothing more to do with them.

When, late in 1919, at the instigation of Archibald Stevenson, of New York City's wealthy and exclusive Union League Club, the New York legislature appointed the Lusk Committee (headed by State Senator Clayton Lusk) to investigate radicalism and sedition in the state, a resident of Harlem wrote to inform Stevenson:

. . . As you know, there is at present a well directed, well organized movement on foot to link up the Negroes of this country with the Radical movement as it now exists. There is one organ through which this work is carried on, the Messenger magazine. If something can be done to cripple this organ without invoking the sympathy of the masses of the colored people for the magazine, the movement can be stopped just where it is now. A committee of young colored men, of whom I am the Chairman, has been secretly organized to help stamp out this radicalism among Negroes and consequently we have been studying the Messenger, and its personnel with a view to finding its weak point. . . . We feel that we are in a sound position to advise you how this magazine can be put out of business if you are willing to cooperate. . . . This is our plan: There is one man more than anyone else who is keeping the Messenger going and that is the business manager, Victor R. Daly; he is the one weak link in the chain and he is at the same time the one making the magazine go. Daly is a young man of about 24 years old, a Cornell graduate and a former officer in the Army, a fine fellow well liked and very popular among the people up here. . . . The Editors, Owen and Randolph have neither managing ability nor thrift and if Daly were taken away the whole thing would fall like a house of cards. The time is ripe now, for I believe Daly is a little disgusted with some of the statements of the Editors in regard to the part the Negro played in the war. Daly's interest lies along the lines of business; he specialized in banking and finance at college. He spoke a few Sundays ago at a public meeting up here on the "need of a bank in Harlem." That is his weak point. If through some of your wealthy friends in the Union League Club, you could organize a bank up here with Daly (he has some little money) or if you could place him down town with a large banking house, you could do more to wipe out Bolshevism among Negroes than by any one thing else. . . . Won't you look into this matter, Mr. Stevenson! . . . We have even found out his home address for you, 261 West 134th Street, New York. . . .

Sincerely yours,
A staunch American

Nor was the alarm confined to New York's black community. Said the *Atlanta Independent,* in October, 1919.

We have read a story in the New York *World* to the effect that the IWW, an industrial society, is inciting the Negroes throughout the country to rise up against the white folks . . . and that articles in the *Crisis* and *Messenger* —two New York Magazines—are evidences that the Negroes are contemplating an uprising against the whites. . . . The *Crisis* and the *Messenger* and other radical Negro papers no more represent the thought, character and intelligence of the twelve million Negroes in this country than Emma Goldman, Debbs and other Bolshevists represent the conservative and intelligent class of our white neighbors. Congress is unduly alarmed.

"We have not become tainted with the iconoclasm of the Bolsheviks," the *Cleveland Advocate* declared the same month. "We do not plan to rebel against orderly government." In Knoxville, Tennessee, Bishop

George C. Clement told a class at Morris Brown University, "I would urge all members of my race to obey the law and keep clear of Bolshevism and all incendiary suggestions." And a black resident of Randolph's home town recalled years later that "when the people in Florida heard that Randolph was a revolutionary, an organization in Jacksonville sent him a note, with a red and black hand on it, saying he'd better not set foot again in Florida."

The white press, which did not, as a rule, pay much attention to what went on in the black community, was also startled. "The publication in the U.S. spreading this insidious propaganda among Negroes," said the *Providence Sunday Journal,* in June, 1919, "is the Messenger. It is published at 2305 Seventh Avenue, New York City, by two as well read, well educated and competent Negroes as there are in the United States." The *New York World* was no less concerned:

The radical forces in New York City have recently embarked on a great new field of revolutionary endeavor, the education through agitation of the southern Negro into the mysteries and desirability of revolutionary Bolshevism. . . . The chief established propaganda is being distributed through the Messenger, [which] with the exception of the Liberator . . . is the most radical journal printed in the U.S.

But the most serious attention—though serious only because of the source—came from the government. It would find nothing startlingly new to say, nor would it prosecute, but the language of the government's findings survives today as the gravest judgments ever passed upon the *Messenger* and its editors. After Congressman James Byrnes, of South Carolina, had advised the House of Representatives that the editors— whose magazine had smuggled the idea of social equality into his home state—were a pair of black Bolshevists, the Lusk Committee and the Department of Justice reported on the investigations that they had been conducting, since mid-1919, into radicalism, sedition, anarchy, and the activities of persons and groups advocating the overthrow of the government.

Somewhat mildly, yet as ominously as if it had just confirmed a serious threat to the survival of the state, the Lusk Committee concluded, early in 1920, that the *Messenger* not only was "distinctly revolutionary in tone," but also was "committed . . . to the proposition of organizing negroes for the class struggle." The language of the Justice Department had been sharper. Toward the end of 1919, its report, titled "Radicalism and Sedition Among Negroes As Reflected in Their Publications," had found that the *Messenger,* "representative of the most educated thought among Negroes," was "by long odds the most dangerous of all the Negro publications."

Now officially associated with forces of subversion, the *Messenger* began to lose the more wavering of its black admirers. (Its white readers were confirmed radicals or left liberals.) The black readership was mainly among the lower-middle-class intelligentsia, since the bulk of the masses were by then reading Marcus Garvey's *Negro World.* The *Messenger's* Socialist radicalism would begin to decline, however, and, by 1923, the magazine would be a mere echo of its former self. But the reduction in its circumstances was also related to the gradual decline of American radicalism, one of the accomplishments of Attorney General A. Mitchell Palmer's ruthless campaign.

Yet the *Messenger* had not allowed itself to be silenced. It had fired back at Congressman Byrnes:

If approval of the right to vote based upon service instead of race or color is Bolshevism, count us as Bolshevists. If our approval of the abolition of pogroms by the Bolsheviki is Bolshevism, stamp us again with that epithet. If the demand for political and social equality is Bolshevism, label us once more with that little barrack behind which your mental impotency hides when it cannot answer argument.

It had assailed the Union League Club, where Archibald Stevenson had dreamed up the Lusk Committee:

You smug plutocrats and silk gloved hypocrites who have time to sit in clubs, steam-heated in the winter and ice-cooled in the summer, are the real causes of discontent among Negroes and among whites and all classes of labor. . . . You are crying stop thief! with the loot under your arms.

It had dismissed the Lusk Committee itself as "a farcical, fossilized and motley crew of ignoramuses." And, in August, 1920, when it seemed that Attorney General Palmer's popularity had begun to fade, it had eulogized him: "Even in America, his public career is all but ended. The shades of private life are awaiting him, and even there he will remain a hated and detested memory." The *Messenger* was voice, to the end, of Harlem and New Negro radicalism.

9 / Marcus Garvey:
Crisis of the New Negro

Hubert Harrison, oldest of the New Negro radicals and "father" of socialism in Harlem, seems also, during the war, to have become one of the community's intellectual progenitors of black nationalism. When he broke with the Socialist party in 1917, Harrison was no longer convinced that socialism contained the answer to the race problem. "The roots of Class-Consciousness," he was to address the Socialist party in his magazine, "inhere in a temporary economic order; whereas the roots of Race-Consciousness must of necessity survive any and all changes in the economic order." He believed, therefore, that it was the duty of all black radicals to sever their ties to the Socialist movement, freeing themselves to follow their own race strategies.

The black radicals Harrison chiefly had in mind—though in 1917 he was still friendly toward them—were men like Randolph, Owen, and W. A. Domingo. They were, as Harrison saw them, "selected Negro spokesmen on whose word" the Socialist party relied "for information as to the tone and temper of Negro political sentiment." In a clear reference to the *Messenger* and Domingo's *Emancipator,* Harrison—after the rise of the Garvey movement—would accuse the Socialist party of subsidizing "both a magazine and a newspaper to attempt to cut into the splendid solidarity Negroes are achieving in response to the call of racial necessity." *

Leaving the Socialist party "to work along lines of his own choosing"

---

* In May, 1920, the *Bulletin,* an organ of the Socialist party, recommended that the national office "push the sale among locals and branches of copies of the monthly magazine, the 'Messenger,' and the weekly paper, the 'Emancipator,' calling their attention to the fact that these Negro periodicals can be procured at such prices as will make their sale profitable."

—as he wrote—Harrison founded the Afro-American Liberty League, in June, 1917, to propound his new doctrine of race first. When, soon after, he started the *Voice,* a monthly magazine, to serve as the organ of the league, Mary White Ovington—a Socialist, and secretary of the Harlem branch of the NAACP—wrote to tell him she saw no reason for another organization or another paper, unless, of course, it printed "straight Socialism." Harrison was indignant. "These good white people," he replied in the *Voice,* "must forgive us for insisting that we are not children, and that while we want all the friends we can get, we need no benevolent dictators. It is we, not they, who must shape Negro policies." In a strong statement of his position, Harrison also informed the Socialist party during the war: "The writer . . . is also a Socialist; but he refuses in this crisis of the world's history to put Socialism or your party above the call of race."

On March 23, 1916, Marcus Garvey, a young man of twenty-eight, arrived in New York. Two years earlier, in his native Jamaica, he had formed the Universal Negro Improvement Association and the African Communities League, to unite, he later said, "all the Negro peoples of the world into one great body to establish a country and Government absolutely their own." He had been inspired to launch such an organization, Garvey said, after reading Booker T. Washington's autobiography, *Up from Slavery,* and after traveling through half of Europe. "I now asked: 'Where is the black man's Government?' 'Where is his King and his kingdom?' 'Where is his President, his country, and his ambassador, his army, his navy, his men of big affairs?' I could not find them, and then I declared, 'I will help to make them ' "

After setting up the UNIA in Jamaica, Garvey "got in touch with Booker T. Washington and told him what I wanted to do. He invited me to America and promised to speak with me in the Southern and other States to help my work. Although he died in the Fall of 1915, I made my arrangements and arrived in the United States." In New York, he visited "some of the then so-called Negro leaders," and found that "they had no program, but were mere opportunists . . . living off their so-called leadership while the poor people were groping in the dark." On a tour of thirty-eight states, Garvey "found the same condition" everywhere. And after visiting Tuskegee to pay his respects "to the dead hero, Booker T. Washington," he returned to New York.

One of the "so-called" leaders Garvey had visited was Dr. W. E. B.

Du Bois, at the office of the NAACP. He was "dumbfounded" to find that "but for Mr. Dill, Du Bois himself and the office boy," he could not tell whether he was in "a white office or that of the National Association for the Advancement of 'Colored' People." It was his first shock at "the advancement of hypocrisy," and, after talking with Du Bois, he "became so disgusted with the man and his principles" that a probability he hadn't contemplated before now "entered his mind—remaining in America to teach Du Bois and his group what real race pride meant."

Back in Harlem—to test the ground for a New York branch of his UNIA—Garvey sought out the company and the platforms of the men he probably considered the genuine race radicals. He struck one of the first men he called upon in Harlem as "a little sawed-off, hammered down black man, with determination written all over his face, and an engaging smile that caught you and compelled you to listen to his story." More than one Harlemite has claimed credit for introducing Garvey to the public forums of the community. Randolph is one of them. He had "the pleasure and opportunity," he likes to say, of "presenting Garvey to the American people in his first meeting on the corner of 135th Street and Lenox Avenue, in 1916." He recalls the meeting:

I was on a soapbox speaking on socialism, when someone pulled my coat and said, "There's a young man here from Jamaica who wants to be presented to this group." I said, "What does he want to talk about?" He said, "He wants to talk about a movement to develop a back-to-Africa sentiment in America." I said, "Yes, I'll be glad to present him," and after I'd spoken a few more minutes I told the people I had a surprise for them. It was a tremendous crowd, and I told them about the young man from Jamaica and what he wanted to talk about. I could hear a dubious rumble of "Oh" run through the crowd. I said, "Well, it is good for us to get his position on this question, because we don't know a lot about Africa ourselves." Garvey got up on the platform, and you could hear him from 135th to 125th Street. He had a tremendous voice. When he finished speaking he sat near the platform with a sheaf of paper on which he was constantly writing, and he had stamps and envelopes, ready to send out his propaganda. I could tell from watching him even then that he was one of the greatest propagandists of his time.

At first, says Edmund David Cronon, Garvey's biographer, "skeptical Harlemites paid scant attention to the stocky black Jamaican. . . . The sidewalk crowds loitering on Lenox Avenue ignored his harangues and dismissed him as just another West Indian carpetbagger." But as Garvey persevered, he met and became closely attached to Hubert Harrison, in whose "race first" doctrines he could hear a distinct echo of his own ideas. Thus in June, 1917, when Harrison launched his Afro-American Liberty League, at the Bethel AME Chapel, in Harlem, he presented Garvey as one of his guest speakers. James Weldon Johnson, then a columnist for the *New York Age,* later described the occasion:

This was Harlem's first real sight of Garvey, and his magnetic personality, torrential eloquence, and intuitive knowledge of crowd psychology were all brought into play. He swept the audience along with him. He made his speech an endorsement of the new movement and a pledge of his hearty support of it; but Garvey was not of the kidney to support anybody's movement. He had seen the United States and he had seen Harlem. He had doubtless been the keenest observer at the Liberty League organization meeting; and it may be that it was then he decided upon New York as the centre for his activities.

It was soon after this speech that Garvey founded the New York division of the Universal Negro Improvement Association, with headquarters on 135th Street.

For a while after Garvey had started the UNIA in New York, he and Randolph—despite basic differences in political philosophy—worked closely together. Toward the end of the war, they collaborated in a group called the International League of Darker Peoples, and drew up a list of demands in behalf of colonized peoples to be presented to the colonial powers at the peace conference in Versailles. Randolph was even selected by the UNIA to go to France. The *New York Times* of December 3, 1918, reported:

A proposal to send two Negro delegates to France to present to the Versailles Peace Conference the ideas of the UNIA and African Communities League was adopted last night at a meeting of 5,000 Negroes in the Palace Casino on East 135th Street. . . . A fund of $3000 was subscribed at the meeting and the officials of the League were authorized to ask the State Department for passports and permission to send the . . . delegates to France to work for the cause of Negroes throughout the world. The delegates chosen . . . were Asa Philip Randolph, editor . . . and Mrs. Ida Wells Barnett, a Negro teacher in Chicago. . . . Marcus Garvey, President of the Association said the party would sail for France within ten days if the State Department gave permission. At the Peace Conference the delegates propose to submit a set of resolutions adopted by a meeting of the League on November 11, and sent to the rulers of the allied nations. These suggested that the German colonies in Africa be turned over to the Negroes under the rule of Negroes educated in this country and Europe; social, political, and industrial equality wherever Negroes live in the same country with another race of people; freedom of education everywhere; with no discrimination and with self-determination in all countries.

But the State Department, which could hardly have been enamored of his activities during the war, refused to grant Randolph a passport. Noting that representatives of more conservative black organizations had been issued passports, Randolph wrote bitterly in the *Messenger:* "Moton [of Tuskegee Institute], Du Bois and Lester Walton [of the Urban League] could go even though nobody wanted them but President Wilson. In other words, 'good Socialists' and 'good niggers' could go." But it was not so much this failure as Garvey's subsequent "success" that would mark the end of his collaboration with Randolph.

By the "red summer" of 1919, as blacks began flocking in droves to the UNIA, and as its leader's message of African redemption and black self-determination reached across the country, Garvey claimed the remarkable membership of 2 million. According to Edmund Cronon, "American Negroes were ready for any program that would tend to restore even a measure of their lost dignity and self-respect." Thus the time was ripe for Garvey to launch one of his most spectacular enterprises, the Black Star Line, "to own, charter, operate, and navigate ships of various types in any part of the world and to carry passengers, freight, and mails." Among the vessels of the Black Star Line were the *Yarmouth* (renamed the *Frederick Douglass*), the *Orion* (*Phyllis Wheatley*), the *Kanawha* (*Antonio Maceo*), the *General G. W. Goethals* (*Booker T. Washington*), and the *Shadyside*. These ships sold passenger and freight space, and scheduled trips to the West Indies and excursions up the Hudson River. The Black Star Line, says Cronon, was "a supremely audacious move that aroused the greatest excitement in the colored world. Here was an enterprise belonging to Negroes, operated by and for them, that gave even the poorest black the chance to become a stockholder in a big business enterprise." Another of Garvey's enterprises was the Negro Factories Corporation, designed, according to the *Negro World,* the UNIA newspaper, to "build and operate factories in the big industrial centers of the United States, Central America, the West Indies, and Africa to manufacture every marketable commodity."

All of this—plus the colorful regalia of the UNIA's officers, marching band, African Legion, Motor Corps, and Black Cross Nurses, as well as the pomp and ceremony of the organization's public affairs—captured the emotions of millions of blacks in the United States, Central America, the West Indies, and even parts of Africa. By August, 1920, when the largest of all UNIA conventions drew delegates from all over the world, and 25,000 blacks filled Madison Square Garden to hear "the Provisional President" of Africa, Garvey had, by his own estimate—though by no means his alone—"become known as a leader of his race," and "over 4,000,000 persons had joined the movement." Commenting upon the growth of the UNIA by 1920, Garvey's biographer says the organization "seemed the answer to the hopes and prayers of countless generations of oppressed and downtrodden blacks."

After visiting Garvey at his headquarters in December, 1921, Herbert J. Seligman—then publicity director for the NAACP—wrote the following account for the *New York World,* reprinted in the *New York Age:*

There in 135th Street, New York City, is the center of it all, of such dreams of African hegemony, of share vending, of idealist talk as it would be difficult to imagine, let alone duplicate. At the center of those dreams, spinning them like so many webs, writing, traveling across the City to Liberty Hall . . . is Marcus Garvey, West Indian Negro. To walk into those offices is to enter a fantastic realm in which cash sales of shares and the imminence of destiny strangely commingle. Not that there is anything bizarre about Marcus Garvey, despite the green and purple robes he sometimes affects. He might, to judge by his appearance, be a politician or a professional man. Of medium height, his head set close down upon broad shoulders, his slender, longish arms terminating in narrow hands, he presents a sedentary almost studious type—except that one feels the orator if not the actor not far beneath his surface. His manner is easy and his voice agreeable, with a slightly English intonation that falls strangely upon the ears of Americans unaccustomed to natives of the British West Indies. Nor is there anything bizarre in Marcus Garvey's talk. It is fluent, even compelling if one does not stop to check him up. And this one is tempted to do. . . . He has no illusions about the commonplaces that pass for realities in our civilization. In fact, he is quite calmly waiting for the present white civilization to go to pieces, and in fifty years he believes the native population of Africa will have seized their continent because the white governments—England, France, Italy—that now hold African territory will have been overthrown. Mr. Garvey sees the problem in the large. Nothing less than continents and hundreds of millions of people will stead him. His imagination is capacious, active. There is something of the poet in his ability to think in terms of the crassest Realpolitik, of power, and of might makes right—such morality as white Christian civilization has taught the black man—and out of these elements to conjure the destruction of Europe and the rise of invincible and eternal Ethiopia.

By 1920, however, Randolph and Owen—along with most black intellectuals, radical or moderate—were becoming increasingly troubled by the strides and ventures of the Garvey movement. In December of that year, as rumors of irregularities in the conduct of the Black Star Line began to circulate, Randolph found it necessary to explain the nature of his earlier relationship with Garvey. He wrote in the *Messenger:*

. . . it might not be amiss to observe upon the past relations of the editors of the Messenger to the [Garvey] Movement. At one time, the editors . . . spoke from the same platform with the moving spirit of the organization. . . . Then, the Black Star Line idea was no part of its effects. Nor were the slogans "Negro First" and "African Empire," "Back to Africa," and extreme race baiting prominent in its program. The representation of Negroes at the Peace Conference was employed as the basis for generating considerable Negro consciousness. . . . Moreover, it is no little illuminating that the organization selected as one of its representatives to the Peace Conference one of the editors of the Messenger, a well-known exponent of Socialism. . . . The editors of the Messenger have never been members of or affiliated with, in any way, the Universal Negro Improvement Association and African Communities League. In speaking from the same platform with the founder of the Movement, we were chiefly interested in educating its membership in the class struggle nature of the Negro problem, and retaining the sympathetic attitude of the Movement toward Socialism.

Not only had they failed to infiltrate the UNIA membership with class ideas, but also, as Randolph explained two years later—after Garvey was indicted, in February, 1922, on charges of using the mails to defraud prospective stockholders in the Black Star Line—he "didn't know then that Mr. Garvey was untrustworthy."

The break between Garvey and the editors of the *Messenger* was inevitable. It would have been surprising if Randolph and Owen, struggling at least since 1917 to build a Socialist mass movement in Harlem, did not feel a certain jealousy—though neither of them confessed to such a feeling—over the mass movement Garvey had organized. While their reasons were those of Socialist radicals whose philosophy had been rejected, they were hardly alone in their critical judgments of Garvey's movement. W. E. B. Du Bois, for example, who was himself no admirer of radicals like Randolph, was no less critical. And, as Edmund Cronon writes, "upper-class Negroes, conscious of their status in colored society and anxious to improve their position in the eyes of the white world," felt an increasing hostility and jealousy as Garvey, "an upstart foreigner

. . . adapted his program to the superstitions and resentment of the lower-class blacks." It would have been equally surprising if Garvey and the editors of the *Messenger*—exponents of warring social ideas, class versus race—had been able to dwell together in harmony for any length of time.

Thus although the dispute between Garvey and the editors of the *Messenger* would flare most acrimoniously around incidental issues—Garvey's handling of the Black Star Line, his relationship with the Ku Klux Klan, his attempt, in a sense, to read "light-skinned Negroes" out of the black race, and the conflict that developed between black West Indians and black Americans—it had its source in fundamental differences of political and economic belief.

"Africa for the Africans" was not the most serious of these differences. Randolph wrote in 1922 that at the end of the war he and Owen "were the theoretical exponents of achieving the goal of 'Africa for the Africans' . . . reinforced by an alliance with the white radicals, liberal and labor movements of the world." This may or may not be disputed. What seems beyond dispute is that their commitment to the cause of "Africa for the Africans" was not as thoroughgoing—nor, in a sense, as radical—as Garvey's.

Theirs was simply an anticolonial position, an advocacy of the right of the indigenous African populations to political liberation and self-determination. Garvey's, in going beyond that, entailed notions of a pan-African empire—with himself, the "Provisional President," conceivably at the head—and the repatriation of Afro-Americans to the ancestral homeland. Since, Randolph and Owen felt, a return to Africa was unachievable for all but a relative handful of blacks in this country—and since, they also felt, social democracies were preferable to empires—the encouragement of Garvey's ideas was a visionary and emotional distraction from the necessary struggle to win political and human justice in America.

Nor were Randolph and Owen insensitive to what was creative in the cultural and psychological aspects of Garvey's nationalism. Despite their reservations about an exclusively racial politics in the United States, they praised Garvey for "having put into many Negroes a backbone where for years they have had a wishbone," for "having stimulated race pride," and for having inspired "an interest in Negro traditions, Negro history, Negro literature, Negro art and culture."

By far the most serious of the differences, at least from the viewpoint of Randolph and Owen, were those around economic philosophy. Garvey's emphasis on black capitalism ("Capitalism is necessary to the progress of the world, and those who unreasonably and wantonly oppose or fight against it are enemies of human advancement") could scarcely have failed to evoke the intense opposition of the *Messenger*'s editors, men whose entire hopes for social progress were invested in democratic socialism.

As long as capitalism was so central a difference, there would also be a clash on such other issues as social equality and labor unionism. On both these issues, Randolph and Owen maintained (a) that "black workers should use the same instrumentalities to save themselves as white workers," and (b) that "if Negroes admit they are the social inferiors of white people, they ipso facto admit they are entitled to inferior treatment." Garvey's position, on the other hand, was (a) that

If the Negro takes my advice he will organize by himself and always keep his scale of wages a little lower than the whites until he is able to become, through proper leadership, his own employer; by so doing he will keep the goodwill of the white employer and live a little longer under the present scheme of things. If not, between Communism, white trade unionism and workers parties he is doomed in the next 25, 50, or 100 years to complete economic and general extermination.

and (b) that

It is a vicious and dangerous doctrine of social equality to urge, as certain colored leaders do, that black and white should get together.

These two points illuminate as well as any others the conflicts and complexities of black leadership in the early 1920's. The accommodationist legatees of Booker T. Washington—aspects of whose thought had inspired Garvey's early career—were, understandably, in substantial agreement with Garvey's position on labor unionism (though, because they were not militant on the race question, they were among those whom Garvey dismissed as "so-called" leaders). But neither would the middle-class, or Talented Tenth, protest leadership, which had come into being upon a rejection of Washington's racial conservatism, differ seriously with Garvey on the trade union question (though they held the black nationalist character of his movement in utter contempt). What united them on that question was an essentially conservative approach to political ideas—and the racist behavior of the organized labor movement itself. On the issue of social equality, however, the middle-class leadership saw eye to eye not with Garvey, but with the Randolph-Owen school of radicals. Not only was social equality an important part of Randolph's and Owen's Socialist commitment, but also, together with most of the middle-class leadership, they had retained it as part of the protest legacy all young black intellectuals had received from Du Bois.

All of this suggests, however, that Randolph was right when he wrote in 1923—though one cannot be sure whether he meant it to apply to himself as well—that "the Negro schools of thought are torn with dissension, giving birth to many insurgent factions. . . . All are engaged in a war of bitter recriminations . . . while the long-suffering masses . . . [are] victims of the vanities, foibles, indiscretions, and vaulting ambitions . . . of the various leaderships."

The eruption of anti-Garvey feeling—among black radicals as well as among the black bourgeoisie—came during the summer of 1922, after Garvey had been indicted on twelve counts of fraudulent use of the mails, and after he had visited Atlanta, Georgia, for a secret meeting with Edward Young Clarke, Imperial Wizard of the Ku Klux Klan. Public criticism had been mounting since his indictment in February, and Garvey did not help his own cause when he was quoted in the July 10, 1922, issue of the *New York Times* as saying, "The Ku Klux Klan is going to make this a white man's country. They are perfectly frank and honest about it. Fighting them is not going to get you anywhere." This brought down a torrent of condemnation on Garvey's head, for, as Theodore Vincent, another historian of the Garvey movement, says, "Members of the black establishment and white liberals and leftists would choose to visit the devil in hell before fraternizing with the Ku Klux Klan."

William Pickens, an NAACP intellectual, a former friend of Garvey's UNIA, and later a member of the *Messenger*'s editorial board, now refused an honorary award from Garvey. "I cannot," Pickens wrote, "feel myself quite bad enough to accept any honor or alliance with such an organization as the Ku Klux Klan or the Black Hand Society. You compare the aim of the Ku Klux Klan in America with your aim in Africa— and if that be true no civilized man can endorse either one of you." Garvey, wrote Dr. Du Bois in the *Crisis,* "is, without doubt, the most dangerous enemy of the Negro race in America and the world."

The UNIA leader maintained his attitude toward the KKK, however, dismissing such criticisms with the reply that "I regard the Klan, the

Anglo-Saxon clubs and White American societies, as far as the Negro is concerned, as better friends of the race than all other groups of hypocritical whites put together. I like honesty and fair play. You may call me a Klansman if you will, but, potentially, every white man is a Klansman, as far as the Negro in competition with whites socially, economically and politically is concerned, and there is no use lying about it."

But it was the editors of the *Messenger*—both in their magazine and through a group they had founded, called the Friends of Negro Freedom —who, upon the slogan of "Garvey Must Go," launched a campaign to banish the Jamaican, either from political leadership or from the United States. In one of their strongest editorials on the subject, Randolph and Owen urged "all ministers, editors, and lecturers who have the interests of the race at heart to gird up their courage, put on new force, and proceed with might and main to drive the menace of Garveyism out of this country." This was followed by another editorial in which they declared that "when a Negro leader leagues with Negro lynchers as did Marcus Garvey in his alliance with the Ku Klux Klan, then it is time for all decent self-respecting Negroes to league together for the purpose of driving out that Negro. . . . The clock has struck . . . the New Negroes must resolve each day: 'Garveyism must be destroyed.' "

Two of the prominent Friends of Negro Freedom who helped to push the "Garvey Must Go" campaign, in the *Messenger* and in public meetings in Harlem, were William Pickens and Robert Bagnall, both of the NAACP. According to the *Messenger*, throughout the "hot and rainy" month of August, 1922, "more then two thousand people came out at 3 o'clock every Sunday afternoon and listened to scholarly addresses upon the emptiness of Garvey's claims, the impossibilities of his schemes, the insincerity of the man, the unreliability of his word, the littleness of his accomplishments, the mischief and menace of his attempted deal with the race's worst enemy—the Ku Klux Klan."

Garvey, of course, fired back with his own heavy oratorical artillery at "these so-called Negro intellectuals." Aiming a deadly shot at the insolvent editors of the struggling *Messenger*, he wrote in his newspaper, the *Negro World*: "Before Owen and Randolph can speak of the failure of any business and the incompetency of any individual to do business they should first prove their success and their competency to handle business." And on August 5, 1922, the *Negro World* struck fear in the hearts of Garvey's critics when it warned: "We say . . . to the Negro enemies of the past we are ready for you, and before the 31st of August comes we are going to give you your Waterloo. . . . So you will understand, whether it be Pickens or whether it be Chandler Owen, the Universal Negro Improvement Association has no fears of anybody and when you interfere . . . you will take the consequence."

What may or may not have been part of the "consequence" arrived on the afternoon of September 5, when Randolph, sitting in the *Messenger*'s office, received a brown paper package, with a New Orleans postmark, addressed to him "From a Friend." Opening the package, Randolph noticed a "whitish powder" falling out, and fearing—because of the anonymity of the sender—that someone had sent him a bomb, he called the Thirty-eighth Police Precinct, on 135th Street. Detectives arrived, placed the package in a container of water, to avoid any possible explosion, and, "to the utter amazement and horror of everyone," Randolph reported later, "upon opening the package a human hand was found."

Carrying the story the following day, the *New York Times* described the hand, "covered with red hair," as "evidently that of a white man." And the *New York Herald* reported that "more than once during the last few months, Randolph has been threatened that he would be killed. . . . The most recent was at a Friends of Negro Freedom meeting . . . [when] an unidentified Negro rose to his feet and shouted he was going to 'get' Randolph. . . . As the troublemaker was firmly led out of the New Douglass Hall, at 142nd Street and Lenox Avenue, Randolph says the man shouted 'I'll get you and be glad to do 15 years in the pen for it.' "

Randolph printed in the *Messenger* the covering letter that, he said, came with the package:

Listen Randolph — We have been watching your writings in all your papers for quite a while but we want you to understand before we act. If you are not in favor with your own race movement you can't be with ours. There is no space in our race for you and your creed. What do you mean by giving us a nigger? Do you know that our organization is made up of all whites? We have sent you a sample of our good work, so watch your step or else. . . . Now let me see your name in your nigger improvement association as a member, paid up too, in about a week from now. Don't worry about lynching in the South. If you were here you wouldn't talk about it. Now be careful how you publish this letter in your magazine or we may have to send your hand to someone else. Don't think we can't get you or your crowd. Although you are in New York City it is just as easy as if you were in Georgia. If you can't unite with your own race we will find out what's the matter with you all. Don't be selfish. Give your friends a tip.

K.K.K.

Clearly, Randolph told the press, the "Klan had come to the rescue of its Negro leader, Marcus Garvey."

But Garvey had his own theory. When a reporter from the *New York Herald* called on him at his 133 West 129th Street apartment, to interview him on the incident, "the African Potentate" was "sitting 'in a council' . . . in his famous Chamber of 1000 Vases in his luxuriously furnished apartment. Large palm plants were all about the room, which was virtually filled to overflowing by vases and bric-a-brac of every possible description and period design." Asked for his views on the package from New Orleans, Garvey replied, "I know nothing about it, but I can venture just about what the whole thing is. It looks to me like a good publicity stunt which Randolph and Owen have pulled to get some notoriety." The identity of the sender would never be ascertained, but the *Herald* later quoted the police as saying that the package "might have been mailed in the city, in spite of the New Orleans post mark."

All this merely intensified the "Garvey Must Go" campaign. As the anti-Garvey language of the *Messenger* increased in vitriol, Owen, in 1923, called Garvey an "ignoramus" and a "rascally renegade and scoundrelly traitor." And Robert Bagnall, in perhaps the most sustained diatribe ever printed against Garvey, described him in the *Messenger* as

a Jamaican Negro of unmixed stock, squat, stocky, fat, and sleek, with protruding jaws, and heavy jowls, small bright pig-like eyes and rather bull-dog-like face. Boastful, egotistic, tyrannical, intolerant, cunning, shifty, smooth and suave, avaricious; . . . as adept as a cuttle-fish in beclouding an issue he cannot meet, prolix in the nth degree in devising new schemes to gain the money of poor ignorant Negroes; gifted at self-advertisement, without shame in self-laudation, promising ever, but never fulfilling, without regard for veracity, a lover of pomp and tawdry finery and garish display, a bully with his own folk but servile in the presence of the Klan, a sheer opportunist and demagogic charlatan.

The *Messenger*'s attacks also took on a sharp anti-West Indian edge. "I think," Randolph wrote in January, 1923, "we are justified in asking the question, that if Garvey is seriously interested in establishing a Negro nation why doesn't he begin with Jamaica, West Indies." And an editorial in the same month's issue of the *Messenger* referred to Garvey as "A Supreme Negro Jamaican Jackass."

Remarks of this sort would rupture one of the *Messenger*'s oldest and most valuable relationships—the one it had enjoyed from its birth with its Jamaican contributing editor, W. A. Domingo. Domingo, who had helped to edit Garvey's *Negro World* soon after its founding—during the period when the black Socialists were speaking on Garvey's platforms in the hope of educating the UNIA membership in the class struggle—had quit the paper in the fall of 1919, when it became clear to him that the UNIA was committed irrevocably to the priority of race. Domingo, who claimed to have resigned over the "execrable exaggerations, staggering stupidities, blundering bombast and abominable assinities of our black Barnum," was later denounced by Garvey as a "barber shop rat," and—by his account—was set upon and beaten up by a group of Garveyites.

One of the Harlem radical groups that attacked Garvey as bitterly as the *Messenger*'s editors were doing was the African Blood Brotherhood —an odd collection of ex-Socialists who now considered themselves partly Communist and partly militant black nationalists. Led by men like Cyril V. Briggs, Richard B. Moore, Lovett Fort-Whiteman, and Otto Huiswood, former colleagues of Randolph and Owen who had gone over to the American Communist (Workers party) movement at its inception, in 1921, the African Blood Brotherhood hated the editors of the *Messenger* quite as much as they hated Garvey. As Communists, the Blood Brotherhood differed from Randolph in their revolutionary radicalism; and, as black nationalists, they differed from Garvey in their demand for militant self-defense and for a separate black republic not in Africa, but in the American South.

Though he did not become a member, Domingo had allied himself with this group soon after its formation. Not only was it made up predominantly of West Indians like himself, but its community of anti-Garvey feeling—because it was shared by West Indians—was more congenial to his own animosities than the *Messenger* community's. And, as Domingo was to disclose, it was not Americans, but West Indians— chiefly members and friends of the Blood Brotherhood—who had secretly engineered Garvey's downfall by reporting the activities of the Black Star Line to the American legal authorities.

In March, 1923, however, Domingo could no longer tolerate the *Messenger*'s strident anti-West Indian tone, and protested to the editors in an

open letter, which led to the end of their relationship, and which illumi-
nates some important aspects of the dissolution of New Negro radicalism
in Harlem. "My position is, I think, clear," wrote Domingo:

Garvey's doctrines are dangerous to Negroes everywhere, but more so to
those in the United States and Africa; his doctrines and many disgraceful
failures have resulted in giving partial confirmation to the Negrophobists'
claims as to our essential inferiority and have been the means of weakening
us politically, financially, and racially by driving away white friends and im-
porting schisms into our ranks. But I am not discussing Garvey's doctrines.
. . . I am concerned about the doctrines of the Messenger. I am a West
Indian. I am so through no act of mine, and neither proud nor ashamed of
what is purely an accident. It is not the fault of Mr. Randolph that he was
born in Jacksonville and not Rosewood, Florida. . . . Despite his [Garvey's]
Jamaican birth, I, a Jamaican, find myself differing from him even as most
native Negroes no doubt differ from Perry Howard, whom you have brack-
eted with Garvey as being of the same sinister sort. . . . Since the Messenger began its belated fight to rid the race of the disgrace of Garveyism, I
have noticed that many of the articles dealing with that subject have stressed
Mr. Garvey's nationality. . . . The persistent and regular recurrence of this
particular emphasis forces me to ignore past relationships and register my
emphatic protest. . . . In the January Messenger there is an editorial entitled "A Supreme Negro Jamaican Jackass," which reads in part: "Of course,
no American Negro would have stooped to such depths. . . . It was left to
Marcus Garvey from Jamaica, etc." Yet in another editorial . . . speaking
of Perry Howard of Mississippi, you say, "Negroes of this country . . .
should hereafter class him with Marcus Garvey." . . . If Howard is equal
to Garvey in infamy then Jamaica is not the only place to produce jackasses
of Garvey's type. . . . I will not point out that it is incompatible with your
professed Socialist faith for you to initiate an agitation for deportation or to
emphasize the nationality of anyone as a subtle means of generating opposition against him, but I certainly maintain that to oppose Garvey on the
score of his birthplace is to confess inability to oppose him formidably upon
any other ground. By the penalties you advocate and the arguments you
stress against Garvey one can determine what you regard as his greatest
offense, namely, his nationality. Certainly there is enough error and weakness in Garveyism for you to find a more intellectually dignified method of
assault; and certainly the people you hope to rouse against this monstrous
thing are sufficiently intelligent as to be entitled to a higher form of propaganda. The Messenger for which I wrote and which I loved prided itself
upon its internationalism and valued this quality as its hallmark of superiority; but today it seems to have fallen from its former high estate. . . . It

is surprising to learn at the forum of the Friends of Negro Freedom that West Indians are a menace to the progress of American Negroes. Perhaps such careful, modest, and reliable scholars as W. E. B. Du Bois and Carter Woodson are in error when they stress the part "played by West Indians" in the upbuilding of the race in this country. Have you ever read the famous passage in *The Souls of Black Folk* in which the author refers to the contributions by West Indians in the early portion of the last century in formulating the manhood policies of native Negroes? . . . Since when has meritorious achievement become a detriment to progress? And what of those like James Weldon and Rosamond Johnson, William Stanley Braithwaite, and Robert Brown Eliot with foreign-born parents? And Du Bois with his Haitian-Bahaman ancestors? . . . Let us face certain facts regarding Garvey. . . . Who are the bitterest and most persistent opponents of Garvey? Aren't they West Indians like Cyril V. Briggs, R. B. Moore, Frank R. Crosswaith, Thomas Potter and myself? Who caused his arrests and indictments? West Indians: Grey, Warner, Briggs and Orr. Who conducts the *Crusader* Service, Garvey's veritable Nemesis? Briggs, assisted by this writer. The January *Crisis*, in justice to truth and elevated journalistic principles, concedes part of the work I did in unmasking Garvey. . . . Is it hoping too much that . . . the Messenger will change its new policy of shifting personal responsibility to a group and penalizing a people who, despite their many faults and their misfortune in not choosing to be born in Mississippi or Alabama . . . are, when all is said and done, just as human as their brothers in the United States?

Chandler Owen could not permit some of Domingo's remarks to go unanswered:

. . . Mr. Domingo remarks: "Since the Messenger began its belated fight to rid the race of the disgrace of Garveyism . . ." Let us stop right there. The Editor of the Messenger was the first person to suggest and inaugurate the fight upon Garvey's nebulous schemes and dreams. . . . Mr. Domingo's national bias is evident. . . . There is no objection to our referring to Garvey as a jackass; none to his racial identity as a Negro; but mention of his nationality is taboo. Here our contributing editor is more concerned about nationality—the great island of Jamaica—than the entire Negro race. Is Jamaica a more sensitive and tender darling than the Negro? . . . America is certainly capable of producing Negro and white jackasses. She has produced enough for centuries to come. Still it can hardly be gainsaid that Garvey at present holds the unenviable distinction of having handed the palm to Jamaica. . . . Mr. Domingo also shows that he is strongly nationalistic in pointing out the large number of West Indians who have achieved. This is perfectly correct. The only trouble about Domingo is that he would hail the West Indians when they hit, but not mention them when they miss. . . .

Domingo urges with a show of certainty that Garvey's "bitterest opponents are West Indians." We grant it. The West Indians are probably the bitterest opponents. . . . But who are Garvey's most formidable opponents? . . . Unquestionably . . . American Negroes. . . . We shall continue to hail both West Indians and Americans when they hit and to mention both of them when they miss.

At the end of this exchange, Domingo requested that his name, as contributing editor, be removed from the *Messenger*'s masthead. He had clearly had the better of the debate. Randolph himself, before receiving the package with the human hand, had written an editorial opposing "unfair . . . attacks upon Garvey's nativity." The merits and demerits of Garveyism, he had said, "are not lessened or increased because he is a West Indian. . . . A man has a right and a duty to fight to improve conditions wherever he is. . . . West Indians are among the foremost fighters in all cities for racial rights. They are assiduous workers, vigorous fighters, diligent and able students." Still, one must ask, hadn't Domingo read that? And how consistent was Randolph, considering that as late as January, 1923, he had written: ". . . if Garvey is seriously interested in establishing a Negro nation why doesn't he begin with Jamaica, West Indies"?

Garvey was brought to trial in 1923, was found guilty, and, after an unsuccessful appeal, entered the Atlanta penitentiary, in 1925, to serve a five-year term. The sentence later commuted, he was deported to Jamaica. After a number of abortive efforts to rebuild his movement from his homeland, he left for London, where he died in 1940.

Among the surviving protagonists of the New Negro political tragedy of the early 1920's are Randolph himself and Garvey's widow, Amy Jacques Garvey, in Jamaica. Her political resentments undiminished after almost five decades, she said, in July, 1970, in a letter to this writer:

Chandler Owen was Secretary of the Committee that wrote that infamous letter to the Attorney General pleading with him to push the case against Garvey, and to extirpate his movement.* . . . The "Negro Intellectuals"

---

* On January 15, 1923, while Garvey was awaiting trial, Owen was one of eight prominent blacks who signed an open letter to U.S. Attorney General Harry M. Daugherty, calling upon him to use his "full influence completely to disband and extirpate this vicious movement," and to "vigorously and speedily push the government's case against Marcus Garvey." The return address was listed as 2305

of the 1919–1930 on the whole were a self-opinionated, isolationist minded set who felt that "integration"—miscegenation—was an easy way out as a solution to the "Negro problem." They hated Garvey as a "foreigner" who had a positive programme of African Redemption and race rehabilitation, and who had millions of followers among the masses, for whom he spoke, wrote and interpreted their sufferings, ambitions, and fears. Those "Intellectuals" and Local leaders never came to Garvey and discussed his programme; they hurled abuse and ridicule at him with their pens and in their speeches. . . . Mr. Randolph was among this set, and Owen did most of the dirty work. . . . Randolph and others . . . in their hey-day regarded American Negroes as Americans, Africans as savages, and West Indians as Monkey-Chasers. Poor dupes—mouthing the white man's thoughts to keep the race apart, and destroy them more easily. Yes, they made Garvey's life a living hell in America.

Randolph, though his opinions on Garvey's politics have changed very little since, looks back on those vanished passions with no residue of animosity. "I had nothing to do with the letter to the Attorney General, and I had nothing against West Indians. I even defended West Indians against people who were attacking them on grounds of nationality. But I don't see how we could have avoided mentioning Garvey's nationality. For one thing, he was doing something no American Negro would do—dividing the race between the light-skinned and the pure black. All of us had to admit, though, that he was an organizational genius. He organized more Negroes than any other single Negro in the history of this country. His impact upon black pride and consciousness—though not always with the best result—was tremendous. A lot of people really believed that their problems would be solved by simply going back to Africa. What you needed to follow Garvey was a leap of the imagination, but socialism and trade unionism called for rigorous social struggle—hard work and programs—and few people wanted to think about that. Against the emotional power of Garveyism, what I was preaching didn't stand a chance."

Seventh Avenue, the *Messenger*'s office, suggesting that the letter had been written there and that the idea for it had originated with Owen. Other signers were Harry H. Pace, a Harlem phonograph salesman; Robert S. Abbott, publisher of the *Chicago Defender;* John E. Nail, a top Harlem real-estate broker; Julia P. Coleman, president of a cosmetic company; William Pickens, field secretary of the NAACP; Robert Bagnall, NAACP director of branches; and George Harris, member of the New York City Board of Aldermen. Garvey described the letter as "the greatest bit of treachery and wickedness that any group of Negroes could be capable of."

10 / The End of Radicalism

The New Negro was not, as we have seen, born during the Harlem, or Negro, Renaissance—that period, between the early and late 1920's, when the work of black artists, chiefly in Harlem, began radiating racial self-awareness and self-assurance, and vibrating with mass experience. He had been born earlier, amidst the issues and crises of the war and postwar years, when the economic radicals and black nationalists inspired the emergence of a more militant black temperament and consciousness. Thus what happened during the Renaissance may be seen as the cultural flowering of an earlier political insurgency. The failure of the Garvey movement in the mid-1920's—though it lingered a while longer —was merely part of the general collapse of New Negro insurgency.

Among the casualties was the Socialist radicalism of the *Messenger* and its editors. Although the magazine would not fold until 1928, and would not wholly lose its interest in the politics of the left, it would never again be as politically brisk and provocative. Where in previous years its pages had been dominated by "economics and politics," from 1924 on the *Messenger* became a cultural organ of no great force or distinction— printing mostly the satirical railleries of George Schuyler; profiles of black communities around the United States; poetry and fiction of uneven quality; and the results of Chandler Owen's resurgent fascination with the life of the rich and the successful. Several years later, Langston Hughes, in his autobiography, would describe the *Messenger* of that period as "a Negro society magazine and a plugger for Negro business, with photographs of prominent colored ladies and their nice homes." Hughes may well have been reminded of portraits like the one, in 1924, of Edward Cooper Brown—a black Philadelphia banker—and his wife,

138

in which Chandler Owen glowed with admiration over the Browns' "beautiful residence of twelve large rooms, three baths, a billiard room, garage and two cars—one a Stutz and the other a Marmon."

As early as February, 1920, the *Messenger* had stopped calling itself "The Only Radical Magazine Published by Negroes"—a belated recognition that ever since the war it had been sharing that distinction with Cyril Briggs's *Crusader,* Hubert Harrison's *Voice,* William Bridges's *Challenge,* and W. A. Domingo's *Emancipator.* It began announcing itself instead as "A Journal of Scientific Radicalism," and continued to do so until June, 1923, when it suddenly became "The New Opinion of the New Negro." Less than a year later, it made an even larger claim, "The World's Greatest Negro Monthly." By then, sadly, it was nothing of the sort. It was more like a faded beauty denying, with delusions and her old photographs, the evidence in her face. In fact, Langston Hughes, in considering the magazine's decline, would describe it around that time as "God knows what." The *Messenger*'s fate was a result of the failure of socialism to catch on in Harlem. Contributions and advertising from Socialist-oriented unions downtown fell off, and the magazine began struggling more desperately than ever to raise money and stay alive. One way of staying alive was to open its pages to the new surge of interest in black culture.

In the black world, the time of "economics and politics"—the *Messenger*'s time—had seemingly passed. It appeared now—during the onset of the Harlem Renaissance—to be the time of "music and art," and, therefore, the time of the only magazines that could then reasonably claim to be the world's greatest Negro monthlies, the NAACP's *Crisis* and the Urban League's *Opportunity.* No magazine was doing as much as they were to encourage and publicize the work of the artists and writers of the cultural Renaissance.

Between 1917 and 1923, Randolph and Owen started more than a half-dozen political and trade union organizations. It was not because they loved so much to start new things, but because hardly anything they started lasted very long. One of these organizations was the Friends of Negro Freedom, formed in May, 1920, to conduct political and labor forums for the education of the masses, and to "proceed from cities and towns" across the United States. But the Friends failed to catch on nationally, spending its first two years as little more than a paper organization. It was not until 1922, when it launched its public campaign against Garvey, that the Friends of Negro Freedom came alive. It was a short life, though, for after the Garvey campaign few people beyond its own leadership ever heard of it again.

What it became was a sort of private intellectual forum for Randolph and friends of the *Messenger*. Saturday afternoons, a few of them held bull sessions in the *Messenger*'s office, or in an empty storefront next to the Lafayette Theater, on Seventh Avenue. Occasionally they sponsored lectures at the Harlem YMCA and YWCA, on 135th and 137th streets, and invited speakers like Norman Thomas, then director of the League for Industrial Democracy; Algernon Lee, of the Rand School of Social Science; Will Durant, historian of philosophy; Alfred Adler and John B. Watson, psychologists; James O'Neal, editor of the New York *Call;* Walter White, of the NAACP; and Jean Longuet, French Socialist and member of the Chamber of Deputies.

None of its members needed the Friends of Negro Freedom more than Randolph did. He had few interests that were not political, and the Friends became, until its demise, the center of his social and intellectual life. Gertrude Elise Ayer—a Socialist in the 1920's, and a contributor to the *Messenger*—recalled that Randolph was then "wholly intellectual, didn't go around dancing or bother with the ladies," and had his mind on nothing but "the general political and economic situation."

On Sunday mornings, Randolph invited members of the Friends of Negro Freedom over to his apartment—then on West 142nd Street, between Lenox and Seventh—for breakfast and political discussion. The regulars were the disputatious Owen; Frank Crosswaith, a Socialist graduate of the Rand School; the priestly Robert Bagnall and the scholarly William Pickens, of the NAACP; George Schuyler, an acidulous young Socialist who, recently arrived from Syracuse, was finding his way among the *Messenger* intellectuals; Joel A. Rogers, a professorial Jamaican-born historian and Africanist; and Theophilus Lewis, soft-spoken, Edwardian in manners, avid reader of the *Smart Set,* drama critic of the *Messenger*—who sometimes left his listeners dangling from the middle of a sentence while he reached into his pocket for a box of Dr. Romney's snuff.

Also present was Randolph's brother, James, who was now sharing the apartment with Randolph and his wife. James, at the age of thirty-five, had arrived in 1922 to enter City College, after working for several years as a Pullman porter based in Jacksonville. Theophilus Lewis, who became his closest friend in New York, remembered him as "tall and handsome," with "a thick shock of hair . . . refined and morally clean, having an encyclopedic knowledge of practically everything, and able to argue with anyone about anything. He was much smarter than Asa, but lacked Asa's passionate interest in politics and race saving. His line was scholarship."

To Lewis, the Sunday-morning discussions were "something like Samuel Johnson's arguments in the coffeehouse." And George Schuyler, who had never been a part of anything so intellectually heady before, described them later as "Athenian conclaves" presided over by the "dapper" Asa Randolph, whose "deep drawl poured oil over the stormy waters of dispute." Nothing, according to Schuyler, "escaped the group's probing minds, and witty shafts."

When the conclaves adjourned, in early afternoon, Schuyler liked to accompany Randolph out to Seventh Avenue, to watch or join the Sunday-afternoon promenades, which were then a fashionable part of Harlem's social life. James Weldon Johnson, in his history of black Harlem, recalls:

Strolling in Harlem does not mean merely walking along Lenox or upper Seventh Avenue or One Hundred and Thirty-Fifth Street; it means that those streets are places for socializing. One puts on one's best clothes and fares forth to pass the time pleasantly with friends and acquaintances and, most important of all, the strangers he is sure of meeting. One saunters along, he hails this one, exchanges a word or two with that one, stops for a chat with the other one. He comes up to a laughing, chattering group, in which he may have only one friend or acquaintance, but that gives him the privilege of joining in. He does join in and takes part in the joking, the small talk and gossip, and makes new acquaintances. He passes on and arrives in front of one of the theatres, studies the bill for a while, undecided about going in. He finally moves on a few steps farther and joins another group and is introduced to two or three pretty girls who have just come to Harlem, perhaps only for a visit; and finds a reason to be glad he postponed going into the theatre. The hours of a summer evening run by rapidly.

It was the kind of spacious old-world evening that appealed to Randolph's sensibility, and harmonized with his own social style. He took a certain pleasure in being finely turned out himself. His "hello's," "how-are-you's," and the doffs of his hat were as courtly and as elegant as his carriage. And, like people who were raised in warm and intimate black communities, he retained memories of an entire boyhood of Sunday evenings when one put on one's best clothes, called leisurely on one's neighbors, or took some of the outside world into the dark rooms of the old and the sick.

Walking down Seventh Avenue, he and Schuyler delighted in the spectacle of men "wearing gaiters and boutonnieres and swinging canes," and women in knee-length dresses and fur coats. Nor was "a monocle or lorgnette" an uncommon sight. It must have been a rare democratic concourse, where the classes of Harlem came out to mix their fashions with the masses—for what would militant Garveyites, say, be doing in gaiters, boutonnieres, monocles, and lorgnettes, or twirling urbane walking sticks? Garvey himself—with his flair for sartorial drama and splendor —maybe; but his legions?

Some Sunday evenings, Randolph and Schuyler, who became quite close, rode an open-top bus down Fifth Avenue to Washington Square and back. And occasionally, after the stroll or the trip downtown, they took in a vaudeville show at the Loew's Alhambra theater, on West 126th Street. That was the least pleasant part of the day. Orchestra seats at the Alhambra were reserved for whites, blacks being allowed the freedom of the balcony. Despite the convention, however, Randolph never gave up trying to get orchestra seats. Entering the lobby, Schuyler later reported, Randolph "would flatten himself against the wall near the ticket window, toss in the money, and ask for two orchestra seats." Sometimes it worked, and two orchestra tickets would appear; but, more often, the teller would catch a glimpse of his hand, and would simply shove out tickets for the balcony.

The Friends of Negro Freedom began to disperse soon after Randolph lost his father and Owen's brother died. About the same time, Owen, claiming that white Socialists had turned their backs on him, renounced his radical beliefs.

Owen's brother, Toussaint, a master tailor, from Columbia, South Carolina, had also arrived in New York in 1922, a few months after James Randolph. His once successful tailoring business in Columbia had failed, and Chandler had encouraged him to come to New York, where, with the Messenger's connections with the Socialist movement, he would be sure to find employment through one of the needle trades unions. The Messenger's connections proved less than useful, however, and Toussaint, failing to find work after several months, died in March, 1923.

Embarrassed, disillusioned, and bereaved, Owen dropped out of the radical movement, toward the end of 1923, and left for Chicago.

On September 13, 1924, the Reverend James Randolph, who had been suffering for seven months from heart and kidney complications, died in Jacksonville, at the age of sixty. Randolph paid tribute to his father ("In Memoriam to Our Fallen Comrade") in the October issue of the *Messenger:*

Gentle in nature, broad in vision, philosophical in thinking, devoted to his family, his entire being ever devoted to the cause of Negro emancipation; loved, honored and respected, the Reverend James William Randolph passed into the unknown at his home in Jacksonville. . . . He represented that sturdy, stable, old sterling fighting stock of the race and America, which after a long and faithful life, to the country in general and the Negro in particular, is passing. The death of such beautiful, rugged and stalwart, sacrificing characters is one of the tragedies of our period.

This would, no doubt, have pleased "the Reverend," except, perhaps, where it was noted that he had "passed into the unknown." Such a view of the afterlife may have been obligatory to a young leftist; but it is hardly likely to have been shared by a man who had spent so much of his life in the service of Christian theology.

When the minister died, his wife, Elizabeth, arrived in New York to join her sons and daughter-in-law. This made the Randolph apartment no longer suitable for Sunday-morning conclaves, and the Friends of Negro Freedom broke up soon afterward.

When Owen left New York, he continued working for the *Messenger* for more than a year, writing occasional pieces and selling advertising space to black businesses in Chicago and Philadelphia. After that, however—though his name would always remain on the *Messenger*'s masthead as coeditor—he would take no further active part in the magazine's affairs. In Chicago, he became an editorial writer for the *Bee,* a black newspaper, and a ghost writer and public relations functionary for both Republican and Democratic ward politicians. The *New York Age* even wrote, in 1924, that he had become president of a business firm called the California Development Company. But this report was never substantiated. He and Randolph remained close friends. Years later, when Randolph was spending a good deal of his time in Chicago, he would pass some of it with Owen, and would observe that Owen had "a joyous social life" and that his associates were "people of money and station."

More than forty years after George Schuyler himself had recanted his Socialist beliefs—never strongly held*—and had become one of America's most prominent black conservatives, he would write that Owen had "seen through and rejected the Socialist bilge" after his brother, Toussaint, "had been unceremoniously brushed off by one of the Marxist clothing unions," and that "Owen became more interested in saving Owen than in saving the masses."

With Owen in Chicago, Randolph started leaning heavily on George Schuyler for help in running the magazine. Many of Schuyler's traits reminded him of Owen's: cynicism, combativeness, and an enormous capacity for shouldering laborious detail. Schuyler, an admirer of Mencken's writing—and later on a contributor to *The American Mercury*—was also a writer of biting satire, and would, in Randolph's view, add an exciting dimension to the *Messenger*'s social commentary. Thus he offered Schuyler $10 a week to join the *Messenger* as a contributing editor—which meant, as it turned out, that Schuyler would take over the practical end of running the magazine, while writing his monthly column of "calumny and satire," called "Shafts and Darts." "To me," Schuyler has said of this column, "nothing was above a snicker, a chuckle, a smile, or guffaw."

Working for the *Messenger* was, financially, about the worst offer Schuyler had ever had. After paying "half that much for a small room," he calculated, there would be "little left for food and laundry." He accepted, however, for he had developed a great admiration for Randolph, and felt the *Messenger* was "a good place for a tireless, versatile young fellow to get plenty of activity and exercise."

But Schuyler almost regretted the decision when he saw the *Messenger*'s office, on the third floor of 2305 Seventh Avenue: "The furnishings were nondescript, the files were disorganized, back copies of the magazine were scattered about indiscriminately, and finding anything was a chore. There was about one typewriter, a battered old Underwood." Nor had he anticipated the extent of his duties: sweeping and mopping the office, opening and answering mail, reading manuscripts and proofs, taking edited copy to the Brooklyn Eagle press, handling subscriptions, dis-

---

* Randolph: "Schuyler was a Socialist when I met him. But he never took it seriously. He made fun of everything—including socialism. But he had an attractive writing style."

tributing the magazine to newsstands, and taking Randolph's dictation on the old Underwood.

Working alongside Randolph every day, Schuyler now found him even more likable: "One of the finest, most engaging men I had ever met . . . undemanding and easy to get along with . . . leisurely and undisturbed, remaining affable under all circumstances, whether the rent was due and he did not have it, or whether an expected donation failed to materialize, or whether the long-suffering printer in Brooklyn was demanding money. He had a keen sense of humor and laughed easily, even in adversity. . . . However the *Messenger* might feel the fell clutch of circumstance, Randolph showed no dismay, and his aplomb seemed impenetrable. . . . He calmed all tension, anger, and insistent creditors."

Despite the decline in his political fortunes, Randolph evoked a similar esteem among other Harlemites. One of them was Noble Sissle, a contemporary, who, as a young vocalist and lyricist, was then—with his partner, the pianist and composer Eubie Blake—enjoying great fame and fortune on Broadway with his hit musical, *Shuffle Along*. "When you looked at Randolph," Sissle recalls, "his rich voice fitted him. It went with everything about him, even his facial expression, which was one of great dignity. And his vocabulary: I don't care who he sat amongst. He might use a lot of ten-cylinder words, but the layman was crazy about him, because he was so different. He had a little beat-up office up there, a raggedy desk and a few chairs. But he sat down just as the President would sit down at his desk in the White House. You'd forget about his little raggedy desk the moment you saw him sitting there. You were way off in another world. He might have sounded like a Yale or Harvard graduate with his talk, but there was a ring of sincerity to it and brotherly love to it, and you were proud to have someone like that to talk to you."

Upon the average Harlemite the *Messenger* had made a considerably smaller impact. Randolph himself would admit that the magazine "went over the heads of the masses of the people." To black actor Leigh Whipper, "it was a fine publication, but the community was not up to it." And Theophilus Lewis, its drama critic, says that "the general population of Harlem did not pay much attention to it."

Despite that, Lewis adds, the *Messenger* was "a distillation of the intellectual atmosphere of Negro life in the early 1920's, particularly at the beginning of the Harlem Renaissance." Though the *Messenger*'s role in that cultural movement was less important than those played by the

Crisis and *Opportunity* magazines, it published the work of many of the young artists and intellectuals of the time—E. Franklin Frazier, Roy Wilkins, Claude McKay, Countee Cullen, Jessie Fausset, Wallace Thurman, and Langston Hughes. Unlike the *Crisis* and *Opportunity,* it was based in Harlem, and, for all its poorer quality and lesser impact, was more closely identified with the life of the community. Langston Hughes, for example, would admit that before he became widely known the *Messenger* bought "my first short stories."

In the January, 1925, issue, the young Paul Robeson praised the trail-blazing career of black tenor Roland Hayes as "infinitely more of a social asset than many who 'talk' at great length. . . . If I can do something of this nature I shall be happy. . . . For it is within my power to make this unknown trail a somewhat beaten path." And in the same issue, Eugene O'Neill paid an extraordinary tribute to black actors like Robeson, though he was not so generous toward black playwrights:

My experiences as author with actor have never been so fortunate as in the cases of Mr. [Charles] Gilpin and Mr. Robeson. . . . I would say that the Negro artist on the stage is ideal from an author's standpoint. He interprets but does not detract—and when his own personality intrudes it is usually (unless he has learned too much rubbish in the conventional white school of acting) an enrichment of the part. I think Negroes are natural born actors (speaking in generalities) while whites have to learn to lose their self-consciousness before they begin to learn. As to voice and innate lyric quality of movement and expression, there is no comparison. You have it "all over us." I have seen it in my own plays and I know. But where are your playwrights? I have read a good number of plays written by Negroes and they were always *bad* plays—badly written, conceived, constructed—without the slightest trace of true feeling for drama—unoriginal—and, what revolted me the most, bad imitations in the method and thought of conventional white plays!

Still, the *Messenger* circulated chiefly among well-read blacks, and was the talk of the more socially conscious middle-class homes. And, as Chandler Owen once admitted, only one-third of the magazine's readership was black, the rest made up of white liberals and radicals. Thus some of the finest tributes paid the *Messenger* during its lifetime came from the white left. The *Call,* organ of the Socialist party, once said the *Messenger* was "one of the most valuable and unique Socialist publications that has appeared in this country." Roger Baldwin, of the American Civil Liberties Bureau, said the magazine contained "a lot of good

A. Philip Randolph in New York, 1911 or 1912
(Courtesy A. Philip Randolph)

James Randolph in his early twenties (Courtesy
A. Philip Randolph)

Lillie Whitney (Courtesy Dr. James Parker)   Mary Neff (Courtesy Dr. James Parker)

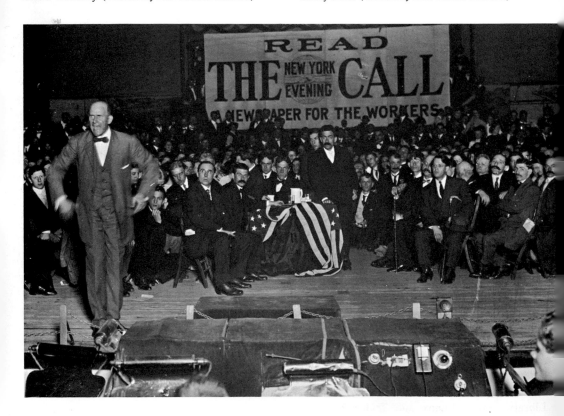

Eugene V. Debs speaking at a meeting in New York (Brown Brothers)

W. E. B. Du Bois (Courtesy Schomburg Collections, The New York Public Library, Astor, Lenox and Tilden Foundations)

A. Philip Randolph, about 1918 (Courtesy Schomburg Collections, The New York Public Library, Astor, Lenox and Tilden Foundations)

Chandler Owen, about 1918 (Courtesy Schomburg Collections, The New York Public Library, Astor, Lenox and Tilden Foundations)

Marcus Garvey, 1921 (Culver Pictures, Inc.)

Vol. II.   No. 7   JULY, 1918

THE

MESSENGER

"ONLY RADICAL NEGRO MAGAZINE IN AMERICA"

Edited by

Chandler Owen — A. Philip Randolph

LIBERTY NUMBER

15c. per Copy   *$1.50 per Year*

Cover of July, 1918, issue of the *Messenger* (Courtesy Schomburg Collections, The
New York Public Library, Astor, Lenox and Tilden Foundations)

The Messenger

Published monthly by The Messenger Publishing Co.,
513 Lenox Ave., New York City

A. PHILIP RANDOLPH,
President.

CHANDLER OWEN,
Secretary-Treasurer.

———— : o : ————

CONTENTS

Entered as second class mail matter at New York Post Office, N. Y., March, 1917,
under the act of March 3, 1879.

Contents page of first issue of the *Messenger*, November, 1917 (Courtesy Schomburg Collections, The New York Public Library, Astor, Lenox and Tilden Foundations)

Richard B. Moore (Courtesy Schomburg Collections, The New York Public Library, Astor, Lenox and Tilden Foundations)

Hubert Harrison (Courtesy Schomburg Collections, The New York Public Library, Astor, Lenox and Tilden Foundations)

Bennie Smith (left), Randolph (center), and Ashley Totten (third from right), with supporters of the struggling Brotherhood of Sleeping Car Porters, about 1926 (Courtesy A. Philip Randolph)

Officers of the Brotherhood in the 1930's: unknown, Bennie Smith, Ashley Totten, T. T. Patterson, Randolph, Milton P. Webster, C. L. Dellums, and E. J. Bradley (Courtesy Chicago Historical Society)

William Pickens (Courtesy Schomburg Collections, The New York Public Library, Astor, Lenox and Tilden Foundations)

The Reverend George Frazier Miller (Courtesy Schomburg Collections, The New York Public Library, Astor, Lenox and Tilden Foundations)

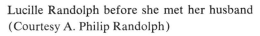

Lucille Randolph before she met her husband
(Courtesy A. Philip Randolph)

Lucille Randolph in the late 1920's (Courtesy
A. Philip Randolph)

stuff." H. W. L. Dana, an ex-professor of comparative literature at Columbia, praised the "skill and vivacity of its writing" and "the courage and significance" of its message. Algernon Lee, of the Rand School, wished that the *Messenger* "had a million readers, white as well as colored." Oswald Garrison Villard, of *The Nation,* admired its "integrity" and "earnestness." Writing from France, Randolph's friend the Socialist Jean Longuet called it "a periodical which can support most representatively the comparison with the best Reviews and Magazines of the International Socialist, Labor and . . . Political Movement." From England, the Labour party's Ramsay MacDonald wrote to congratulate Randolph for his "efforts to eradicate from the minds of certain sections of people that one race is more worthy than another." To the "Rebel Girl," Elizabeth Gurley Flynn, the *Messenger* was "the only rebel voice" of the black American worker. And Eugene Debs wrote to praise the editors for doing "a splendid work in the education of your race and in the quickening of the consciousness of their class interests."

Yet the editors of the *Messenger* had failed to achieve any significant "quickening" of class consciousness among blacks. As the conservative George Schuyler says today, "Despite all the talk about black and white unite and fight, it didn't quite pan out." Several reasons have been advanced for the failure. An old resident of Harlem attributes it to the language of the black Socialists. "Socialism," he says, "did not appeal to the Negroes, because the leadership did not speak the language of the masses. Also because a lot of them were West Indians, and they were so pompous they antagonized the Negroes. The Socialists should have learned to speak the language of the masses. They should not have been standing in front of churches; they would have been better off in poolrooms and bars."

Sterling D. Spero and Abram L. Harris blame the failure as much upon the "instability" of Socialists like Randolph and Owen as upon "the Negro's orthodox religious traditions; the growing prevalence of Negro middle-class ideology; and racial antagonism between white and black workers." And much of what Spero and Harris say is borne out by the kind of middle-class ideological leadership that Dean Kelly Miller of Howard University was offering as late as 1925:

There is every indication that it is the intention of the great industries to foster and favor the Negro workman to the fullest extent of his merit and efficiency. For the Negro wantonly to flout their generous advances by joining the restless ranks which threaten industrial ruin would be fatuous suicide. At present the capitalist class possess the culture and conscience which hold even the malignity of race passion in restraint. There is nothing in the white working class to which the Negro can appeal. They are the ones who lynch and burn and torture him. He must look to the upper element for law and order. . . . Whatever good or evil the future may hold in store for him, today's wisdom heedless of logical consistency demands that he stand shoulder to shoulder with the captains of industry.

Despite the errors of the black Socialists and the political reserve or conservatism of the general black population, the white radical movement itself bears a large part of the blame for the failure of class politics to engage the serious interest of the black community. Given the good intentions of the white radical movement, this failure was tragic. Notwithstanding the fullness of the Socialist party's commitment—at least, after the war—to racial and economic equality, it failed to make a realistic appraisal of the two essential aspects of the black struggle—one against the kind of economic deprivation that could be alleviated by inclusion in the trade union movement, and the other against the kind of bigotry that barred all but a token handful of blacks from that movement. Thus while the Socialist party stood firmly behind the principle of trade union solidarity, it failed—except with the few unions closely allied to it—to devote any special effort to the organization of black workers.

In view of the party's policy, this failure was inevitable. No American Socialist had been as committed to the principle of racial equality in the labor movement as Eugene Debs. The St. Louis race riot of 1917 was, in his view, "a foul blot upon the American labor movement." Had the labor movement "freely opened their doors to the Negro instead of barring him," Debs argued, "the atrocious crime of East St. Louis would never have blackened the pages of American history." And, a year later, Debs declared that any Socialist who failed to speak out "for the Negro's right to work, live and develop his manhood, educate his children, and fulfill his destiny". equally with whites "misconceives the movement he pretends to serve or lacks the courage to live up to its principles." But it would be difficult to fulfill these principles as long as Socialists saw no need to make a special address to the race problem. The party's policy toward that problem had been stated as early as 1903 by Debs himself: "We have nothing special to offer the Negro, and we cannot make separate appeals to all the races. The Socialist Party is the party of the whole working class, regardless of color—the whole working class of the whole world."

Because black workers had learned from their experience with organized labor that they were not considered part of the "whole working class of the whole world," Socialists would not succeed in overcoming the ingrained political conservatism of the black community, let alone quickening its consciousness of class interests and identity. This, in part, was why Randolph, by 1925, had withdrawn from Socialist activism and lost interest, if not in socialism, in the party. "The Socialist party," he says, explaining his withdrawal, "had no effective policy toward Negroes, and didn't spend enough time organizing them." Ernest Rice McKinney, a black Socialist himself, and a former contributing editor of the *Messenger,* concurs in this view: "As understanding as Debs was of these problems, he apparently didn't understand this one: that Negroes had two disabilities, one being Negroes, and one being workers; that Negroes had to struggle on both fronts and probably more vigorously on the front against discrimination. Randolph's main effort, as I remember, was to try to get this notion in the head of the Socialist leadership."

Thus despite the eloquence of Socialist declarations on the race question, if these could not be matched by practical effort—to say nothing of success—then it wouldn't be possible to recruit any significant number of blacks to the social struggle, or to persuade them that the future which white Socialists had seen would work—or was meant—for them.

By 1925, not one of the political or trade union organizations that Randolph and Owen had founded remained. The Independent Political Council had quietly passed away after the war. The 21st A.D. Socialist Club was defunct. The United Brotherhood of Elevator and Switchboard Operators, founded in 1917, was, the following year, taken over by the Elevator and Starters Union. A National Association for the Promotion of Labor Unionism, announced in 1919, failed to materialize. A National Brotherhood Workers of America, conceived in 1919 as a sort of Negro Federation of Labor, dissolved in 1921. A Tenants and Consumers League ("to meet and settle the problem of high rents and high food") did not survive its first few meetings in the *Messenger*'s office. An attempt to organize a Harlem branch of the Journeymen Bakers and Confectioners Union was rebuffed in 1920. And the Friends of Negro Freedom went their own ways in 1924. All that survived was the *Messenger,* and that—though its life would flicker for three more years—was dying. Even Lucille Randolph's once thriving beauty salon was in decline, her husband's reputation as a "wild-eyed radical" having scared away most of her customers.

For Randolph, by 1925, these were not only the shambles of radical dreams, but the ruins of a career. He had no profession, except that of a propagandist and self-employed journalist, and, as far as he or anyone else can remember, nothing fresh to contemplate. In Harlem, the possibilities of radical propaganda had been exhausted, and in America as a whole, A. Mitchell Palmer—as Arthur Schlesinger, Jr., put it—had slain the liberal dream.

There were consolations, to be sure. As Randolph would say, late in his life, "It was a dark period for us. We were in the wilderness alone. But as Negro radicals, we did not work in vain. We were the very first to shape a working-class economic perspective in Negro thought."

And there was still the *Messenger*. Going there every morning was a way of giving some shape to his day and keeping alive something of what had been the center of his life. Somehow, he managed to keep the magazine afloat—more, apparently, by blind faith than by realism. Advertising was down to practically nothing, and the magazine's close circle— once made up largely of intellectuals—seemed now more like a ring of creditors. Stuart Chase, who came occasionally to look over the accounts, could not understand how the *Messenger* kept going. But, according to George Schuyler, whose salary had, miraculously, been increased to $15 a week, Randolph kept declaring that "the *Messenger* shall never die."

The *Messenger* did dwindle to nothing and die, but not before it had served as the bridge over which Randolph—bearing, like a stubborn refugee, the essence of his former political commitments—crossed to a new beginning.

IV / The Case of the Pullman Porter

Now what are you going to get in this country? As I see it, the colored brother is going to get what he can take. You are not going to be able to take anything unless you are going to be able to pay the price to take it. Nobody else in this country got anything unless they took it. They took Manhattan island from the Indians and gave them a bottle of whiskey in return. They came here looking for a new haven, and they drove the Indian back. They died, suffered and sacrificed. They cut the trees, lived and suffered in the cold, and they took a country and built it up. They brought us over here in chains. . . . We know that. We are still in chains, to a large extent, light chains. The only way that those chains are going to be broken is we have to break them. That is all. There isn't anybody else going to do it for us.

      —MILTON P. WEBSTER, First Vice President of
        the Brotherhood of Sleeping Car Porters

The first condition to being worthy of help from others is for an individual, race, or nation to do something for itself. . . . I consider the fight for the Negro masses the greatest service I can render to my people, and the fight alone is my complete compensation.

           —A. PHILIP RANDOLPH

Even those fellows who thought you were doing great didn't have nothing to do with you once you commenced forming a union. We thought Randolph was crazy. You going to fight the Pullman Company? You going to unionize the Pullman porter? Randolph going to fight Pullman's millions of dollars when half the time he didn't have a dime in his pocket?

            —NOBLE SISSLE

11 / "George"

One morning in June, 1925, two months past his thirty-sixth birthday, and with his political future apparently behind him, Randolph was walking from his new apartment, at 314 West 133rd Street, up Seventh Avenue, on his way to the *Messenger*'s office. At the corner of 135th Street, he was stopped by a man who doffed his white Panama hat, introduced himself as Ashley Totten, and asked to have a word.

Ashley L. Totten was a tall, powerfully built black man, with the kind of strong, decisive, and handsome face some people like to call honest. The Panama hat was the crown of one of his favorite ensembles—white gabardine suit, flowered red or blue tie on white shirt, carried off, or along, by a pair of white shoes. Totten, approaching his forty-first birthday, was a native of Christiansted, St. Croix, in the Virgin Islands, had been living in Harlem since 1915, and had worked for most of the time since then as a Pullman sleeping car porter, out of the New York Central district. Aggressive and outspoken, he had, by 1925, developed a reputation among New York porters as "a firebrand."

Totten further introduced himself as someone who had read the *Messenger* for several years and who had once been a regular listener at Randolph's soapbox forums. What he had on his mind was this: would Randolph consider coming to the Pullman Porters Athletic Association one evening, and speaking to the members on the subject of trade unionism and collective bargaining? Randolph said he would be glad to. He made a date, and resumed his walk to the *Messenger*'s office, carrying away the image of Totten's manner that had most impressed him: "a sort of fearlessness."

The meeting was not an accident. Totten had been thinking for several months of approaching Randolph, and was, in fact, on his way to the

Messenger's office when he ran into the editor. His mission and his invitation to Randolph grew out of a widening unrest among sleeping car porters in New York and other cities over their working conditions and, specifically, over the functioning of the Pullman Company's five-year-old Plan of Employee Representation—a glorified company union, which Pullman had imposed upon the porters. The previous year, Totten and Roy Lancaster—two of the porter delegates on the Plan of Employee Representation—had returned from a wage conference at the Pullman headquarters, in Chicago. The conference, they felt, had been a sham: there had been no genuine attempt at bargaining; the representatives of the Pullman Company—supported by a number of "weak-kneed" porter delegates—had simply made a take-it-or-leave-it offer, to become effective on April 1, 1925. Totten had come back to New York angry, disgusted, and determined to find a way of organizing a bona fide trade union among the porters.

Randolph's talk to the Porters Athletic Association was well received, and it encouraged Totten in his resolve. Yet he and his colleagues in New York knew only too well the dangers and difficulties of what they wanted to attempt; every previous effort by Pullman porters to organize themselves had been crushed by the company and the ringleaders fired. Historically, it was not the policy of the Pullman Company to recognize bona fide labor organizations. The company simply fixed its wage rates and working conditions, and employees were free either to accept them or to quit.

But the more Ashley Totten and his disgruntled colleagues thought about their need for a genuine labor union, the more it occurred to them that there was no better man to undertake the task than A. Philip Randolph. He had some formidable liabilities, to be sure. The impeccable dress, the "Harvard" accent, and the cultivated manners of an Edwardian gentleman were scarcely compatible with the popular conception of a labor leader or a champion of the cause of the workingman. Yet he also possessed assets that were remarkably to the purpose. Totten knew, from reading the *Messenger* and from listening to Randolph's old soapbox speeches, that no one in Harlem had a deeper understanding of the need for labor unionism or a greater concern for the problems of the black workingman. As a public speaker, Randolph was one of the best that Harlemites had ever heard. He also had a magazine, a ready-made mouthpiece for any new labor organization. And, most important, he wasn't a Pullman porter. There was an irony here, of course. If you considered such things as rapport and experience in common problems, then a Pullman porter was really the best man to organize his peers. But as history had shown, no Pullman porter could survive the attempt. Randolph's pre-eminent credential was that he could not be picked off by the Pullman Company.

A few weeks after Randolph addressed the Porters Athletic Association, W. H. DesVerney—one of the older and more prosperous porters —invited Randolph to a secret meeting at his home, on West 139th Street. Four other porters were there: Totten; Roy Lancaster; Thomas T. Patterson, a tall, courtly, and ascetic-looking Jamaican (called, by one of his colleagues, "a student of metaphysics"), who worked out of the New York Central district; and R. R. Matthews, a part-time Christian Science reader, and inveterately prounion in sentiment. During the meeting, Totten and DesVerney put it squarely to Randolph: would he undertake to organize the porters?

Randolph said that, flattered though he was by the request, he was sorry; he had no further interest in organizing anything. He told them of all his previous unsuccessful efforts, and that he was now satisfied to consider himself merely a propagandist for the idea of unionism. Then again, he said, the *Messenger* was now his whole life, and he was fully occupied in the struggle to keep the magazine going. Moreover, he added, he couldn't see himself jumping into a fight with a company like Pullman, "one of the most powerful Brahmins of American business." Nevertheless, he would not close the door. He would like to give the matter some more thought, and, in the meantime, would prepare a series of articles for his magazine calling public attention to the plight of the porters.

In the early 1850's, railroads in the United States linked only the East Coast and the Middle West. To get from California to New York, for instance, it was necessary to take a steamboat down the Pacific coast to San Juan del Sur, in Nicaragua, travel by mule, wagon, and boat across the jungle to the eastern shore, and sail from there to New York. The journey, when not impeded by bad weather, could take as much as four weeks. Even the railroad trip from Chicago to New York City was something of an ordeal. A passenger rode one train from Chicago to Cleveland, changed there to another, for Buffalo, transferred at Buffalo to one headed for Albany, and took another from Albany to New York City. And if, in the process, he had to change from one primitive sleeping car to another, it was a still greater ordeal.

One cold night in 1853, George Mortimer Pullman, twenty-two-year-old woodworker, living in Albion, New York, was traveling in a sleeping car between Buffalo and Westfield, a distance of some fifty-eight miles. It was an uncomfortable experience. The car had neither sheets, blankets, nor pillows. Lying in his clothes and shoes, and trying to sleep on the rough mattress, the young Pullman—who, according to one observer, grew up "conveying the impression that the world rested on his shoulders"—was thinking to himself how such a car might be improved.

It was one of the earliest sleeping cars. Stanley Buder, a Pullman historian, describes them as

ordinary coaches with a few crude extras added. Three wooden shelves were permanently fixed to the sides in a tier arrangement so that the sleeper could not be used for day travel. Lacking privacy and adequate bedding, the passenger would climb fully dressed onto a shelf. . . . Everyone knew that the problem was to build a sleeping car that could be used comfortably day and night. What was lacking, however, was the know-how.

George Mortimer Pullman provided that know-how. His first chance at doing so came in 1858, when he went to Bloomington, Illinois, and converted two old passenger coaches into sleeping cars, for the Chicago and Alton Railroad. Though they were not much of an improvement upon the existing sleepers, he converted several more, and persuaded a few railroads to use them. When passenger travel fell off, during the Civil War, Pullman left for the gold fields of Colorado, where he ran a trading post from 1862 to 1863, and saved his money. With his savings, he returned to Chicago toward the end of the war, determined to build "the biggest and best car ever."

This turned out to be the "Pioneer." It was built at a cost of $20,000, five times more than any previous sleeping car had cost. Many who had seen it under construction had laughed it away as "Pullman's Folly." But when Pullman unveiled the "Pioneer," it was hailed as "the wonder of the age." "Never before," writes Joseph Husband, one of Pullman's biographers, "had such a car been seen; never had the wildest flights of fancy imagined such magnificence." The floor was covered with a rich red carpet, the seats upholstered with brocaded fabrics, the doorframes made of polished woods, the berths paneled with ornamented wood, and the entire car lit with silver-trimmed oil lamps and hung with gilt-edged mirrors. Arthur Dubin, of Chicago, a collector of Pullman memorabilia, says, "There was a sense of order about this man which must have been in his personal life. He was a very religious man. He built seminaries and left money to churches. George Pullman was a lover of beautiful things. That's an interesting facet to a man considered by so many to be ruthless."

For a time, the "Pioneer" seemed to be the wonder of the age in more ways than one. Because it was too large to fit between any of the existing station platforms, the railroad companies displayed little interest in it, and people started wondering what on earth Pullman was going to do with his sleeper. It was the assassination of President Lincoln that provided an answer, and opened up a future for the "Pioneer." When the body of the slain President arrived in Chicago, on its way to Springfield, Illinois, state officials looked around for the most splendid conveyance to bear Lincoln on the final leg of his journey. And, of course, there was nothing more splendid in Chicago at the time than the "Pioneer." Platforms along the way were hurriedly widened. The dead President was placed aboard the "Pioneer," and the magnificent sleeper received everywhere an outpouring of publicity and acclaim that exceeded even George Pullman's most optimistic dreams.

"From that day on," says Arthur Dubin, "the Pullman car was very much accepted, and somehow I feel that George Pullman always felt that this break, this accident of Lincoln's death, contributed somehow to the development of his company. So that the attorney for the company at one time was Robert Todd Lincoln. And the minute George Pullman died, Robert Todd Lincoln was elected president of the company. All kinds of romantic stories grew, many of which proved fallacious. But Robert Lincoln was very tight-lipped about anything to do with his father."

Moving quickly to exploit the publicity gained during the President's funeral, the Chicago and Alton Railroad hired the "Pioneer," on Pullman's terms, and placed it in service. Pullman now built several more cars, some even more luxurious than the "Pioneer," and hired them out to a number of other railroads. By the end of 1866, he had forty-eight cars in service, and had become the leading sleeping car builder and entrepreneur in the Midwest. People now called him "the prince of railroads" and "a missionary of civilization" who had made railroad passenger travel "both a comfort and luxury." On February 22, 1867, the Pullman Palace Car Company was incorporated, and by 1870, when the first through train crossed from the Atlantic to the Pacific, George Pullman dominated the sleeping car business in the entire United States.

By the mid-1860's, according to Joseph Husband—quoting a writer of the day—a typical Pullman conveyance was

lighted by gas throughout . . . equipped with a compartment buffet sleeping car, a drawing room sleeping car, reclining chair cars, and a combination coach and smoking car. The smoking room of the buffet car is finished in African vermilion wood of exquisite grain, relieved by embossed gold-leather panels and frieze, with carpeted floor and finely decorated ceiling to match. A fire-jet gas chandelier of deflecting mirrors accentuates the silk draperies and the vermilion and gold finish. The buffet is finished in light mahogany, and the state rooms, with all the conveniences of fine dressing rooms, are finished in bright pea green stippled with gold, broken by embossed and decorated plush panels of tint to match. The upholstery, carpets, and the decorated ceiling, in the center of which is a gas chandelier of deflecting mirrors, harmonize with the green and gold tints.

In Pullman's own words, these hotels on wheels were "the finest trains on earth."

Yet what was anything so fine without Pullman's own ambassadors of hospitality? At first, the comfort and luxury of a Pullman traveler were in the hands of conductors, but conductors alone—or, perhaps, because they were white—could not provide the sort of hospitality Pullman had in mind for his passengers. There had to be a few maids to render personal services to women and children; and, above all, there had to be porters to help receive and discharge passengers, handle baggage, prepare beds and berths, care for linen and equipment, keep the cars tidy, and wait upon a passenger's every wish and desire. In 1867, when he first felt the need for such a service, George Pullman turned to what he considered a uniquely appropriate source: the recently freed slaves. Thus from the very beginning the porter's job was "a black man's job."

Succeeding generations of porters would have their own words for describing a "black man's job," though their meaning would not, in essence, be very different from Pullman's. According to one porter, a black man's job was a job in which "the work was hard, the hours long, and the pay poor." Another porter would add, "And where the boss man was mean." When it occurred to Pullman that blacks were singularly suited to fulfill his requirements for what a sleeping car porter should be, it was because—certainly at the end of slavery—he saw the history of their servitude and habits of obsequiousness as distinctly qualifying black men above all others. And as long as this was so, it also followed that they were used to hard work, long hours, poor pay, and mean boss men.

George Pullman's surpassing interest in the ex-slaves revolved around what he could reasonably predict of their manners as porters: that fine point of their situation where the need for employment, gratitude, and the cake of social custom would converge to produce in them an unfailing courtesy. His biographer Joseph Husband confirms it. Pullman, he says, chose blacks as porters because they had been "trained as a race by years of personal service in various capacities," and because they were "by nature adapted faithfully to perform their duties under circumstances which necessitate unfailing good nature, solicitude and faithfulness."

Still, for the sake of the record, one must acknowledge that motives more selfless have been assigned to Pullman. As late as 1935, one of the company's executives, in Chicago, sent the following reply to an inquiry from D. A. Crawford, the president:

There is a story sometimes heard which, so far as I can find out, is wholly apocryphal, that Mr. Pullman created the job for the emancipated slave. There is another story, which has had some currency, that Abraham Lincoln suggested to Mr. Pullman the employment of colored men as porters, but recent inquiry to Mrs. Lowden [daughter of Pullman] concerning this elicited the reply . . . that so far as she knew her father never had known or even met Mr. Lincoln; that she was entirely sure the latter had not suggested such employment.

Whatever the motives, they seem, economically, to have worked out fairly well—at first—for the ex-slaves, and spectacularly so for the Pullman Palace Car Company. By the early 1920's, the company had become the largest single private employer of black labor in the United States. And during the same decade—the company now one of the industrial giants of the country—C. R. Harding, another of its executives in Chicago, described the porters as "Pullman's greatest assets."

As the years passed, the ex-slave porters—those "with the wicker-lamp, wooden-car mind," as Randolph would describe them—had gradually been replaced by elementary and high-school graduates, students working their way through college, and more than a few young men with bachelor's degrees—to whom America could offer nothing finer than a place in Pullman's livery. "Among this army of porters," one of them

said, "may be found skilled mechanics, lawyers, doctors, scientists, theo-
logians, philosophers, orators, men of ability in the field of literature; in
fact, every line of human endeavor." They would all become romantic
legends, both to Pullman's pleased patrons and to their neighbors in their
own communities.

On the trains, the porters came to be trusted for their honesty, praised
for their reliability, and romanticized for their unfailing politeness. And
since some of them—the college graduates, no doubt—had been found
remarkable for intelligence and refinement, it was not infrequently said
by satisfied travelers that the porter was "a higher grade of Negro."

Among his neighbors, by the early 1920's, the porter was regarded, on
the whole, as a model of solid black citizenship. He had a secure job;
mixed with white people—those of wealth and distinction, no less; usually owned his own home—even if he had to take in boarders to pay off
the mortgage; was a pillar in the local church; saved to send his children
to college; voted the Republican ticket; subscribed to the American way
of life; and, as far as people could tell, never messed around with any
woman but his wife. Here also, not long ago, is E. D. Nixon, an ex-
porter, talking to Studs Terkel:

Everybody listened because they knowd the porter been everywhere and
they never been anywhere themselves. In cafes where they ate or hotels where
they stayed, they'd bring in the papers they picked up, white papers, Negro
papers. He'd put 'em in his locker and distribute 'em to black communities
all over the country. Along the road, where a whole lot of people couldn't
get to town, we used to roll up the papers and tie a string around 'em. We'd
throw these papers off to these people. We were able to let people know what
was happening.

In his community, the porter was not, to be sure, on the same social level
with the black middle-class professional—at least, the black middle-class
professional, who saw the porter as something of a joke, did not think so.
But many people who lacked professional credentials—and who held a
less exalted estimate of their status—saw the porter as an example of
what black men could make of their lives, within the limits of what their
situation allowed.

For several years, however, the majority of porters had not been as
happy with their situation within the Pullman service as passengers and
admiring friends seemed to be. A few of them had stopped smiling not

only at their situation, but also at the passengers. Such men meant business; they wanted to change both their working conditions and their public image.

The roster of their names is long, and some were crushed by the Pullman Company for daring to think aloud among their fellow workers. But a few would survive, in or out of the Pullman service: men like Milton Webster and John Mills, of Chicago; Benjamin ("Bennie") Smith, of Omaha; "Dad" Moore, of Oakland; and Ashley Totten and Thomas T. Patterson, of New York. What Murray Kempton would later write of the porter, and, in particular, of T. T. Patterson, would indicate, in one way or another, something of why all these men were bound, one day, to throw away their masks of contentment and defy the traditions of their service to Pullman:

The Pullman porter rode his car, silent with all the chaff around him, always most agreeable when he was of the old school. . . . A sensitive white man might look at him, at once deferential and removed, and wonder what he was really like. There was a certain thrill to the notion that he might be a Communist or a murderer or even an emperor— a doomed emperor of course —if his chance came and the constituency were inferior enough. But he was, after all, only a man beneath his station, as every servant is a man beneath what should be his station. The resources of any of us being what they are, he might very well dream other dreams than those of the sort of man who sits up late drinking in a Pullman lounge. . . . The pleasures of fantasy were not open to Thomas Patterson. He could not afford, as an instance, to nurse the hope that he of all Negroes might ever be treated as though he were white. Any white man who spoke to him spoke consciously to a Negro, which is a terrible barrier even for the best of men. Thomas Patterson's life was a process of enforcing recognition of his personality from a world which treated him as possessed of color without feature. It was always mixing him up with the porter in the car ahead and asking him in simple bewilderment if he was its porter, because he was, after all, only a piece of furniture set out for the convenience of persons who saw no need to be connoisseurs of this sort of furniture.

And yet why would the guests of Pullman feel a need "to be connoisseurs of this sort of furniture" when the Pullman Company itself did not? Consider the porter's working conditions. In 1915, when his minimum monthly wage was $27.50, the chairman of a U. S. Commission on Industrial Relations asked the company's general manager, L. S. Hungerford, "Do you consider $27.50 a month sufficient for a man who is required to discharge all the duties you have detailed here and to follow all the rules referred to?" Hungerford replied, "All I can say is that you can get all the men you require to do the work." Between 1915 and 1919, the porter's wage rose to a minimum of $47.50 a month. And in the latter year—following a ruling by William Gibbs McAdoo, Director-General of Railroads under Woodrow Wilson—the porter started making $60 a month, still considerably below what a New York Factory Commission study had set as a decent minimum for an American family. Pullman justified its policy of substandard wages on the following grounds: faced with the urgent need to supplement his wage with tips, the porter would not be able to afford any slackening in his attentions to the passenger.

The results of such a policy were psychologically disastrous. "Pullman made hustlers out of us," recalls one ex-porter in Chicago. "They had us constantly on our knees. You had to do that to survive." In November, 1916, a porter wrote, in a letter to the *New York Age:* "The Pullman Company . . . relies upon the custom that the porters collect from the travelling public money enough. . . . We argue not for favor, but rather make a claim for fairness. Let the laborer be rewarded for efficiency, not color." Writing in *Coronet* magazine, in April, 1948, several years after their retirement, ex-porters Jake Wolf and Weldon Melick revealed that the "porter caters first to your *mental* comfort. He massages your ego, flatters your vanity, helps you enjoy your trip. . . . Most porters would be out of work if they didn't add applied psychology to their job of running errands. . . . The best-liked porter is the one who answers his bell before it rings." A New York porter remembers that "passengers used to have the porters doing the buck and wing, cutting up on the platform, and so forth. The porters would do it for the extra tip. They had to scuffle, however they could." All of which, as Milton Webster would suggest, merely worsened the comical aspect of the porter's public image: "They would depict the Pullman porter as a clown even if he was a hero in a wreck. They depicted him as using dialect that even Negroes didn't know anything about."

Nor was that the sum of the porter's exploitation. The basic work month consisted of 400 hours or 11,000 miles, whichever was logged first. No overtime was paid until a porter exceeded one of these figures— and then at the rate of only sixty cents for every extra hundred miles. It is hardly surprising that few porters—a favored handful who were given extra runs—managed to log either 400 hours or 11,000 miles a month, let alone qualify for overtime. Out of his salary and tips, a porter paid for his own meals, and bought his own uniforms and equipment—down to the polish he used to clean the passengers' shoes. And if he ran out of polish on the job, he was reported by the white conductor, and penalized.

A porter was also expected to run several hours or hundreds of miles a month without pay. This was called "deadheading." It worked this way. A porter scheduled to leave New York at 12:30 A.M. on a train for Washington, D.C., say, was required to report for duty at 7:30 P.M. He spent these hours preparing the train for departure and receiving passengers. His paid time, however, did not begin until 12:30, when the train pulled out. And if, at 12:30, there were no passengers, the porter was also required to "deadhead" into Washington, in the hope that there would be passengers coming back.

Then there were the times when the porter had to "double out," whether he liked it or not. That is, whenever he returned from a long run—which may have lasted for as long as a week—he could be ordered out on the very next train, without a rest period, and at a lower rate of pay. This, of course, gave him no time to see his family, or even to shower, shave, and change his clothes. But if, while "doubling out," he was found untidy, unclean, or asleep, he was either docked, suspended, or fired.

A porter could also be ordered to run "in charge." On such runs, he performed not only his own duties, but also those of the conductor. If he was "lucky" enough to run "in charge" for a month, he received $10 above his basic salary. This was a considerable saving to the company, for a conductor's salary in, say, 1920 was $150 a month.

"Then, too," a porter from Jacksonville recalls, "there was this thing of 'George.' No matter who you were, or how old, most everybody wanted to call you 'George.' It meant that you were just George Pullman's boy, same as in slave days when if the owner was called Jones the slave was called Jones. It got so you were scared to go into the office to pick up your check, for fear some little sixteen-year-old office boy would yell out 'George.' "

"This thing of 'George,' " however, infuriated quite a few passengers—mainly those who also answered, legitimately, to the name George. They were tired of looking up suddenly from their newspapers or cups of coffee only to find that it was not *they* whom their neighbors wanted, but "George." One of them, a Chicago lumber merchant named George W. Delaney, decided to do something about it—though apparently more in

fun than anger. In 1916, he launched an anti-"George" campaign by
forming the Society for the Prevention of Calling Sleeping Car Porters
George. In later years, the society's letterhead would carry such names
as Senator George, of Georgia; George Arliss; George Ade; George M.
Cohan; George Cardinal Mundelein; King George V; Georges Carpentier;
George B. Cortelyou; King George of Greece; and the "Babe," of the
New York Yankees. The society's patron saints were the first president
of the United States and the builder of the "Pioneer." By 1941, George
Delaney claimed a membership of 33,000 Georges, after which nothing
more was heard of his society. It probably exploded from an excess of
frivolity.

In any event, because of all of their grievances, porters had been trying to form a union since 1900. Milton Webster would recount the history:

It was told to me by old porters that as far back as 1900 efforts were put
forth to organize. . . . The first concrete effort . . . was manifested along
about 1912. This effort took the form of petitions which were circulated
among the porters throughout the country, virtually begging the Company
for some consideration and relief from the very meagre wage which at that
time was $25 per month. We found that there were many porters at that time
too timid to sign even a begging petition. However, as a result of this first
petition, an increase in pay was given to the porters of $2.50 per month,
making their salary $27.50, which was not a big salary in 1912. Several years
later another petition was submitted to the Company which, it is believed,
brought forth an additional increase of $2.50 per month. . . . At this rate
the porter's wages remained until the year 1917 when a 50% increase was
granted . . . raising wages to $45 per month. . . . Shortly thereafter the
Pullman Car Lines became part of the United States Railroad Administration
[when President Wilson nationalized the railroads during the war], under the
direction of Director-General William McAdoo. The porters were receiving
the lowest classification of pay that was obtained in the Railroad Administration at the time and were paid $47.50 per month, the rate that was paid
to office boys. One of the first proclamations issued by the Railroad Administration was that employees of the Administration, seeking consideration with
respect to wages and working conditions, must come through organized
groups, and that the Railroad Administration would not deal with individuals,
and the Lane Wage Commission was set up by the Railroad Administration
on all matters concerning wages and working conditions. Following the edict
of the Railroad Administration, an organization, a number of organizations

sprung up among the Pullman porters, namely, the Brotherhood of Sleeping Car Porters Protective Union; several local organizations in the American Federation of Labor organized under the Hotel Workers Alliance and the International Railroad Men's Benevolent Industrial Association, of which the writer was an official for several years. Most of the activities of the various porters' organizations of that period were taken up in each telling what the other could not do for the porters. . . . However, during the period of the United States Railroad Administration the Pullman porters were raised from $47.50 a month to $60 . . . and placed on the eleven thousand mile basic month. . . . At this rate the porters' wages remained until . . . 1924. At the conclusion of the United States Railroad Administration and the passage of the Transportation Act of 1920, the Plan of Employee Representation of the Pullman Company was set up and presented to the porters in the various districts throughout the United States.* Many porters, because of the chaos and confusion that existed among the several organizations at that time, accepted the Pullman Plan of Employee Representation, and among the early members were such men as Frank Boyd of St. Paul; A. Briggs of Denver, Colorado; A. L. Totten of New York City; John C. Mills of Chicago, and others. During . . . 1924 another effort was made to organize the porters into a bona fide labor union, and shortly thereafter there was called by the company the first so-called joint conference under the Pullman Plan of

---

* The plan, designed and supervised by the Pullman Company, was an attempt both to comply with and to circumvent the War Labor Conference Board's report of March, 1918, giving Pullman employees the right to collective bargaining by representatives of their own choosing, a right that was not to be "denied or abridged or interfered with in any manner whatsoever." In the case of the conductors, Pullman did not interfere with this right; it recognized and bargained with the Order of Sleeping Car Conductors (all-white). But when the company saw that the porters could not choose among the different organizations vying to represent them, it took the opportunity to rush in with its own Plan of Employee Representation. This plan contained no provision for genuine collective bargaining between the company's and the porters' representatives. The company, after *pro forma* discussion with the porters' representatives, simply made an offer, and the porters either accepted it or went away with nothing. Representatives who refused to sign the "agreement" were either fired or disciplined in other ways. At these wage conferences—as the meetings between porter and company representatives were called—the porters throughout the country were represented by twenty delegates, while four or five company representatives held twenty votes by proxy. Since the majority of the porter delegates were usually afraid to vote against the company's wishes, Pullman held an easy majority in every wage conference. Nor did the porter delegates have any say over when one of these wage conferences would be called. They simply rushed to Chicago whenever the company was disposed to meet with them.

Employee Representation. Pullman porters throughout the country made an effort to select the best possible men to represent them, and there were included among those in the first conference such good . . . men as John C. Mills, C. S. Wells of Cleveland, M. C. Oglesby of Boston, and A. L. Totten.

It was what transpired at this wage conference that convinced Ashley Totten that a new effort to organize a bona fide porters union would have to be made, and that led him, on his return to New York, to seek the aid of A. Philip Randolph. Here is Totten's memorable report of what happened at the conference:

Delegates were treated like the dignitaries of Europe visiting America. We were met by an army of guards, calamity howlers and self-seekers who belonged to the official staff of the Pullman Company. . . . We had to be guarded while we slept, lest evil spirits in the form of labor leaders ran away with us. We ate the best meals, slept in good beds at the YMCA and smoked the best cigars, but we did not have to pay one cent to anybody. . . . Big Negroes held elaborate banquets in our honor, supposedly at their own expense. . . . The Pullman Porters Band played for us. We were paid $5 a day in addition to our regular wages and an extra allowance for taxicab and other expenses. We were told of a number of new jobs to be created and if we behaved ourselves we would be promoted. We listened to Pullman officials who called us the chosen children of the Pullman Family and the Big Negroes who advised us of the dangers of a labor union. Thus fourteen of the twenty well-fed delegates walked into the conference ready to vote for anything that the management wanted and against anything that the porters were asking for. . . . We prayed and listened to a welcome address by L. S. Hungerford, Vice President. They passed the cigars around. F. L. Simmons [a Pullman executive] felt it was fair that the four members of management should have twenty votes in order to balance the twenty votes of the porter delegates. Old man [J. D.] Bannister, porter delegate from Philadelphia, agreed with Simmons, indicating that if put to a vote there would be 21 against 19, in favor of management, so there was no use for any further debate. . . . The twenty delegates in a caucus meeting had conflicting opinions, it was easy to see that the element of fear had been established in the minds of most of them. . . . Principal demand was for the 240-hour work month. Delegates Bannister, [James] Sexton, [D.] Bass, and [James S.] Morris . . . were opposed to it because they knew the Company would not grant it. Bannister said . . . "The Company is good to us. Show me another corporation that would let us choose our own representatives and pay them besides to fight for their own brother porters." And then they passed the cigars around. . . . Our next task was to get them to vote on the 240-hour month. We begged and beseeched them to no avail. . . . Someone had a bottle of Gordon's gin which was passed around. Jim Sexton of New Orleans likes gin—evidently two good hookers made him quite merry and his mind seemed to be in a receptive mood. Others began to make similar promises but [Albert] Fisher brought his fist down on the table with the statement— "By God," said he, "if I'm the only one I'm going to vote with the management." . . . Old man Bannister took the same position. It was then that M. C. Oglesby of Boston . . . who deserves the lasting respect of every Pullman porter, burst into tears, dropped on his knees and with hands outstretched as if in appeal to Heaven, prayed and pleaded with the delegates, but to no avail. . . . Fisher remarked that if Christ himself appeared in the room as an advocate of the 240-hour work month it would not change his position. . . . It requires 20 votes to effect a tie. This would at least prove to the management that the porters were opposed to 11,000 miles of railroad as a basis for a month's pay. We thought about Perry Parker [an ex-porter who had been appointed by the Pullman Company as a welfare officer]. Would he help us? We asked the management to make him a member of the conference and they agreed to do so. This gave the management five representatives, each with four votes. Would Perry Parker vote on the side of the porters and maids? . . . When the management representatives entered the room with Perry Parker we gave a wild cheer. F. L. Simmons [management] announced that Perry Parker had something to say, after assuring us that there is no man in whom management had any higher regard than its national welfare worker. Perry thanked us for the applause and requested that he sit with the management, but reminded us that he would have also to protect the side his bread and butter came from, and left the room. The conference put on the appearance of an armed camp. The six delegates determined to fight to the bitter end for the 240-hour work month. We held the floor all morning in an effort to keep our week-kneed opponents quiet and to keep the management from calling for a vote any too soon. The late superintendent Leach announced that there was a delegation of porters outside with a protest against the 240-hour work month. They were seeking admission, he said. The statement made us fighting mad. We would not yield.

But it was all in vain. Totten's forces were routed, and when the conference was over the basic work month remained 400 hours or 11,000 miles. What the porters received was nothing more than what the company had come prepared to offer: a $7.50 increase, raising their monthly wage to $67.50.

And, as Milton Webster said later, "This was the beginning of the Brotherhood of Sleeping Car Porters."

12 / "The Sea Is Ruff..."

After looking into the history of the porters' grievances, Randolph wrote and published two articles—"The Case of the Pullman Porter" and "Pullman Porters Need Their Own Union"—in the July and August, 1925, issues of the *Messenger*. They aroused such interest among porters in New York that Ashley Totten renewed his pressure upon Randolph to take on the job of organizing a union. And this time Randolph agreed. An organizing committee was set up, with himself as general organizer; W. H. DesVerney, deputy general organizer; and Roy Lancaster, secretary-treasurer. Lancaster also became business manager of the *Messenger,* which Randolph agreed to transform into the voice of the new union. Totten, Thomas Patterson, and R. R. Matthews continued working on the railroads.

Randolph's decision to lead the new movement had turned mainly on two considerations. First, no one else seemed willing to take up the porters' cause. And, second, on further reflection, he saw the porters as his last and, possibly, best chance to promote the idea of labor unionism among black workers. "The Pullman porter," he told Benjamin Stolberg a year later, "seems to be made to order to carry the gospel of unionism in the colored world. His home is everywhere."

The Brotherhood of Sleeping Car Porters was launched on the night of August 25, 1925, in the auditorium of the Imperial Lodge of Elks, at 160 West 129th Street. The New York *Amsterdam News* called the gathering of 500 "the greatest labor mass meeting ever held of, for and by Negro working men." But not all were well-wishers and potential members. According to the *Amsterdam News,* there were also "a few of the Company's spies and several hat-in-hand porters, waiting to get information to carry back to the Pullman offices." Because of this, the inaugural meeting had to be a cautious and restrained affair. Randolph recalls it:

I told the men I didn't want one porter to open his mouth in the meeting, lest the stool pigeons reported them to the Pullman Company. So I ran the whole meeting myself. I told them I would now give the invocation, and I gave it. I told them I was going to sing the Brotherhood's song, "Hold the Fort," and I sang it. I told them I was going to make the announcements and introduce guest speakers,* and I did. I told them now I was going to make the main speech, and then I did. At the end of the meeting, I moved the vote of thanks, said the benediction, and told everyone to go home and not hold any discussions on the street corners.

Randolph also told the porters what the Brotherhood would be demanding: recognition of the union and abolition of the company's Plan of Employee Representation; an end to tipping, and a minimum monthly wage of $150; a basic work month of 240 hours, compensation for "deadheading," and an end to "doubling out"; conductor's pay for conductor's work; and, "by no means least, that porters be treated like men."

The following day, more than 200 porters came to the *Messenger*'s office—also headquarters of the new Brotherhood—to join the union. The initial enthusiasm was so great that within two months the Brotherhood would claim a majority of the porters in New York.

But the message had to be spread. Porters in Pullman terminals all over the country had to be organized. There seemed no way, at first, for this to be done, for the Brotherhood had no money to conduct a national membership drive. The parent organization, in New York, took in just enough dues to keep itself alive. Here Randolph turned to his connections among white Socialists and liberals in New York; and the Garland Fund, a supporter of liberal causes—of which Roger Baldwin and Norman Thomas were members—came through with a grant of $10,000. In mid-October, Randolph left New York on the first leg of his first national organizational tour, on which Chicago, Oakland, and St. Louis—three of the largest Pullman terminals outside New York—would be the most important stops.

---

* W. J. Orr, special organizer for the Brotherhood of Locomotive Engineers in New York; Frank Crosswaith, secretary of the Trade Union Committee to Organize Negroes; S. E. Grain, an ex-porter, who would become a special organizer for the new union; Roy Lancaster; and George S. Schuyler.

The man to see in Chicago, Totten had told Randolph, was an old porter named John C. Mills, one of the few delegates who had tried to hold out against Pullman during the 1924 wage conference. But Mills, having neither taste nor talent for organization, called, instead, upon the one man in Chicago who could get porters together: Milton Webster.

At the age of thirty-eight, Milton Price Webster was as tall as Ashley Totten—whom he knew—and even more powerfully built. Not too long before, Webster, who had worked as a Pullman porter for twenty years, had been "canned" by the company, as he put it, for attempting to organize porters in the Railroad Men's Benevolent Association. He was blunt-speaking, gruff, had a formidable-looking head, and, with a cigar frequently in his mouth, seemed like a man who was most at home in the back rooms of political clubhouses. His stern face inspired fear, and declared its owner to be a man who fed on power and who was guided by the philosophy that "you get nowhere unless you push people out of the way." "He was not a college man," one of his admirers has said, "but he was smart." And he later struck a journalist from New York as having "no rein on his tongue."

It was not by accident that Webster seemed to recall the political clubroom. He had spent the most recent years of his life there. Webster, who was born in Clarksville, Tennessee, in 1887, and his father had been "chased up north by the crackers," as he once told an audience. For most of his years in the North, he had worked as a Pullman porter, out of Chicago, and supporting the black Republican machine in that city. Since being fired by Pullman, he had been working as a bailiff and as the Republican leader of Chicago's Sixth Ward—which was why, as he once said, he had come to know "all the crooks and all the different angles around" the city.

It was also why John C. Mills felt Webster was the best man in Chicago to "get the boys together" for a meeting with Randolph. But Webster was not enthused over Mills's mission, and almost sent him away. He had no further desire, he informed Mills, to tangle with the Pullman Company. Besides, he asked, who the hell was this Randolph, and what did *he* know about Pullman porters? Wasn't he supposed to be one of those socialistic soapbox boys from Harlem? At that point, Mills's heart may well have sunk, for in the eyes of men like Webster people who were "socialistic" or "atheistic" were far more reprehensible than those who were merely Socialist or atheist. John Mills said that he was a simple man; all he knew was that Ashley Totten was behind Randolph, and if Totten was behind a man, then that man had to be all right. Webster could not easily dismiss that.

So, without surrendering his skepticism, he agreed to round up some porters and organize a public meeting for Randolph. He found, however, that the subject of a porters' union was "so hot" around Chicago that few of the prominent black citizens wanted to touch it. As he reported later, "I went to some forty-five or fifty leading Negroes in the city . . . whom I'd known for years and some of whom I held in the highest esteem. I told them there was going to be a movement started to organize Pullman porters and I wanted them to come out and give us a word of encouragement. Lo and behold, only five agreed to come and speak, and when the time came only one showed up. He [Dr. W. D. Cook, of the Metropolitan Community Church] has now passed on and may the Lord have mercy on his soul."

The meeting—there would be one every night for the next two weeks —was held on the night of October 17, in Dr. Cook's Metropolitan Church hall, at 3118 Giles Avenue. "Randolph came into Chicago looking keen," a porter remembers. "He was a sharp-looking youngster. I remember he had on a blue serge suit. Webster introduced him to the men, stumbling around for a while, because he wasn't the orator that Randolph was. And when he was finished he left the platform and went to sit in the back of the room with John Mills. When Randolph started to speak you could hear a pin drop. He said he saw the day when a Pullman porter would be making 150 dollars a month. Of course, who could believe that? Why, that was almost three times what we were making." Benjamin McLaurin, who would later become an official of the Brotherhood, was also in the audience, and could not himself see the day when the men would have their own union, "let alone be making that kind of money. That was like reaching for the moon." But Milton Webster was impressed. When Randolph finished speaking, he turned to John Mills and said, "That's our man. Count me in."

Launching the movement in Chicago proved more difficult than Randolph, buoyed by the experience in New York, had hoped. Chicago had the largest number of Pullman porters, and would, in time, become the strongest local of the Brotherhood, but the men there were nowhere near as eager to sign up as the New York men had been. And since none of the "big Negroes" would lend the prestige of their presence to the nightly meetings, the only two speakers were Webster and Randolph—"me opening," as Webster said later, "and Brother Randolph closing."

Late in October, the movement received a strong, if unexpected, infusion of life. Perry Howard, black Republican national committee-man from Mississippi, and a special assistant to the United States Attor-ney General, had attacked the Brotherhood as an agent of communism and its leaders as "starving Bolshevists." When, soon after, he challenged Randolph to a debate, Randolph accepted the opportunity to defend "the question of the right and necessity and value" of the Pullman porters' organizing a union. Here is Webster's account:

Randolph and I were holding a lodge of sorrow. We were pretty nearly down and out. . . . We couldn't pray hard enough that the Lord would preserve Mr. Howard's good health until the night of the meeting, and not allow him to change his mind about meeting Randolph. The Lord was with us. Howard showed up all right, in the biggest hall in the Negro section. In almost less time than it takes to tell, Randolph ran him out of gas. I got my coat ripped off helping the police get Howard out.

This effectively launched the Chicago division of the Brotherhood. How-ard's appearance "provided a platform for the first major statement of the porters' case," Randolph has said, and it was followed by a sudden in-flux of new members.

Randolph and Webster were joined the following night by an unex-pected campaigner, Ashley Totten. Arriving on a run from New York, shortly before the debate began, Totten had sought permission to remain overnight in Chicago. As a delegate to the Plan of Employee Representa-tion, Totten told a superintendent, he had an "important" mission to carry out in the city that night. No fool, the superintendent guessed the nature of his mission. Every Chicago official of the Pullman Company—which, it was later disclosed, had paid Perry Howard to attack the Brotherhood—knew that a debate was to take place that night, and that porters running in to Chicago would want to stay over to hear it. Totten had been ordered to return to New York immediately, and when he re-fused had been fired on the spot for "unsatisfactory service."

Thus at the following night's meeting, after Webster, as usual, had opened, Totten took the platform to rail against the arrogance of the

Pullman Company. As one of his colleagues remembers, "Totten was fired up. He had no technique, he had never made a big speech before, but he told his story in a dramatic way. He just roamed up and down the platform like a caged lion. He stormed the house." And Webster, watching, with admiration, as Totten "strutted his stuff" up and down the platform, whispered to Randolph—who would soon be leaving to continue his organizational campaign across the country—"Take that man along with you."

Webster was now fully committed to the struggle for a porters' union, but it would be some time before he would wholly lose his reservations about Randolph. And though they would develop into one of the most harmonious two-man teams in the American labor movement, Webster would never completely surrender himself to the authority of Randolph's leadership. He was no more the kind of man to make that concession than Randolph was the kind of leader to demand it.

In 1925, they were strangers in more than the ordinary sense. Webster "was brusque where Randolph was gentle," a close observer of both men has said, "cynical where Randolph was trusting, stripped of illusion where Randolph was a perambulatory dream." Webster, a Republican all his life, followed politics that Randolph had once despised. And Randolph, a Socialist, shared a political faith that Webster, like any "hundred percent American," regarded with distaste. Nor would Webster ever forget, despite Randolph's obvious marks as a leader and inspirer of men, that it was he, Webster, who shared the background and workaday experience of the porters. While this would never be an occasion for jealousy —as would later be the case with W. H. DesVerney, in New York—it would cause some moments of uneasiness.

Webster, a leader of men in his own right—and according to his own homespun lights—would, in later years, bristle over the fact that the Chicago division of the Brotherhood, over which he reigned like a lord, should take orders from the national headquarters, in New York, or contribute as heavily as it did to the national treasury. He would just as soon have had Chicago as the headquarters of the Brotherhood—after all, it was the headquarters of the Pullman Company, and where the largest number of porters were to be found—or, if not, then as his own independent principality. Despite their reverence for Randolph, most porters, especially those in Chicago, looked on Webster as one of their own. Thus within the context of their close comradeship, Webster would sometimes suggest testily to Randolph that he, Randolph, should run New York and leave him, Webster, to run Chicago. "Web was a rough-and-tumble man," says a Chicago porter, "and he was the man that mechanically ran the organization. He was the power behind the throne. In negotiations, when it came to the theoretical and political and economic discussions, people would have to listen to Randolph; but when it came to the rules and regulations and working conditions, Webster was the man."

But as with Randolph's relationship with all his political associates, the heart of his comradeship with Webster was their common devotion to a common cause. Differences of personal style and character were again of little consequence to him; and, in any case, nothing so qualified Webster for the difficult task of organizing a porters' union as his toughness, aggressiveness, and genuine commitment to the imperative that black workers organize themselves. As the years passed, "they became like blood brothers," one porter says. "They trusted each other. Randolph didn't make a turn until he consulted Web, and vice versa. There was hardly a day they didn't write or call each other."

Before Randolph left Chicago to seek new converts in the West and Midwest, he appointed Webster assistant general organizer of the national movement and organizer of the Chicago division. George Price, an ex-porter, was named secretary-treasurer, and John Mills became chairman of the organizing committee. Among the members of the committee were Chandler Owen, now publicist and an editorial writer for the *Chicago Bee,* and C. Francis Stratford, who would become one of the attorneys of the new union. Webster set up headquarters in Dr. Cook's Metropolitan Community Church, the only prominent organization in Chicago that cared to identify itself openly with a movement against the powerful Pullman Company. "I wasn't sure where I was going to get the money to pay for it," Webster said later, "but I did not sit down and wait for the Lord to do our work, as most colored people do." Webster, says Robert Turner, in his *Memories of a Retired Pullman Porter,* "told the porters he was ready to fight till Hell froze over, and then get a pair of skates and fight on the ice."

The most important stops Randolph ("the Saint") and Totten ("the Terrible") made on their Western tour, which lasted through January, 1926, were St. Louis and Oakland. These cities, along with New York, Chicago, and Detroit, would provide the first rank of the union's leadership, and the strongest divisions. Word of Randolph's and Totten's mission had preceded them on the porter grapevine, and when they arrived in St. Louis they found a porter named E. J. Bradley waiting to meet them. Bradley, with thirty years in the Pullman service, was a balding, fair-skinned man, whose thin features and large eyes, set deep in their sockets, gave him the look of a consumptive. But it may simply have been the look of a man who had grown accustomed to living with pain, for Bradley had suffered through most of his life from lumbago— though this had not impaired his efficiency as a Pullman porter, or dampened his enthusiasm for quail hunting.

After Randolph's and Totten's first public meeting in St. Louis, Bradley, says an old porter, "thought the Brotherhood was going to win the next day." Bradley told Randolph he was ready to give up his job on the sleeping cars, in order to organize a division in St. Louis. Randolph replied that he would not think of demanding so great a sacrifice, but that perhaps Bradley could suggest someone with less to lose. Not a chance, Bradley said. "You see," another old porter recalls,

St. Louis was one of the hardest places in the whole United States to organize. They had a superintendent down there who boasted that he whipped niggers. His name was [A. V.] Burr. Randolph begged Bradley not to quit. We needed the support of porters who were financial. Brother Randolph wasn't being supported. Sister Randolph carried him for years. Webster was the most independent, because he was in politics and he had some income. But Bradley quit. He told Randolph, "Ain't nobody can organize St. Louis but me." I used to run in to St. Louis when Bradley's office was in the trunk of his automobile.

But that was later. When Randolph and Totten left St. Louis, Bradley opened an office in Room 208 of the People's Finance Building, at 11 North Jefferson Avenue. For a while, he ran the office out of his own pocket— $22 a month rent and $15 a week for a stenographer. St. Louis was, indeed, one of the toughest towns to organize, for when superintendent Burr heard that some thirty men had been seen going into Bradley's office, he fired them all the same day. The effect of this broke the back of Bradley's organization overnight—for only the bravest of porters would now dare to join up—and it would be several years before either he or the organization recovered. After two months, Bradley was forced to reduce the stenographer's salary to $8 a week; and when she resigned, in protest, he replaced her with a business-school dropout, at fifty cents a day. Several months later, Bradley was evicted from the People's Finance Building, and that was when he started running the office out of the trunk of his automobile.

In Oakland, the man who volunteered to organize a division of the Brotherhood—the only one who was not afraid to "talk union" with Randolph and Totten—was a retired porter in his late seventies named Morris Moore, known to everyone as "Dad" Moore. The Pullman Company provided sleeping quarters in the different cities for porters who could not afford hotel accommodations, and it hired ex-porters to take care of them. The caretaker in Oakland was Dad Moore. He was, according to a Brotherhood booklet, "a tall, raw-bony, plain, blunt, hulk of a man, with stern eyes flashing fires of revenge." A porter who knew him says "he could outcurse a drunken sailor." And another recalls:

Dad Moore didn't have nothing but a pint of moonshine. He was in retirement. They gave him the job of taking care of the two old sleeping cars where porters stayed. He took care of those cars, woke the men up, and saw that they got on the job. The first time Randolph went out there, Dad Moore hooked up with Randolph with his drunk self. But everybody admired the old man. He preached Brotherhood to every man he saw coming in and out of the railroad yard in Oakland. He and the boys would share a bottle of moonshine at nights and he would preach Brotherhood. If you wasn't a Brotherhood man you had a hard time getting in his quarters. He worshipped Randolph. Whenever Randolph went out to Oakland, Dad followed him everywhere, with a bottle of moonshine in his pocket.

The impressions Randolph made upon other porters, as he recruited troops across the country, were similar to the one he had made upon Dad Moore. Samuel Harper, president of the union's division in Jacksonville, who first heard Randolph in Kansas City, remembers: "He gripped you. You would have to be without feeling to pull yourself away from him. You felt by him the way the disciples felt by the Master. You may not know it right then, but when you got home to yourself and got to thinking what he had said, you would just have to be a follower of him, that's all." What most impressed C. L. Dellums, who would succeed Dad Moore as organizer in Oakland, was that Randolph was "a thin guy. He was so thin that sometimes, when speaking, he would put his left hand on his hip and it would gradually slide down. But, you see, that was my idea of a revolutionary leader. I had never heard of a fat one yet. I figured the fat ones must worry about their bellies too much. I thought of that when I had seen a picture of Gandhi. And now here was Randolph. And, of course, he was the best orator I'd ever heard, bar none."

When Benjamin McLaurin first heard Randolph, in Chicago, he felt that this "was just one of those fast-talking fellows from New York," but as he listened he became convinced that "if there was anybody who could help the porters, he was the man." E. D. Nixon, a porter from Montgomery, Alabama—who, several years later, would recruit Dr. Martin Luther King, Jr., to the civil rights struggle—says, of the first time he heard Randolph, "It was like a light. Most eloquent man I ever heard. . . . I never knew the Negro had a right to enjoy freedom like everyone else. When Randolph stood there and talked that day it made a different man out of me. From that day on, I was determined that I was gonna fight for freedom until I was able to get some of it myself."

By the end of 1926, divisions of the Brotherhood had been set up in New York, Chicago, St. Louis, Kansas City, Seattle, Minneapolis-St. Paul, Omaha, Wichita, Oakland, Los Angeles, Denver, Portland, Washington, D.C., Boston, Detroit, and Buffalo.

It had been, and would continue to be, a grueling effort. Often, Randolph had been unable to continue from one city to the next until the porters had "passed the hat" to raise his fare. And not always with success. For instance, on his return visit to Oakland, in March, 1926, he received word that his mother, Elizabeth, had died in New York. "I didn't have a nickel to get back to New York," he says today. "My wife and my brother had to take care of the funeral."

Physically resilient but never, in those days, robust, Randolph had begun to suffer occasional fainting spells. On his first trip to Chicago, he had collapsed from exhaustion during one of the public meetings. Headquarters, in New York, had been alarmed by the news, prompting George Price, the Chicago secretary-treasurer, to assure Roy Lancaster that "we are preserving him as much as possible," because "if we lose him we lose the cause."

The Pullman Company could scarcely— at first—have been alarmed at the news that its porters were attempting to organize a union. The odds were too heavily against their success. Money: The Pullman treasury was sufficient, to say the least, to resist and outlast this latest flight of fancy. The law: There was none in the country that ruled clearly and unequivocally in favor of self-organization among railroad workers. And, perhaps the most important, history: The company had defeated similar efforts in the past. As the saying still went, in America black men had no rights that a white man, let alone a powerful company like Pullman, was obliged to respect. Black workers, the company felt, had never shown themselves to have the spiritual and material resources necessary to sustain a long twilight struggle in behalf of their own interests. When all was said and done, the job of Pullman porter was a virtual monopoly for black workers, and, with the proper threats, they would shrink from any action that would tend to lose them their jobs and jeopardize that racial monopoly. Lastly, the conservative and antilabor sentiments within the black community could always be recruited or suborned by the Pullman Company to denounce and discredit any effort by a bunch of radicals to endanger the security of the only group of black workers in the country who enjoyed a monopoly of the work they did.

But if there was no cause for alarm, there was certainly enough for outrage. A handful of disgruntled and ungrateful porters were trying once again to disrupt the smooth and harmonious relationships of what the company liked to call the Pullman family. And they were being aided and abetted in this by a handful of "agitators," whose sole intention, it seemed, was to defy the historic and almost divine rights the Pullman Company had exercised over its black help since Emancipation. The effort, then, would have to be crushed: to protect harmony, to assert and preserve historic privilege, and, no doubt, to vindicate history.

In moving against the upstart Brotherhood of Sleeping Car Porters, the Pullman Company employed three basic weapons: a spy system, in which loyal company porters—or stool pigeons, as they were called—informed upon union members; threats, firings, and suspensions; and the black church, the black press, and the "big Negroes," as the chief instruments of propaganda against the union and its leadership.

Ashley Totten was once asked to define a stool pigeon. "The thing is so distasteful," he said, "that it baffles the English of the writer." Nevertheless, he tried: "A stool pigeon is a male or a female employed as a decoy to spy on others; a confidence man for the dirty work of the employer; a seller of souls; a traitor to little children. In the Pullman service, a Negro stool pigeon is a low, degraded human being akin to a contemptible skunk."

The stool pigeons did their work so well that in many cities the Brotherhood was forced to operate like a secret society. In New York, after the first few weeks, porters had to slink into the *Messenger*'s office after dark, meet organizers and dues collectors surreptitiously on prearranged street corners, or slip into telephone booths to call in their membership. In St. Paul, Minnesota, where he was recruiting porters, organizer Nat Evans, in his own apartment, "had to draw the shades in broad daylight for fear of the Pullman stooges." Benjamin McLaurin says that "you'd have a man who was a dues-paying member who would slip you his money when nobody was around. But you'd never see him at a meeting, and he would never engage you in a conversation." And there were dues-paying members who crossed to the other side of the street to avoid being seen sharing the same sidewalk with Randolph or his organizers. Loyal company porters would do the same, of course—not just to avoid the risk of being considered fellow travelers of Randolph's movement, but because they fully believed what Pullman said about Randolph: that he was "a Bolshevik hustler" who was merely out to line his pockets with their money.

To support such a claim, the Pullman Company, according to McLaurin, "once cooked up a scheme to get Randolph behind bars. It was arranged for him to be taken off a train at Englewood station [in Chicago] and placed in the custody of the police. There were no charges against him, Pullman just wanted to get a photograph of him behind bars, to circulate it among the porters. But Webster got wind of the plan, and when the train pulled in, Webster, who was a bailiff, took Randolph as his prisoner. They couldn't arrest him then, because he was already in the jurisdiction of the law."

On the whole, says McLaurin, the stool pigeons reported back so promptly and accurately "that if a porter had a fuss with his wife in the morning, the company knew about it in the afternoon. If a porter bought some furniture today, they knew about it tomorrow. They'd call you in and tell you, 'I understand you bought some furniture, so you'd better be careful about your job and be a good porter.' And, of course, to be a good porter meant you should leave the Brotherhood alone."

Across the country, hundreds of porters were fired as Pullman uncovered their membership in the union. There was that day in St. Louis when superintendent A. V. Burr fired more than thirty men, which crippled Bradley's organization for several years. "Sometimes when Randolph came into St. Louis to hold a meeting," an ex-porter recalls, "he would just talk with anybody he saw on the street, 'cause there were no porters there, or none that would come within a mile of him. Every porter that went to a meeting, old man Burr would just line 'em up next morning and fire 'em."

In Oakland, the company took away Dad Moore's job as caretaker of the two old sleeping cars where out-of-town porters slept. To support himself, and to keep the Oakland division of the union going, he opened his own sleeping quarters to compete with the company's. "He went up on Seventh Street," according to his successor, C. L. Dellums, "over an old saloon, got about four little rooms, and had some secondhand furniture put in. He got a big old stove put in the middle of the living-room part, to keep the place warm. The Eastern porters rented the rooms and slept in some old hammocks he had. On the ground floor, behind the saloon, Dad got another small room and set up the Brotherhood office there. But Pullman kept after him. Soon after he opened the office, the company canceled his $15-a-month pension."

To break Dad Moore was to smash the Oakland organization, and the Pullman Company threatened to fire any porter seen patronizing Moore's rooming house. Without his pension and the extra income from his roomers, neither he nor the movement could survive. And both very nearly went under—but for the handful of secret union members who defied Pullman's orders. "I am going to stand by the ship, no matter what happen," Dad Moore wrote Milton Webster in Chicago, in May, 1926, while having a hard time raising money for the rent. "The sea is ruff and the wind are high but I'll stay with her until she make the harbor." A month later he wrote again: "I will not stop until the flag of the Brotherhood fly high in the breeze of victory. . . . If the ship sink I will be on the head end, with such men as yourself . . . and Mr. Randolph."

Even in Chicago, under Milton Webster's fiery leadership, the men were, in his words, "completely cowarded." Benjamin McLaurin, then a porter there, remembers that "grown men trembled like a leaf in a gale of wind." And Ulas Crowder, today the secretary-treasurer of the Chicago division, recalls the day, in 1926, when he was summoned to the superintendent's office:

He asked me, "Do you know a colored man that is going around the country supposedly organizing porters?" I said, "Yes, I know Mr. Randolph. I never met him, but I understand he's a highly educated man, a wonderful speaker, and a brilliant orator." He said, "We think so too." Right then it hit me on top of the head that I'm through. He said, "Are you a member of the organization?" I didn't answer. I remembered just then that a couple weeks before a stool pigeon had stolen my union card out of my billfold on one of my runs. The dues card had twelve months, and each time you paid you punched the card. I had paid up the whole year in advance, so I had what we called then an air-conditioned card—all the holes punched. The superintendent told me, he said, "Brother Crowder, look around see if you see anything here that belongs to you." I hit the ceiling, because I look around and see my air-conditioned card right there on his desk. But I pretend I don't see it. He stood up, turned his back to me, and looked through the window, then spun around suddenly. "You don't see anything that belongs to you?" he said. I said, "I wouldn't know what you're talking about." He picked up the card and handed it to me. I said, "Oh, thank you, that's my union card," and reached for it. He snatched it back. He said, "What you know about the union?" He said, "I'm surprised at you. The favors this company has done you, and now you coming up with one of your Bolshevik cards. This is the beginning of the end for you here." Then he gave me a long lecture. He said I was just bumping my head against a brick wall. "The Pullman Company will never recognize Randolph," he said, "and there's nothing he can do about it. In the first place, your people, colored people, don't know anything about labor organizing. Randolph is too smart for you. The Pullman Company has always taken care of its porters and it always will. We can take care of you, too, if you will work with us. I want you to give this some thought, because there can be a place for you in this setup. I don't want an answer now, but when you make up your mind, come and let me know." Well, right there I see myself on the way out, because I don't intend to mess with the Brotherhood. "Remember," he told me before I left, "this is a white man's country, white people run it, will keep on running it, and this company will never sit down around the same table with Randolph as long as he's black."

In one of its earliest attempts to scuttle the Brotherhood, the Pullman Company called in the porter representatives on the Plan of Employee Representation to a conference in Chicago—from January 27 to February 5, 1926—to "negotiate" a revision of wages and working conditions. Again, as in 1924, most of the representatives were loyal company men, and their sentiments were perhaps best expressed by porter E. Anderson, representing the Atlanta district, who made the opening speech:

We are here today to join with the Pullman Company and not some outside organization. . . . Our hands are extended to the Pullman Company in the interest of good fellowship. . . . We are not here to demand, but requesting. . . . We are not here in an arrogant way, but submissive to the degree that we desire that our wishes be complied with as far as possible. . . . We are quite cognizant of the fact that the Pullman Company has done and are doing more for the Negro race than any corporation in the world.

Nothing so illustrated the need for an independent union. And there can scarcely be any surprise that the loyal porters—far from getting even what they humbly requested—had to take what Pullman offered: a $5 increase, raising their minimum salary from $67.50 a month to $72.50.

Still, no serious complaint was recorded. All but two of the delegates signed the "agreement," and before the conference broke up, porter W. A. Hill, from Cincinnati, rose to applaud "the fairness" the company had displayed "by laying your cards on the table for us to read openly," and pledged to "do all in our power to discredit radicalism." The Pullman Company, Hill said, "has been our greatest benefactor and friend from the dawn of freedom down to the present day." One delegate who had refused to sign was Benjamin ("Bennie") Smith, of the Omaha district, a fact that Pullman would not forget.

Bennie Smith was a tall man of medium build, with a military bearing that accentuated his three-piece suits and the watch chain running across his vest. But his distinguishing physical features were a cool, dark, and solemn face and a head of thick, carefully groomed hair parted in the center—all of which made him appear to be of predominantly East Indian rather than African strain. His grave mien seems to have been deceiving, for, as an officer of the Brotherhood has said, no one was capable of more humor. He was an old friend and colleague of Milton Webster, the two having run together between Chicago and Omaha when Webster was a porter. Smith was a militant, undercover union man. During the Chicago conference, he had served not only as the porters' delegate from Omaha, but also as a spy for the Brotherhood. At the end of each day's session, Smith had taken a taxicab from the Pullman headquarters, at 79 Adams Street, to the Vincennes Hotel, on Chicago's South Side, where Randolph and Webster were waiting to receive his reports. And it was at their instigation that he had refused to affix his signature to the results of the conference—the strategy being for the Brotherhood to claim a victory if Smith succeeded in blocking a settlement.

Less than a year later, however, Pullman evened the score with Bennie Smith—firing him, after several months of harassment. But since no porter of Smith's caliber could be wasted, Randolph immediately hired him, and sent him to help Ashley Totten organize the Kansas City division.

In April, 1927, Randolph recalled Smith from Kansas City and sent him to Jacksonville, with a view to setting up the first division of the Brotherhood in the South. The plan failed, however. Posing as a salesman of the *Messenger* in Jacksonville, Smith was reported to the local authorities by a Pullman stool pigeon, and one day, while holding a secret meeting in the basement of a private home, he was arrested and charged with "preaching social equality in the South." According to Randolph, "social equality then was like communism now." Smith reported later, "I hired a young colored lawyer, and we had a fight on the courthouse steps. He told me to run. I said, 'I paid you $50 to defend me.' He said, 'Well, you'll find out what's going to happen.' . . . The judge said, before he adjourned, 'We know what you're doing down here, and you won't get away with that stuff. We're going to send you to Blue Jay prison farm, and from there we're going to take you to a tree.' "

That night Smith telegraphed his plight to Randolph, in New York, who ordered him to get out of Jacksonville immediately. But leaving so unceremoniously did not appeal to Smith, and he wired Randolph again:

AM FULLY MINDFUL OF GRAVE SERIOUSNESS OF SITUATION AND PERSONAL DANGER. CONSCIENTIOUSLY FEEL BROTHERHOOD CAUSE IS SO RIGHTEOUSLY IMPORTANT THAT A FIRM STAND SHOULD BE TAKEN. HAVE FULLY DECIDED TO REMAIN AND MEET CONSEQUENCES. THIS MEANS THAT I'M WILLING TO MAKE SUPREME SACRIFICE. HAVE SACREDLY DEDICATED MY ALL TO THE BROTHERHOOD'S NOBLE CAUSE. ADVISE AT ONCE.

The advice was the same, but this time it came from Webster, accompanied by $40 for train fare: "Get the hell out of Jacksonville. You can't beat no case down there." Smith was then sent to organize Detroit, where he has remained ever since.

The Pullman Company had no more formidable allies in the black community than the "big Negroes," the church, and the press. As Milton Webster would put it, "Everything Negro was against us."

Dean Kelly Miller of Howard University, remaining, as ever, on the side of the propertied, came out against "Negro unionism," arguing that the best interests of the group would be served by "standing with capital." Melvin Chisum, a prominent Chicago politician, advised porters that they would be better off relying upon the "goodwill" of the Pullman Company. Webster wrote to inform Randolph that Jesse Binga, black president of Chicago's Binga State Bank, had told porters that "George Pullman was comparable only with Lincoln and that he had done more for the Negro industrially and economically than anyone else." Binga, Webster said, had also advised porters that there was "a special department in his bank for porters . . . in need of funds." And the *Messenger* later claimed that the Pullman Company had made a special deposit of $10,000 in Binga's bank.

Most of the prominent black churches outside New York denied their platforms to Brotherhood speakers, while ministers preached openly against the union from their pulpits. In New York, the union was supported by the Reverend Lloyd Imes's St. James Presbyterian Church, the Reverend Frederick Cullen's Salem Methodist Church, and the Reverend Adam Clayton Powell, Sr.'s Abyssinian Baptist Church. The Second Baptist Church, in Los Angeles, the Central Baptist Church, in St. Louis, and the Metropolitan Community Church, in Chicago, also opened their doors to the Brotherhood, but few others did. Webster once tried to obtain a church in Chicago to hold a union meeting:

We went to one of the largest churches . . . and paid the people a hundred dollars for the use of the church on a Sunday afternoon. . . . Through my own espionage system I found out that the head stool pigeon had called on the pastor of this church, and I became concerned. I thought I'd better see the pastor. So I went to the office of the church, knocked on the door and said I wanted to see the Reverend. He said, "Who are you?" I told him and was invited in, and then he asked me what I wanted. So I told him that I understood we were to have a meeting at the church on Sunday afternoon and I just thought I'd come around to see the church and so on. And he said, "Now listen here, Webster, I don't know about that. You know that deal wasn't made with me." Well, I called the brother aside and whispered to him: "You've got a hundred dollars of our money and we've spent a hundred and fifty dollars advertising this meeting. This is Wednesday and the meeting is Sunday, and I'd just like to suggest to you that if we don't meet in this church Sunday you're going to find all these stones in the middle of the street." And I left. . . . I believe we had probably one of the best meetings we ever had in the city of Chicago.

"Any Sunday you went to church," recalls a Chicago porter, "the preachers touched on the Brotherhood. Their slogan was 'Don't rock the boat, don't bite the hand that feeds you.' They said Randolph was just a glib orator, whereas the Pullman Company was a million-dollar outfit. 'The company will never sit down with a man like that,' they told us. 'Look at his record. He was drafted in World War I and accused of treason. Look at the little radical magazine he's putting out. Way out of line.' "

The black press was almost solid in its opposition, the notable exceptions being the New York *Amsterdam News,* the *Chicago Bee* (for which Chandler Owen was an editorial writer), the *Kansas City Call* (where Roy Wilkins worked as a young general reporter), and, briefly, the *Pittsburgh Courier.*

"Randolph's interference in Pullman porters' affairs," said a writer in the *Louisiana Weekly,* "is dangerous to industrial colored America." To counteract the influence of the *Messenger* as mouthpiece of the organized porters, the Pullman Company subsidized the publication among its loyalists of a journal called the *Pullman Porter Messenger.* This journal, in its May, 1926, issue, called Randolph "a lamp post orator," and the members of his union "wormy Pullman fruit, poor, disloyal, yellowed, spotted out, ungrateful, undesirable, beggars for a job, not wanted, exiled, abandoned, slipping around here and there under cover."

The company saw to it that the porters were supplied with the pro-Pullman newspapers from the black community. According to Ulas Crowder, of Chicago, "the *St. Louis Argus,* the *Denver Star,* the *Seattle Enterprise,* the *Chicago Whip,* and the *Chicago Defender* were stacked up high in our sign-out offices. They were full of nothing but Pullman propaganda. All you had to do was walk in and pick up your copy. You didn't need to pay for any, 'cause Pullman was providing them free. And if you didn't pick up a copy, a clerk or somebody like that would yell after you, 'Hey, where's your paper?' "

All of these, Randolph said, unleashed "a pitiless storm of intolerance" against him. One even accused him, he remembers, of preparing to abscond to Russia with $72,000 of the porters' money. By March, 1926, the counterattack having done its work, the early enthusiasm of the union porters began to wane, and dues receipts declined all over the country.

Randolph, an estimable propagandist himself, but lacking Pullman's access to publicity, had to rely upon his circulars to the porters, almost all of which were reprinted in the *Messenger.* In March, 1926, fearing that the all out offensive directed by Pullman might shatter the base of his following among the porters, he threw himself upon their emotions:

When I enlisted in the cause I knew that slanderers would attempt to blacken my character with infamy. I knew that among the wicked, corrupt, and unenlightened my pleadings would be received with disdain and reproach; that persecution would assail me on every side; that the dagger of the assassin would gleam behind my back; that the arm of arrogant power would be raised to crush me to the earth; that I would be branded a disturber of the peace, as a madman, fanatic, an incendiary, a Communist, Anarchist, and what not; that love would be turned into hatred, confidence into suspicion, respect into derision; that my worldly interests would be jeopardized. I knew that the base and servile would accuse me of being actuated with the hope of reward. But I am undaunted and unafraid. The only reward I seek is that your cause secures a full and complete vindication.

This appeal had the effect of arresting the slow erosion of the porters' support; and with the passage, in May, of the Watson-Parker bill as the Railway Labor Act*—protecting the right of railroad workers to organize—dues and membership began to climb again.

———

* Randolph had not appealed to the Railway Labor Board, which then existed under the Transportation Act of 1920. All railroad unions were dissatisfied with its inability to enforce its decisions, and the big railroad brotherhoods, whose support Randolph was interested in seeking, were then moving to secure a new labor law. While awaiting this, Randolph had approached Congressman Emanuel Celler, of New York, to request a congressional investigation of Pullman's labor policies, and Celler had introduced a resolution calling upon the House's Labor Committee "to investigate the wages, hours and conditions of employment of the Pullman porters . . . and to investigate the financial conditions of the Pullman Company." The resolution died in the Rules Committee, however. The same month, in May, the Watson-Parker bill—supported by the big railroad unions and all railroad managements—was passed as the Railway Labor Act of 1926.

13 / "There Seemed No Way to Win"

The heroic preliminaries were over. The real struggle—the Brotherhood's legal effort to upset Pullman's company union, and to be recognized in its place as the rightful bargaining agent of the porters—could now begin.

The Railway Labor Act, passed on May 20, 1926, provided for "the prompt disposition" of all disputes between railroad carriers and their employees. To avoid "any interruption in the operation of any carrier," the act called upon both sides to meet in joint conference to "make and maintain agreements" on rates of pay, rules, and working conditions. Employee and employer representatives were to be designated without "interference, influence, or coercion," and disputes that could not be resolved in conference were to be submitted to a Board of Mediation. The leaders of the Brotherhood were joyful. The Railway Labor Act seemed a clear affirmation of the porters' right to *independent* self-organization. It would be merely a matter of time, they felt—the time it would take to exhaust the due process of the act—before their union was recognized as the bona fide bargaining agent of the porters.

Randolph took the first step on September 20. Writing to E. G. Carry, president of the Pullman Company, he called attention to the provisions of the Railway Labor Act, informing him that porters had "designated and authorized" the Brotherhood to bargain in their behalf, and requesting a conference with Pullman's representatives. The same date, Randolph wrote to Webster, in Chicago, to share what he evidently considered a historic moment in the struggle not only of porters, but of all black workers: "For once, black men are seriously preparing to write their own economic contracts which will benefit their children and their

187

children's children." He had no way of knowing how long they would be preparing.

No reply came from the Pullman Company. That was no reason for alarm, however. The Labor Act required him to write again if no reply was received after ten days, and, on September 30, Randolph sent another letter to Carry. Well aware by now of the contempt in which they were held by the Pullman Company, Randolph and his lieutenants probably expected no reply. In fact, Roy Lancaster, the secretary-treasurer, in New York, was already looking forward to the next move authorized by the Labor Act, in the event Pullman remained silent. "If there is no hearing from the Company by [October 15]," he wrote George Price, in Chicago, "we file with the Mediation Board our brief, from which time the battle will be on." It was on, to be sure, but hardly joined, for the company maintained its silence. On October 15, Randolph notified the Board of Mediation that a dispute existed between the Brotherhood and Pullman, and requested its intervention.

The Mediation Board assigned Edward P. Morrow, a former governor of Kentucky, to investigate the dispute, and a preliminary inquiry was set for December, 1926. The Brotherhood retained Donald P. Richberg, a prominent Chicago labor lawyer—later active in the New Deal—to prepare its brief. Because Richberg, representing the big railroad unions, had helped to write the Watson-Parker bill, which became the Railway Labor Act, Randolph assured his membership that their case was in capable hands, since Richberg knew more about the act "than any living man in America." To provide data for Richberg, Randolph commissioned George Soule, Benjamin Berheimer, and Stuart Chase, of the New York Labor Bureau, at 2 West Forty-third Street, to make a survey of the porters' wage structure and working conditions.

Here, too, was an example of how costly it would be for the fledgling porters' union to challenge the rich and powerful Pullman Company. Out of its very meager treasury—less than half of its fluctuating membership was paying dues—it had to pay token salaries to organizers all over the country, underwrite the expenses of publishing the *Messenger,* pay $5,000 to Donald Richberg and $3,000 to the New York Labor Bureau, and provide retainers for the following legal advisers: C. Francis Stratford, a black attorney in Chicago; Frank P. Walsh, a former chairman of the United States Commission on Industrial Relations; Morris Hillquit, of the New York Socialist party; Samuel Untermeyer, Henry T. Hunt, and Louis Waldman, New York attorneys; and Morris Ernst, of the law firm of Greenbaum, Wolff, and Ernst.

To meet these expenses, Randolph had to make one of the many inspirational fund appeals he would be forced to make to the porters from time to time. "We have reached a milepost it was doubted we would ever reach," he told the porters in a circular. There was "no question" that the union would win, but it would "cost plenty of money," and they would have to give "until it hurts." Above all, Randolph urged, it was necessary to demonstrate to the Pullman Company that black men did not lack "the guts to fight . . . the pride and will to pay for [their] freedom," or the ability to back their own struggle for justice "with their own dollars." All of which may simply have brought a smile to the faces of Pullman's officials as they contemplated their company's prestige, its money, and the lawyers it was able to buy.

When Edward P. Morrow opened the preliminary inquiry, in December, the Brotherhood claimed a membership of 5,763, or, based on its estimate of 10,875 porters in the Pullman service, slightly more than 53 per cent. Of these, the union said, 4,203 had authorized it, in a referendum, to be their representative. But Pullman had its own figures By "actual nose count," it employed 12,354 porters, the company replied. Furthermore, it claimed that, in a poll it had recently conducted, 85 per cent of the porters had voted to be represented by the company's Plan of Employee Representation. Therefore, the Brotherhood "does not now, and never has represented a majority" of its employees. Morrow then adjourned the inquiry, instructing the disputants to await word of its resumption.

The Brotherhood had been totally unprepared for Pullman's claim that 85 per cent of the porters had voted to stick with the company union. There was no question, the union felt, but that the porters had been intimidated into voting for the company's plan, for those very porters had also authorized the Brotherhood to be their representative. Such coercion was a clear violation of the Railway Labor Act, and evidence of it would have to be gathered and submitted to Edward P. Morrow, whenever he reconvened the inquiry. Randolph was reassured by Donald Richberg's advice:

I hope you will point out . . . that no matter what representations the Pullman Company makes regarding the number of porters who voted according to the company plan, nevertheless the . . . facts show that the company plan violates the Railway Labor Act. The form of organization has been drafted by the company, the company conducted the election, the company pays the expenses of the so-called employee representatives. . . . Therefore, the only representatives of the porters who are designated and authorized in conformity with the Railway Labor Act are the officials of the Brotherhood.

As evidence of coercion, Randolph collected some 900 affidavits from the porters, swearing that the Pullman management had forced them to vote against their will. Here are two examples: A porter in St. Paul, Minnesota, swore that superintendent C. C. Healy "told me that the company considered any one who did not vote on their plan as being against them, and that they did not want any one working for them that was against them, and that my job was my bread and butter." And a Chicago porter, asked by a superintendent why he did not vote, asked in return, "Does a man have to vote for this plan?" The superintendent replied, "You do not have to go on the new train; you do not have to work for the Pullman Company unless you want to; and you do not have to live unless you want to."

But some six months later, at the beginning of June, 1927, the Brotherhood had heard nothing further from Edward P. Morrow about when or whether the inquiry would be resumed. The overwhelming import of this, from the Brotherhood's point of view, was that whereas the Pullman Company could afford to wait indefinitely—or forever—for the issue to be resolved, the union could not. Success, or some promise of it, was an imperative if the union was to retain its members' support or sustain their morale—a morale that had never been higher than the previous December, when Randolph had taken their case before the Mediation Board.

In fact, by June, 1927—considering no news to be bad news—the porters' enthusiasm had waned again. Webster had written from Chicago to inform Randolph of "considerable uneasiness" among the men. And Randolph, contending with a similar uneasiness among New York porters, had replied, "I know just what you are up against." Dues paying also having fallen off, Randolph issued another of his inspirational fund appeals, this one aimed specifically at the staunchest members of the union—"the pure gold of the Brotherhood," as he called them. Asking for loans of "$5 immediately," he assured them that "the Brotherhood will surely win," that "our struggle is the supreme test of the race," and that "the eyes of the world are upon us."

But at that point, despite his apparent determination, Randolph himself felt no such assurance. He may even have begun to lose faith in the effectiveness of the Railway Labor Act, for on June 9, when he still had heard nothing from Morrow, he seems to have been shaken. Taking a friendly and amicable tone, he wrote a fifteen-page letter to the president of the Pullman Company, in which he assured E. G. Carry that "the Brotherhood is building a new porter, upstanding, responsible, efficient, with initiative and constructive, practical intelligence, who will work to build up a bigger and better Pullman industry to serve the nation. You will find the Brotherhood ever ready to fully cooperate with you, frankly, intelligently, loyally and honorably to achieve this end, mutually beneficial to the property and human elements of the Pullman industry."

It was a tactical blunder from which it would take him years to recover. With the dispute still technically under mediation, the Pullman Company had no reason to expect a letter from Randolph, let alone a tone of such sweet reasonableness from a man whose voice, from the beginning, had been the essence of trade union militancy—unless, that is, Randolph was weakening. That, in fact, was precisely what the company suspected. As one of its lawyers said in an internal memo to the president—advising that no reply was necessary—"the letter rather indicates that Randolph has lost some confidence in the organization's ability to force through the program in the way he previously announced he would do." This being its conclusion, Pullman, which had, no doubt, remained willing to resume mediation whenever Morrow called upon it to do so, now decided to stand its ground and have nothing further to do with the proceedings. Shortly after the letter from Randolph was received, the company's general manager, L. S. Hungerford, wrote to Morrow:

When the Railway Labor Act was passed . . . there was in effect, and now is in operation, an agreement between the Pullman Company and its porters and maids. This agreement fully meets all the requirements of the law. . . . No dispute, and therefore no situation requiring mediation, exists between the Pullman Company and its employees of the classes mentioned. . . . In these circumstances, and because of the existence of the agreement . . . the Company cannot properly confer [with the Brotherhood].

Thus when, in July, Morrow finally got around to reconvening the Mediation Board's inquiry, he could not have been too surprised that the Pullman Company refused to send a representative. In any case, it left

Morrow no alternative—or so it seemed—but to inform the parties that "efforts to bring about an amicable adjustment of the dispute through mediation have been unsuccessful." The dispute, he advised, was now a matter for arbitration.

Randolph was ready and eager to go along. He had no choice; time was flying, and he yet had nothing to show the porters. But Pullman was now firmly in control. Not only was it free of any urgent need to appeal to the good offices of the federal government, but it also knew something that Randolph and the Brotherhood either did not know or had forgotten: though arbitration was provided for under the Railway Labor Act, it was not mandatory. Therefore, the company simply reiterated to Morrow: "As no dispute existed . . . which required mediation, and the status not having changed, it follows that there is no dispute and therefore no cause for arbitration." Whether Morrow disagreed or not, he knew he had no power to order compliance, and, in effect, he washed his hands of the case. The Mediation Board, he informed both sides, had "exhausted its efforts under the law," and "nothing can be accomplished in the further handling of the case."

It was a crushing defeat for the Brotherhood, and its enemies, particularly sections of the black press, were overjoyed. Said the *St. Louis Argus:*

The outcome of [Randolph's] supposed organization has resulted in just what we had expected, only it was a little late in coming. H? has nothing to show . . . for the thousands of dollars he has collected from the porters and maids. . . . We do not believe that Randolph is sincere. Nor do we believe he has ever been sincere. That he is a good talker there is no doubt. He will now tell the porters and maids that he has just begun to fight. He will call upon them for more money. . . . It may be that he is figuring on getting rich before the porters and maids wake up. The proper thing now for those who have given him money is to demand so much of it back, dismiss him from their case, and try through some other means to get their cause before the proper parties.

The porters' morale collapsed; only "the pure gold" of the Brotherhood continued to pay dues, and, with the exception of men like Milton Webster, Ashley Totten, Dad Moore, C. L. Dellums, and Bennie Smith, Randolph's organizers around the country were dispirited.

They would not be dispirited for long, however, for, despite their disappointment, they stood ready to respond with as many new acts of faith as Randolph requested of them. The initial reserve many of them, all former porters, had felt toward him, a nonporter, had evaporated in the warmth of the devotion he had won from them, especially as they had observed the qualities of his leadership: pride, fearlessness, selflessness, determination, integrity, moral courage. So, as C. L. Dellums said, trying to restore the morale of a group of porters in Oakland, "As long as Randolph stays, I'll stay. And I expect you to stay. He's the brains and spirit. And if there's any way under the sun to win, he'll find it." It also helped that most of his organizers were afraid of losing his respect. They knew how heavily his judgment of men turned on their capacity for courage and sacrifice, as well as the force of their commitment to the causes in which he believed.

Aside from gifts of patience and doggedness, Randolph himself was driven by a sense of duty to the porters, having stirred their discontent, aroused their hopes, and raised their expectations. And because he looked upon the Brotherhood as something more than just an organization of sleeping car porters— as a symbol, in fact, of the struggle by black Americans to build and sustain movements for their own political and economic salvation within the framework of the American social movement—Pullman's intransigence implied, in his mind, a contempt for the right of blacks to choose their own leaders and representatives. He would emphasize this point a year later, in a letter to Milton Webster. After inviting Randolph to speak, in July, 1928, the Catholic Industrial Conference of Cincinnati withdrew the invitation when it heard of his radical activities during World War I. Asked to send someone else, Randolph sent Webster, with these instructions:

One thing I would stress very fundamentally . . . and that is never again will Negroes permit white people to select their leaders for them. I would make it very emphatic that upon that principle we shall not compromise, not only with respect to the Pullman porters but with any Negro movement. Negroes will no more permit white people to select their leaders than will white people permit Negroes to select theirs. I would emphasize the fact, too, that the Pullman porters' organization is a Negro movement, and that it stands for self-expression and interest of Negroes by Negroes for Negroes. I would also indicate to them that it would not matter what the opposition would be, that the question of the right of Negroes to choose their own leaders is as fundamental as the right of life itself. . . . Cater to nobody and make no compromises. . . . Of course, we want the support of everybody we can get, but not at the price of surrendering principles that are vital to our existence.

The *St. Louis Argus* was right when it said that Randolph "will now tell the porters and maids that he has just begun to fight." In fact, four days after the Pullman Company had refused to enter into arbitration, those were almost the words he used. "The fight has just begun," he told the porters, in an open letter. Pullman's refusal to arbitrate was "a challenge to the manhood of every porter. . . . We are now in a fight to the finish and propose to go to the limit to beat the company into submission." Those were brave words—partly meant to revive hope among the porters, and partly an accurate description of his determination.

In speaking thus, Randolph was pinning his hopes on the last resort remaining to the Brotherhood under the Railway Labor Act. The act provided that the powers of the Mediation Board could again be invoked in the event of "any interruption to commerce or the operation of any carrier." In other words, the Brotherhood could now call a strike, or, in the words of its leaders, create "an emergency." The union announced that it intended to do just this, and began regaining members.

But the precariousness of the Brotherhood's situation dictated a strategy so delicate that it was almost bound to fail. Knowing that the porters were afraid of losing their jobs—since the Pullman Company did not hesitate to replace them—and fearing another large-scale desertion by its membership, the union could not demand from them a firm commitment to strike. Thus if the "emergency" was to be created, it would have to be done not by calling a strike, but by indicating the union's ability and readiness to call a strike. The problem was: While that would suggest a threat, it would not, in fact, constitute one. Nevertheless, the Brotherhood, in calling for a strike vote, gave the following assurance to its members:

By a strike vote is meant the indication on a strike ballot that Pullman porters are determined to strike if need be. . . . A strike vote IS NOT A STRIKE. It is a sign of the iron resolution of the men to fight to the finish for their rights. It does not follow that Pullman porters will strike because they take a strike vote. The Telegraphers Union on the Burlington Railroad took a strike vote but did not strike. The United States Mediation Board stepped in and effected a settlement.

That may have been true, but declaring so openly that a strike vote was not a strike posed another problem. Why should the Pullman Company take it seriously? Why shouldn't the company regard it as further evidence of the union's weakness, and design an appropriate counterstrategy? By the end of May, 1928, however, the Brotherhood announced that 6,013 out of 10,994 porters had voted to walk off the cars whenever the word was given.

The support of the white press in New York—especially the *Times,* the *World,* and the *Herald Tribune,* most of whose labor reporters liked and admired Randolph—had built up strong liberal sentiment in favor of the Brotherhood's cause. And in Chicago, the *Daily News* and the *Journal* had taken the union's side. This was in such marked contrast to the continued hostility of most of the black press that Webster wrote Randolph triumphantly: "I don't think we need worry about the *Courier* or any other Negro paper now."

What was this about the *Pittsburgh Courier?* Up until the beginning of 1928, the *Courier* and the New York *Amsterdam News* had been the most devoted supporters of the union among the black press. Suddenly, however, by March, the *Courier* had become a spokesman for the Pullman Company a switch that Milton Webster attributed to the arrival of Pullman's "gravy train."

In April, returning by train from Chicago—where he had gone to study the progress of the strike vote—Randolph was joined in Pittsburgh by Robert L. Vann, editor of the *Courier.* Apparently a secret emissary of the Pullman Company—or "the dark person in the woodpile," as Randolph, with an excess of good taste, later described him—Vann asked the Brotherhood leader, "Would you resign from the Brotherhood if the Pullman Company agreed to recognize the union and sign an agreement with it?" When Randolph said he would be glad to, Vann assured him that the company was ready to recognize the union, but would not do so as long as Randolph, "a Socialist radical," was in control. Far from being the olive branch it seemed, this was just another attempt to smash the union: to create the impression among union porters that Randolph's background was the only obstacle to their success, and thus rid the Brotherhood of the leadership without which it could not continue. On his return to Pittsburgh, Vann telegraphed Randolph in confirmation: "I have authority to say to you that conference will follow immediately after your resignation is announced. Wire at once."

But before wiring, Randolph wrote to Webster, in Chicago:

Of course, I should be perfectly willing to resign from the organization if the Company made a bona fide agreement with the Brotherhood and recognized it fully and completely just as other railroad unions are recognized, if the men wished me to resign. But I shall abide by the wishes of the men. . . . You may depend upon me to see to it that nothing will be done except that which will securely and legally, completely and absolutely, bring victory to the Brotherhood. I am not important in the matter. . . . I should be willing to make any sacrifice which would advance the cause of the organization.

He then wired Vann to say that he was prepared to resign, but only after the company recognized the union.

This was clearly not what either Vann or the Pullman Company had in mind, and, on April 14, the *Courier,* in an open letter, went directly to the porters:

When other papers were silent the Courier took up the fight because it wanted to see something done. The Courier still wants to see something done. . . . For almost two years the company has refused to have anything to do with the porters. . . . There must be a reason for this attitude. . . . Mr. Randolph has been told that the company objects to dealing with him and the reason for their objection is based on the history of Mr. Randolph in this country as a socialist and radical. Perhaps some of the porters don't know what this means. It must be remembered that Mr. Randolph and Mr. Owen are the men who several years ago started the most radical and socialist magazine ever issued by Negroes in this country. . . . These men declared themselves socialists and radicals and bragged about it. We did not make the history of Mr. Randolph. He has made it himself. It is known that American capital will not negotiate with socialists. It has never been so even where white people were concerned. Mr. Randolph has been informed that the Company will not deal with him because of his history as a socialist.

The tactic failed, however, for 6,013 porters obeyed the union's call for a strike vote.

With the results of its poll, the Brotherhood now went back to the Mediation Board. Claiming that its strike vote represented an emergency in the Pullman service, the union appealed to Section 10 of the Railway Labor Act, which empowered the President of the United States to establish an Emergency Board to resolve such a crisis. The Brotherhood expected no obstacles, reminding its members that, in a recent precedent, President Calvin Coolidge had set up an Emergency Board in response to a strike vote among workers on the Kansas City-Mexico-Orient Railroad.

On the morning of June 4, Edward P. Morrow, the Mediation Board's chief investigator, called in Randolph to listen to the Brotherhood's arguments and ascertain the facts. It was purely a formality, however, for by then Morrow's mind was already partly made up. In March, after reading newspaper reports that the union was voting to strike, Colonel Samuel E. Winslow, chairman of the Mediation Board, had dispatched Morrow to Chicago to look into and advise him on the truth of the reports. Morrow, after talking with Pullman officials, had informed Winslow:

The following is a fair statement of their [Pullman's] position. They do not believe that any real strike is threatened by Randolph or those associated with him. They do not believe that Randolph can induce any considerable number of their employees to leave the service, but is taking a fake strike vote in order to induce the Board to believe that large numbers of porters will go out of the service. They believe that his entire plan is based upon the realization that he cannot induce any substantial number of porters to quit their jobs, and therefore could not, as a matter of fact, seriously threaten an interruption of transportation, and that he is seeking a method to induce the Board to believe that an emergency exists when no emergency does exist. It is confidently asserted that trained porters can be immediately put in service to take the place of any striking porters and that more than 3000 ex-porters are known and listed; that the Company has a list of several thousand applications for porters' positions, who have been examined as to education and qualification. Finally, the Company asserts that Pullman transportation will not be interrupted in any way, that they are perfectly able to take care of the situation, provide service and so forth. . . . I do not believe that ten percent of the Pullman employees will quit the service of the Company, am confident that the Company will be overrun with applications for jobs and that they can more than supply any losses from their ranks. If anything approaching a real strike could have been staged with any hope of success, it would have been done long ago. In my opinion, Randolph's movements at this time are for the sole purpose of inducing the Board to request the President to appoint an emergency board.

So, by the time of the formal hearings, in June, the chairman of the Mediation Board had long been satisfied that the union was incapable of producing a genuine emergency. What he had heard from Morrow, in March, was "exactly the information we wanted to get." Nor, by then, could Morrow himself—who, on his mission to Chicago, had not even thought it necessary to consult the Brotherhood—have had much of an open mind on the question.

Nevertheless, in the formal hearings with Morrow, Randolph—who had no idea that the Mediation Board had already held secret talks with Pullman—stressed that 6,013 porters were ready to strike "on a date to be set, by the Brotherhood's chiefs," and suggested that the Mediation Board ask President Coolidge to set up an Emergency Board to resolve the issue and avert the impending disruption of sleeping car service. But, of course, Morrow already "knew" better, and had a few questions of his own. Did Randolph believe he could tie up the Pullman Company? Randolph said he was confident he could. The Pullman Company did not think so, Morrow revealed. Randolph said it was only natural for the company to take that position; after all, it wanted to create "fear and uncertainty" among the porters. Morrow said he would have to check the strike ballots to see whether they were authentic. Moreover, he added, it wasn't sufficient for Randolph to threaten an emergency; he would also have to give the date on which the emergency would occur. Randolph's hand was forced. Setting a strike date was not part of his strategy, but now that Morrow had asked, he came up with Friday, June 8.

On June 5, the morning after hearing Randolph, Morrow called in the Pullman Company, whose representative repeated, in substance, what the company had told Morrow in March: the Brotherhood was incapable of disrupting the Pullman sleeping car service. Further, since it was the company that would suffer the most seriously from an emergency, it was the company, and not the union, that should inform the Mediation Board whether an emergency existed or not.

No one could say, of course, just how many porters would walk off the sleeping cars if a strike was, indeed, called, but there were grounds for Pullman's belief that the number would be small. It was well known that many union porters were not firmly committed to the organization. Theirs was an attitude of: "If the union succeeds we are for it; if it fails we're not." Clearly, no such porter could be depended upon to endure the usual risks—particularly that of a strike—entailed in making any struggling union a success. Here, for instance, is an exchange between two porters in Los Angeles, after the strike date had passed:

HOLLAND: When I joined the union I knew what I was doing; I studied it very well. Mr. Taylor came and asked me on the day the strike was called if I would report for my run. I said, "Mr. Taylor, haven't I always reported all these 18 years?" He said, "Yes, but I want a definite answer." I said, "I will be here." The union has never influenced me one way or the other. Every man has in his heart the desire to benefit himself if possible; I am able to still abide by the Employee Plan until they have been destroyed.

TODD: Holland, you say that you are going to remain loyal to the Employee Plan of Representation until the Plan has been destroyed. Now, if you are loyal to the Employee Plan and you refused to go out on the strike, I would like to know just why you consider it necessary to continue to be a member of the Brotherhood. Let me ask you this question. Assume another strike is to be called tomorrow and you were to go out on the train tomorrow night. Would you say, "I have always been loyal to this company and I will be there tomorrow night"—would you say that?

HOLLAND: Yes, sir.

TODD: It still puzzles me. Why endorse both the Plan and the union? Why stray away from the fold and belong to the Brotherhood, which has been created by somebody who is not a porter?

HOLLAND: I have never said that it was not possible for me to change my opinion, but as long as I was a Brotherhood man I would be as loyal as possible. I also said that I was going to show my loyalty to the company.

Anyway, immediately after leaving the meeting with Morrow, on June 4, Randolph telegraphed Brotherhood organizers all around the country: "A strike shall be declared and enforced on all Pullman property the eighth day of June Friday noon unless there is cause for change of which you will be advised."

That hesitancy again—". . . unless there is cause for change . . ." Words like those did nothing to shake the conviction Edward P. Morrow had already formed that the Brotherhood had neither the means nor the intention to call a strike, that it was merely bluffing. It was not surprising, therefore, that on June 6—a day after his meeting with the Pullman representatives, and two days before the strike date Randolph had given him—Morrow instructed John Merrinan, secretary of the Mediation Board, to send the following letter to Randolph:

After . . . full consideration [of] the presentations made by both parties and in view of the facts and circumstances surrounding the situation, it is the judgment of our Board that at this time an emergency . . . does not exist in this case.

and a copy to the Pullman Company, with this covering note:

I take pleasure in herewith forwarding for the information of your Company copy of a letter which I have been instructed to send today to Mr. A. Philip Randolph.

Merrinan's duty—onerous or otherwise—one could well understand. But his pleasure? Did not that suggest, however slightly, the bias of the Mediation Board?

In any case, it meant that President Coolidge was not going to be requested to set up an Emergency Board, and that the way was now cleared for a power confrontation between the Pullman Company and the Brotherhood of Sleeping Car Porters. As it had assured Edward P. Morrow, in March, the company showed itself "perfectly able to take care of the situation." In New York, for instance, according to Brailsford Brazeal, an early historian of the Brotherhood,

the company required a large number of operating porters . . . to remain constantly under call by sleeping in Pullman cars in passenger stations and in the yards, where they received free meals. Extra porters were stationed at the first stops, which the limited trains make when leaving New York City, to be ready to take the places of any strikers who sought to interfere. . . . Provisions were made to have police guard the New York Central and Pennsylvania yards and stations in New York City. . . . Porters were ordered to report to local sign-out offices where they were asked if they intended to strike or continue to work for the company. Naturally, the men questioned said that they intended to remain on their jobs although a large majority had voted to strike; they had no desire to invite reprisals.

But those, apparently, were the kind of porter who was for the union if it succeeded and against it if it failed. Randolph believed that the union was ready and able to "cripple" the New York yards. On a visit to Kansas City, he found Ashley Totten "in a little hole in a Negro business building" collecting sawed-off shotguns, railroad iron taps, boxes of matches, knives, and billy clubs. Alarmed, Randolph asked Totten what he was going to do with "the ammunition." Totten said he wasn't going to let any strikebreakers into the Pullman yards. Randolph had to beg him "to dispense with the hardware." In Chicago, Milton Webster said he expected an 85-per-cent response to the union's call, and out in Oakland, Dad Moore expected 90 per cent. In Oakland, according to C. L. Dellums, the porters were going to "win the strike, no matter what the cost. We were going to put women and children in front of trains. We had about a thousand volunteers from the University of California, and there weren't five Negroes in that university then. They were going with us on the picket lines and were going to set up soup kitchens. Some of the plans we mapped out cannot be told because, well, the trains just weren't going to get very far if they left Oakland."

All this was averted when William Green, president of the American Federation of Labor, advised the Brotherhood to call off the strike. Green had met Randolph in 1926, when the latter unsuccessfully approached the American Federation of Labor to seek affiliation. Green himself had been sympathetic toward the porters' cause, however, and not only had developed a personal admiration for Randolph, but also had been raising his voice in support of the Brotherhood's fight ever since.

The union, Green now told Randolph, was still not strong enough to carry off a strike against a powerful corporation like Pullman. "For obvious reasons," he said, "a strike at this time would play into the hands of the company." Milton Webster, even more so than Randolph, agreed. "It is almost certain," he wrote, explaining the decision to Dad Moore, in Oakland, "that if we actually interrupted commerce . . . they [the Board of Mediation] would have assumed a 'hand off' policy which would have meant that we would have been face to face with the millions of dollars of the Pullman Company. . . . Had we walked into the trap, the organization would have been seriously crippled."

Looking back, more than forty years later, C. L. Dellums was inclined to agree: "There was no question we were going to win in Oakland. We were also going to win in Kansas City, where Totten was. New York and Chicago would have made one hell of a showing, and they might have won. But the rest of the country would have been wiped out, and that way the whole union couldn't have won. We didn't have enough money. In those days, a white man could pick up a telephone and have a Negro arrested. So they would have thrown all the leaders in jail. I doubt we had enough money to get the leaders out of jail the first day of the strike."

Though the chances of their success had been slim from the beginning, the Brotherhood's leaders felt that their strike-threat strategy might still have worked but for the racial bias of the Mediation Board. Ashley Totten was forthright on this point. Noting that the board had failed to follow the precedent it had set in the case of a group of white railroad workers, Totten wrote from Kansas City "to congratulate" the board "for the very splendid work you are doing to adjust grievance of *white* workers on the railroad. The appointment of an emergency board in the case of the Orient & Mexico railroad . . . which has resulted in a settlement was indeed remarkable, since the mere threat of a strike by the latter indicated an emergency which would have seriously interrupted interstate commerce all over the country. Thus the United States Mediation Board, appointed by a Republican administration, is rendering valuable service in the adjustment of disputes between carriers and *white* railroad workers in America."

Randolph shared Totten's view. "No union," he wrote Morrow, "can present any greater evidence of a threat of interruption . . . than the Brotherhood presented; namely, an overwhelming strike vote, with date and hour of strike fixed and announced. Certainly, the Board has no right to go behind the strike vote of the porters and assume that the porters would not strike, that the votes don't mean what they say, because the Company said so." After hurrying to Washington to confront the Mediation Board, Randolph sent the following report to Webster:

I asked when was a condition fraught with danger? They said when it was certain that men would walk out and substantially interrupt interstate commerce. I asked what enabled them to be certain that men would walk out and substantially interrupt interstate commerce? They were then stalled, and hedged. I asked wasn't a strike vote an evidence of this certainty, and the only evidence they could act upon? They said it was a part of the evidence with the Kansas City, Mexico, Orient Road and not with the Brotherhood. They said that the Kansas City . . . was a different situation, as in that case the carrier itself petitioned for the Emergency Board to prevent the men from walking out. . . . Then I asked if the Emergency Board was established only upon petition of carriers. This floored them. They replied, of course not. I asked them if organizations of the travelling public were to petition them for an Emergency Board in our case, would they have set one up? They said that they could not say. . . . It is obvious that the Pullman Company got a man who was big enough to go to Washington and tell that Mediation Board and perhaps the President himself that the Pullman Company was not going to stand for any Emergency Board; that it was going to stir up the Negroes of this country and make them cocky, so that they would feel their power and that this would cause the business interests to have trouble with their Negro workers.

And when, in July, the Mediation Board formally "retired" the case, Randolph wrote them his final opinion of their conduct: "May I say that your decision is not calculated to increase the respect of Negro American citizens for the spirit of fair-play of Government agencies where their interests are involved."

Still, it meant that the Brotherhood had failed again. After almost three years of nursing the porters' hopes, it had no tangible gains to show them. And, having exhausted the procedures of the Railway Labor Act, it had no idea where to turn next. Heavy with a sense that he had let down the porters, and that his and their faith had been betrayed by the Board of Mediation, Randolph said it was "next to the saddest moment" of his life up to then.

The saddest moment had come earlier in the year, in January, 1928, when his brother, James, died of diphtheria, in New York. James, at forty-one, had completed 107 credits toward a bachelor of arts degree at City College, and had planned, after graduation, to enter the University of Berlin, to continue his studies in mathematics and languages. According to a Harlem resident, James "had the reputation of being one of the best-read men in New York." Despite the measure of national renown he had achieved by then, Asa Randolph continued to stand in awe of his elder brother's intellect, and still retained much of the deference he had felt toward James when they were boys in Jacksonville. "I cannot bear to live in a world without my brother," he told a friend in Harlem after James died. And, writing to a friend in St. Paul, Minnesota, he said it was easier to "fight a dozen Pullman Companies" than to overcome his personal loss.

But it was not in Randolph's character, or in the nature of his pledge to the porters, to surrender the struggle against the Pullman Company. Sad though he was, he kept his feelings hidden from his colleagues in the union's leadership. A frequently inscrutable face and an unflappable manner—masks he assumed with ease—enabled him to behave in the presence of awkward or unpleasant situations as if they did not exist. One of his organizers, who found the trait both mystifying and reassuring, said "he could put up a front as if nothing happened." And as for his pledge to the porters, he was committed to an unyielding struggle to "put the Brotherhood over the top." Randolph would need every ounce of that commitment, for the union would now encounter such adversity that at times it seemed not to exist at all, except as a fact of his imagination or—as far as many people could tell—in the form alone of his own tenacity.

No sooner had the strike been called off than the American Negro Labor Congress, a Communist-oriented group established to infiltrate the American labor movement—and led by Randolph's former Socialist colleagues Otto Huiswood, Richard B. Moore, and Lovett Fort-Whiteman—charged the Brotherhood's leadership with selling out the porters to William Green and the American Federation of Labor. "The present leaders of the Brotherhood," the ANLC said—in a flier advertising an anti-Randolph public meeting at St. Luke's Hall, in Harlem— "have followed the trail of Green. They have forsaken the policy of militant struggle in the interest of the workers for the policy of class collaboration with the bosses and bluffing with the strike—with the present result."

Such propaganda, part of a broad campaign to discredit the Brotherhood, was also spread in Chicago and Oakland, two of the stronger divisions of the union outside of New York. In Oakland, old Dad Moore, having no experience of sophisticated Communist strategy, resisted out of what he knew best—loyalty. He wrote Milton Webster, in Chicago:

I was in A meeting of the Communist. The Speaker said it was a clare sell out to Mr. Green. I listen to his talk then I got up and said that I was an old man 75 years old and I Dared eny one in the Sity of Oakland or the State of California to say my hands was tainted with half a penny of bad money. And it went for Mr. Randolph for I would stand by my leader if it cost my life. I told them I would die in the street before I would go against my leader.

Webster wrote back to reassure him:

That group is a group of opportunists who have no apparent destination and according to reports, are supposed to have actually originated in Russia and they are believers of accomplishing the purposes of labor by actual force, that is to say, by fighting. We have an organization here in Chicago and also one in New York of the same group, which have been broadcasting the story that Randolph and Webster sold out the Brotherhood. . . . That is all tommyrot, because Green does not need the Brotherhood and there wouldn't be anything accomplished by selling out to Green. . . . It is simply a ballahoo of a group of opportunists. . . . All these folks want is a chance to raise a roughouse, regardless as to what the merits would be. . . . It is on the members of the Brotherhood that depends its success and not on any daily workers, or communists.

Perhaps Randolph, who knew far more about Communists than Webster did, had not told him that the Communists in the American Negro

Labor Congress were after much more than just "a chance to raise a roughouse"; that what they really had in mind was to take over the Brotherhood, or, failing that, destroy it. "Effective action must be taken at once to strengthen the position of the porters," said the ANLC flier quoted earlier. "Their cause is our cause. Save the union from the bosses attack and the misleaders of labor." What else could that have meant?

Randolph had been alert to Communist designs upon the organized labor movement as early as August, 1923, two years before the founding of the American Negro Labor Congress, when he had written an editorial in the *Messenger* attacking the Communists as a "menace" to labor. And in January, 1927, he had written to Abraham Shiplacoff, chairman of the Committee for the Preservation of the Trade Union Movement: "It is my hope that your vigorous and formidable attacks upon the destructive methods of the Communists, bent upon a rule or ruin policy, at the behest of Moscow, will completely break their power and liberate the trade union movement from their fell clutches."

Now, after the ANLC's attacks upon the Brotherhood, he wrote to advise Webster: "We cannot temporize with the Communist menace. It's a sinister and destructive crowd which will stop at nothing in order to realize its aim, which is to wreck and ruin every organization which is not Communistic. . . . Instruct Brotherhood men who run into Oakland to denounce and condemn the crowd. We shall kill this reptile at the very outset. . . . Everything moves promisingly forward."

Promisingly! If anything in the affairs of the Brotherhood was moving at all, the direction was backward. The Pullman Company, acting—in the wake of its victory—as if it meant now to crush the union once and for all, was firing or suspending every porter who—as far as the company could ascertain—had voted to strike. Thus over the next two or three years, aggravated by the onset of the Depression, the Brotherhood would lose almost all its membership. Porters who did not desert the union because of disappointment, or those who did not abandon it to escape reprisals, simply dropped out because they were unemployed. It was not the first time this had happened, of course, but never before had it happened in such large numbers. By 1932, the union's membership, which had risen to almost 7,000 in the early months of 1928, dropped to 771. Almost every divisional office was deep in debt, and offices had to be closed in Denver, Omaha, Cincinnati, Louisville, Pittsburgh, Columbus, Norfolk, Albany, and Buffalo.

"It has been necessary for us to call upon some of the members for a

loan in order to keep things going" in New York, Randolph wrote Webster. But though the Chicago division remained the strongest—of the
771 members in 1932, Chicago alone had 300—it, too, had serious
financial problems. Webster wrote Randolph, toward the end of 1928,
that if a way could not be found to stop Pullman's reprisals against the
porters, "there is going to be a serious handicap . . . in maintaining an
organization." By 1931, Webster was writing to Spencer Watson, who
had succeeded Ashley Totten as organizer in Kansas City: "I am having
serious difficulty in getting carfare. It was promised from headquarters,
but now I'm informed they haven't got a nickel." A few months later, he
wrote to Watson again: "We are still wrestling with that same question.
What are we going to do for money?"

In August, 1928, the *Messenger* had folded. The disappointed porters
had stopped reading it, and as the union's membership dwindled there
had not been enough money to keep it going. It had also lost its readership among white liberals and radicals, as well as the black middle class.
According to C. L. Dellums, "They couldn't take the *Messenger* any
more. Too much Brotherhood in it." The following year, the *Messenger*
was succeeded by a tabloid newspaper, which appeared irregularly,
called the *Black Worker*. It was not only the new organ of the Brotherhood, but also, as it called itself, "The Mouthpiece of the Negro Workers
of America."

Ashley Totten was recalled to New York, in April, 1929, because, as
Milton Webster once put it, "his head was beaten into a pulp" in Kansas
City. Dellums tells the story:

A couple of thugs ambushed him and beat him down with a loaded billy.
Totten was a powerful man, and even when he fell to his knees, he grabbed
on to the club. But they kicked him loose from it, and he never got over those
blows. They caught him right across the face and knocked out some of his
teeth and fractured both jawbones. He suffered for the rest of his life. His
tongue was never the same, we could always tell it.

A few weeks later, Randolph transferred him to a desk job in the New
York headquarters, where, after being elected a vice president of the
union, he succeeded Roy Lancaster as secretary-treasurer.

Meanwhile, Bennie Smith, in Detroit, was receiving no salary. Milton
Webster had been fired from his job as bailiff and from his Republican
ward leadership in Chicago—for spending too much time with the union.
And E. J. Bradley was practically starving in St. Louis.

During these years, the union was faced with two urgent imperatives: to find money to keep itself alive, and to do something—anything—to show the porters that it was, indeed, alive. In short, survival was now the first priority. Later, if it endured well enough, it could start thinking about victory again. But the Brotherhood's survival, Randolph stressed among his organizers, should be sought only through "honorable means."

Though the union's first national membership campaign had been launched with a grant from the Garland Fund, Randolph now revised his policy toward accepting support from white organizations. The Brotherhood would welcome moral and psychological support, he said, but not financial. Black workers should "pay the price and bear the brunt of their own struggle." As C. L. Dellums reports, "Randolph said Negroes have never put over a major job in this nation without the aid of white men when the effort was sinking. John L. Lewis offered us all kinds of money. He said the Brotherhood must not fail. But we refused to accept his money—at least, Randolph did, for I was ready to take it. He said this was one fight Negroes must win on their own."

Instead, the union organized concerts, picnics, baseball games, and boatrides up the Hudson to raise funds. The New York *Amsterdam News* sponsored fund-raising benefits in Harlem. The handful of determined union members were approached for loans, though only a handful of them had anything to lend. One of them replied to Randolph, "There is such little money coming in, I can only keep my rent and table going." "The average man who had a job," says Dellums, "was so frightened he thought the Depression was hurting him too." Randolph wrote and circulated a weekly news bulletin, in which black businesses in Harlem and Chicago were asked to advertise, and for which porters were to "give something." But despite the poverty of the union, there were certain kinds of advertising Milton Webster, in Chicago, was not about to accept in the bulletin. He wrote to tell Randolph, while the first issue was being prepared, "One undertaker has already asked me if we didn't have something he can advertise in. However, I am not particularly interested in advertising undertakers."

Hoping to raise a contribution of $1,000 from the black Elks, as well as to obtain a political endorsement that might "turn Negro sentiment around," Randolph asked J. Finley Wilson, the Grand Exalted Ruler, for permission to address the Elks' 1929 convention, in Chicago. Wilson—

who, Randolph later learned, was a fraternal politician "who can't be trusted too far"—said he had no objections, but first Randolph would have to join the Elks.

Considering it a small price to pay, Randolph applied for membership, and underwent the rigors of initiation at the Elks Hall in Harlem. It was only then he realized how high the price was. "They made me an Elk all right," he wrote to Webster. "They nearly killed me. I would never go through an ordeal like that again. I am still sore and stiff and can hardly navigate." And no price is so high as that which is exacted for nothing. Despite several letters, Randolph could get no further word from J. Finley Wilson. Had Wilson changed his mind? If so, there could be only one reason, as Randolph wrote to Webster:

I find that in New York an opponent of Mr. Wilson's is going to be put forward, and he comes out of the same lodge I have recently been made an Elk in. Therefore, I assume that Mr. Wilson is perhaps uncertain about having me speak in the Convention because he does not know whether I would support this competitor of his or not. It may be that he may think that it was a conspiracy on the part of the New York Elks to get me in, in order to back this candidate from New York for the Grand Exalted Rulership.

Webster, who knew fraternal politicians the way Randolph knew political radicals, was not surprised at all. "I have never thought so favorably of them, anyhow," he told Randolph. "I don't know as I ought to talk to you about that now since you are an Elk. However, there is more politics in these grand conventions than there are in the Republican and Democratic Parties, and in the final analysis you will find it is simply a grand scramble for favorable positions."

In 1928, the Brotherhood's need for moral and psychological support —and its search for the kind of prestige that might impress the porters— took Randolph, once again, to William Green, president of the American Federation of Labor.

When Randolph had approached Green the first time, early in 1926, to seek affiliation with the AFL, his application had been blocked by the Hotel and Restaurant Employees' Alliance, which claimed jurisdiction over the porters. Sleeping car porters, the Alliance said, were not railroad workers, but merely hotel workers on wheels, and, as such, belonged in a hotel and restaurant union. Sympathetic to this claim, William Green had offered to affiliate with the Brotherhood, but only through the Hotel Alliance. Randolph and Webster had refused. Porters *were* railroad workers, they insisted. They would accept affiliation only on those terms and only under their own leadership. Besides, Webster said, "if we belonged to them, they should not have left us lying around loose so long." One of the reasons the Hotel Alliance had left the porters "lying around loose so long" was that it had a clause in its constitution barring black members. Thus if it was now interested in the porters, it was not because the Alliance was ready to organize them on the basis of equality, but simply because it wanted to preserve its claim on them as potential dues payers, to be organized in a segregated auxiliary union. Nevertheless, the claim of the Hotel Alliance did rest on sound legal grounds. The international charter it had received from the AFL had, in fact, granted it jurisdiction over sleeping car porters.

The impasse could be resolved only by amending the Alliance's AFL charter. And when Randolph reapplied in 1928, William Green did just that, making it possible for the Federation to affiliate with the Brotherhood as an independent union. But since the porters' organization had neither enough members nor enough money to meet the AFL's requirements for an international union, it was accepted into the Federation as a group of thirteen federal locals, under the direct jurisdiction of William Green and the AFL Executive Council. It was something less than what Randolph had wanted—full international status—but, as he told Webster, it was the most the Brotherhood could get at the time, and, in any case, the union had now "demonstrated to the world that we are on a solid foundation and that we are here to stay."

Not all the world saw it that way. Black Communists and black middle-class intellectuals ridiculed the Brotherhood's entry into the AFL. How, they asked, could Randolph accept affiliation with one of the bastions of American race prejudice, an institution that he himself, only a few years earlier, had denounced in the *Messenger* as "the American Separation of Labor" and "the most wicked machine for the propagation of race prejudice in the country"? Randolph replied that he had, indeed, attacked the AFL's policies of racial exclusion, but now that an opportunity had come for him to fight those policies within the AFL it would be foolish not to accept. It was true that the record of the Brotherhood inside the AFL would be one of relentless opposition to race bigotry. Yet when he entered, in 1929, that had not been Randolph's predominant motive. Nothing was so important to him then as saving the union's life; and, as it appeared, affiliation with the AFL was one of the best ways of doing so. The Brotherhood in the AFL would no longer be a lonely collection of black porters crying forlornly in the wilderness of American corporate power, but, rather, a union that was part of the organized labor movement, and, therefore, entitled to its moral and political backing.

Milton Webster's reply—a few years later—to the critics of the Brotherhood's relationship with the AFL was, in its pragmatic directness, as effective as any Randolph had given:

You can get an eight-column write-up any day about the prejudice of the American Federation of Labor. . . . Those who are so loud in their condemnation of the prejudice in the AFL . . . condone that same prejudice in other institutions in the United States. . . . You will find in the universities and schools of the nation the same prejudice that you find in the AFL. Everybody wants to get into Harvard, Yale, and Princeton where that same prejudice is. Nobody says we should not participate in these things because there's prejudice there. . . . Now the American Federation of Labor is a typical American institution . . . and anytime we have an American institution composed of white people there is prejudice in it. . . . In America, if we should stay out of everything that's prejudiced we wouldn't be in anything.

Exploiting its new prestige as a member of the organized labor movement, the Brotherhood embarked upon a number of activities designed to enhance its standing in the eyes of the porters. In 1929, it called its first national convention, in Chicago, where it hammered out a constitution, set up a formal chain of command, and held its first election of officers. Randolph was elected president; Webster, first vice president; Ashley Totten, Bennie Smith, S. E. Grain, E. J. Bradley, Paul Caldwell, and C. L. Dellums, vice presidents—second through seventh, respectively; and Roy Lancaster, secretary-treasurer.

Though the union was still practically broke, it was necessary, Randolph said, to do something to demonstrate to the porters that the organization was on "sound footing," and to provide some "evidence of permanency." Thus mortgages were obtained in Chicago and New York on permanent headquarters for the Brotherhood.

And since, as Randolph believed, "high-powered propaganda can make people believe the devil is Jesus Christ," the Brotherhood would have to speak and act boldly. Webster, he wrote to Chicago, should talk up the Brotherhood's alliance with the AFL "for all it's worth." Nor, despite its lack of funds, could the union afford to seem cheap. Its public-relations activities should appear expensive, down to the quality of paper the union used for its letterheads. "Good quality paper," Randolph told Webster, "may cost a little more, but experienced advertising experts attest that it pulls results. The public does not give much consideration to anything that looks cheap, regardless of its merits. . . . The psychology of the public is that it only thinks a thing is big if it is done in a big way."

To all this, Randolph added his usual inspirational appeals to the porters: "The lesson that Pullman porters in particular and Negroes in general must learn is that salvation must and can only come from within." Ashley Totten pitched in: "Those of us who have read American history know that when the US finished the War of Revolution the people were ragged, the wives and children were barefoot, the homes had not even window panes to keep out the cold; but America had her independence just the same."

None of it seemed to work. The union's membership continued to dwindle, even when, in desperation, entrance fees were lowered from $5 to $3. By 1933, Chicago, with 250 members, still had almost half the entire membership of the Brotherhood—and it was mainly upon the slight income from this division that the union would subsist through the darkest days of its and the country's depression.

In Oakland, there were just eighty members. And Dad Moore, who had pledged to "fite to the finish" and to stick with the Brotherhood "until Deth carry me to my last Restin place," had died, in January, 1930. In one of his last letters to Milton Webster, he had written:

My back is against the wal but I will Die betore I will Back up one inch. I am fiting not for myself but for 12,000 porters and maids, and there children. . . . I has bin at Starvasian Door but it had not change my mind, for just as the night follows the Day we are gointer win. Tell all the men in your Dist that they should follow Mr. Randolph as they would follow Jes Christ.

"We have received no greater inspiration in our lives," Randolph had said in eulogy, "than from the life and spirit of Dad Moore."

The leadership of the Oakland division had passed into the hands of C. L. Dellums, the young man whom Dad Moore had once praised to Webster as "a square shooter," whom he had personally selected as his successor and had pushed into a vice presidency at the 1929 convention in Chicago. Dellums was a battler from a different mold. Unlike Dad Moore's, or even Randolph's, his style was not to resist with quiet and indomitable will, but to blast away at his enemies; not to cling to principle with an unbreakable grip, but to flail away in defense of it, with his fists, if necessary—like the "roughneck" he liked to call himself. Light-skinned and powerfully built, Dellums had a large, shiny, and formidable head, flashing eyes, a toothbrush mustache, and a severe, unsmiling face that could look—when he wanted—as truculent as a clenched fist. Unlike Randolph, say, he was not spun from gossamer, but cut from the rough canvas of men like Ashley Totten and Milton Webster.

In St. Louis, by 1933, hardly anything was left of E. J. Bradley's division. He was evicted from his headquarters, on North Jefferson Avenue, and his office records were thrown away and the furniture sold to meet his back rent. "I notified our Chicago office," he recalled later, "that I would not be able to carry the rent and other expenses of the local any longer. The international office advised me to close up St. Louis permanently. . . . I refused . . . because that would have shown weakness in St. Louis, and if we closed the Pullman Company would feel that it had won a signal victory. . . . By late 1933, I was flat broke, and my wife put me out."

On a visit to St. Louis, about this time, Milton Webster found Bradley without "a nickel to pay car fare." He had lost even the automobile that he had used, for a while, as his office. According to Ulas Crowder, of the Brotherhood's office in Chicago, "They took away Bradley's car in payment of debt. After that he was carrying his office around in his pocket. He lost his two homes, and his wife quit him when he couldn't support her. He had mortgaged the houses to support the Brotherhood. He lived with his daughter and anybody who would put him up. Bradley was a good quail shooter, and that's what he ate off for many days. He used to say the last thing he would give up was his shotgun. And he damn near lost everything, including his shotgun." Recognizing such sacrifices, the Brotherhood's leadership would later refer to Bradley as "the noblest Roman of them all."

In New York, when the Brotherhood was unable to maintain the mortgage payments on its new headquarters, at 239 West 136th Street, it, too, was evicted, and its office records and furniture thrown out into the streets. Benjamin McLaurin, who had moved to New York from Chicago, was now an organizer in the New York office. He recalls:

I picked up the pieces and moved into an apartment on 140th Street. There were five rooms in this apartment and we used the two front rooms for offices. I lived in one room, and we used the kitchen and the dining room for recreation, on weekends. I promoted a weekly rent party, to get money to pay rent. It was the only income we had. . . . We used to go from house to house holding rent parties. I had learned to cook somewhere . . . and Saturday mornings I spent preparing food and most of the day cooking. I cooked chitterlings and pigs feet. They were the best things. I used to cook a hundred pounds of chitterlings, plenty of stew and potato salad. . . . I cooked so much of that stuff that it nauseates me now, I don't want to be around if anybody is cooking it. I could bake, and we had pastry and foods of that kind. It was on this income, for two years at least, that we kept the headquarters together. We couldn't hire stenographers. Everybody had to do his own typing. . . . There were many days when we didn't know where the next mouthful was coming from. But it wasn't important. We would live on a bottle of milk and a loaf of bread. Chicago was in the best financial condition, and Webster did his best to keep the wolf away from the door. . . . If Brother Randolph had to make a trip somewhere and there wasn't but ten dollars, the trip came first. And if we had to have stamps and stationery, that's where the money went. Many days Randolph left the office to go to the Public Library to research an article, and he had to come back to the office because he didn't have enough car fare.

O. W. Bynum, a porter who had joined the New York office as an organizer when he was fired for his prounion leanings, remembered that "one Christmas Totten didn't even have carfare to visit his wife and children out in Queens. He and I slept in the office, on Randolph's desk, the one he had brought over from the *Messenger*. We spread newspapers on it for a mattress and slept there that Christmas. It was the one time I saw a grown man cry. Totten just broke down and cried."

The New York office continued to subsist on the results of Benjamin McLaurin's rent parties; scraps from the lean table of Webster's Chicago division; donations from sympathizers in Harlem; and loans and gifts from the handful of men who remained fiercely loyal to the Brotherhood. Two such men were R. R. Matthews and Thomas Patterson, who had helped found the union in 1925. Porters still speak with pride of the day when Matthews, having run out of ready cash, took off his gold watch and diamond ring, and pawned them to help the Brotherhood out of an emergency. Between 1929 and 1933, Patterson is said to have loaned the union more than $2,000 out of his savings. Patterson, who named one of his sons after Randolph, was as devoted to the Brotherhood's president as he was to the union. In 1933, says McLaurin, when "the bread-bin was pretty low" in the Randolphs' apartment, Patterson took extra runs between New York and Chicago, and used part of the income to buy groceries for the Randolphs.

This was necessary partly because Randolph's salary from the union was only $10 a week—sometimes less, and sometimes nothing—and partly because his wife, who had once been the breadwinner of the household, now had little or no income of her own. Her once thriving beauty-parlor business—which had declined after the war, because of her husband's reputation as a radical—had completely collapsed.

Though Randolph did not seem to mind the deterioration in his appearance, the porters and organizers, who were used to admiring him as a "sharp dresser," were now embarrassed to observe, as McLaurin says, that "he had no soles on his shoes. He couldn't afford to buy any clothes. Like many of us, he just went from what he had to rags. There were so many patches on his pants he didn't know where to put the next patch. He used to love his blue serge suit, which was the best thing he had, but he wore it so long that it began to shine like a looking glass." Samuel Harper, of the Jacksonville division, says that "one night, when he was going to speak, two men went out and bought him two shirts when they saw how soiled his shirt was. He knew you saw his condition, but it didn't seem to be important to him. But those men said, 'We ain't going to let him speak with that shirt on.'" C. L. Dellums saw much the same thing when Randolph went out to Oakland: "He came out sometimes with just his fare, one way. He had nothing else. He did not even have a change of socks or underwear. Sometimes he would sleep at my house, and my wife would look around for his socks and his underwear, and she wouldn't see any. Later on, when she went into the bathroom, she would see his socks and underwear all washed and hanging up to dry. And his shirts were frayed around the collar. But he still had that dignified bearing; he didn't care what his clothes looked like."

After he became mayor of New York City, Fiorello La Guardia, who had known Randolph when they were both Socialists, offered him a job with the city government, at a salary of $7,000 a year. According to McLaurin, "La Guardia said, 'Phil, you have holes in your shoes. It will take a lifetime to organize the porters. Take a job with the city. You need to eat and pay your rent. You can carry out your organizing activities while you work for the city.' But Randolph turned the job down. He said he already had a job."

By 1933, as far as the public could tell—and where the majority of porters were concerned—the Brotherhood was dead. In fact, its obituary had already been written—two years earlier, when Sterling Spero and Abram L. Harris said in *The Black Worker,* their book on the Negro and the labor movement: "The great pity of the virtual collapse of the porters union lies not merely in its effect upon porters who have grievances which sorely need correction but in its effect upon Negro labor generally. The hope that this movement would become the center and rallying point of Negro labor as a whole is now dead." Dellums himself, recalling the dark night of the struggle, says today that "there seemed no way to win."

But in Randolph's imagination the union and its cause were as alive as ever. His health impaired and—if he was human at all—in touch with despair, Randolph kept declaring that "nothing can keep us from winning." To people who lived by the evidence of their eyes, it must have sounded like madness, for there was little or no sign of life in the Brotherhood of Sleeping Car Porters.

14 / Then Came the New Deal

And then Roosevelt came along, started the New Deal, and they started passing laws. ——C. L. DELLUMS

Though Randolph's union was probably the shakiest in America during the early thirties, it was not the only one that had been thwarted by company unions, or retarded by the failure of the Railway Labor Act to guarantee the right to collective bargaining.

Despite the hopes it had raised in 1926, the encouragement its language had given to the prospects of self-organization, the Labor Act had seemed, in the end, to be more helpful to railroad managements than to workers. As the Brotherhood had found, the Railway Labor Act, while it provided for the arbitration of disputes, lacked sufficient teeth to compel management to come to the arbitration table. In the words of a member of the Mediation Board, the Railway Labor Act was "as full of holes . . . as Swiss cheese." Thus in 1932, six years after the passage of the act, workers in 147 of the 233 largest railroad enterprises were still formally represented by company unions, or plans of employee representation. The American Federation of Labor itself had become disenchanted with the act, and, as William Green had told Randolph, was waiting for a favorable opportunity to press for its amendment. That opportunity came in 1932, when, with the strong support of organized labor, Franklin D. Roosevelt was elected president.

Soon after Roosevelt took office, Donald Richberg—general counsel of the railroad unions, and one of the architects of the Railway Labor Act—called a group of labor executives together in Washington to discuss possible legislation to "strengthen the right of self-organization and the power of collective bargaining as already provided in the Railway

Labor Act." And when, not long after, the President appointed a committee to draft legislation for a national recovery program, Donald Richberg, along with the results of his meeting with the labor executives, was included. Thus, as the representative of the railroad union interests, Richberg would be largely responsible for one of the most important sections of the national industry recovery bill, which the committee drafted.

That was Section 7a, plainly stating that "employees shall have the right to organize and bargain collectively through representatives of their own choosing and shall be free from the interference, restraint, or coercion of employers of labor, or their agents, in the designation of such representatives or in self-organization . . . no employee and no one seeking employment shall be required as a condition of employment to join any company union or to refrain from joining, organizing, or assisting a labor organization of his own choosing." These provisions became the law when the National Industrial Recovery Act was passed, and were also included in the Emergency Railroad Transportation Act—which specifically banned company unions and yellow-dog contracts. Together they constituted one of the most impressive victories railroad unions—and the labor movement in general—had ever won. The *New York Times* saw labor as having jumped into "sudden power." William Green, head of the AFL, considered it labor's Magna Charta. And John L. Lewis described it as the emancipation proclamation of the organized working-class movement.

Re-energized by what others called Roosevelt's legislative revolution, the labor movement—including the Brotherhood of Sleeping Car Porters —launched the most vigorous organizational campaign in its history, founding new unions and rebuilding shattered memberships. By mid-1933, porters were flocking back to the Brotherhood, as Randolph, waving the promises of the National Industrial Recovery Act and the Emergency Railroad Transportation Act, assured them that victory was now near, that the Brotherhood had finally "licked" the Pullman Company. Still, triumph would remain elusive.

Randolph now wrote the Pullman Company again: "As the duly authorized representatives of the majority of the porters and maids, the Brotherhood of Sleeping Car Porters requests a conference to negotiate an agreement on wages and rules governing working conditions . . . in conformity with the principles promulgated by the Railway Labor Act, the Railway Emergency Act and the general program . . . outlined under the National Recovery Act." Once again, as with every letter he had written to Pullman since September, 1926, he got no reply.

Taking the next logical step, Randolph called upon Joseph B. Eastman, co-ordinator of railroad transportation, to intervene and enforce the Emergency Railroad Transportation Act. But Pullman must have realized all along what Randolph now learned from Eastman: as defined by the ERTA, the Pullman Company was not a railroad, but a common carrier; thus the emergency legislation applied neither to the Pullman Company nor to its sleeping car porters.

The news came like an explosion in Randolph's face. What it meant was that the Brotherhood had been let down again—this time not by Republican bureaucrats, such as those who ran the Mediation Board under Calvin Coolidge and Herbert Hoover, but by Randolph's own friends in organized labor. In all the definitions, recommendations, and demands that Donald Richberg and the labor movement had had written into the emergency acts, the plight of sleeping car porters had been either overlooked or ignored—despite the fact that for almost a decade it was the porters' struggle that had focused attention most dramatically upon the inequities of the company union and the inadequacies of the Railway Labor Act. In the words of men like Benjamin McLaurin, the Brotherhood had been sold out in Washington.

Eastman, however, was sympathetic to the position in which Randolph now found himself, and offered to co-operate with any effort the Brotherhood cared to make to seek changes in the emergency railroad legislation. Encouraged by Eastman's promise, Randolph wrote to President Roosevelt and to friends of the Brotherhood on Capitol Hill, protesting the exclusion of the Pullman Company and its sleeping car porters from the provisions of the railroad legislation. And at the fifty-third annual convention of the AFL, in Washington, D.C., he called upon the Federation to urge President Roosevelt "to issue an Executive Order interpreting the Emergency Railroad Transportation Act, 1933, to include within its scope sleeping car companies, thereby correcting a situation that results in the Pullman Company occupying a favored status."

Embarrassed by Randolph's demands, railroad labor executives—as well as officials within the administration—threw their weight behind the Brotherhood's efforts to rectify the omissions, and, early in 1934, the Senate's Interstate Commerce Committee opened hearings, with a view to amending the Emergency Railroad Transportation Act and the Railway Labor Act. During the hearings, twenty-one railroad unions urged that the acts be changed to include "sleeping car and express companies." According to C. L. Dellums, the railroad unions backed the Brotherhood only because "they couldn't let this Negro [Randolph] lead a fight and get the credit for strengthening the Railway Labor Act. But we needed the help and we needed the law, and we didn't give a damn about credit. We let them take it and go with it because they had the power to put it over and we didn't."

One of the strongest supporters of the Brotherhood on the Interstate Commerce Committee was its chairman, Senator Clarence C. Dill, of Washington. Dill wanted to go even further than the proposed amendments. Reacting to the Pullman Company's practice of hiring Japanese and Filipinos to replace union porters, Dill had introduced a bill in the Senate, as early as March, 1933, "to require the employment of American citizens in observation cars, club cars, and sleeping cars used by railroad in inter-state commerce." But that was more than Randolph wanted. "Personally," he wrote Walter White, of the NAACP, "I am opposed to any exclusion legislation based on race, creed, nationality, or color."

Despite Pullman's argument that it was more "an innkeeper" than a railroad enterprise—and thus had been properly exempted from the emergency legislation—the ERTA and the Railway Labor Act were amended. "The term 'carrier,' " the amendments now said, "includes any express company, sleeping car company, carrier by railroad, subject to the Interstate Commerce Act. . . . The term 'employee' as used herein includes every person in the service of a carrier."

Suspecting that it was about to lose the long battle against Randolph's union, the Pullman Company suddenly started laying off hundreds of porters, especially those whose loyalty to the company was in doubt— wanting to lessen the number of porters trooping back to the Brotherhood. And still hoping, within the letter of the new law, to frustrate its spirit, the company hand-picked a few loyal porters and authorized them to form their own "independent" union, the Pullman Porters Protective Association, as a legal alternative to the Brotherhood. Since the NIRA forbade companies to contribute to the upkeep of any union, Pullman allowed the Protective Association to charge its own monthly dues, a mere twenty-five cents—"as though," Randolph observed, "any national labor union could conduct its business on such a meager income." The Protective Association was, in fact, another glorified company union— controlled by porters who were controlled by Pullman. Randolph had a few other words for it: "a mushroom sprung fully grown out of the fertile soil of Pullman gold." So did Brotherhood members, who referred to the Protective Association as "the voice of Jacob but the hand of Esau."

On November 13, 1934, Randolph wrote to the president of the Pullman Company again, requesting a conference, and, for the first time since 1926, received a reply. It was not the one he had hoped for, however. The Brotherhood was not "the duly authorized representative" of the porters, F. L. Simmons—the company's supervisor of industrial relations—wrote. Therefore, "there is no occasion for a conference with you." What Simmons meant, no doubt, was that it was the Pullman Porters Protective Association which was "the duly authorized representative" of the porters, and not the Brotherhood.

When Randolph now wrote to the Board of Mediation pointing out that the Brotherhood was the porters' authorized representative—under the amended railroad acts—the Pullman Porters Protective Association entered a similar claim in its own behalf. To resolve the conflicting claims, the Board of Mediation ordered a secret ballot, and from May 27 to June 27, 1935—almost ten years after the Brotherhood had begun its fight for recognition—porters voted in sixty-six Pullman terminals around the country.

Victory for the Brotherhood was by no means just around the corner, but it was nearer now than ever. And, sensing this, Randolph wrote to the NAACP's Walter White, during the balloting:

This is the first time that Negro workers have had the opportunity to vote as a national group in an election, under federal supervision, for their economic rights. It is an extraordinary occasion. It is the result of 10 years of militant, determined and courageous fighting by a small band of black workers against one of the most powerful corporations in the world. It may be interesting for you to know that on the Pullman Board sit J. P. Morgan, R. K. Mellon, Alfred P. Sloan, George F. Baker, Harold S. Vanderbilt, George Whitney, and others. These men rule Wall Street, America and practically the world of capitalist finance and industry. And yet the Brotherhood of Sleeping Car Porters has, in the face of nameless opposition and terror, stood its ground through one of the worst depressions ever witnessed in America, and has come to the point where it has caused a national election to be called to determine the organization the porters really want. . . . This election . . . will mark an historic point in the efforts of the Negro workers in the trade union movement. . . . The porters . . . are the vanguard of the black workers of America.

When the ballots were counted—on the night of June 27, in the Consumers Building, in Chicago—89 were void, 1,422 had been cast for the Pullman Porters Protective Association, and 8,316 for the Brotherhood of Sleeping Car Porters. Randolph exulted once more to Walter White, in a telegram: "First victory of Negro workers over great industrial corporation." And, on July 1, the Mediation Board finally certified the Brotherhood as "duly designated and authorized to represent the porters and maids of the Pullman Company."

This time, Randolph heard from L. S. Hungerford, general manager of the Pullman Company: "This company is agreeable to meeting in conference, for discussion of the question of an agreement concerning rates of pay, rules and working conditions of its porters, with the duly authorized representatives of your organization." "No labor leadership in America has faced greater odds," wrote Elmer Carter in the August, 1935, issue of the Urban League's *Opportunity* magazine. "None has won a greater victory."

At ten o'clock on the morning of July 29, 1935, New York's Randolph, Chicago's Milton Webster, Detroit's Bennie Smith, St. Louis's E. J. Bradley, Oakland's C. L. Dellums, and two operating porters—Thomas Patterson and Clarence Kendrick—walked into Room 412 of the Pullman headquarters, on Adams Street, in Chicago. It was, understandably, their finest moment in ten years. They had forced the proud Pullman Company to do what one of their detractors had said the company would never do: sit down around the same table with "a bunch of black porters."

Yet it must also have been a frightening moment for them. What did they know about bargaining? They knew quite well what they wanted; but did they know how to get it, or whether they would be equal to "the high-priced brains"—as one of them put it—who would be sitting across the table from them? Ten years of fighting in the streets, so to speak, had made them some of the toughest guerrillas of the labor struggle. Only Randolph had ever set foot in a college classroom; only he and Thomas Patterson knew how to turn a fine sentence; and none of them, except Randolph, had ever sat around a table with "high-priced brains." In Benjamin McLaurin's words, "We had no experience with high finance, we didn't know what a million dollars was like." "Here," says Dellums, "was this handful of guys around Randolph. None of us was prepared, none had any special training, none really educated. But here we were around this wonderful man."

As it turned out, their lack of polish was their greatest strength. And there were no better symbols of this strength than Milton Webster, "the strongman of the Brotherhood," who could growl like a bulldog in the face of any man, and C. L. Dellums, whose light-skinned face could redden at the mere suspicion of provocation, and who could wield home-spun repartee with the truculence of a club in a dark alley. These men were never so at home as in situations that called for the "rough stuff." * In such talents, of course, their leader was spectacularly deficient. His role during the negotiations would be to orchestrate the instruments at his disposal: to rein tongues like Webster's and Dellums's—when that seemed in the urgent interest of the proceedings—and to unleash them when his own softer passages evoked no response.

Anyway, it would take them two long years to negotiate an agreement with Pullman. As Webster said, "The company was messing around, handing it to us line by line. We couldn't get a full paragraph. We had a thousand sheets of paper with two lines on it." Pullman, says Benjamin McLaurin, "just could not conceive of Negroes sitting across the table talking to them as equals. It took months and months to get by that stumbling block." Before that stumbling block could be passed, the Brotherhood had to break off negotiations. On October 4, 1935, after weeks of angry exchanges, Randolph and his men walked out of the Pullman headquarters, and referred the dispute back to the Mediation Board.

Entering the case the following day, the board ordered mediation to begin on January 23, 1936. But the company had reasons for stalling,

---

* When Webster substituted for Randolph at the Catholic Industrial Conference in Cincinnati, in 1928, he prepared a speech, for the first time in his life. "Having heard Brother Randolph speak many times," he said later, "I thought since I was going to represent him I ought to prepare something pretty good. I spent a couple of weeks getting stuff together, including some poetry." But when Webster arrived on the platform and saw a Pullman superintendent among the guest speakers, it looked to him, he said, "like the Company is mixed up in this thing." Then "a high-powered lawyer . . . got up and made a speech on the constitution, and then read from a written draft, in which he said, 'experience teaches us that the Company union form of organization is the best for the Negro.' I took that speech I had prepared for two weeks and tore it up. I said to myself, this doesn't call for any speech. It calls for the same old rough stuff. So I have never attempted to prepare a speech since that time."

and informed the board that because of other negotiations at that time it would be unable to comply. Knowing how frequently porters had deserted the Brotherhood in the past, Pullman believed that a long delay in the negotiations would cause the porters to become impatient again, forcing the Brotherhood to withdraw the case from mediation and take whatever offer the company was willing to make. The constitutionality of the amended Railway Labor Act was also being tested in the courts, and if the amendments were declared unconstitutional, then the status of the Brotherhood would revert to what it had been previously, thus making it unnecessary for the company to continue negotiating with the union.

When, several months after its initial refusal, the Pullman Company decided to go along with the mediation proceedings—though only half-heartedly, since the courts still had not ruled upon the amended Railway Labor Act—its representatives behaved so contemptuously that once even Randolph lost his renowned self-control. C. L. Dellums recalls it:

[E. G] Carry was just about as vulgar as a drunken sailor on the water front, and when he would come into the conference room he would rear back and he would vulgarly prop his foot up against the table and he'd start his vulgarity. And here is Brother Randolph, this man who was having a hard time saying "hell," and a man I have never seen angry. But one day he and Carry got at it. Carry is shaking his finger about twenty feet away; he's shaking his finger at Randolph, and he's cursing, and he's raising hell; and Randolph had his fist doubled up, and he's shaking it back at Carry. Carry is all red, and I don't know what color the Chief [Randolph] is any more. But he was boiling over. And finally, he looked around at me and said, "C. L., did you want to make an observation?" But I knew what he meant. He meant that this baby [Carry] needs some cursing now, and the Chief couldn't do it. And he knew that was right down my alley. Well, I gave it to that Carry. I gave it to him so good that two minutes later the mediator broke up the meeting.

When the mediator adjourned the meeting, the Brotherhood men refused to return. "We got tired," Webster said. "We told them, 'We've been here long enough. We are going to take a strike vote.' We had strike ballots printed. We distributed them to every district, and told them to await the order, and all the members of our negotiating committee went back to their respective homes. The mediator handling the case came out. . . . He said, 'You know, Mr. Carry is quite concerned about this strike vote. He said if you people don't come back there and get together on this thing, he is going to tell the porters that they can get two million dollars a year increase, and you are standing in the way.' I said, 'Since you brought a message you can go back and tell Mr. Carry we don't give a damn what he does. We are going to do what we want to do.' "

It was about this time, while Randolph was back in New York, that a story started circulating that the Pullman Company had sent him a blank check, redeemable in six figures, to abandon the Brotherhood. Today, only one man declares that the story is true. Randolph himself has neither admitted nor denied it, perhaps because—as Roy Wilkins once said, while telling the story at an affair in Randolph's honor—"Mr. Randolph is a modest man." C. L. Dellums says, "It is one of those stories you can't publish, because everyone would deny it." The man who says it's true is William Bowe, a charter member of the New York Brotherhood, who succeeded Ashley Totten as secretary-treasurer. Bowe knows it's true, he says, because "I was present at the attempt to purchase Randolph." It was, he recalls, "in the Harlem apartment of a porter named Owens. There were four of us there. Owens, Randolph, the porter stool pigeon who brought the check, and myself. Randolph had me hiding in another room. The stool pigeon, a porter working out of Philadelphia—I won't call his name—didn't know I was witnessing the transaction. He gave Randolph the check and told him all he had to do was fill in the amount. And Randolph, with his poker face, said, 'Take this blank check back to where you got it and tell them I'm not for sale.' " Randolph confines himself to the comment that "it was a feat to avoid being corrupted by the Pullman Company, because those fellows could corrupt Jesus Christ."

But, as one of the Brotherhood's organizers—O. W. Bynum—has said, recalling what every union porter felt at the time, "Randolph could not be bought. He had no interest in worldly goods. He would walk away from the Empire State Building if you gave it to him." Then, too, aside from his genuine disregard for "worldly goods," Randolph—as he had written in an internal office memo, in 1931—considered "the Brotherhood a high public and racial trust and I propose that its work shall always be conducted upon a high plane of honor, integrity and character."

It was not until April 1, 1937, three days after the Supreme Court had upheld the constitutionality of the amended Railway Labor Act, that the Pullman Company started bargaining in good faith. And it was not until August 25—the twelfth anniversary of the Brotherhood—that E. G. Carry announced to the mediator and the Brotherhood's negotiators,

"Gentlemen, the Pullman Company is ready to sign." The agreement, the first ever signed between a union of black workers and a major American corporation, called for a reduction in the work month from 400 to 240 hours, and an annual wage package of $1,250,000.

E. G. Carry may not have realized that August 25 was the union's birthday, or, as the Brotherhood men suspected, he would have held out another day. Nevertheless, after twelve years of one of the bitterest struggles in American labor history, the Brotherhood of Sleeping Car Porters had finally been recognized.

Almost overnight, Randolph became the most popular black political figure in America. A year earlier, the Brotherhood had become a full-fledged member of the AFL when, anticipating its victory, William Green had awarded it an international charter. After the union's victory, New York's Mayor Fiorello La Guardia, receiving a delegation of porters at City Hall, praised Randolph as "one of the foremost progressive labor leaders in America." And a few years later, the Brotherhood would help to win for blacks a place in American society that the Pullman porter of old had not known and could hardly have foreseen.

V / New Masses

It wasn't so many years ago that Brother Randolph and I could walk from 145th Street to 125th Street and nobody would say a word to us. Now Brother Randolph starts to go to his office and he is stopped a half-dozen times. . . . Everybody wants in on us now. We are riding the crest of the wave. So many people on the platform the other Sunday, it was about to break down. And so hot up there. Everybody sweating to death. People we never heard of before want to sit on the Brotherhood platform. They took us down to the Waldorf Astoria, a hotel that I have just been passing by for the last twenty years. Had everything from Coca-Cola to champagne on the house. —MILTON P. WEBSTER

There was no other group of Negroes in America who constituted the key to unlocking the door of a nationwide struggle for Negro rights as the porters. Without the porters I couldn't have carried on the fight for fair employment, or the fight against discrimination in the armed forces. —A. PHILIP RANDOLPH

15 / The Red and the Black

Since the collapse of Garveyism, in the mid-1920's, there had been nothing resembling a black mass movement in America. But signs of a new one—though quite different in character and purpose from black nationalism—had begun to appear in the late 1930's. And when, by 1941, it had emerged fully, in the form of an economic mass movement, there was probably more than a little irony in the fact that the main source of its leadership and sustenance was the once passive and despised Pullman sleeping car porter.

In May, 1935, a conference on the "economic status of the Negro" was held at Howard University, cosponsored by the university's division of social sciences and an organization called the Joint Committee on National Recovery. The idea for the conference had originated with Ralph Bunche, chairman of Howard's department of political science, and John P. Davis, executive secretary of the Joint Committee on National Recovery—formed in 1933 to represent the interests of black workers before the agencies of the New Deal.

The Howard conference found that there was a need for a closer collaboration among the existing black organizations—political, fraternal, and religious—and a need, as well, for a central organization to articulate the broad objectives of the racial struggle. It was decided, therefore, to form a National Negro Congress. It would not, the founders agreed, replace or duplicate the work of any existing organization, but would "give strength and support" to all the progressive programs of all the black groups. John P. Davis was appointed national secretary, and among the prominent black leaders around the country whose support he enlisted were Lester Granger and Elmer Carter, of the National Urban League; Alain Locke, of Howard University; James A. Bray, R. A. Car-

ter, and W. J. Wells, black churchmen; M. O. Bousfield, of the Rosen-
wald Fund; and A. Philip Randolph, of the Brotherhood of Sleeping Car
Porters. Replying to Davis, Randolph praised the idea of a National
Negro Congress, and promised his support "in any way possible."

The first meeting of the Congress took place in the Eighth Regiment
Armory, in Chicago, on February 14, 15, and 16, 1936. There were 817
delegates from 585 political, fraternal, religious, and labor organizations, and more than 5,000 visitors, including a large number of white
Communist sympathizers.

A week before the Congress opened, the presiding committee, headed
by the Reverend Adam Clayton Powell, Jr., had drafted Randolph as its
first president. This was in recognition not only of what Davis called
Randolph's "brilliant victory" over the Pullman Company,* but also of
the fact that he had become by then the most widely known spokesman
for black working-class interests in the country.

Randolph was then ill at home. The long struggle against the Pullman
Company had left him in poor health, and he was suffering from a respir-
atory infection, a fever of 103 degrees, diseased tonsils, chronic laryngi-
tis, and a persistent cough. Dr. George Baehr, of Mount Sinai Hospital,
had recommended a tonsillectomy, and had cautioned Randolph against
the abuse of his vocal cords and too much public speaking. Still, at forty-
six, he was, as Dr. Baehr noted in a consultation report, "a well developed and well nourished man." His body, slender through most of his
life, had begun to broaden and flesh out; and his eyes—though their
early mixture of diffidence and optimism had given way to a trace of
melancholy—mirrored an inner calm, in a face that retained the youthful
appearance of a man in his early thirties.

Randolph wired the Congress that, because of illness, he was unable
to accept the presidency. That was not the only reason, however; it was
simply the easiest to explain. He was still tied down in tough negotiations
with the Pullman Company over a contract for the porters. And while his
colleagues in the union, especially Webster, had made it clear they would
not impose their wishes upon him, they were not at all in favor of his
dividing his attentions between the Brotherhood and what they called
"outside organizations." But one of the executive members of the Na-

---

* A reference to the jurisdictional ballot in June, 1935, after which the Brotherhood was certified as "duly designated and authorized" to represent the porters.

tional Negro Congress was Charles Wesley Burton, a personal friend of Randolph's, and one of the few black Chicagoans who had supported the Brotherhood from its inception. Urging Randolph to change his mind, Burton assured him that illness was not a serious obstacle, since it was not absolutely necessary for him to come to Chicago in order to accept the presidency of the Congress. Randolph then decided to accept.

Despite his initial reluctance, there was nothing—next to the presidency of the Brotherhood—that Randolph would have liked more at the time than the presidency of the National Negro Congress. Throughout the struggle against Pullman, he had regarded the Brotherhood as not merely a labor organization, but the vanguard of a black political movement. The presidency of the Congress—which, among other objectives, was pledged to organizing black workers in industrial unions—was attractive not only because he could use the office as a mouthpiece for organizing black workers, but also because the NNC itself would be an expression of the collective black political will. George S. Schuyler, a conservative today, and no longer reverent in his feelings about Randolph, has attributed an even vainer motive: "Randolph had never quite been accepted by the NAACP Brahmins up to that time, and he was panting for leadership."

It was not all vanity, however. It was true he held a rather high estimate of himself as a spokesman—one of the things, no doubt, upon which leadership feeds—and it may or may not have been true that he felt insufficiently recognized by the NAACP elite. But he seems also to have been deeply committed to what he felt his leadership of the NNC might achieve. Then, of course, there were others—the NNC's presiding committee included—who felt that he was the best man to lead the organization. As Claude McKay said in the late 1930's, of Randolph's capacity to lead broad coalitions:

. . . more than any other Negro leader, [he] has a comprehensive understanding of the vast conquests of modern industry and the grand movement of labor to keep abreast of it. And he is aware that the Negro group is in a special position and has a special force. His outlook remains unblurred by passion and prejudice. He takes a long, balanced view of men and affairs. He could not be tagged with radical,* chauvinist, nationalist, or reactionary labels, or with any other slanderous names such as the Communists and the

---

* By "radical," McKay probably meant Communist.

other labor henchmen attach to those colored people who oppose their unscrupulous exploitation of Negro organizations in the interest of Soviet Russia. . . . He believes that the mainspring of the Negro group lies within itself.

McKay's was a rather accurate estimate, except—as events were to prove—in his belief that Randolph could not be tagged with "slanderous names."

Randolph wrote his presidential address, and sent it to Charles Wesley Burton, who read it at the opening session of the Congress. The address, ranging widely over current political and racial issues, called for the preservation of democratic institutions against Hitlerism and Fascism, and for the organization of black workers—particularly in industrial unions, which, unlike most craft unions, had no constitutional clauses barring black members. The speech, suggesting Randolph's continuing attachment to democratic socialism, was particularly tough on the New Deal: "It does not seek to change the profit system. It does not place human rights above property rights, but gives business interests the support of the state. It is no insurance against the coming of Fascism or the prevention of war or a recurrent depression, though it be more liberal than the Republican Tories."

Then, taking note of the shift in Communist policy, in which American Communists had joined liberals in a "united front" against Hitlerism and Fascism—and because of which black and white Communists had endorsed the National Negro Congress—Randolph's speech warned:

The United Front does not provide for weakness or timidity, or reliance by any one organization upon the others who comprise it, but, on the contrary, it affords an opportunity for the contribution of strength by each organization to the common pool of organizational power for a common defense against the enemy. Thus the Negro people should not place their problems for solution down at the feet of their white sympathetic allies . . . for, in the final analysis, the salvation of the Negro, like the workers, must come from within.

The NNC seems to have been thinking along similar lines at the time, for one of the several resolutions it passed before it adjourned was "that in the words of our national secretary, John P. Davis, 'The National Negro Congress goes on record that it is not and will never be dominated by any political faction or political party.' "

Randolph's warning had not been entirely unnecessary, for in the audience, though not formally affiliated with the NNC, were scores of Communist sympathizers. According to John P. Davis, they were there only because of "the need for cooperation with friendly organizations . . . of other races to solve the common economic problems facing all." To the Communists, however, their presence was part of a grander design. In his study *The Negro and the Communist Party,* Wilson Record writes:

The Communist Party realized that its change in line during and after 1935 would enable it to approach, possibly penetrate, "reformist" Negro organizations. However, it soon saw that it would be impossible to capture such organizations as the NAACP and NUL (National Urban League), or to work out any program of joint action, satisfactory to itself. Even had this been possible, it is quite doubtful whether the Party would have attempted it. The Communists' aim was a broad Negro "people's movement," and these organizations were regarded as too narrow in scope to fulfill this goal. It was necessary for the Party to assist in building an over-all Negro organization whose primary purpose would be the unification of varied Negro groups around the immediate problems confronting the race, and around the general united front program.

The National Negro Congress was seen as this "over-all Negro organization."

Though the Communists were no doubt resourceful enough to have found their own means of penetrating the NNC, the task was made much easier for them by the non-Communist membership. Many affiliated groups—especially the religious and fraternal—did not wish to contribute to the financial support of the organization. Disturbed by the endorsement the NNC had received from the Communists, they were fearful of the potential left-wing influence upon the Congress. This seemed to leave the NNC no viable alternative—or perhaps none more sustaining—except to take money and services from the Communists, who stood willing and ready to give. But they were not giving for nothing; and they invested so wisely and generously that, by 1940, they were able not only to penetrate the Congress, but to control it. As Irving Howe and Lewis Coser point out in their study of the American Communist party: "At first, the Communists stayed ostentatiously in the background, deliberately refraining from too obvious control. But from the very beginning their ability to provide organizational forces, experienced personnel, and a variety of skills assured them a powerful role. The non-Communists might show up for meetings and congresses, *but the Communists were there every day.*"

Randolph had no idea, soon after assuming the presidency of the NNC, that the Communists were contributing so heavily to its support and slowly dominating its internal machinery—though, from his experience with labor organizing, he could not have been naïve about their motives in endorsing the organization in the first place. Replying, at the end of the 1936 meeting, to conservative critics like Kelly Miller, of Howard University, he had denied that the Congress was Communist influenced. The NNC, he said, "is, as its name implies, a Negro movement, and has been projected to fight for Negro rights. It was not, is not, and will not be dominated by either Communists, Republicans, Socialists or Democrats. Being a Negro movement, it naturally includes Negroes of all political faiths as well as Negroes of various religious creeds and denominations."

Between meetings of the Congress, Randolph played little part in the operation of the organization, concentrating largely upon the affairs of the Brotherhood. This accounted for his ignorance of the extent to which Communists were taking over the NNC. At the end of the second meeting of the Congress, in 1937—held in the Philadelphia Metropolitan Opera House—he still had found no reason to believe the Congress was anything but "a Negro movement." It was only shortly before the Congress convened for the third time—in the auditorium of the Department of Labor, in Washington, in April, 1940—that he realized the full extent of Communist penetration. By then, the Nazi-Soviet pact had been signed, the Communist party line had changed again, and American Communists were no longer interested in the popular front against Hitlerism and Fascism.

At the opening of the third meeting, in Washington, the keynote of the new politics was struck when John L. Lewis, the guest speaker, demanded that the United States stay out of the war in Europe, stressed the need to fight for democracy at home, and urged the NNC to affiliate with Labor's Non-Partisan League.* Lewis's speech, as Ralph Bunche recalled, "received a tremendous ovation."

---

* Labor's Non-Partisan League had been founded in April, 1936, by John L. Lewis, with the immediate objective of supporting the re-election of President Franklin D. Roosevelt. By 1940, however, Lewis had become an isolationist and a bitter opponent of the President's foreign policy. Thus Labor's Non-Partisan

It was the beginning of the end of Randolph's presidency. Here is Ralph Bunche's eyewitness report:

Randolph followed John L. Lewis, and in a very carefully prepared manuscript titled "The World Crisis and the Negro People Today" analyzed the direction of Negro interests in the present day. Randolph was fully aware of the temper of the Congress and knew that the position he would take would be very unpopular. It had been bruited about for some months that there was internal dissension in the Congress and that Randolph, the President, and John Davis, the Secretary, were at odds on policy. The Auditorium was packed with 1,700 people at the opening meeting when Randolph began his paper. No more than one-third of this audience remained at the conclusion of Randolph's address. But it cannot be said that the audience left only because of the length of Randolph's talk. Within the first fifteen minutes of his paper it was noticeable that an exodus began and this coincided with Randolph's first statement to the effect that the Soviet Union is pursuing power politics and that what is in the national interest of the Soviet Union is not necessarily in the interest of world peace and democracy. . . . When Randolph grouped the Soviet Union with the other imperialist and totalitarian nations, many in his audience became offended. The first exodus was led by white delegates of whom there were a great many present. But throughout his address there was continued restlessness and a gradual disappearance of the audience. Hostile criticisms and murmurs were heard throughout the audience whenever Randolph made any uncomplimentary remark about the Soviet Union.

As a matter of fact, Randolph's speech was a very fair one. He merely cautioned the Negro that it would be foolish for him to tie up his own interests with the foreign policy of the Soviet Union or any other nation of the world. Nor would the Negro be sensible in hoping that through tying himself to any American organization, political or labor, he would find a ready solution for the problems. He cautioned the Congress against too close a relationship with any organization, mentioning the major parties, the Communist Party, the Socialist Party (of which he is a member) and the CIO. He expressed the view that the Negro Congress should remain independent and non partisan, and that it should be built up by Negro effort alone. He ridiculed the assumption that the Communist Party, aligned with the political course of the Soviet Union, could pursue a constructive policy with regard to Negro interests here. He pointed out the whimsy and capriciousness characteristic of the foreign policy of the Soviet Union as reflected in the "party line" of the

---

League was now a mouthpiece of Lewis's isolationism and anti-Roosevelt sentiments; and its own position on the war in Europe coincided with the line the Communist party had adopted after the Nazi-Soviet pact of 1939.

Communist Party here. He made it clear that he believed in the program enunciated at the very first meeting of the Congress; viz., the development of a minimum program of action on the basis of which all Negro organizations might unite in a common effort to establish an effective national Negro pressure group. Randolph vigorously attacked the Dies Committee* and just as vigorously emphasized the loyalty of American Negroes to America. He made the express statement that in a conflict between the United States and the Soviet Union the Negro people would go to war against Russia, just as they would join a war against any other. He appealed for a leadership in the Congress that would be "free of intimidation, manipulation or subordination, with character that is beyond the reach and above the power of the dollar . . . a leadership which is uncontrolled and responsible to no one but the Negro people." . . .

Randolph's speech threw a bombshell into the Congress. . . . It became apparent immediately that Randolph would either have to resign or would be put out, since the sentiment of the Congress was so definitely in pursuit of different objectives. This, of course, is explained by the composition of the delegates. The vast majority represented the unions, and these were almost entirely CIO unions. The Negro rank and file did not know what it was all about, except when perfervid speeches were made demanding anti-lynching legislation, the franchise, and full democracy for the Negro. The more subtle aspects of the line that was being followed were over the heads of most of the rank and file, but the Congress was well organized. . . . John Davis, it is said, stayed up all Friday night writing a reply to Randolph's address, as the report of the executive secretary to the Congress. This report devoted a minimum of attention to the work of the Congress, but was a deliberate attempt to reply to the statements made by Randolph the night before. It embraced an attack upon the Dies Committee, a demand for the realization of Democracy at home, opposition to American participation in the "imperialist" war abroad, and a repetition of the slogan of the Congress (which is also the current slogan of the Communist Party) . . . "The Yanks are not coming." . . .

One of my former students who was not aware of my disgust at the proceedings and of my sentimental attachment to the Congress, due to the fact that I had helped John Davis organize it, came up to me and indulged in a sort of religious confessional which ran something like this: "Oh, Mr. Bunche, I am no longer naive and uninformed now. I have a point of view and I will never be unprogressive again. Don't you think it's grand?" I didn't

---

* The House Un-American Activities Committee, chaired by Congressman Martin Dies. Established in 1938, it investigated and attacked popular-front groups, youth and antiwar organizations, the CIO, and certain prominent liberals of the New Deal.

know what to reply, but started to say, "Peace, sister, it's wonderful!" . . .

The real drama of the Congress occurred . . . when the Resolutions Committee presented its report and when Randolph resigned from the presidency. . . . Edgar Brown, a Negro government employee . . . arose and defended Roosevelt's peace policy and his policy toward Negroes when the resolution on imperialism was up for consideration. As soon as he mentioned President Roosevelt he was denounced in a roar of boos and hisses. Randolph, who was presiding, had to chastise the audience and demand tolerance. Brown received only mild applause when he thanked Randolph. He praised Randolph as the greatest Negro labor union leader (and, he might have added, the *only* Negro labor leader in the Congress). Brown later stated, "I know that I speak for the Negro people, although I do not speak for some of the white communists in the audience." . . . Randolph then scolded Brown for his personal reference.

John Davis spoke on behalf of the resolution on the imperialist war and it was adopted by acclaim. Randolph spoke in opposition to the resolution on unity with Labor's Non-Partisan League. He stated: "I am in opposition to the resolution on the grounds that it is in violation of the minimum program of the Congress because it introduces a controversial issue. A minimum program is one on which all members can agree. By aligning the Congress with the League you are breaking up the Congress. It is impossible to rally the Negro masses behind a partisan program. I know the temper of this Congress but I would not be true to you if I did not register my exception and my opposition to this resolution. I am opposed to the Congress making alliance with any party or with any political group. . . ."

When the report of the Resolutions Committee was adopted as a whole, a dozen people who were standing on the floor went without recognition. Randolph arose to make a few remarks just before the report of the Presiding Committee was given. His remarks were extemporaneous, as follows: "When the Negro Congress was organized, I was urged by Mr. Davis and Dr. Burton to serve as President. I at first refused, but later accepted reluctantly. . . . Now we have come to a point in the development of the organization where a departure from the principle of minimum demands is reached, and where policies are adopted to which I am opposed. For these reasons it is impossible for me to continue as President of the Congress. I wish to make it clear that the reports in the press of personal differences between John P. Davis and me are untrue. There are no personal differences between us. We are friends and I have high regard for the ability of Mr. Davis, but we do disagree on certain policies of the Congress. We disagree, for example, on the alliance of the Congress with Labor's Non-Partisan League. We disagree on the policy of tying up the Congress too closely with the CIO, for I believe that whenever the Congress is tied up too closely with any organization it loses its mass character. I am compelled also to warn the delegates of this Congress against the tie-up with any political organization. . . . We have received donations from the Communist Party, and that is not a healthy condition. I believe that this Congress should be dependent upon the Negro people alone, for wherever you get your money, you get your policies and ideas. The Congress will be responsible to the organization from which it gets its money. I also disagree with the policy towards the Soviet Union. I oppose any cooperation with the Soviet Union. It has been said that if there was a war between the United States and the Soviet Union the Negro people would not fight against the Soviet Union. John Davis and I disagree on that. For these reasons I have concluded that I can no longer serve."

There was an embarrassing silence and no applause when Randolph concluded. It was apparent that the whole thing was cut and dried, for while Randolph was speaking, Max Yergan moved up to the front row. Immediately following Randolph's remarks the Presiding Committee presented its report and named for President, Max Yergan. There was an immediate ovation, and Randolph, who had retired very graciously, promptly handed the gavel of the Presiding Officer to Yergan. . . . I could not help but reflect while this transpired that the one Negro among all those present who had really worked and sacrificed in the labor movement among Negroes, and who was thoroughly steeped in Negro working-class lore, was being replaced by a rank neophyte, a former YMCA Secretary, who had long engaged in missionary work in South Africa, and who now can only parrot the slogans laid down in the party tracts. . . . In my estimation, the Negro Congress dug its own grave at this meeting. It will now be reduced to a Communist cell. . . . I think that this third Negro Congress was an historic meeting and in it Phil Randolph played the most dramatic role. It took both courage and honesty to do what he did.

Randolph's position on the war in 1940 was, of course, the direct opposite of the doctrinaire one he had taken during World War I. The reason, he explained, was that the threats which Hitlerism and Fascism posed to democratic institutions in 1940 were far more serious than those posed in 1918, and made it imperative for blacks to support the war against Nazism. "What does the Battle for Britain mean to America?" he wrote in 1940. "What does it mean to the Negro? Does it matter whether Britain lose and Germany triumph? . . . Does it matter if Britain, the last stronghold of democracy and liberty, fall under the fury and fire, death and destruction of Nazism? The question carries its own answer to a civilized and free people. The answer is, is it a matter of life and death to democracy, and freedom as we know it?"

That same year Randolph resigned briefly from the Socialist party—which had maintained a doctrinaire antiwar position—because, as he said, he could not in good conscience support the party's decision to remain neutral in a war between the Western democracies and Nazi Germany. It was interesting, nevertheless, that, in 1940, it was John P. Davis who was saying what, in effect, Randolph had been saying in 1918: "The American Negro will not fight abroad; he will fight for his survival here at home."

Thus it was now time for Randolph to be tagged with the "slanderous names" that, Claude McKay said earlier, Communists attached to "those colored people who oppose their unscrupulous exploitation of Negro organizations." No sooner had the NNC's Washington meeting adjourned than Randolph was being attacked nationally as a "red baiter," "a frightened Negro bourgeoisie," and "a traitor" to the cause of his race. Under the bombardment, he was forced to release a statement explaining the stand he had taken in Washington, D.C.:

I am opposed to the National Negro Congress depending upon the Communists or CIO for its financial maintenance, because I am opposed to the Congress being dominated by either. . . . The Congress should be uncontrolled and responsible to no one but the Negro people. But it will not be . . . unless the Negro people supply the money for its maintenance. When the NNC loses its independence, it loses its soul, and has no further reason for being. . . . It will shatter the hopes and aspirations of the Negro people who yearn and pray for the Negro Congress not to sell out either to labor or capital, Communists or Republicans or Democrats. I do not oppose domination of the Congress by the CIO because I am opposed to the CIO. I would be opposed to the domination of the Congress by the AFL or any other white organization. . . . I quit the Congress because I was opposed to it or its officials expressing sympathy for the Soviet Union, which is the death prison where democracy and liberty have walked their "last mile," and where shocking "blood purges" wipe out any and all persons who express any dissenting opinions from Dictator Stalin. . . . I quit the Congress because it is not truly a Negro Congress. . . . Movements that claim to be fighting the battles of the American people, and seek their allegiance and support, should be honest enough to sail under their true colors, and the people should at least know what and who they really represent.

If the flow of congratulatory letters Randolph received was any indication, then he had struck a responsive chord among most black Americans. Here are a few. Mary McLeod Bethune: "I see you more now as my ideal. I am proud of the stand you took regarding the Congress. It will go down in history as one of the courageous acts of your life." La-Comtiss Brown: "Your resignation . . . should counteract definitely the thought that all Negro leaders will eventually sell out. It should prove to them that Negroes can lead and at the same time maintain honor and integrity." Frank Horne: "You have certainly done your damndest to teach Negroes to stand on their own hind legs . . . as for me, I'll string along with you." A. J. Johnson: "You came through as one of the greatest men in my race. . . . History will remember you as a brave general who knows when to retreat and when to stand your ground at any cost."

All of this was, in a way, a broader recognition of Randolph's emergence as a national leader. It was also an omen of the popular mass support he would soon be able to call upon, while the National Negro Congress was—as Ralph Bunche had predicted—shrinking into a Communist front.

16 / "Let the Negro Masses Speak"

For the majority of black Americans, the New Deal had turned out to be a revolution only in their expectations—some notable exceptions being those who had found it easier to organize trade unions, or to gain admission to the more progressive ranks of the labor movement.

By late 1940 and early 1941, with Hitler's armies marching across Europe, America's defense industry began to boom. "We Americans," President Franklin Roosevelt assured the threatened European democracies, "are vitally concerned in your defense of freedom. We are putting forth our energies, our resources and our organizing powers to give you the strength to regain and maintain the free world. We shall send you in ever increasing numbers, ships, planes, tanks, and guns." But the Americans reaping the benefits of the industrial boom—getting the jobs to build the ships, the planes, the tanks, and the guns—were almost entirely white. Turned away at the gates of defense plants, the masses of blacks remained largely on relief—what most of them had gotten out of the New Deal—or in temporary emergency work.

Recalling those days, the magazine *American Labor* said, in August, 1968:

Building contractors begged for construction workers but 75,000 experienced Negro carpenters, painters, plasterers, cement workers, brick-layers and electricians could not get employment. It had been announced that 250,000 workers would be absorbed in supplying defense needs, but there was little place for Negro workers, regardless of training. The president of North American Aviation set forth the industry's thinking in a press interview, declaring that "regardless of training, we will not employ Negroes in the North American plant. It is against company policy." Standard Steel Corporation told the Kansas City Urban League: "We have not had a Negro worker in twenty-five years, and do not plan to start now." From the June, 1942, issue of the Federal Security Agency publication: "Over 500,000 Negroes who should be utilized in war production are now idle because of the discriminatory hiring practices of war industries. Several million other Negroes engaged in unskilled occupations are prevented from making greater contributions." When Negroes of Seattle . . . demanded the elimination of the union color bar at the Boeing Aircraft plant, the district organizer of the International Association of Machinists declared: "Labor has been asked to make many sacrifices in this war and has made them gladly, but this sacrifice . . . is too great." In a Newport, Rhode Island, war housing project, where it was required to admit all families of war workers, it was said: "In these critical times it is more important than ever to preserve the principle of white supremacy." In Shreveport, Louisiana, the mayor rejected a Federal grant because of the provision that skilled Negro workers be given a chance to work on its construction. He said: "Of equal importance to winning the war is the necessity of keeping Negroes out of skilled jobs."

Nor were the hands of the federal government much cleaner. According to Will Winton Alexander, formerly of the Resettlement Administration, when complaints of discrimination started pouring in, Sidney Hillman, codirector (with William Knudsen) of the Office of Production Management, was urged to write antidiscrimination clauses into the contracts the government was awarding defense plants: "We said, put it in the contracts. Put the responsibility for enforcement on the contractors. But Hillman wouldn't do it. He was just timid . . . didn't have any confidence in himself in the field of politics." And when blacks began to enlist in the military—comprising 16.1 per cent of all enlistments in 1940–41—they were sent mostly to Jim Crow units in Jim Crow training camps, or assigned mainly the duties of laborers and servants. In fact, Milton Webster felt that "the greatest culprit in the discriminating practices against Negroes was the federal government itself. It was a pattern —this government under the New Deal or any other kind of deal; so far as Negroes were concerned, the deal was just the same."

Yet, despite the effect all this had upon black morale, President Franklin Roosevelt—benefiting from the great esteem in which his wife, Eleanor, was held—remained the most widely admired white American among black citizens. Though the New Deal had not altered fundamentally the plight of black Americans, there was a feeling among them that here, for the first time in the present century, was an administration whose rhetoric and whose liberal philosophy suggested a genuine concern for their problems. Said the magazine *Crisis,* in its election issue of

1940: "The most important contribution of the Roosevelt administration to the age-old color line problem in America has been its doctrine that Negroes are part of the country as a whole. The inevitable discriminations notwithstanding, this thought has been driven home in thousands of communities by a thousand specific acts. For the first time in their lives government has taken on meaning and substance for the Negro masses."

But there were others not so ready to pass lightly over the "inevitable discriminations." "Early in July [1940]," writes Joseph P. Lash, Mrs. Roosevelt's biographer,

Mrs. [Mary McLeod] Bethune came to Eleanor with a bundle of papers citing chapter and verse on discrimination against Negroes in the armed forces, and the covering memorandum said there was "grave apprehension among Negroes lest the existing inadequate representation and training of colored persons in the armed forces may lead to the creation of labor battalions and other forms of discrimination against them in the event of war." Mrs. Bethune urged that the newly appointed Secretary of War, Henry L. Stimson, name an outstanding Negro as his aide to ensure fair treatment of Negroes in the armed services. A few days later Pa Watson [of the President's staff] called Mrs. Bethune, and, on the basis of a directive he had received from General Marshall's office, informed her that as part of the increase in the Regular Army there were to be several new Negro units. The Negro leadership bristled at this response. Walter White . . . hurried to Hyde Park to see Eleanor. They left with her a letter Thurgood Marshall had sent Stimson which listed the services that excluded Negroes and warned that when conscription was enacted, Negroes who were refused the right to serve in all branches would prefer to go to jail.

And none were less ready to pass over the "inevitable discriminations" than the leaders of the Brotherhood of Sleeping Car Porters. Among the resolutions the union passed at its fifteenth anniversary convention—at the Harlem YMCA, in September, 1940—was one calling upon the President, the Congress, and heads of departments "to see to it that no discrimination is practiced against American citizens entering all departments of the Army, Navy and Air Corps on account of race or color." One of the guests at the convention was Mrs. Roosevelt. On September 16, the night after the resolution was passed, she addressed the convention's labor dinner, in the Mecca Temple, at 135 West Fifty-fifth Street. Stressing "the fineness of people," she promised to co-operate with any effort "to make this a better country, not for you alone but for all of us."

As her husband's ambassador to black America, Mrs. Roosevelt no doubt reported to the President on what had transpired at the Brotherhood's convention. If so, it was a further reminder to a memorandum she had sent him earlier, after hearing that a request from the black leadership for a cabinet-level meeting on the armed services question had not been granted. In any case, two days after she addressed the Brotherhood's anniversary dinner, she telephoned Stephen Early, secretary to the President, to relate to him the result of a conversation she had just had with Roosevelt. Early was to arrange a meeting at the White House with the President; the Undersecretary of War, Robert Patterson; the Secretary of the Navy, Frank Knox; Walter White, of the NAACP; T. Arnold Hill, of the National Urban League; and Randolph, of the Brotherhood. Mrs. Roosevelt said the meeting was "important and immediate," and its purpose was "to discuss the rights of Negroes—their rights to volunteer, their rights under the Conscription Act, their general rights to participate in the whole structure of national defense, but particularly the Army and Navy."

But the meeting, on the morning of September 27—at which White, Hill, and Randolph submitted a memorandum calling for the immediate and complete integration of all defense preparations—produced nothing to match the swiftness and concern with which Mrs. Roosevelt had acted. In fact, despite White's feeling that progress had been made, Mrs. Roosevelt's good intentions were hopelessly mangled in the intransigency and clumsiness of the administration's policy and public-relations machinery. Almost two weeks later, on October 9, Stephen Early called a press conference to announce "the War Department policy in respect to Negro participation in national defense." "You will remember," Early told the press, "that . . . the President held a conference . . . with Walter White and, I think, two other Negro leaders. . . . As a result of that conference the War Department has drafted a statement of policy with regard to Negroes in national defense." The statement said, in part, that "the policy of the War Department is not to intermingle colored and white enlisted personnel in the same regimental organizations." Faithfully reporting Stephen Early's announcement, newspapers immediately informed the country that "the segregation policy was approved after Roosevelt conferred with Walter White [and] two other Negroes."

Blacks were outraged. It was painful enough to understand that a liberal New Deal administration had upheld a policy of segregation. But were they to understand, as well, that their own representatives had concurred in such a policy? Since, in the circumstances, it was scarcely possible for them to understand anything else, White, Hill, and Randolph were condemned across the country as a bunch of "sellouts."

Of course, it would have been absurd, to say the least, for White, Hill, and Randolph to have supported a policy of segregation. Why had they gone to the White House in the first place? And why had they bothered to submit a memorandum calling for the immediate and complete integration of the armed forces and "equitable participation" in all defense work? But the black public did not know why they had gone, or what they had submitted. Nor was it ever a part of blacks' political habit to trust their leaders behind closed doors—especially when those leaders were closeted with whites, and at a place like the White House.

Randolph was "shocked and amazed" at the impression Stephen Early's announcement had created. And Walter White telegraphed a strong protest to Early. When no public denial of any kind came from the White House, White wrote Early again to insist that "a moral obligation rests upon the White House to correct the implication for which it is responsible." There was still no public denial. Early merely wrote to assure White, "as emphatically and as honestly as it is possible for any man to speak to another, that there was no disposition or intention on my part . . . to cause you or your colleagues any embarrassment whatsoever."

By then it was rather difficult to accept Early's protestations of honor. As White said later, in his autobiography, the Democratic party had feared the damaging effect Early's announcement might have upon Roosevelt's re-election campaign, and this turned into "consternation when shortly afterward Early kicked in the groin a New York City Negro policeman who had been assigned to protect the President, when the officer refused to permit Early to cross a police line." Realizing that this could cost the Democrats millions of black votes, Walter White now tried to drive a tougher bargain with the White House: instead of calling merely for a retraction of Early's statement, he demanded that the President fire Early from his staff—clearly, as the price for black support in the election.

But, as everyone well knew, black support for Roosevelt was so solid that not even Stephen Early could have kicked it apart. He kept his job in the White House, and, soon after, Roosevelt wrote White, Hill, and

Randolph, expressing regret "that there has been so much misinterpreta-
tion of the statement of the War Department Policy" and that "your
position, as well as the attitude of both White House and the War Department, has been misunderstood. The plan . . . on which we are all
agreed is that Negroes will be put into all branches of the service, com-
batant as well as supply. Arrangements are now being made to give,
without delay, training in aviation to Negroes. Negro reserve officers will
be called to active service and given appropriate commands. Negroes
will be given the same opportunity to qualify for officers' commissions as
will be given to others."

All of that was welcome, but it failed to touch the main issue that had
brought the three men to the White House, and on which they had been
misunderstood by their own people: segregation in the armed forces and
exclusion from jobs in the defense industry. Consequently, the War Department's essential position had not been misunderstood, for Roosevelt's letter did not deny what Early had said on October 9: "The policy
of the War Department is not to intermingle colored and white enlisted
personnel in the same regimental organizations."

Randolph thanked the President for his letter, and all three men
quoted it in public statements, in order to clear their names.

Walter White appears to have been satisfied with the President's clari-
fication of the armed services question, for, according to Joseph P. Lash,
"the Monday before election he sent Eleanor a note: '. . . I would be
grateful if you would give the President the enclosed personal note of
thanks for what he did in the matter of integration of Negroes in the
armed forces of the United States.' And to the President he wrote, 'I
want to send you this personal word of thanks for all you did to insure a
square deal for Negroes in the defense of our country. . . . I am certain
tomorrow will reveal that Negroes know our country. We have worked
night and day during recent weeks to take personally to the people the
things you did and wrote. I am certain tomorrow will reveal that Negroes
know the truth.' He was right. An analysis of fifteen Negro wards in nine
northern cities showed that Roosevelt had captured four in 1932, nine in
1936, and fourteen in 1940."

But Randolph was not at all happy with the result of the White House
conference. He began to feel, in fact, that it was probably a mistake to
continue such modes of protest—public statements, strongly worded
telegrams to Washington, and conferences with White House officials.
To him, the recent one with Roosevelt had been no more successful than

the first one he attended at the White House, in 1925, when Monroe Trotter led a black delegation to make representations to President Coolidge:

Trotter was a superradical, left of Du Bois on race. He knew Coolidge and wanted to tell him what Negroes were then thinking with respect to federal legislation on lynching. So Trotter got together about twenty-five leaders in the country. I wasn't a leader, he just happened to know me, and wanted me in on the group. So we went in, and Trotter walked up and introduced himself to Coolidge. After we were seated, the President said, "Mr. Trotter, will you tell us what's on your mind?" And Trotter got up and started a tremendous oration against white America in general. Negroes, he said, were living in the worst form of tyranny, slavery, and brutalization. If Coolidge did not do something about it, he said, we were going to have trouble in this country. President Coolidge looked on stolidly, as if there was no sensation at all going through his mind. "Have you finished?" he asked Trotter. Trotter said yes. "Well, Mr. Trotter, I'm glad to see you," Coolidge said. "I'm glad to meet your delegation, and I wish you all success. And now I must say good day, gentlemen." Trotter got up and walked out, and we all trooped out behind him. It was hilarious. I had no idea what was going to happen. It was a new experience to me, but I was glad to be in it, because I wanted to be in on something that was going to create some trouble.

So, remembering all such White House delegations—though, for him, there would still be more—Randolph felt that what was now needed was mass action by black people themselves.

In December, 1940, Randolph and Milton Webster left Washington by train to visit Brotherhood divisions in the South. As the train rumbled through Virginia, both men were silent. Whatever was on Randolph's mind, Webster, a self confessed "loud-mouth" who "talk[ed] too much sometimes," was consulting old memories. "I always," he said later, "get a deep feeling, a funny feeling whenever I cross the Potomac River, and I'm always silent. They ran me and my old man from down South when I was a boy and I haven't been particular about going down there since."

Randolph finally broke the silence. "You know, Web," he said, "calling on the President and holding those conferences are not going to get us anywhere."

The remark pleased Webster. He was still, despite the Brotherhood's experience under Coolidge and Hoover, a staunch Republican, "and anything said against a Democrat was all right with me."

"We are going to have to do something about it," Randolph went on.

This changed Webster's mood. "Here it comes again," he said to himself, warily, remembering that "Brother Randolph was always figuring out something for us to do, sticking his nose in everything to see where he can stir something up." Wondering what Randolph had "up his sleeve" this time, Webster did not reply, but kept looking out across the Virginia landscape.

Randolph continued: "I think we ought to get 10,000 Negroes to march on Washington in protest, march down Pennsylvania Avenue. What do you think of that?"

Webster replied, guardedly, that it was a good idea, "but where are you going to get 10,000 Negroes?"

"I think we can get them," Randolph said, and both men resumed the silence.

On their first stop, in Savannah, Georgia, the Brotherhood's leaders called a public meeting to announce that they were "gathering 10,000 Negroes to march on Washington to demand jobs in the defense industry." Since, in the black belt, discretion in such matters was still, by consensus, the better part of valor, people in Savannah helped the two Northerners arrange the meeting, and then withdrew in silence—much like taking cover after lighting a fuse. "It scared everybody to death," Webster reported. "The head colored man in Savannah opened up the meeting and introduced me, and ran off the platform to the last seat in the last row. And when I looked up there a second time, he was gone." From Savannah, they went on to Jacksonville, Tampa, and Miami, preaching march at each stop. Black newspapers picked up the story, and when Randolph and Webster returned to New York, the idea, according to Webster, "had caught on fire."

Striking while the idea was hot, Randolph issued a statement to newspapers around the country on January 15, 1941:

. . . only power can effect the enforcement and adoption of a given policy, however meritorious it may be. The virtue and rightness of a cause are not alone the condition and cause of its acceptance. Power and pressure are at the foundation of the march of social justice and reform . . . power and pressure do not reside in the few, and intelligentsia, they lie in and flow from the masses. Power does not even rest with the masses as such. Power is the active principle of only the organized masses, the masses united for a definite purpose. Hence, Negro America must bring its power and pressure to bear upon the agencies and representatives of the Federal Government to exact their rights in National Defense employment and the armed forces of the country. . . . I suggest that TEN THOUSAND Negroes march on Washington, D.C. . . . with the slogan: WE LOYAL NEGRO AMERICAN CITIZENS DEMAND THE RIGHT TO WORK AND FIGHT FOR OUR COUNTRY. . . . No propaganda could be whipped up and spread to the effect that Negroes seek to hamper defense. No charge could be made that Negroes are attempting to mar national unity. They want to do none of these things. On the contrary, we seek the right to play our part in advancing the cause of national defense and national unity. But certainly there can be no national unity where one tenth of the population are denied their basic rights as American citizens. . . . One thing is certain and that is if Negroes are going to get anything out of this national defense, which will cost the nation 30 or 40 billions of dollars that we Negroes must help pay in taxes as property owners and workers and consumers, WE MUST FIGHT FOR IT AND FIGHT FOR IT WITH GLOVES OFF.

The idea "grew like Topsy," recalls Benjamin McLaurin, who, as an officer of the Brotherhood, would become one of the chief organizers of the march. "It got out of hand almost overnight. People began writing us, 'What can we do?' How could they go about getting groups together?"

Randolph then went to Walter White, of the NAACP, and Lester Granger, of the National Urban League, to enlist their support. Of Randolph's approach to these major civil rights organizations, Herbert Garfinkel, historian of what was to become the March on Washington movement, writes:

This was not the kind of action which the predominantly conservative Negro leadership was likely to welcome with enthusiasm. The recruitment and organization of Negroes into a disciplined mass movement was unfamiliar even to the more militant Northern Negroes. Yet the proposal for a March on Washington was made to a quite conservative group, and it was made by an already prominent figure in the Negro world. In the words of the executive secretary of the National Urban League, Lester Granger: "It was Randolph's immense prestige among all classes of Negroes that made this idea something more than a pretentious notion." It is a measure of the extreme desperation of the Negro leaders that the proposed March was agreed to, however reluctantly.

A March on Washington Committee was formed, with Randolph as director, as well as a Sponsoring Committee, comprising Walter White; Lester Granger; the Reverend William Lloyd Imes, of Harlem's St.

James Presbyterian Church; Frank Crosswaith, of the Negro Labor Committee, and a former organizer of the Brotherhood; Richard Parrish, as youth organizer; Dr. Rayford Logan, of Howard University; J. Finley Wilson, Grand Master of the Order of Elks; the Reverend Adam Clayton Powell, Jr., pastor of the Abyssinian Baptist Church; E. E. Williams, of the Blasters and Drillers union; Noah A. Walters, of the Laundry Workers Joint Board, and Layle Lane, a vice president of the American Federation of Teachers. Regional committees were set up in cities across the country, supported by local divisions of the Brotherhood. In Harlem, Brotherhood organizers fanned out through the streets, shops, bars, and beauty parlors, publicizing the march and raising money. And, around the country, the union's leaders were asked to donate part of their salaries to help finance the movement.

The support of the NAACP and the Urban League appear to have been less than Randolph had hoped for. According to Herbert Garfinkel:

The reluctance of the NAACP and Urban League leadership in agreeing to the March was plain. During the entire period that the agitation for the demonstration was taking place . . . it was given no attention in the official journals of these organizations. It was not until the July issue of the Urban League's *Opportunity* that any mention was made of the March. . . . The NAACP's *Crisis* also did nothing to recruit members. There was no notice of the March until a very small item appeared in July.

But, Garfinkel adds, both groups did "contribute financially to the March on Washington Committee; more significantly, White and Granger were important spokesmen and negotiators."

In March, 1941, Randolph issued the official call for the march, to take place on July 1:

. . . be not dismayed in these terrible times. You possess power, great power. Our problem is to hitch it up for action on the broadest, daring and most gigantic scale. In this period of power politics, nothing counts but pressure, more pressure and still more pressure. . . . To this end we propose that 10,000 Negroes MARCH ON WASHINGTON FOR JOBS IN NATIONAL DEFENSE AND EQUAL INTEGRATION IN THE FIGHTING FORCES. . . . Mass power can cause President Roosevelt to issue an Executive Order abolishing discrimination.

William Dufty, in the *New York Post,* has described the preparations:

Some $50,000 was laid on the line. Union members sparked committees, hired buses and trains, undertook the formidable logistic planning required to move the equivalent of an army division. . . . No mightier pressure had ever been brought to bear in the political history of the American Negro. Yet there was still no evidence that official Washington was heeding any of the noise. On the stump in Harlem one spring day, Randolph had a sudden recollection of other meetings in other streets years before. . . . "I had reason to believe my personal movements were under surveillance by the Federal Bureau of Investigation," he says. . . . Randolph in 1941 decided the FBI could be a great help in the problem of communications. Instead of burying himself in strategy conferences and administrative matters, Randolph stayed on the streets. He trekked up Seventh Avenue, down Lenox, up Eighth. He walked into beauty parlors and said a few words; he invaded pool rooms and spread the message; he rallied inhabitants of bars, shops, and restaurants. He spoke in street corners and theater lobbies. He quit talking in terms of 10,000 marchers—responsive audiences were raising the ante. Word of public response to his exertions would, he hoped, reach Washington in a form in which they could be believed: in the dull, routine, time-place-and-nose-count reports of the vigilant FBI.

By the end of May, Randolph, responding to pressure from supporters, had, indeed, raised the ante. He was calling now for 100,000 marchers: "When 100,000 Negroes march on Washington, it will wake up Negro as well as white America. . . . I call upon Negroes everywhere . . . to gird for an epoch-making march and demonstration. . . . Let the Negro masses march! Let the Negro masses speak!"

Some of Randolph's old critics, especially in the black press, were not impressed, however. To the *Pittsburgh Courier,* the march was "a crackpot proposal," which would accomplish nothing, except to give business to railroad companies and to the gas stations in Washington. "We doubt," the *Courier* said, "if these people have plans to handle 5,000 visiting Negroes, let alone 50,000."

Official Washington was not only impressed, but also quite alarmed. Whether or not the capital had received any intelligence from the FBI, people like Frances Perkins, Secretary of Labor; Sidney Hillman and William Knudsen, of the Office of Production Management; Henry Stimson, Secretary of War; and Eleanor Roosevelt could no longer dismiss the march as pure talk after they received letters from Randolph inviting them to address the concourse he proposed to lead to Washington on July 1.

Mrs. Roosevelt replied immediately to say that she had taken up the matter with the President, "and I feel very strongly that your group is making a very grave mistake at the present time to allow this march to take place. I am afraid it will set back the progress which is being made. . . . I feel that if any incident occurs as a result of this, it may engender so much bitterness that it will create in Congress even more solid opposition from certain groups than we have had in the past." William Knudsen sent a copy of his letter to Stephen Early, at the White House; and Early, after consulting the President, wrote to Wayne Coy, of the Office for Emergency Management, asking whether "it would not be possible, since this movement originates in New York, for you to appeal to Mayor La Guardia to exercise his persuasive powers to stop it." Early said he was not suggesting any "arbitrary action," but since La Guardia had "great influence with New York Negroes," he might be able to convince them of "a better means" of presenting their case than in "this march on Washington."

La Guardia's "great influence with New York Negroes" was indeed a fact. And he had an even greater influence among the leadership and the New York membership of the Brotherhood of Sleeping Car Porters. As a congressman, in the 1920's, he had been one of their most reliable supporters in Washington. As an attorney, he had once assured Randolph, during the Brotherhood's struggle for recognition, that his services were available to the union without charge. He had never turned down an invitation from the porters to speak at their conventions. And he was a personal friend of Randolph and his wife, Lucille. In January, 1941, when it had been rumored that La Guardia might not seek re-election, Randolph had written to him: "Your friends in the Harlem community . . . have a high regard for the best administration any Mayor of New York has ever given." So if there was anyone in New York who stood a good chance of persuading Randolph to call off "this march on Washington," it was the mayor. Thus a meeting was arranged at City Hall of La Guardia, Mrs. Roosevelt, Walter White, and Randolph.

That would not be the only attempt to discourage the march. Wayne Coy urged Roosevelt to support a bill, introduced in February by Senator W. Warren Barbour, of New Jersey, that sought to establish a committee to investigate discrimination in national defense. If such a committee were set up, Coy felt, it "would give Negroes a continuous forum," and the drive behind the march "will be largely dissipated." Sidney Hillman, of the Office of Production Management, sent a circular to defense plants entreating them to hire black workers. Roosevelt sent similar circulars, asking the plants to "take the initiative to open the door of employment to all loyal and qualified workers, regardless of race, creed, or color." But Randolph, refusing to be appeased, said he would accept nothing less than an executive order, "with teeth in it."

For different reasons, the Communists were also attacking the march. As late as mid-June—during the period of the Hitler-Stalin pact—the Communists' position was that, while they favored the principle of a mass movement, the March on Washington should be a mobilization not for jobs, but against the country's entire war program. Besides, the Communists felt, the objective of the march—an increase in employment—would only tend to sap the energy among blacks for more radical social agitation. By June 22—when Germany invaded Russia, thus voiding the Hitler-Stalin pact—the Communists had reversed their policy. They now attacked the proposed march as damaging to the war effort against Nazism and Fascism.

"Those Negro leaders," wrote Irving Howe and Lewis Coser, "who felt that the struggle for the rights of their people could not be suspended in the name of war were ferociously attacked by the Communists. The very organizations that James W. Ford [one of the black leaders of the Communist party] had previously scorned for deluding Negroes into support of 'the imperialist war' were now found to be 'sabotaging the war effort,' 'aiding the Axis camp,' and endangering 'the unity of the American people.' In Stalinist eyes the most dangerous of these organizations (because most intelligently led) was the March on Washington Movement headed by A. Philip Randolph. This group, wrote Ford, was creating 'confusion and dangerous moods in the rank and file of the Negro people and utilizing their justified grievances as a weapon of opposition to the Administration's war program.' "

Nor was that all. The Communists also attacked Randolph as a black chauvinist, for saying he did not want whites to take part in the march. "We shall not call upon our white friends to march with us," he had said. "There are some things Negroes must do alone. This is our fight and we must see it through. If it costs money to finance a march let Negroes pay for it. If any sacrifices are to be made . . . let Negroes make them."

The charge of black chauvinism overlooked or exploited Randolph's rather complex attitude toward the nature of the black struggle in American society. Black chauvinism was certainly not consistent with—nor had it been a mark of—his campaign for integration, his public philosophy as a democratic Socialist, and his history as a labor union propagandist and activist. Even those who had criticized him for building an all-black union had overlooked the fact that he had merely organized a group of workers whom no one else had cared to organize, and who were, in any case, doing what had been designed by their employer as a black man's job.

As for his reasons for wanting to exclude whites from the march, they appear to have been mainly tactical and psychological. Excluding whites was, tactically, a way of virtually excluding Communists, who, Randolph feared, might try to subvert the Washington demonstration the way they had subverted the National Negro Congress. Psychologically, it was necessary, he felt, to dispel one of the prevailing notions in the country, namely, that blacks were incapable of building anything for themselves, or sustaining any effort on their own, without the major participation of whites. Those who suffered the most from the denial of freedom, he said, were called upon to bear the major burden in the struggle to achieve that freedom: "The Negro must supply the money, pay the price, make the sacrifices, and endure the suffering to break down his barriers." C. L. Dellums recalls: "We told our white friends over the country why this had to be a Negro march. It had to be for the inspiration of Negroes yet unborn. We told them all we wanted was their moral support, to stand on the sidelines and cheer us on. We were unalterably opposed to segregation, but we also knew that Negroes needed an example of Negroes doing something for themselves. We didn't go for no separation stuff. That's South African."

When all this has been said, it would be surprising, anyway, if all blacks in the Western world—despite their many differences in political outlook and cultural attitude—were not, when the chips were down, brought in touch with the strong reserves of black nationalist feeling that the experience of white racism produces and feeds. In Randolph's case, he had, from his youth, been connected to a certain strain of black nationalism that ran through his social and religious heritage: through the African Methodist Episcopal church—"the first wavering step of a people towards organized group life"—established as "a church of men who support from their own substance, however scanty, the ministrations of the word they received"; through black religious and political stalwarts like Bishop Henry McNeal Turner; through his own father, that home-grown social and moral eclectic, preaching his biblical dream of Ethiopia's redemption. It is a wonder that black nationalism did not become the central activating force and principle of Randolph's political life.

Randolph's meeting with Mayor La Guardia and Mrs. Roosevelt took place at New York's City Hall, on June 13, 1941. Walter White was also there, and, possibly, Aubrey Williams, head of the National Youth Administration, and Mrs. Anna Rosenberg, of the Social Security Board. According to Joseph P. Lash, Roosevelt had also called in Aubrey Williams and told him, "Go to New York and try to talk Randolph and White out of this march. Get the missus and Fiorello and Anna and get it stopped."

Lash gives this account of the meeting: " 'You know where I stand,' Eleanor said to Randolph and White. 'But the attitude of the Washington police, most of them Southerners, and the general feeling of Washington itself are such that I fear there may be trouble if the march occurs.' When White explained that they had tried unsuccessfully all spring to see the president about Negro grievances, she assured him she would get in touch with the president immediately, 'because I think you are right.' " But, though he enjoyed a higher standing in the White House than Randolph, White was merely one of the supporting characters in the drama of the threatened march. It was Randolph who was the main protagonist, and his account of the City Hall meeting, more detailed, suggests on whom the spotlight of the discussion was focused:

"Mrs. Roosevelt reminded me of her sympathy for the cause of racial justice, and assured me she intended to continue pressuring the President to act. But the march was something else, she said: it just could not go on. Had I considered the problems? she asked. Where would all those thousands of people eat and sleep in Jim Crow Washington? I told her I myself did not see that as a serious problem. The demonstrators would simply march into the hotels and restaurants, and order food and shelter. But that was just the point, she said; that sort of thing could lead to violence. I replied that there would be no violence unless her husband ordered the police to crack black heads. I told her I was sorry, but the march would not be called off unless the President issued an executive order banning discrimination in the defense industry."

Mrs. Roosevelt reported back to the President, and Mayor La Guardia informed the White House that, as far as he could see, nothing would stop the march unless Roosevelt called in Randolph and White to "thresh it out right then and there" with his cabinet aides. The President and Mrs. Roosevelt agreed, and that same day he announced to one of his assistants that "I will see Stimson, Knox, Knudsen, Hillman, White and Randolph." The following day, Aubrey Williams, of the National Youth Administration, called Randolph in New York to inform him that the President wanted to meet the march leaders, but that it would be helpful to the spirit of the coming discussions if Randolph immediately suspended all preparations for the march. "I could not do that," Randolph telegraphed Roosevelt. "The hearts of Negroes are greatly disturbed . . . and their eyes and hopes are centered on this march, and the committee must remain true to them. We feel as you have wisely said: 'No people will lose their freedom fighting for it.' "

The White House meeting was held on June 18. Present were Roosevelt, White, and Randolph; Henry Stimson, Secretary of War; Robert Patterson, Undersecretary of War; Frank Knox, Secretary of the Navy; William Knudsen and Sidney Hillman, of the Office of Production Management; Anna Rosenberg; Aubrey Williams; and Mayor La Guardia. According to Mrs. Roosevelt's biographer, before the meeting began "the president saw Anna Rosenberg, who had become his link with La Guardia and who briefed him on what the Negro leaders wanted, which was essentially an order that would make nondiscrimination in defense industry not only a matter of policy but of mandate, with a Fair Employment Practices Committee set up to enforce it. The upshot of the June 18 conference was that the president asked the Negro group to meet with La Guardia, Williams, and Mrs. Rosenberg to draft the kind of order they thought he should issue."

According to the accounts of Randolph and others, however, it had not been so easily won. Here is a reconstruction of several accounts Randolph has given of the meeting:

"Hello, Phil," the President said. "Which class were you in at Harvard?"

"I never went to Harvard, Mr. President."

"I was sure you did," Roosevelt replied. "Anyway, you and I share a kinship in our great interest in human and social justice."

"That's right, Mr. President."

Roosevelt, a man of great charm, had merely embarked upon one of his favorite filibuster stratagems. But, finding he could not engage Randolph in small talk, he turned raconteur and started regaling his audience with old political anecdotes. Randolph, unfailingly well-mannered, allowed himself to be entertained. But the clock was running, the President's time was no doubt well budgeted, and Randolph had no way of knowing when Roosevelt might suddenly inform the gathering that it was time for him to leave for another appointment. So, with as much graciousness as he commanded, Randolph broke in:

"Mr. President, time is running on. You are quite busy, I know. But what we want to talk with you about is the problem of jobs for Negroes in defense industries. Our people are being turned away at factory gates because they are colored. They can't live with this thing. Now, what are you going to do about it?"

"Well, Phil, what do you want me to do?"

"Mr. President, we want you to do something that will enable Negro workers to get work in these plants."

"Why," Roosevelt replied, "I surely want them to work, too. I'll call up the heads of the various defense plants and have them see to it that Negroes are given the same opportunity to work in defense plants as any other citizen in the country."

"We want you to do more than that," Randolph said. "We want something concrete, something tangible, definite, positive, and affirmative."

"What do you mean?"

"Mr. President, we want you to issue an executive order making it mandatory that Negroes be permitted to work in these plants."

"Well, Phil," Roosevelt replied, "you know I can't do that. If I issue an executive order for you, then there'll be no end to other groups coming in here and asking me to issue executive orders for them, too. In any event, I couldn't do anything unless you called off this march of yours. Questions like this can't be settled with a sledge hammer."

"I'm sorry, Mr. President, the march cannot be called off."

"How many people do you plan to bring?" Roosevelt wanted to know.

"One hundred thousand, Mr. President."

Roosevelt seemed torn between alarm and disbelief. Perhaps this was a bluff. He turned to Walter White, as if to a man whose word he could trust, looked White squarely in the eye for a few seconds, and asked, "Walter, how many people will really march?"

White's eyes did not blink. He said, "One hundred thousand, Mr. President."

[It may, at that, have been a bluff. Randolph and White certainly expected a march of thousands. March committees around the country could have turned out at least 10,000 marchers. The question was whether they could, indeed, muster an army of 100,000. Then, too, what is one to make of what William Bowe, one of Randolph's lieutenants in the Brotherhood, said later? "Personally," Bowe said, with a twinkle in his eyes, "I don't know how far we could march. I didn't think we could go as far as South Ferry."]

"You can't bring 100,000 Negroes to Washington," Roosevelt said. "Somebody might get killed."

Randolph said that that was unlikely, especially if the President himself came out and addressed the gathering.

Roosevelt was not amused. "Call it off," he said curtly, "and we'll talk again."

Randolph said he had a pledge to honor with his people, and he could not go back to them with anything less than an executive order.

Budging somewhat, Roosevelt suggested that Randolph and White confer with his presidential assistants over some way of solving the problem with defense contractors.

"Not defense contractors alone," Randolph broke in. "The government, too. The government is the worst offender."

This, Roosevelt seemed to feel, was going a bit too far, and he informed the president of the porters' union that it was not the policy of the President of the United States to rule, or be ruled, with a gun at his head.

"Then," Randolph replied, "I shall have to stand by the pledge I've made to the people."

It was Mayor La Guardia who broke the impasse. "Gentlemen," he said, "it is clear that Mr. Randolph is not going to call off the march, and I suggest we all begin to seek a formula."

Roosevelt welcomed the opening, and asked Mrs. Rosenberg, La Guardia, and Aubrey Williams to take the group to an anteroom and work out a solution. But the solution proposed was the one Randolph had already rejected—the President's promise to call up the heads of defense plants and urge them to follow a nondiscriminatory policy. When both Randolph and La Guardia dismissed the proposal, a committee of five was appointed to draw up an executive order to be submitted to the President. This satisfied Randolph, and he left for New York—to continue preparing for the march, at least until he was assured that the President would sign the order.

It took a few days to work out a draft of the order that was acceptable to Randolph—one that had "teeth in it" and could be enforced. The chief legal draftsman for the government was a young lawyer in the Office for Emergency Management, named Joseph L. Rauh. Every draft that Rauh prepared was sent back to him as being not strong enough. They had all been read over the telephone to Randolph, in New York, and he had rejected every one. Rauh could no longer contain himself when what he considered his best and final draft was thrown back at him because, once again, it was not strong enough for Randolph. "Who the hell is this guy Randolph?" Rauh exploded at his superiors. "What the hell has *he* got over the President of the United States?" Rauh would later come to know, admire, and work with Randolph in a number of public causes, and would say, "I don't know that I've met a greater man in my life."

Randolph liked Rauh's very next effort, however, and on June 25, six days before the march was scheduled to take place, the President signed and issued Executive Order 8802—declaring it to be the policy of the United States "that there shall be no discrimination in the employment of workers in defense industries or government because of race, creed, color, or national origin," and that "it is the duty of employers and of labor organizations . . . to provide for the full and equitable participation of all workers in defense industries." To enforce the order, the President appointed a temporary Fair Employment Practices Committee to "receive and investigate complaints of discrimination" and to take "appropriate steps to redress grievances." Mrs. Roosevelt wrote Randolph to say she was glad the march had been called off and to hope that "from this first step, we may go on to others." On July 19, the President appointed the Fair Employment Practices Committee, chaired by Mark Ethridge, of the *Louisville Courier-Journal,* and including Milton P. Webster, first vice president of the Brotherhood of Sleeping Car Porters. Randolph had declined to serve on the committee.

But Randolph's decision to cancel the march was hotly contested by the more militant elements of his following. Chief among these was the Youth Division of the March Committee, led by Richard Parrish, and made up of young radicals like Bayard Rustin, who had recently joined the Youth Division, after quitting the Young Communist League at the City College of New York. Protesting Randolph's failure to consult them before calling off the march, the young militants accused him of selling out to Roosevelt, and demanded that he reschedule the march to take place within ninety days.

Challenged for the first time by young black activists more militant than himself—his critics in the National Negro Congress had been older men—Randolph was forced to issue a public statement. The march had been called off, he explained,

because its main objective, namely the issuance of an Executive Order banning discrimination in national defense, was secured. . . . The Executive Order was issued upon the condition that the march be called off. . . . The purpose of the march . . . was not to serve as an agency to create a continuous state of sullen unrest and blind resentment among Negroes. . . . There is sufficient of this. Its purpose was to achieve a specific and definite thing. . . . It would have constituted a definite betrayal of the interests of the Negro if the March Committee after receiving . . . the main object of its struggle . . . had defiantly waved it aside and marched on to Washington. Such a strategy would have promptly and rightly been branded as a lamentable specie of infantile leftism and an appeal to sheer prima donna dramatics and heroics.

The majority of Randolph's following, however, applauded his handling of the march strategy. As one newspaper commented, he had "demonstrated to the Doubting Thomases among us that only mass action can pry open the iron doors that have been erected against America's black minority."

Among the black intelligentsia, in 1941, the predominant feeling was that Eleanor Roosevelt was the decisive moral force behind the President's apparent espousal of the principle of equal opportunity in wartime industrial employment. "I don't think you'll find that he had any love for Negroes as such," says Benjamin McLaurin, of the Brotherhood. "I think his wife had a much deeper sense of justice and fair play, and while she was not in a position to do very much . . . as a result of her own persuasion he had to take a look at some of the problems. But President Roosevelt never did anything as such for Negroes."

After acknowledging that Roosevelt, in Executive Order 8802, "directly pays his respects to racial discrimination," Roy Wilkins wrote, in 1941: "If the record be searched, it will be found that . . . Roosevelt himself has uttered very few words upon Negroes. Even when he has discussed problems which vitally affect Negroes he has been careful in nearly every case to speak in general terms. His condemnation of lynching falls in this category. He mentioned no specific lynching. He mentioned no race or section of the country. He did not advocate a Federal anti-lynching law. The President has let Mrs. Roosevelt 'run interference' for him on the Negro question and she has done a good job. . . . I believe she has been sincere and genuinely interested in fitting the race into the American scheme. . . . The President reaped the benefit of Mrs. Roosevelt's activities and pronouncements on the Negro. But he never said a word."

Though the executive order said nothing whatever about segregation in the armed forces—an issue that had played as important a part as discrimination in defense industry in the origins of the March on Washington movement—it represented one of the historic break-throughs of the black struggle. No longer could blacks be barred from equal opportunity in federal employment or in any institution fulfilling government contracts. In 1941—after the betrayals of Reconstruction, the disillusionments of 1919, the privations of the Depression, and the unmet expectations of the New Deal—the order was the first major act by the national government to remedy distinct abuses suffered by black citizens. "Never in the history of the United States," Roy Wilkins wrote, "has a President issued an Executive Order which is at once a condemnation of racial discrimination as a policy and a powerful aid, economically, to the well-being of Negro citizens."

The movement to achieve all this—mass action, or the threat of it—was equally significant, in that it represented a transition from previous modes of black protest activity. "Up until then," writes Lerone Bennett, Jr., the historian, "the dominant issues in Negro life were poll tax legislation, anti-lynching legislation, 'separate-but-equal' school facilities and the white primary." But from 1941 on, Bennett observes, "Negro strategy would be based, implicitly and explicitly, on the necessity for decisive intervention by the federal government. It would be based, too, on the need for unrelenting pressure on the government."

17 / Man of the Hour

Randolph now became, and would remain for almost a decade, the most popular and sought-after black political figure in America. Two weeks after he had won the executive order, the New York *Amsterdam News* ranked him "along with the great Frederick Douglass. His name is rapidly becoming a household word. The rise of A. Philip Randolph to a new and loftier position in the affairs of the race appears to presage the passing of the leadership that has controlled the Negro's identity for the past 25 years. . . . We regard A. Philip Randolph as the man of the hour." In 1943, W. E. B. Du Bois, to whom the younger Randolph had once been a radical nuisance, now praised his action "which compelled the issue of Presidental Order 8802" as "the most astonishing in our later leadership." And Murray Kempton, recalling the Brotherhood's role in the events of 1941, would write years later that the union "had become a kind of cathedral," and that Randolph, who "might have been nothing except a voice insistent and off the beat," became, as president of the Brotherhood, "a paladin of the Negro community."

Amidst the applause that greeted the news of Roosevelt's executive order, Randolph announced that the March on Washington Committee would become a permanent movement. Its objectives, he said, were to serve as a watchdog over the enforcement of the order, to carry on a campaign for a permanent Fair Employment Practices Commission,* to represent the temper of the masses at the time, and to engage in other protest activities. Since one of these activities would revolve around "the refusal of Negroes to obey any law which violates their basic citizenship

---

* For a detailed account of this campaign and the march movement's activities in the 1940's, see *When Negroes March,* by Herbert Garfinkel.

rights," Randolph declared that the march movement would adopt Gandhi's tactics of nonviolent civil disobedience and nonco-operation—which prompted newspapers to start referring to him, approvingly, as "the American Gandhi." Not all newspapers were pleased, however. Randolph's old enemy, the *Pittsburgh Courier,* said his call for a civil disobedience movement was "the most dangerous demagoguery on record," and would give "irresponsible and vicious elements an excuse to slaughter thousands of colored citizens." Randolph dismissed this as the whinings of "the petty black bourgeoisie," who wanted "results without risks, and achievements without action."

While most of the followers of the March on Washington movement were swept along by the social emotions of the day and by the spirit of Randolph's leadership, they did not have much of a sense of belonging to a formal organization. "The power of the new movement," wrote Edwin Embree, a contemporary commentator, "is mysterious. It has almost no organization, no big machine for promotion and publicity. Yet it grips the people's imagination and holds their loyalty. Masses of the darker common people are looking to Randolph as the modern Messiah."

At times, however, this loyalty would undergo a severe strain, for it was not easy for a March on Washington movement to satisfy its followers. That is, as long as people belonged to a movement that went by such a name, they fully expected to be marching. No matter how many school and bus boycotts it called, or how many picket lines it threw around city hall, if the movement didn't march to Washington, then it wasn't the kind of movement people thought they had joined. Yet it made no sense for the movement to march if there was no pressing reason to do so. When it came into being, early in 1941, its immediate objective had been to march on the capital to force President Roosevelt's hand. Now that the executive order had been won, there was no urgent new demand being made on Washington. The threat of a march was simply being dangled over Washington's head—in case there was any temptation to slacken enforcement of the executive order, and to lobby for a permanent Fair Employment Practices Commission. When Randolph persisted in holding out the threat of another March on Washington, many of his followers became impatient. "What kind of a march movement is this," they asked, "which doesn't march?" But if the movement was to survive, the threat of a mass march—its most intimidating weapon—could not be withdrawn, and Randolph had no choice but to continue dangling his threat.

By April, 1942, however, after American emotions had flared over the attack on Pearl Harbor, and the country had entered the war, those who had been calling impatiently for a march were being drowned out by those who declared that a march at that time would damage the national interest. Even the *Amsterdam News,* one of Randolph's most loyal and consistent champions since 1925, felt that "it would not be tactful at this time to organize another march," since it would "play directly into the hands of Hitler and other enemies of our country and our cause."

In view of the patriotic pressure, Randolph could now stop threatening to march. But the movement had to be kept together and its major objectives sustained. So, shelving the march idea for the time being, he began calling instead for a series of mass rallies throughout the country —to demonstrate to Washington that the march movement had lost none of its energy and that, while respecting the demands of patriotism, it had not abandoned its goals. These rallies, held in the summer of 1942, marked the peak of the movement's popularity.

The largest were held in the Chicago Coliseum and in New York's Madison Square Garden. On June 16, the night of the New York rally, Randolph called upon businesses in Harlem to dim their lights and close their doors; and, for fifteen minutes, the community was, in his words, "dark, silent, and dry." In Madison Square Garden, the crowd of more than 20,000 was addressed by leaders of almost every important civil rights, religious, fraternal, labor, and liberal organization in New York City—so many, in fact, that Randolph, the main attraction, did not get to speak.

Some observers report that Randolph's thunder was stolen by the Reverend Adam Clayton Powell, Jr., who not only made the longest speech, but also announced his intention to run for Congress from the Harlem district. This made Randolph's lieutenants angry. Powell, according to Laurence Ervin, chairman of the New York March Committee, had done nothing to help organize the meeting, was jealous of Randolph's popularity, and, in using the occasion to announce his own candidacy, meant to forestall plans that were then being made to run Randolph for the congressional seat. In fact, says Ervin, Randolph had not only been warned of Powell's intentions, but also had been urged to keep him off the program. Randolph, however, had refused to bar the minister, saying he was an authentic voice of the community and should be heard.

But though he did not get a chance to speak, Randolph's leadership was recognized in the reception he received when he entered the Garden.

As he moved up the aisle, ushered by one hundred uniformed porters in front and fifty Pullman maids behind, the crowd of more than 20,000 stood and applauded, while the Brotherhood's marching band played the union's battle song, "Hold the Fort for We Are Coming." Joel A. Rogers, the veteran Harlem historian and journalist, had not seen anything like it "since the days of Marcus Garvey." And, writing to Webster, in Chicago, a few days later, Randolph described the Garden mass meeting as "the biggest demonstration of Negroes in the history of the world."

The March on Washington movement would continue into the late 1940's, and would be described by Herbert Garfinkel as "one of the most remarkable mass movements in American political history." But it would never be as remarkable again as it had been during the summer of 1942. In the words of one of its participants, it "had reached a peak; from that time on its strength either seeped away or was funneled in different directions." Randolph's personal popularity would last much longer, but it, too, would never be as great and unchallenged again as it had been on the night of June 16, 1942.

Less than a month later, Randolph was being attacked by sections of the black community more bitterly than at any time since his struggle to win recognition for the porters' union. At the NAACP convention in Los Angeles, in July, Carlotta Bass, a prominent delegate, attacked the march movement as dangerous to national unity. "Mr. Randolph," she said, "does not, in truth, give a damn whether the war is won or lost." And, raising the specter of disloyalty, she reminded her audience that Randolph had been arrested for criticizing the country during World War I and for being "the most dangerous Negro in America."

On August 1, George S. Schuyler joined the attack, writing in the *Pittsburgh Courier:*

Mr. Randolph knows how to appeal to the emotions of the people and to get a great following together, but there his leadership ends because he has nowhere to lead them and would not know if he had. . . . He has the messianic complex, considerable oratorical ability and some understanding of the plight of the masses, but the leadership capacity and executive ability required for the business at hand is simply not there. The original March on Washington move is now admitted to have been a failure else the current agitation would not be necessary. . . . Organization is not merely a matter of ballyhoo and oratory, it is a Science, and one that is largely a closed book to Mr. Randolph. Mass leadership in times like these also requires a little more guts than any of the Negro leaders possesses. I know of none willing, like Nehru and Gandhi, to go to jail.

By 1943, the *Courier* was calling upon Randolph to disband his movement "and leave the field to the NAACP—with its 600 branches and 160,000 members—which has demonstrated its ability as a fighting representative of the American colored people since 1909."

Dissension had also developed within the march organization itself. A member of the committee in Washington, D.C., addressed Randolph, in an unsigned letter: "My Dear Philip Lord Randolph . . . you've lost your fire—your power to inspire is getting increasingly sporadic. Hell, of course you can bring 20,000 people to their feet, but that's on past performance . . . stop being so God-damned bossy, and petered out, and petulant . . . you're getting vain. You're setting yourself up as a judge, as an oracle. . . . Your trouble is you're too close to fawners. You're not Jesus Christ, and you shouldn't let people tell you that you are."

An officer of the organization in New York wrote Randolph to complain that she was "getting fed up with listening to grievances by members of the New York local who feel that you have a gravy train and they want to get aboard to get the gravy. Since I have come to this office I have heard nothing but 'Mister, when thou cometh into Thy Kingdom who will sit on the Left and who on Thy Right.' I have tried, and with little avail to tell the New York group that they are not alone in the Movement."

Milton Webster and the Chicago March Committee were fighting bitterly over the Brotherhood's role in the movement. He told Randolph, in a series of letters:

The March on Washington around here is getting to be a nuisance. There are strenuous objections to the Brotherhood having too much to say about the running of the show. . . . The question has been asked as to what have I got to do with the March on Washington. In the first place, if the Brotherhood hadn't furnished a couple of thousands of dollars to put this mass meeting over, they wouldn't have the two or three hundred dollars they have now, and the way that is earmarked they will be broke in the next few weeks. If the March on Washington functions, the Brotherhood will have to finance it again. There are too many women mixed up in this thing, anyhow. . . . Your March on Washington Committee is getting way out of line again. It was intimated in the meeting the other night that why should the Brotherhood have so much to say about the March on Washington . . . and why I stuck my nose in it. . . . I told them that the March on Washington was so much a part of the Brotherhood I had to be in everything that the Brotherhood was in. . . . I think these people ought to be straightened out one way or the other and they won't take anything as authentic unless it comes from you. I think they ought to be told the part the Brotherhood intends to play in this thing and let those who don't like it get out now. . . . This thought occurs to me, as I think over this matter, whether or not it is worth our while to create a lot of bitterness among our people when it is really doubtful whether we can save the race and maybe it would be better if we just saved the Brotherhood. I suppose you will be flooded with a bunch of protests and etc. But I did not relish the idea of spending all that money in New York, getting all those people there and not one word being said about the Brotherhood. . . . I don't intend for these women to be pushing us around, because I know, and they ought to have sense enough to know, that if it was not for the Brotherhood there would not be any March on Washington Movement now.

The Chicago women did, indeed, send protests of their own. Accusing Webster of violating democratic procedures, they wrote Randolph: "If it is true that the Brotherhood owns and controls the movement and does not intend to allow democratic techniques, then we have been led upon a blind alley." But there was probably no one alive at the time with whom Randolph would have sided against Milton Webster, his closest friend and colleague. Replying to the ladies in Chicago, he simply asked them to remain faithful to the cause.

Nor did many of the porters approve of the Brotherhood's playing so central a role in the March on Washington movement, or of Randolph, their president, spending so much of his time in "outside activities." As one of them said, "We are paying Randolph to negotiate and sign contracts, not to run around like a West Indian Communist agitator and dreamer." This was a minority opinion, to be sure, but Benjamin McLaurin —who himself was dividing his attentions between the Brotherhood and the march organization—considered it serious enough to remind union members that though "Brother Randolph is the president of the Brotherhood, we should not own and control him body and soul. All of his interests are interrelated with our struggle for a better life."

Still, arenas of public service were opening to Randolph, which—despite their relation to the broader "struggle for a better life"—his obligations as president of the Brotherhood kept him from entering. Late in 1942, Mayor La Guardia appointed him a member of the New York

City Housing Authority, but Randolph declined, on the grounds that he had to be out of town "frequently and at extended periods." La Guardia appointed Frank Crosswaith instead, from a list Randolph submitted which included Roy Wilkins, of the NAACP, Lester Granger, of the Urban League, and Ashley Totten, of the Brotherhood.

In 1944, though Adam Clayton Powell, Jr., had announced two years earlier, a strong bipartisan and grass-roots movement developed in Harlem to nominate Randolph as the candidate from New York's Twenty-second Congressional District. The district had been recently redrawn to facilitate the election of a black congressman. For Randolph, going to Congress would have been, as Dorothy Norman wrote in the *New York Post,* "a fitting climax to his life-long fight in behalf of Negro workers and other minorities." Besides, at the age of fifty-five, he was then earning all of $3,600 a year as president of the Brotherhood—half as much as the lowest-paid union leader in the country.

The prospect of going to Washington did not seem to excite Randolph, however, partly because he had lost his appetite for elective office, and in larger part because he knew his colleagues in the union's leadership would not approve. Anyway, he asked them what they thought of the idea. E. J. Bradley, of St. Louis, said he saw "nothing wrong with it," felt, in fact, that it would be "great to have one of our own group in Congress." But the typical reply came from Bennie Smith, of Detroit:

I am yet convinced that your candidacy . . . is a leap in the dark. I fully realize the pressure being brought to bear to induce you to accept, nor do I question your possible success, but beyond that, this coming campaign, in my judgment, is going to be the dirtiest, muck-raking campaign that America has witnessed in her life time. Nor am I unmindful of the fact that we have not gained many more real friends in either high or low places despite your unmatched contributions to the cause of mankind. In the final analysis, when one comes out as a candidate for Congress in this smeary campaign, every self-seeking interest of every walk of life will use every trick in the bag, even if unable to defeat, to minimize the great good you have done. It is also to be remembered that in our own organization we have some politically minded locally and we could wake up to find our organization being used as a "Political Football."

Randolph informed his bipartisan supporters in Harlem that he did not care to run for Congress, since he did not wish to divide the officials of the Brotherhood. Nor did he wish to become involved in the "entanglements" of politics and politicians: the "pay-offs necessary to get ahead in public office" involved compromises "which may strike at the basic convictions, ideals, and principles that one has held dear all his life." That November, Powell was elected to the first of his several terms in Washington as the Congressman from Harlem.

At the Socialist party conference in Reading, Pennsylvania, in June, 1944, Randolph was nominated to run as the party's vice presidential candidate, with Norman Thomas. But, in a message to Harry Fleischman, the party's national secretary, Randolph declined the nomination because of "my obligations to the Brotherhood of Sleeping Car Porters." He did so with "keen regret," however, for "nothing would give me greater pleasure than to share in the national campaign as part of the Socialist ticket, not to achieve immediate office, but to build the intellectual and spiritual foundation for the development of a broad political movement in America in the pattern of and comparable to the Canadian Commonwealth Federation."

But Randolph's popularity was not so universal in the South. In November, 1943, when a group of black citizens in Memphis invited him to address a mass meeting, in the Mount Nebo Baptist Church, he arrived to find that the meeting had been called off. E. H. ("Boss") Crump, who ran the Memphis political machine, had ordered Sheriff O. H. Perry to close down the church, and to see to it that Randolph spoke nowhere in the city. To Crump's functionaries, Randolph was "a blatherskite and rabble rousing race demagogue of the first rank," who was no good for race relations "in this part of the country." Making sure no one was tempted to violate Crump's wishes, Sheriff Perry called a group of black preachers to the courthouse, showed them a row of empty jail cells, and reminded them of the good things Memphis had done for its "coloreds." Moreover, Perry said, he had a dossier on Randolph showing that he was "a dangerous impostor, a graduate of Oxford and the holder of a law degree from Harvard who was going around the country passing himself off as an ex-Pullman porter," and who had made speeches that were "nothing but 'social equality of the races' propaganda." The preachers were then sent home, the sheriff having excused them from asking any questions.

Back in New York, Randolph wired William Green, head of the American Federation of Labor, to report the "unjustifiable interference" with his right of free speech, and to seek the AFL's support in organizing another public meeting in Memphis. Green tried for several weeks, but it was not until March, 1944, that he found someone willing to associate himself with an affair at which Randolph was to speak. His name was George Goode, and he was a Southern organizer for the AFL. With the co-operation of the Tennessee Tenant Farmers Association, Goode arranged a public meeting at the First Baptist Church, on Beale Street.

If Crump knew of these arrangements, he made no attempt to interfere. The night of March 31, a crowd of over 700—mostly black citizens, but including white newspaper reporters and officials of the Tennessee State AFL—turned out to hear Randolph lambaste the "dictatorial" political system of Memphis, and Crump himself as a political boss "who out-Hitlers Hitler." This was not only during wartime, when Hitler was the most hated name among Americans, but also during an era in the South when black men were not permitted the luxury of such bravado.

Randolph left Memphis satisfied that he had vindicated his right to free speech, and it was only after returning to New York that he realized how serious was the lurch in which he had left some of his sponsors. "Had I known the Negro Randolph was going to make such a black-guarding speech," Sheriff Perry announced next morning, "I would have pulled him out of the pulpit." Having missed Randolph, Perry turned on the Reverend G. A. Long, who had allowed his church to be used for the anti-Crump meeting. Calling the Reverend Mr. Long "a sassy and fresh preacher from Chicago," the sheriff promised to run him out of Memphis. At this, the other black preachers panicked, and, to protect themselves from the wrath of the Crump machine, got together and issued a public statement: "Did the speech delivered by Randolph in which he lambasted and vilified E. H. Crump represent the attitude of the colored people of Memphis? We say NO."

The statement was more than a mere effort by the black preachers to save their skins. It suggested, as well, something of the mood that still prevailed within the black religious establishment, particularly in the South, where controversial questions of race and politics were concerned. After its militancy during the nineteenth century—especially as displayed by the race-conscious leadership of the African Methodists—the black church, in the early decades of the new century, had fallen into a political slumber, and had been dreaming mainly not of the earthly rewards of struggle, but of the heavenly rewards of endurance. It was not until the 1950's that the black church, stirred by the example of preachers like the Reverend Martin Luther King, Jr., began to reawaken.

The Reverend G. A. Long may well have been one who prefigured that reawakening. Abandoned by his ministerial colleagues in Memphis, and jeopardized by the anger of the Crump machine, he stood firmly by the principle on which he had opened up his church to Randolph. "I would like Mr. E. H. Crump to know," the Reverend Mr. Long announced, "that I am an ambassador of Jesus Christ and take my orders only from Christ. The issue raised by Crump in Memphis is the issue around the world—Freedom. Thousands of my group are dying around the world for that freedom. If they can take it there, I can take it here."

The Reverend Mr. Long was to pay a high price for trying to take freedom in Memphis in 1944—though nowhere near as high as the one the Reverend Martin Luther King, Jr., would pay for trying to take it there almost twenty-five years later. As part of the plan to run the preacher out of Memphis, "Boss" Crump's fire chief, A. J. Schaefer, visited Long's Beale Street Baptist Church, found "violations" that would cost $2,500 to correct, and informed Long that his church would be condemned as a fire hazard unless the "violations" were corrected immediately. The church was almost as good as condemned, because it was a poor church, and the Reverend Mr. Long had only $500 in the treasury.

Since it was Randolph who had gotten the church into trouble, he now felt obliged to come to its assistance. Appealing to the sleeping car porters and to the Tennessee State AFL, he quickly raised $2,000 and sent it to the Reverend Mr. Long. It was the Brotherhood's duty, he told the porters, "to stand by this courageous minister in the deep South." We are not told whether the sheriff kept his threat to run Long out of Memphis.

An aspect of the enormous political popularity Randolph enjoyed in the 1940's was the increased attention he received from women—"increased" because, with his fine looks and manners, he had never lacked female admirers. How seriously he took all this is hard to say. There are few of his contemporaries who admit to any knowledge of his private life, and fewer who are disposed to discussing anything that is not consistent with his public image of monumental dignity.

Perhaps an indication of how little importance Randolph attached to the attention he received from women all over the country is the number of private letters he passed on to his secretary to be filed away among the Brotherhood's papers. One, from Washington, D.C., tinged with jealousy: "As for me; keep me waiting—it's okay. There are sights along the road for me to see, but that road leads to you—and don't forget it. Of that, I'm as sure as I am of your vision." One from Chicago: "When are you coming over for dinner? . . . I have an apartment now and can cook a meal." From St. Louis: "I look at the wine and think of you. I'll never open it." Someone in Iowa, who wanted to arrange a tryst with him in Chicago, quoted Omar Khayyám: "Here with a Loaf of Bread beneath the bough / A Flask of wine, and a Book of Verse—and Thou / Beside me singing in the Wilderness / And Wilderness is Paradise enow." Another from Washington: "I should be very happy to receive a telephone call from you, during your next visit to 'Dee Cee' and most highly honored to have luncheon with you, 'leader of the American Negro.' " From Nashville: "I was too smart to let my passion for you sever our friendship as long as the feeling wasn't reciprocally related. Again I was informed by . . . that you were so very interested in lots and lots of beautiful women that a person with no beauty or charm were merely hoping in vain for admiration from you . . . there's something so mystical about you." And from Los Angeles: "Remember it is a promise. When you again come to the Coast, you are to visit the poet. . . . We will have not merely a chat, but a conversation that will sizzle the atmosphere."

An account of his response to similar attentions is given by C. L. Dellums:

I don't think a man ever lived who women begged and chased more than that man. They tried everything but rape. Webster and I had a joke between us, that we followed Chief around to handle the overflow. And they were the most beautiful women. Lots of times he would lean on one of us and whisper, "You all get me out of here." It was always depressing having to get out of there. I've seen women try everything to get him, plead with him to come up to their hotel room for a nightcap or something. He would just say, "Sorry, I'm tired. Had a hard day. We better call it a night." Sometimes I'd say to him, "Chief, you kidding me?"

Randolph's apparent avoidance of such involvements was a result not only of his devotion to "my beautiful wife"—as he always referred to her, even from public platforms—but also of the caution he had developed during the days of his struggle against the Pullman Company, when attractive women were sometimes sent up to his hotel room with instructions to seduce him into compromising situations. "He tried to teach us in the early days of the Brotherhood," Dellums says, "that we can't take the chance of getting involved in any kind of scandal, that women were one of the frames they used to get you. He was a man of great moral principles. Even when he was the number-one Negro in America, and people were offering him everything, you couldn't get him to abandon his principles. He is the only man I know that nothing could buy."

18 / We Won't Go

Though President Roosevelt's executive order of June, 1941, did not touch upon the problem of segregation in the armed forces, Randolph and the March on Washington movement had decided against pressing a desegregation campaign. They felt that such a campaign, in arousing public feeling—black feeling, at any rate—against the military, might tend to embarrass the nation's war effort. Two years after the war, however, when Roosevelt's successor, Harry Truman, called for a peacetime draft, a new opportunity arose for Randolph—if not the declining march movement—to wage a crusade against the racial practices of the armed services.

The 1947 draft bill, proposing universal military training, contained no provision for a ban against segregation. This, Randolph said in a statement to the press, was "pregnant with indecency"; and, that November, he and Grant Reynolds, Commissioner of Correction for New York State, founded the Committee Against Jim Crow in Military Service and Training—which expanded, early in 1948, into the League for Nonviolent Civil Disobedience Against Military Segregation.

Next to Randolph and Reynolds, the most important figure in the league was the man who actually ran it, Bayard Rustin, the executive secretary. At thirty-eight, Rustin, one of the young militants who had denounced Randolph for calling off the 1941 march, was a confirmed pacifist, a member of the Society of Friends, cosecretary, with James Farmer, of the Race Relations Department of the Fellowship of Reconciliation, and field secretary of the Congress of Racial Equality, founded in 1942. In 1948, when he joined Randolph in the League for Nonviolent Civil Disobedience Against Military Segregation, Rustin had recently finished serving a three-year sentence in Lewisburg Penitentiary, as a conscientious objector during World War II. "Conscription for war," he had written his draft board, "is inconsistent with freedom of conscience, which is not merely the right to believe, but to act on the degree of truth that one receives, to follow one's own conviction. Today I feel that I must use my whole being to combat by nonviolent means the ever-growing racial tension in the United States." After reading Rustin's statement, Randolph had written to "applaud" him for his action: it "will give heart and spirit even to those who may disagree with your philosophy."

Rustin's career as a radical and dissenter went further back. In June, 1941, when he joined the Youth Division of the March on Washington Committee, Rustin, an evening student at City College—supporting himself by singing with Josh White and Leadbelly—had recently resigned from the Young Communist League. The YCL was one of the many leftist groups on the CCNY campus, and Rustin had joined it in 1938, when, as he later said, "Communist organizations appeared genuinely interested in peace and in racial justice," and when, as a consequence, pacifists could feel relatively comfortable in the YCL. Soon after he joined, Rustin had been assigned by the YCL to organize a committee against discrimination in the armed forces. But in June, 1941, after Hitler invaded the Soviet Union, the YCL, consistent with the reversal of Communist policy, had called in Rustin and ordered him to disband the committee. "You can all go to hell," Rustin says he told them. And before he walked out, he added, "I see that the Communist movement is only interested in what happens in Russia. You don't give a damn about Negroes."

It was then, disillusioned, that he had gone to see Randolph, to offer his services to the March on Washington Committee. Despite their differences—soon after Rustin joined the march movement, and again in 1948, as will be seen later—he and Randolph would retain an abiding respect and admiration for each other. Rustin recalls their first meeting: "The thing that impressed me the most was this man of great dignity and inner beauty, who, when I walked into his office, he stood up, came out from behind his desk, met me in the middle of the room, shook hands, offered me a seat—and I was nothing but a nobody. I spent about an hour with him, and all he wanted to know was how I thought. It wasn't until I got back outside that I realized that the man knew everything about what I thought and I didn't know a thing about his ideas." Their ideas concerning political action were quite similar, however, and in the years ahead they would become extremely close political collaborators.

On March 22, 1948, after Randolph had made it clear that the civil disobedience movement would be satisfied with nothing less than an executive order against military segregation, President Truman invited a group of black spokesmen to the White House to discuss the subject. Among them were Randolph, Walter White, Mary McLeod Bethune, Lester Granger, and Charles Houston, a special counsel for the NAACP.

As Randolph remembers, the meeting had been proceeding smoothly and amicably, until he said to Truman, "Mr. President, after making several trips around the country, I can tell you that the mood among Negroes of this country is that they will never bear arms again until all forms of bias and discrimination are abolished."

In a battle of bluntness Harry Truman came out second to no man, and he told Randolph, "I wish you hadn't made that statement. I don't like it at all."

Charles Houston intervened: "But, Mr. President, don't you want to know what is happening in the country?" Truman said he certainly wanted to know what was happening in the country; a president attracted more than enough yes men.

"Well, that's what I'm giving you, Mr. President," Randolph said, seizing the advantage before it disappeared again. "I'm giving you the facts." When the President allowed him to proceed, Randolph ran headlong into Truman again: "Mr. President, as you know, we are calling upon you to issue an executive order abolishing segregation in the armed forces." At this point, Truman simply thanked his visitors for coming, and said there didn't seem to be much more that they could talk fruitfully about.

But Truman's rebuff merely aroused Randolph's defiance. Testifying, nine days later, during hearings on the universal military training bill, Randolph (appearing with Grant Reynolds) told the Senate Armed Services Committee:

This time Negroes will not take a jim crow draft lying down. The conscience of the world will be shaken as by nothing else when thousands and thousands of us second-class Americans choose imprisonment in preference to permanent military slavery. . . . I personally will advise Negroes to refuse to fight as slaves for a democracy they cannot possess and cannot enjoy. Let me add

that I am speaking only for myself. . . . But Negro leaders in close touch
with GI grievances would feel derelict in their duty if they did not support
such a justified civil disobedience movement—especially those of us whose
age would protect us from being drafted. . . . I personally pledge myself to
openly counsel, and abet youth, both white and Negro, to quarantine any jim
crow conscription system, whether it bears the label of UMT or Selective
Service. . . . On previous occasions I have seen the "national emergency"
psychology mow down legitimate Negro demands. . . . Many veterans, bitter over Army jim crow, have indicated that they will act spontaneously in
this fashion, regardless of any organized movement. "Never again," they say
with finality. I shall appeal to the thousands of white youth in schools and
colleges who are today vigorously shedding the prejudices of their parents
and professors. I shall urge them to demonstrate their solidarity with Negro
youth by ignoring the entire registration and induction machinery.

One of Randolph's admirers on the committee, Senator Wayne Morse,
of Oregon, was distressed:

MORSE: . . . let us assume this hypothetical. A country proceeds to attack
the United States or commits acts which make it perfectly clear that our
choice is only the choice of war. Would you take the position then that unless
our Government granted the demands which are set out in your testimony, or
most of the demands . . . that you would recommend a course of civil disobedience to our Government?

RANDOLPH: . . the Government now has time to change its policy on segregation and discrimination and if the government does not change its policy
. . . in the interests of the very democracy it is fighting for, I would advocate that Negroes take no part in the Army.

MORSE: . . . I understand your answer to be that under those circumstances
even though it was perfectly clear that we would have to fight then to exist as
a country you would still recommend the program of civil disobedience?

RANDOLPH: Because I would believe that that is in the interest of the soul of
the country. . . .

MORSE: . . . do you have any doubt then that this Government as presently
constituted under the Constitution that governs us would necessarily follow a
legal course of action of applying the legal doctrine of treason to that conduct?

RANDOLPH: I would anticipate nationwide terrorism against Negroes . . .
but I believe that that is the price we have to pay for democracy that we
want.

MORSE: But on the basis of the law as it now exists . . . the doctrine of
treason would be applied to those people participating in that disobedience?

RANDOLPH: Exactly. I would be willing to face that doctrine on the theory and on the grounds that we are serving a higher law than the law which applies the act of treason to us when we are attempting to win democracy in this country and to make the soul of America democratic.

MORSE: But you would fully expect . . . that there would not be any other course of action of our Government to follow but indictments for treason?

RANDOLPH: . . . we would participate in no overt acts against our Government . . . ours would be one of non-resistance. Ours would be one of non-cooperation; ours would be one of non-participation in the military forces of the country. . . . We would be willing to absorb the violence, absorb the terrorism, to face the music and to take whatever comes, and we, as a matter of fact consider that we are more loyal to our country than the people who perpetrate segregation and discrimination upon Negroes because of color or race.

MORSE: . . . this is not the time and place for you and me to argue the legal meaning of aiding and abetting the enemy. . . .

If it was part of Wayne Morse's intention to frighten Randolph out of his purpose, he did not have to wait very long for the news that he had failed. On his way from the Armed Services Committee hearings, Randolph stopped off at the old March on Washington headquarters, in the capital, to address a group of young people who had gathered to await his report of the confrontation with Morse. "I am prepared," he told them, "to oppose a Jim Crow army till I rot in jail." And, upon returning to Harlem, he launched a series of public meetings, at the corner of Seventh Avenue and 125th Street, in which he counseled young men to refuse induction in a segregated army. In giving such counsel, he said, he was fully aware he was violating the Selective Service Act. "My exemption from the draft," he told one of the meetings, "is merely by accident of birth. And it imposes on me and others a special responsibility, a special moral obligation, not to expect of our younger brothers a conduct that the rules of self-respect and human decency preclude."

The black community had mixed feelings about all of this. Once more, Randolph lost the support of his old friends at the *Amsterdam News*. It was difficult to understand, said editor and publisher C. B. Powell, in a signed editorial, why Randolph and Grant Reynolds "should advocate a line of action that could easily lead to the rule of the minority, violence or revolution. . . . To counsel Americans not to enlist in the armed forces could so weaken the defense of the nation that a powerful totalitarian state could be tempted to step in and take over." A prominent stockbroker in Washington, D.C., wrote to assure Harry Truman that Randolph spoke only for himself and a handful of others, and that "you or anyone else who presumes that he did speak with authority did me an injustice, and . . . insulted the intelligence and loyalty of the colored citizens of this our country." Calling Randolph's the "extremist" viewpoint among black citizens, the *Pittsburgh Courier* said: "The Negro has never produced any traitors, and we do not believe he ever will." In a statement expressing "grave concern," the National Urban League warned that Randolph's campaign "would weaken the foundations of law on which our democratic processes rest." And, in an article in the *Amsterdam News,* Lester Granger, the Urban League's executive secretary, further warned: "Enemies of the Negro's progress . . . will use the Randolph statement as proof final of their claims that 'Negroes are not really 100% Americans,' and are not to be relied upon in time of crisis."

While Walter White, of the NAACP, did not, as he said, go "the whole hog" with Randolph—"our Association is not advising Negroes to refuse to defend their country if it is in danger"—he objected to Wayne Morse's criticism. "We would have valiant allies," White wrote Morse, "if you and some of your allies in the Senate could darken their faces and don a uniform for six weeks." Congressman Adam Clayton Powell, though no great admirer of Randolph, sent a statement to the Armed Services Committee asserting that Randolph's testimony "did most emphatically state the mood of the vast majority of the 15,000,000 colored Americans. He did not overstate it . . . . We are not going to be frightened by the cry of 'Treason.' If the finger of treason can be pointed at anyone, it must be pointed at those of you who are traitors to our Constitution and to our Bill of Rights. There aren't enough jails in America to hold the colored people who will refuse to bear arms in a jim crow army." Writing in the *Amsterdam News,* New York City Councilman Earl Brown said that "millions of other Negroes . . . feel even more bitter about the raw, undemocratic deal they got and are still getting in the armed services than Reynolds and Randolph. They may not be as articulate as these two men, but in their souls they hate the Army, the Navy, and the entire military set-up of the United States. . . . A man, white or black, cannot fight for his country with any heart or courage unless he knows he has the respect of his country."

But the most telling endorsement of Randolph's campaign came from those immediately affected. A poll of young black men, in Harlem, showed that 71 per cent favored a civil disobedience campaign against the draft. It only proved that Max Lerner had been correct when he wrote in the newspaper *PM* that "Randolph and Reynolds come closer to the true feelings of the masses of American Negroes than their more cautious and circumspect colleagues."

In July, 1948, while Hubert Humphrey, at the Democratic National Convention in Philadelphia, was waging his historic fight against the Dixiecrats to obtain a strong civil rights plank in the party's platform, scores of blacks, led by Randolph, were picketing the convention hall. Randolph's own picket sign read: PRISON IS BETTER THAN ARMY JIM CROW SERVICE.

Under the combined pressure of the Randolph campaign, the Humphrey civil rights floor fight, and the need to retain the black vote in the November election, President Truman, on July 26, issued Executive Order 9981, calling for an end to military discrimination "as rapidly as possible." The language was not clear, however—the word "segregation" had not been used—and Randolph wanted to know from Truman whether "you interpret your Executive Order on Armed Services to mean that its policy and purpose is to eliminate discrimination and segregation." When Truman replied, through Senator J. Howard McGrath, one of his spokesmen, that the order did indeed ban segregation, Randolph called off the civil disobedience campaign, and wired congratulations to the President for his "high order of statesmanship and courage."

But, as had happened in the summer of 1941, Bayard Rustin and the radical pacifist wing of the civil disobedience movement again refused to go along with Randolph's decision to call off the campaign. Since the order was neither strong nor positive enough, said Rustin and his supporters, they would carry on the disobedience campaign, with or without Randolph. Randolph told the rebels they were free to proceed by themselves if they wished, but that he himself was not only calling off the campaign; he was also disbanding the League for Nonviolent Civil Disobedience.

Again, Rustin balked. Disbanding the league, he argued, would be unfair to those blacks who were still in jail for refusing to serve in the armed forces. The most publicized case was that of Winfred Lynn, a Long Island landscape gardener, and brother of Conrad Lynn, a prominent civil liberties attorney. Winfred Lynn had been imprisoned after informing his draft board that while he was "ready to serve in any unit of the armed forces of my country which is not segregated by race," he would "not be compelled to serve in a unit undemocratically selected as a Negro group." Rustin and his supporters felt that both the campaign and the league should remain in existence, to press for the release of prisoners like Winfred Lynn as well as for an "unconditional law stating that non-segregation in military service is the national policy."

Randolph replied that he was bound by honor to keep his word with the President; he had demanded an executive order as the condition for discontinuing the campaign, and his demand had been met. Thus there was no further need for the campaign or the league. He did "not believe in civil disobedience for its own sake, but merely as a drastic last resort." On August 17, 1948, he asked Rustin to call a press conference for four o'clock the following afternoon, in order that he might announce the dissolution of the league.

Rustin agreed, "but what we didn't tell Randolph," he said later, "was that at ten o'clock in the morning we were going to call a press conference of our own, where we were going to denounce him as an Uncle Tom, a sellout, a reactionary, and an old fogey who did not understand the spirit of young people. So we had our press conference, and in the afternoon Randolph had his, and, of course, it was we who got the big headlines."

When, as late as October, 1948, Rustin and his followers were still sending out correspondence on League for Nonviolent Civil Disobedience stationery, Randolph was called upon to explain why a movement he had publicly disbanded was still functioning, in apparent defiance of his orders. Randolph issued a statement saying the league was being used by "a pacifist nucleus . . . to resist military segregation as a front for ulterior purposes." By "pacifist nucleus," Randolph was referring not only to Rustin and his followers, but also to A. J. Muste, a major influence upon the evolution of Rustin's pacifist ideas. Randolph explained that the pacifists had been welcomed into the league because he had felt their philosophy "would help to keep a potentially violent movement nonviolent in spirit and action." They had helped to do that, he said, but "we became very much disillusioned with the unethical tactics within the pacifist nucleus. . . . Good faith demands aboveboard dealings with draft-age youths and a separation of pacifist aims as such from an anti-jim crow campaign."

The League for Nonviolent Civil Disobedience finally collapsed in November, 1948. "Without Randolph," Rustin recalls, "we didn't have the strength to carry on or the clout to raise money." The young rebels dispersed, and Rustin, "feeling rotten over what I had done," avoided Randolph for more than two years. "When I finally got up the courage to walk into his office one day," Rustin says, "he was, as usual, standing at his desk, with arms outstretched, waiting to greet me. 'Bayard,' he said, 'where have you been? You *know* I've needed you.' Such character! He never said a word about what I had done to him."

What happened in 1948 was probably the last public disagreement between the two men. Since then they have worked so closely in their public activities that, especially over the last ten years, Rustin—whom Randolph describes as "innovative, creative, and a person of dreams and integrity"—has come to regard himself, and to be regarded as, the older man's protégé.

VI / In the Parliament of Labor

The labor movement cannot afford to be split along any lines. This society, left to itself, cannot, and will not, cure the basic ills of the masses. And there is no movement in the country which can get as much as possible out of the free-enterprise system as a movement of the working classes. Only the masses can, if they choose, bring about real change. The professors and the intellectuals can't do it by themselves. They can talk about principles but they alone can't change society, because they have no power. The masses have power, and only groups with power can challenge the power which oppresses them. The labor movement has that power, but first it must represent the economic needs and aspirations of all the masses. —A. PHILIP RANDOLPH

19 / Black Thorn

Despite the Brotherhood's desperate need for the support of organized labor, and its leader's belief that blacks had no choice but to fight racism within the AFL, it was nevertheless ironic that Randolph should have found a home there for the rest of his life. When he entered, in 1929, the AFL was dominated not only by unions that excluded black members, but also by the craft union philosophy, to which he, an advocate of industrial unionism, had never subscribed.

It must also have been quite difficult for Randolph to entertain any faith in the integrity of an organization that, though it had gone on record, in 1890, as looking with "disfavor upon trade unions having provisions which exclude from membership persons on account of race or color," claimed itself powerless to do anything about unions that engaged in such a practice. It was partly because of the AFL's failure or inability to enforce its official policy on race that, back in 1919, Randolph had written in his magazine, the *Messenger:* "The dissolution of the American Federation of Labor would inure to the benefit of the labor movement in this country in particular and the international labor movement in general. It is organized upon unsound principles. It holds that there can be a partnership between labor and capital. . . . It stands for pure and simple unionism as against industrial unionism. . . . The present American Federation of Labor is the most wicked machine for the propagation of race prejudice in the country." Nevertheless, whatever the apparent contradictions of his membership, Randolph as part of the AFL—even in later years when he became part of its leadership—would never be silent on the practices he had once condemned as an outsider.

Though Randolph's was the loudest and most insistent voice for racial justice in the AFL, it was neither the only nor the strongest one for industrial unionism. Among the minority of industrial unions in the AFL —all of which organized black workers on a basis of equality—were the United Mine Workers, the Amalgamated Clothing Workers, and the International Ladies' Garment Workers. And there was no more forceful spokesman for industrial unionism in the AFL than John L. Lewis, the leader of the Mine Workers, which, when Samuel Gompers was president of the AFL, had had more than half of the total black membership in the Federation.

It was partly because of William Green's origins in the Mine Workers that, as president of the AFL, he had felt so sympathetic toward the struggle of the Brotherhood of Sleeping Car Porters that he had cajoled the AFL into admitting Randolph's union in 1929. The rest of his concern for the Brotherhood had been inspired by the personal admiration he and Randolph shared for each other. But whatever early Mine Workers influences had shaped his social attitude as a trade unionist, and however personally likable he was, Green was able to give little or no support to Randolph's struggle in the AFL, mainly because as president he had virtually no power.

An ex-secretary-treasurer of the Mine Workers, Green had been elected president of the AFL at the age of fifty-two, when Samuel Gompers died in 1924. A mild-mannered man, he had the air of someone who would have been much happier discharging the duties of a country parsonage than reigning over contentious labor princes. In fact, before joining the Mine Workers, as a young man, he had thought of entering the Baptist ministry, and had taught one of the largest Baptist Bible classes in Coshocton, Ohio, where he was born. Thomas R. Brooks, a labor historian, has described Green as "a decent and humane man with a warm sympathy for the oppressed," who "could not command the respect of his tough-minded peers." It was because they were convinced that in Green they had found a weak president—one who would not dominate them—that his "tough-minded peers" had elected him to succeed Samuel Gompers. There could hardly have been a better choice than a man whom it pained severely to have to mediate contending claims, or who, as he did during one heated AFL debate, would plead, "Please, please, avoid this awful controversy." Green was hardly the man to put the prestige of the AFL presidency behind Randolph's struggle against discrimination in the powerful craft unions.

Considering his later experiences, Randolph's very first impression of an AFL convention was reasonably accurate. In 1926, not long after he started organizing the porters, he had traveled to Detroit, scene of the Federation's forty-sixth annual convention, to see what went on at such gatherings. He had been disappointed by "the absence of any hot intellectual battles on the floor," and had recorded his impressions in the *Messenger:* "Everything seems to have been ironed out in committees. . . . Green . . . has much the manner of a theolog. He is markedly dignified. He seems to be yet feeling his way as leader of the Federation. I felt that the Negro workers needed a strong man whose voice would be heard and respected in that parliament of American labor. There was not a word on their problems although the American labor movement cannot reach its goals without them."

By 1929, it was clear that it was Randolph who would be that strong black voice in the annual councils of organized labor, and at the session at which the Brotherhood was admitted to the Federation, he warned the delegates that the porters' union intended to function as "the spearhead which will make possible the organization of Negro workers."

At the beginning, it seemed a rather hopeless undertaking. For all the power and attractiveness of his voice, hardly anybody listened. Where most craft unions were concerned, their constitutions were their own business—not the AFL's—and they would bar black members for as long as they pleased. Randolph, however, according to John Brophy, of the Mine Workers, would continue to be "a thorn in the side of prejudice and discrimination and some union officials. It didn't deter him from introducing an annual resolution on the subject and to continue to call for fair treatment for the Negro in the interests of interracial justice. Randolph was a magnificent orator . . . with great powers of reasoning. Idealism radiated from him. He emphasized the ethical as well as what was practical for the trade union."

Progress was slow. As late as 1944, Herbert Northrup, in his *Organized Labor and the Negro,* pointed out that there were four chief methods by which national and international unions—the majority of them affiliated with the AFL—excluded black members: by provisions in their rituals; by provisions in their constitutions; by tacit consent; and by placing blacks in segregated, or auxiliary, unions. By Northrup's count, there was one union barring blacks by a provision in its ritual, thirteen by provisions in their constitutions, nine by tacit consent, and nine by setting up segregated locals.

The antidiscrimination resolutions Randolph introduced at almost every AFL convention contained two main demands: that the Federation pursue a more vigorous policy of organizing black workers; and, more important, that unions guilty of excluding black members be ordered by the AFL to end the practice—especially since it was in violation of the Federation's own stated principles—or, if they failed to comply, be expelled.

The AFL's response to these demands was that its member unions were autonomous bodies and that it had neither the power nor the right to dictate policies to them. This, as Randolph once replied, was "baloney": the AFL *had,* from time to time, overruled the autonomy of its member unions, when they had been found to be engaging in corrupt practices. Why, then, could not the Federation overrule its unions' Jim Crow policies?

For example, at the 1934 convention, in San Francisco, Randolph called upon the Federation to "go on record for the elimination of the color clause and pledge from the constitution and rituals of all trade and industrial unions," and to "expel any union which violates the constitution" of the AFL "by maintaining said color bar." Roy Burt, of the Laundry Workers International Union, replied that the AFL "cannot interfere with the autonomy of National and International unions. The American Federation of Labor cannot say who are eligible or who are not eligible to membership in National and International unions. That is the right of the . . . union itself, of which it cannot be deprived."

Year after year, craft unionists endorsed this position. Said Hugh E. MacGowan, of the Boiler Makers, at the 1943 convention, in Boston: "This institution [the AFL] is, as its name implies, a federation of autonomous and independent and self-governing international unions. It is, as its founders have often declared . . . a purely voluntary organization, and as long as it remains voluntary and concedes to each international union the right to manage its own affairs it will remain the guiding star of the American labor movement." In 1944, at the convention in New Orleans, William Green himself endorsed the prevailing philosophy: "The American Federation of Labor is not an organization; it is a federation of organizations and each organization, constituting a federated part of the federation, is clothed with autonomous authority to formulate, shape, and administer its own affairs. . . . Now, if Brother

Randolph has any quarrel, it must be with other organizations affiliated with the [AFL], not with us."

Randolph's speech at the Tampa, Florida, convention, in 1936, was typical of his many replies to such arguments:

Autonomy is not something absolute. . . . You have this doctrine of autonomy with respect to states' rights, and yet there are limitations set upon states' rights. . . . No state is permitted to ignore the income tax law. No state is permitted to set up a separate postal arrangement of its own. . . . If the American Federation of Labor can say to an international union that you cannot go out and organize workers without the scope of your jurisdiction, by invading the field of another union, it seems to me that the American Federation of Labor ought to be able to say to a national or international union that you cannot remain . . . if you go out and proceed to organize a given group of workers and exclude from that organization workers that come within the scope of your jurisdiction. . . . The white and black workers in the South cannot be organized separately as the fingers on my hand. They must be organized altogether, as the fingers on my hand when they are doubled up in the form of a fist. . . . If they are organized separately they will not understand each other, and if they do not understand each other they will fight each other, and if they fight each other they will hate each other, and the employing class will profit from that condition.

Although, as he told the 1941 convention, in Seattle, it was true that the constitution of the AFL itself frowned on discrimination, "it is difficult for the public to differentiate between the American Federation of Labor discriminating against Negroes and international unions affiliated with the AFL discriminating against Negroes." And, at Boston, in 1943, he told the delegates:

The [AFL] cannot continue to exist with a part of its members who are white as first-class union men and another part who are colored as second-class union men. This division of the house of labor is fatal to its existence and future. . . . Even though these international unions are autonomous it [the AFL] ought to have the courage to say to them, "Your policy is wrong and it is up to you to bring your policy in harmony and in conformity with the basic principle of the American Federation of Labor, as expressed in the constitution." . . . If the AFL claims that it is the house of labor then it cannot escape criticism for the wrongs committed in that house. If the AFL is justified in claiming credit for numerical increase in general membership, it must bear the guilt for the lack of increase in Negro union membership because of a narrow racial policy.

Besides, Randolph said, the unions' appeal to the right of autonomy was a mere cover-up for their racial bigotry. Nor could this bigotry have survived, he said, had the AFL exerted in behalf of racial integration one-tenth of the energy it spent defending the exclusive jurisdiction of its unions.

Under Randolph's persistent attacks, many craft unionists did, indeed, crawl out from under their "cover-up" of autonomy and reveal their racial motives. At one convention, a Southern delegate, replying to Randolph, said, "You can't mix oil with water, even if you want to." At another, John P. Frey contended that the American people could not be forced "to do things that run strongly against the grain." And Andrew Furuseth, of the Seamen's union, once told Randolph that race, after all, was "the most terrific force in the whole of human life."

During the years of William Green's presidency, Randolph was never more severely reprimanded than at the Seattle convention, in 1941, at Boston, in 1943, and at New Orleans, in 1944. At Seattle, three months after President Roosevelt had issued Executive Order 8802, barring discrimination in defense industry, Randolph urged the AFL to appoint a committee to investigate race bias "in unions or employment opportunities." In doing so, he named several unions whose racial policies were in violation of the President's executive order. The most guilty, he said, were the Painters, Plasterers, Cement Workers, Metal Workers, Machinists, Boiler Makers, and Carpenters.

He also singled out certain trade unionists for special comment. Turning to John P. Frey, head of the AFL's Metal Trades Department, Randolph said, "Now, no doubt, we all know that Mr. Frey has a fine spirit and believes in sound trade union principles, but when it comes to the application of these principles with relation to the Negro they do not seem to hold up." Of Harvey Brown, delegate from the Machinists, he observed that "Brother Brown has an obligation to make a statement to America on this matter. . . . If the Machinists union is going to persistently defy the President's Executive Order, then the AFL ought to put the Machinists union out." Finally, he told the entire convention, "Negroes are not begging you for anything. We are calling upon you for these things on a basis of right. We have earned the right to call for liberty and equality of consideration on matters of work and other issues affecting the citizens of this country."

John P. Frey was the most indignant. Randolph's remarks, he said, disturbed me more than any statements in connection with the racial problem in this country which have ever been made in a convention of the American Federation of Labor. It is evident that the delegate came here with one specific object in mind, and that was to present an indictment, and that considerable research work has been done, and now we have the indictment as part of our record. . . . The delegate . . . has an advantage over every other delegate who is present. He is the only one who has had the full advantages of an education in Harvard University. He studied logic, he studied philosophy, he studied ethics, he studied the humanities and human nature as well, and I again express regret that a trade union delegate should rise and present the type of indictment which this highly cultured individual presented this morning. . . . If there is any institution in these United States to whom the colored race owes more than any other, it is this American Federation of Labor. The delegate's organization could not have come into existence, in all likelihood, had it not been for the assistance given . . . by organizers of the American Federation of Labor. . . . And yet, instead of hearing one word of appreciation for what the [AFL] and its constituent unions have done . . . all we listen to is an indictment. And let us look some facts in the face. . . . The delegate's organization is composed exclusively of members of the colored race, and no white individual is permitted to become a member. So we have a gentleman rising here and accusing us of willful, deliberate race prejudice when the great organization he heads will not permit a white person to become a member. . . . Racial prejudice was developed in these United States long before the American Federation of Labor came into existence. The [AFL] cannot change men's minds and men's attitudes in every portion of the country . . . It almost seems as though he was deliberately endeavoring to inject a statement into this convention which would make our task of organizing the Negro workers ten times more difficult than it has been in the past.

"I am able to sustain every charge I have made on this floor," Randolph replied, "and . . . I don't retract a single one I have made."

At the 1943 convention, in Boston, Randolph delivered another lengthy indictment of segregated unions, and ended by saying:

The race problem is the number one problem of America today. It is the number one problem of American labor. It is the number one problem of the American Federation of Labor. . . . And brothers let me warn you that unless a sound, unequivocal and definite position is taken on the question of democracy for Negroes in the [AFL] and other agencies, the tides of Fascism are going to rise in this country and wipe out not only the Negroes but organized labor as well. . . . Fascism will use the Negro as scapegoat, but while they are attacking Negroes today they will attack the Jews tomorrow and they will attack the Catholics the next day.

Confessing his inability to speak "in polished Harvard accents, nor in the refined cultural language of the Washington drawing rooms," Hugh MacGowan, of the Boiler Makers, said that Randolph, as a "professional Negro," was "one of the greatest causes contributing to the failure" of his people. The delegate of the Electrical Workers said it was "getting tiresome in convention after convention to hear someone who is out shouting from the housetops. Maybe he thinks he is doing a good job for the people he is representing, but I share the views of the others that he is doing them a disservice. He is agitating and not doing anything concrete." But, once again, it was John P. Frey whom Randolph had angered the most:

. . . something was done here . . . which I feel is the greatest injury done the Negro race since the question has come into these conventions. There was deliberately put into [the] record a statement calculated to place the American Federation of Labor in a false position as to its basic policy. . . . To me, that is little short of a moral crime. . . . Delegate Randolph may not realize it, but . . . he rendered the greatest disservice to the colored race that has ever been rendered at any time since the Negro became a free man.

Randolph felt that this called for a reply:

There seems to be some spirit in the convention . . . that criticism of policies that are obviously unsound is unjustified. Now whenever an organization that proposes to be democratic takes [that] position . . . then that organization is moving backward. . . . Certainly it is recognized that in the arena of criticism sound policies, truth and programs are developed. . . . Nothing has been said on this floor that causes me to retreat from the position I have taken. . . . Auxiliary unions based upon race are not necessary, they are undemocratic and un-American, and upon that we rest our case.

It was not, however, the kind of case that could be rested for long—especially since the AFL was doing virtually nothing about it; and at the New Orleans convention, the following year, Randolph again demanded that the Federation condemn those of its affiliates which maintained segregated unions:

This Federation cannot maintain a dual form of membership. Either the second-class membership will eventually prevail and become normal or the first-class membership will become normal and prevail. . . . It is a species of dangerous discrimination, it is unethical and opposed to democracy. . . .

When this Federation of labor puts its stamp of approval upon second-class trade union membership, typified by the auxiliary union, it is aiding and fostering the spread of trade union fascism in America. Discrimination based on religion, nationality or race cannot live in the same country together. Therefore, some choice must be made and the choice is not made solely in the interest of the Negro workers, but from the point of view of the growing power and strength of the labor movement, because unless that is done, no one can predict the future of the labor movement of America. . . . You cannot condemn the existence of the CIO and yet permit and countenance . . . the existence of a dual union in the American Federation of Labor. Your position is inconsistent, it is unsound, illogical. As a matter of fact, it is a joke.

Hugh MacGowan said that he had been attending AFL conventions since 1913, "and never in all those years have I listened to a more offensive address." Randolph's remarks, he said, were "arrogant and insolent," and "some of us are getting just a bit tired of being kicked around by professional agitators. . . . I wonder if he is in the right organization? I wonder if he is in sympathy with the American Federation of Labor or its aims and objects?" Lev Loring, a delegate from the Tennessee State Federation of Labor, recognized no race problem in the AFL, "only the race problem that is brought up by Delegate Randolph. He goes up and down the length and breadth of this country preaching social equality. . . . We are the sole judge of who shall become our members. . . . I think it is high time we should stop this professional agitation in the labor movement. White people are not raising the race question. It is the Negroes themselves."

But Randolph was unrepentant:

I don't care what you say about professional agitators. I will continue to denounce discrimination and condemn the auxiliary unions on the floor of this convention as long as there is breath in my body and I am in this convention, and there is no delegate . . . that can intimidate me. I don't care who you are . . . if anyone thinks that Negroes are going to wait a thousand years in this country to get their rights, they have another thought coming. We are going to continue to fight with all our might to change this despicable and contemptible situation. . . . Get as mad as you want to. I don't care how mad you get, I will continue to tell the truth.

Except for Milton Webster (who had accompanied him to every convention since 1936), C. L. Dellums (who went occasionally), and John L. Lewis (before he and the Committee for Industrial Organization were suspended from the AFL), Randolph had little or no support on the floor of the annual conventions. Regarded by many as "a troublemaker," he was often hissed when he got up to speak, or interrupted by the rumble of chairs as some delegates took the opportunity to repair to the bar for a drink. Webster would recall that "nobody spoke to him. When he passed anyone at the convention, they would say 'there goes the number one hell-raiser in the AFL.'" Randolph says that "John L. Lewis was the only one who would have anything to do with the Brotherhood delegation. He would leave his seat among the other vice presidents on the platform and come down on the floor to sit at our table. It used to make the rest of the big unionists mad. For we were not only black, you see, we were small. We were nothing, in size, compared to those big unions."

According to Julius Hochman, of the Dressmakers union, "There is no question that Randolph had a very hard time, but it never really touched him, he couldn't be humiliated." A. H. Raskin, of the *New York Times,* who covered several of the conventions, remembers that "John P. Frey used to get up and mock Randolph in a terribly degrading way. Frey had a mean look about him, and invented a lot of background about Randolph. It was just miserable. But Phil took it all with his usual dignity, no personal bitterness. He and Webster were always together. Webster was more of the get-along type, hale fellow, very likable guy, though a good deal tougher. At least, he gave the appearance of toughness, but his basic quality was, I suspect, geniality. He and Phil made a good team, having qualities that supplemented each other. But they really weren't part of the closeness of the conventions. You could see that they were isolated, sort of strangers clinging to one another. They were really alone all the time. Whenever they were with the others, there was a sort of strain."

Recalling Randolph's speech at the 1934 convention, Jacob Potofsky, of the Amalgamated Clothing Workers, says, "His oratory was terrific . . . but there was no action . . . he was a voice in the wilderness." And James Wechsler has written of the 1941 convention, which he covered for the *New York Post,* that Randolph "rose in lonely valor at that session to plead his case against discrimination. . . . He spoke with an eloquence and passion that no one else approached. . . . No one was moved to speak in his support. He betrayed no outward anguish about the silence; I may have felt lonelier than he did."

Randolph speaks in a different key, however, of his annual frustrations of the AFL conventions. "We gave them hell every year," he says today, apparently enjoying the memory. "They didn't pass our resolutions, but we brought them religion."

Though, as labor historian Walter Galenson observes, Randolph "profoundly influenced" the "evolution of AFL racial policies during the 1930's," it would not become noticeable until later, particularly during the 1950's, when a number of craft unions removed the color clauses from their constitutions, and black membership in organized labor showed a dramatic increase. Still, even through the fifties and early sixties, Randolph continued to press his brand of religion upon the labor movement, and he would arouse the AFL's new president, the volatile George Meany, in a way that he had never moved the complaisant William Green.

20 / Life with Meany

In October, 1935, after the AFL convention had rejected a resolution aimed at converting it to a policy of industrial unionism, John L. Lewis began his withdrawal from the Federation, and Randolph lost one of his few friends at labor's annual meetings. On November 9, Lewis formed the Committee for Industrial Organization, made up of unions in the AFL that shared his philosophy; on November 23, he resigned as a vice president of the Federation; in 1937, following a two-year debate of the industrial union issue, the AFL expelled all unions belonging to the Committee for Industrial Organization; and, in 1938, the Committee became a new labor federation, the Congress of Industrial Organizations.

On his way out of the 1935 convention, Lewis, as he often did, stopped at the table of the Brotherhood of Sleeping Car Porters to exchange greetings with Randolph. "Phil," he said, before leaving, "are you coming with us? You know you belong with us." It was true, for the two men shared the conviction that mass production workers should be organized according to the industry in which they worked, rather than according to individual crafts. It was also true because the pro-Lewis group of unions in the AFL did not discriminate against black workers— certainly did not bar them from membership. And, during one of the debates on the industrial union question, Randolph had told the convention, "Our people believe in the United Mine Workers and John L. Lewis, no matter what other people say about him." Nevertheless, Randolph now told Lewis he was sorry; the Brotherhood could not go out with the CIO. "I have no quarrel with your unions," Randolph said. "You organize black workers. My fight, the fight to organize Negro workers, is in the AFL. I must stay here and carry on that fight."

Lewis had once described the AFL as standing still with its face to the past, and it was doubtful whether a small and weak union like the sleeping car porters could—on the question of race, anyway—do what the larger and more powerful unions could not do: turn the AFL around. But leaving the Federation would, in Randolph's mind, have been an admission—one he was not ready to make—that he had failed in the major task he had set himself: if not to turn the Federation around, then to move it substantially in the direction of racial democracy. Besides, it was doubtful whether within the CIO, a potential community of friends, his voice as the spokesman for black labor could have retained the resonance it had achieved while rebounding off the moral and political intransigences within the AFL.

In remaining with the Federation, Randolph continued to be not only the voice of racial democracy, but also one of the few delegates who argued that the principle of a united labor movement took precedence over the interests, however real, of the contending craft and industrial factions. Here is what he said at the 1937 convention, shortly before the AFL expelled the CIO unions:

If these unions in the CIO are put out we are going to transfer this controversy from the arena of discussion, reason and sanity to the field of vituperation and violence, and perhaps bloodshed. . . . The main question before the convention is not . . . democratic control and procedure, it is not the question of communism, but . . . of the right of the members of the CIO group to organize the mass production industries along industrial lines. . . . I believe that unity is more important than craft unionism. I believe that unity is more important than industrial unionism. . . . I appeal to President Green to exercise his influence in this tremendous conflict. What are you going to do when you expel the members of the CIO? You are simply going to mess up the labor movement. . . . If you adhere merely to the letter, the letter killeth, and only by interpreting this great question in the spirit of unity will you have life in the American labor movement.

The rift was not healed until 1955, when the AFL and the CIO came together again in the merged federation it is today. On the questions of civil rights and race prejudice in organized labor, the new federation adopted a more progressive position than the AFL alone had taken. Randolph, the AFL's nominee, was one of the two blacks elected to the twenty-nine-member Executive Council, labor's top leadership. The other was Willard Townsend, of the United Transport Service Employees, nominated by the CIO. The constitution of the AFL-CIO called for the formation of a Committee on Civil Rights "vested with the duty and responsibility to assist the Executive Council to bring about at the earliest possible date the effective implementation of the principle . . . of non-discrimination." As Walter Reuther, of the United Automobile Workers, told the inaugural convention, in 1955, "I believe that this labor movement of ours will make a great contribution in the field of civil rights."

Though discrimination was still widespread among the unions, the degree to which Randolph had "profoundly influenced" the racial policies of the AFL was now evident: all the unions, except three, had dropped from their constitutions the clauses barring black members.

When William Green died, in 1952, he was succeeded, in the presidency of the AFL, by George Meany, a fifty-eight-year-old ex-plumber, who had been the Federation's secretary-treasurer since 1940. A blunt, plain-speaking, pragmatic craft union man, Meany had been practically raised in the plumbers' local his father once headed in the Bronx, New York. His ideas and personality, unlike Green's, were not only congenial to the prevailing craft union spirit of the AFL; they were also able to dominate the conventions as only those of Samuel Gompers, the first president, had done. The "burly" and "ham-fisted" Meany, as Thomas R. Brooks describes him, "seemed to be the perfect embodiment of the AFL 'leave 'em alone' bureaucrat, the least likely union leader to upset the ancient traditions of the craft-oriented federation. . . . He does not waste time with subtleties."

While Randolph and Meany would eventually develop a deep mutual admiration, it would not be as spontaneous as the one Randolph and Green had felt for each other. But it would be more productive—even though, unlike Green, Meany would sometimes denounce Randolph, in bitter and offensive language, from the chair of the convention. Perhaps it was because the Meany-Randolph admiration would be forged against serious conflicts of political belief and formidable differences of personal style and character that it would be far stronger. As Randolph has said, what he came to admire the most in Meany were his "candor and honesty" and his readiness to "deliver" once he had committed himself to a course of action.

But anyone watching their bitter clashes at the September, 1959, convention, in San Francisco, would have found it difficult to discern that they had by then, as they claimed, developed warm feelings toward each other. The first clash took place on the afternoon of the fourth day, when, during the debate on a resolution to readmit the International Longshoremen's Association—which had been expelled from the AFL for corruption in 1953—Randolph told the convention that though he favored readmission, the ILA was "guilty of some incredible and unspeakable discriminatory practices against Negro and Puerto Rican workers," and should be ordered, as a condition of readmission, to end such practices.

Meany, who, like most of the delegates, may have been sick and tired of such remarks, replied:

Now in regard to Phil Randolph, I would like to say a word to him personally. I think it is time he got on the team. I think it is time he joined the organized labor movement and became part and parcel of the AFL-CIO. He is a member of our Executive Council. We appointed a Committee of the Executive Council in February to investigate this thing. . . . That Committee worked for eight months. Phil Randolph never came to me with any complaint. He attended the meetings of the Executive Council. He made no complaint. . . . I never knew of discrimination in the ILA. It has had Negro officers, Negro members as long as I've known them. Its first Vice President for many years was a Negro. And to come at this late date, where he has an audience . . . and come up with this material, I just don't think that is playing the game. I don't think that is playing on the team. . . . But I would like Brother Randolph to stay a little closer to the trade union movement and pay a little less attention to outside organizations that render lip service rather than real service.

Meany did not entirely dismiss Randolph's complaint, however, saying, "We can look into that and we certainly will expect the ILA to look into it also."

At the next morning's session, Randolph, Webster, and Dellums moved that the Brotherhood of Locomotive Firemen and Enginemen and the Brotherhood of Railroad Trainmen—two of the three unions that still had clauses in their constitutions barring black members*—be expelled from the AFL-CIO, "unless they eliminate the color bar from their constitutions within six months." When the resolutions committee recommended, instead, that the Executive Council should "work with these organizations to obtain, at the earliest possible date, compliance . . . with the civil rights requirements," Randolph took the floor

---

* The other was the International Brotherhood of Locomotive Firemen and Engineers.

to register my exception to the [resolutions committee's] report on the grounds that it does not provide any time limit for the elimination of the color bar. . . . I submit to this convention that in the mid-20th century the color bar in any trade union is absolutely incompatible with the basic principles and ideals of free trade unionism. . . . It is my opinion that even though these organizations be strong, history shows that liberty is indivisible, and the right to work belongs as much to a black locomotive fireman as it does to a white locomotive fireman. . . . For a long time, the delegates of the Sleeping Car Porters have been fighting racial discrimination on the floor of the conventions of the AFL-CIO and the AFL particularly. Nobody knows better than George Meany that the delegates of the Brotherhood of Sleeping Car Porters will never back up in their fight on racial discrimination in the affiliates of the AFL-CIO, regardless of opposition. . . . I have absolutely no question about the commitment of George Meany to the great values of human freedom and human dignity, and I believe that if a particular case of discrimination is brought face to face to him he will do the right thing. . . . Nevertheless, the responsibility of keeping this question alive in the labor movement is the responsibility of the Negro trade unionists. . . . I submit that the color bar is a mockery of trade union democracy. . . . The question has been raised about giving the unions time to take the color bar out . . . let me advise you that the unions have had the color bar in their constitutions for over 50 years. How much more time do they want? . . . What kind of trade union democracy is that? . . . I understand that you don't want to put anybody else out of the AFL-CIO, and before it has been suggested that if you put them out, you will make them mad. Well, if you keep them in you will make us mad.

More coolly this time, Meany rebutted Randolph:

. . . until a few years ago, these unions had officers who were in favor of keeping the color bar. . . . The heads of these unions now do not favor the retaining of the color bar and have indicated that by their public statements and by their actions. . . . Now the question is, do we try to make some further progress or do we try to work with them under a deadline hanging over their heads? It is my thought that all efforts . . . to work with them would end the minute we give them an ultimatum or give them a deadline, because then we are playing into the hands not of the officers, who are sound, and who are with us on this question, but playing into the hands of those people in those organizations who are determined to keep this color bar. After all, these are human institutions, and you set a goal for yourself and you keep striving for that goal. I admire Phil Randolph for striving for his goal. And while he has made progress . . . none of us is going to live long enough to reach the state of perfection where we say this matter has been entirely and completely eliminated from the social structure of our country. We just won't live that long, and we know it.

But the convention really exploded later that day, when Randolph, Webster, and Dellums introduced another resolution, demanding "that racially segregated local unions be liquidated and eliminated . . . regardless of contention that some members of racially segregated local unions desire to maintain" such unions. The resolution continued: "It is just as unsound and indefensible for national and international unions . . . to tolerate, countenance and maintain racially segregated unions on the grounds that the members of the said unions desire to maintain them as it would be for national and international unions . . . to tolerate . . . unions under Communist domination and corrupt influences, on the grounds that the members of the said unions wish and desire said unions."

The resolutions committee said it would support the motion if the word "liquidated" was deleted. But Harry Bates, of the Bricklayers union, was not going to vote for the resolution in any form. "Many of these colored unions," he said, "own their own halls and are strong financially and the membership does not want to be bothered. They want to maintain those unions the same as they have over the years. . . . We are going to keep those unions and maintain those conditions because if we don't we can't maintain the conditions of the white unions." Meany calmed Bates's fears. The AFL-CIO, he said, "does not intend to force national unions, despite their constitutions, to expel from membership unions that have every legal right to membership."

This brought Randolph to his feet:

This resolution is a declaration of a new policy and it is a policy against racially segregated unions. Now, either we are for or we are not for segregated unions. It isn't logical to permit an organization to carry on a given type of behavior merely because the members want it. If it is true then a Communist-dominated union is perfectly legitimate in the AFL-CIO. A union under corrupt influences would be legitimate if the members wanted it. Therefore we cannot conclude that because a group of Negro members . . . want a racially segregated union, that is proper and sound and in harmony with the constitution . . . of the AFL-CIO. That is just as simple as day is day and night is night. . . .

MEANY: I can say, Brother Randolph, if you mean what you say you certainly made it very simple. As I understand it, it is your position that you put the desire of the Negro members to maintain their union as it has been maintained over the years in the class with corruption and communism. Will you consider it a violation of this policy if the Bricklayers union did not attempt to eliminate these segregated unions that they have had for so many years because the members do not want them eliminated? Is this your idea of a democratic process, that you don't care what the Negro members think? You don't care if they want to maintain the union they have had for so many years? I would like an answer to that.

RANDOLPH: Yes.

MEANY: That is not my policy. I am for the democratic rights of the Negro members. Who appointed you as the guardian of the Negro members in America? * You talk about tolerance—

RANDOLPH: Just a minute.

MEANY: Do you think this union should destroy the locals that have lasted so many years despite the fact that the members want to maintain them? You say "Yes," and you call it democracy. It is not my type of democracy. These Negro members have the same rights as any other members even though you think you should think for them.

RANDOLPH: I say this, and I want to make it clear. We don't have to become emotional about it. I don't believe that the members of a union have a right to maintain a Jim Crow local. I don't believe that a group of Negro members of a union have a right to maintain a Jim Crow local if we believe in an accepted trade union policy.

MEANY: That is up to them. They have as much right to think as you have.

RANDOLPH: What about a group of members in a union who want to have a communist-dominated union?

MEANY: They can't have it and belong in this Federation.

RANDOLPH: But then they ought not to have it as a Jim Crow local either.

MEANY: This is where you and I part company, Phil. I think these Negro members have some rights and have a right to think for themselves.

In passing the resolution with the word "liquidated" omitted, the convention, in effect, killed it. Very few of Randolph's antidiscrimination resolutions had ever been passed, let alone in their original form. Thus the delegates had supported his latest resolution only after they made sure that, in pulling its teeth, they had preserved the privileges the resolution was designed to destroy. The objective of the resolution, as Ran-

---

* This remark, taken from the official record of the convention proceedings, differs slightly from what was reported in the newspapers the following day. In his story to the *New York Times*, A. H. Raskin quoted Meany as saying, "Who the hell appointed you as the guardian of all the Negroes in America?"

dolph explained, "was to destroy the old principle of local trade union autonomy by which the local union membership had sole and final authority over the policy of their union. My position was that the local unions were a part of a larger trade union movement and if each local union were allowed absolute autonomy in matters pertaining to membership, it would not only limit the growth of a trade union movement, but it would kill the chances of nonwhite workers to become part of a national trade union movement. Everybody knew that as long as you conceded that kind of power to the local unions they would use it to keep out blacks and other ethnic minorities. And if the national trade union movement allowed that to happen, then they were in some way acquiescing in the practice. A trade union movement begins to court extinction when it begins to limit membership. If it cannot continue to grow, then it weakens its position as the only countervailing force in America against the power of big business."

Meany's outburst at San Francisco—"Who [the hell] appointed you . . . ?"—brought a strong reaction from the liberal press and the black community. The remark, said the *New York Post,* "was not only intemperate and abusive, but an offensive echo of Southern sophistry. . . . Randolph speaks for millions of colored people throughout the nation in and out of his union . . . his authority to voice his people's aspirations for an end to discrimination is incontestable." The *Baltimore Afro-American* called Meany's statement "shocking and distasteful," and likened his position to that of Senator James Eastland, of Mississippi, and Senator Richard Russell, of Georgia. The Trade Union Leadership Council—"composed of Negro trade unionists from all sections of the labor movement"—wrote Meany "to make it unmistakably clear . . . that we unqualifiedly support the position of Brother Randolph and that we are at a complete loss to understand yours. . . . We also want to clear you up on the matter that seemed so vexing to you, the question of Brother Randolph's 'appointment' as guardian of all Negroes in the labor movement. . . . Brother Randolph was accorded this position by acclamation of the Negro people in recognition of his having devoted almost half a century of his life in freedom's cause." And the NAACP told Meany, in a wire, that it "fully supports Randolph's demand for positive action against discrimination."

To give Meany an opportunity to explain his position, William Walker, publisher of the *Cleveland Call and Post,* arranged an off-the-record luncheon in Washington, D.C. His remark to Randolph, Meany told the group of black civil rights officials who attended the luncheon, had been nothing more than "convention language." His differences with Randolph, he assured them, were differences of tactics, not of objective. "Phil is a friend of mine," he concluded, "and an honest man. I am willing to rest my case on the judgment of honest men." Recalling the San Francisco incident, twelve years later, Meany maintained that "it was just a flare-up of the moment. I kind of blew my top. It has done nothing to mar my relationship with Phil Randolph, nothing at all. A few weeks after the flare-up, he and I flew together to a meeting of the International Confederation of Free Trade Unions, in Brussels. Phil and I were even discussing the remark on the plane, and we were quite amused by it."

Randolph's public statements were similar to Meany's. A. H. Raskin, who interviewed him after the convention, recalls that "Phil was hurt, because he had respect for Meany. But when I asked him how he felt about the whole thing, he took a very forbearing view of what Meany had said. 'I know George didn't mean it,' Phil said. 'When he thinks it over, he'll regret it.' He was hurt, but there was no vindictiveness in him." Randolph also told a reporter, a few days after the convention, that Meany's language was "the way of life in the trade union movement. It in no way affects my regard for him. I am now convinced that he is absolutely committed to the position I took at the convention. He now agrees that I was right. He is a tough man, but he is able to recognize when he is wrong and acknowledge it. Regardless of his views, he is honest. I don't know that I've had as sharp conflicts with any man in any movement as I've had with Meany, but I don't know of any one in the organized labor movement with more integrity."

Meany's integrity was something that even his harshest critics conceded. The *New York Post,* in the same editorial that deplored his outburst at San Francisco, also observed that "Meany's decency and integrity have often been demonstrated." And a few months later, A. H. Raskin wrote in the *New York Times* that "the unhappiest aspect of the bitter exchange was that it created the outward appearance of a rift over principle between the two men who had been most conspicuous in the implementation of this no-discrimination drive. . . . Actually, their differences have never been over which way the federation should go, but over how fast its progress should be and how much pressure it should exert to make it faster."

But so long as these basic differences remained, there would continue to be serious conflicts between Randolph and George Meany. Soon after the 1959 convention, even while they were making public declarations of mutual esteem and good feeling, Randolph was preparing to accept the presidency of a new black trade union organization—the Negro American Labor Council, conceived partly in response to the incident at San Francisco—which would again incur Meany's displeasure.

The chief aims of the NALC, which held its inaugural convention in May of 1960, in Detroit, were "to fight and work for the implementation and strengthening of civil rights in the AFL-CIO and all other bona fide unions"; to "secure the right of membership of Negro workers in the unions"; to "increase the opportunity for Negro employment and promotion on the job"; and to "encourage qualified Negro trade unionist participation in the executive, administrative and staff areas of the union."

The following are excerpts from a statement by Randolph to the steering committee of the proposed NALC, in the Hotel Carnegie, Cleveland, on November 14, 1959:

. . . the position of the National Negro Labor Council [the name was changed soon after to the NALC] which is in the process of development must be governed by basic premises relating to trade unions and civil rights. This proposed movement would have no reason for existence were it not committed to the support of and cooperation with the AFL-CIO as well as the national and international and local unions in affiliation with this body. By the same token there would be no reason for this movement were it not committed and dedicated to the abolition of racial discrimination and segregation in the labor movement, together with the achievement of fair representation and participation by Negro trade unionists in the various areas of the movement. Hence, the following basic premises are pertinent to the values of the proposed movement. . . . 1. Free labor unions are indispensable for human welfare in an industrialized society whose economic life is largely dominated by giant corporate business and financial interests. 2. Labor unions, like other human institutions, are imperfect. Their weaknesses and abuses, when clearly established, should be subject to vigorous and fair criticism. . . . 3. Free labor unions are essential to the strength, health and progress of our democratic society. . . . 4. The free private, voluntary organizations of economic enterprise, involving as they do great segments of the lives of all citizens, must also conform to the standards of justice, freedom and equality of opportunity that society establishes. . . . 5. Racial discrimination is basically incompatible with labor union democracy. 6. Racially seg-

306 / IN THE PARLIAMENT OF LABOR

regated or jim crow unions are morally wrong since they affront the dignity of the personality of Negro workers by attaching the stigma of racial inferiority to workers of color. . . . What can the [NALC] achieve? It can give Negro trade unionists a sense of unity, both among themselves and with their white brothers. . . . It can struggle to bring about the desegregation of the racially segregated unions. . . . [The NALC] is necessary because the AFL-CIO, though committed to a national policy against discrimination and segregation based upon race and color, will not voluntarily move toward the implementation of this policy unless it is caused to move, and it cannot be caused to move except through an organization which is committed to the elimination of discrimination and segregation. This is no reflection upon the leadership of the AFL-CIO. . . . The fact is, racial discrimination and segregation has reached the stage of institutionalization in the labor movement. It is taken for granted. It is viewed with utter complacency, apathy, unconcern, if not indifference. This has been true from the very foundation of the labor movement in the United States.

Because its leadership contained a number of young labor militants who did not share Randolph's loyalty to the AFL-CIO, the NALC would be torn by serious tactical and philosophical differences. Whereas Randolph wanted the new organization to function as a black pressure group within organized labor, the younger militants preferred to see it as a black federation of labor—not only separate and distinct from the AFL-CIO, but also opposed to it.

In any event, despite Randolph's assurances to the AFL-CIO—that the NALC's over-all objective was merely to strengthen the prestige of the trade union movement among blacks and to keep the labor federation faithful to its constitutional pledges against discrimination—it was not his voice that set the tone of the NALC, but that of the militants calling for an all-out war against Meany's organization.

In light of such rhetoric, Meany, who had turned down Randolph's invitation to attend the founding convention, in Detroit, denounced the NALC as a form of dual unionism, black separatism, and black nationalism. If black trade unionists wanted to form their own council, Meany said, it was up to them, but they should "keep out of our business and attend to their own."

Because Meany did not at first dissociate Randolph from what he considered the objectionable tone of the NALC, the relationship between Randolph and the AFL-CIO leadership had, by 1961, become more tense than at any time since the 1959 explosion at San Francisco. In the spring of 1961, Randolph submitted a memorandum to the Executive

Randolph leading pickets in demand for strong civil rights plank in Democratic party platform, Philadelphia, 1948 (UPI photo)

Randolph with Eleanor Roosevelt and Fiorello La Guardia at an FEPC rally, New York, 1946 (UPI photo)

Grant Reynolds and Randolph testifying before a Senate committee, Washington, 1948 (UPI photo)

Randolph addressing AFL-CIO national convention, 1961 (AFL-CIO)

George Meany, Randolph, and Milton Webster at the rostrum during AFL-CIO national convention (A. Philip Randolph Institute)

Bayard Rustin and Randolph announcing plans
for the March on Washington for Jobs and
Freedom, 1963 (A. Philip Randolph Institute)

Randolph and Roy Wilkins, with New York
civil rights leader Anna Hedgeman, planning
strategy for the March on Washington (UPI
photo)

At the White House after the 1963 March on Washington: civil rights leader Dr. Martin Luther King, Jr., Rabbi Joachim Prinz, chairman, American Jewish Congress, Randolph, President John F. Kennedy, and Walter Reuther, vice president, AFL-CIO (UPI photo)

Whitney Young and Randolph with President Lyndon Johnson, August, 1965, preparing for White House Conference on Civil Rights (UPI photo)

Announcing Randolph's Freedom Budget at the White House Conference in 1965: Morris B. Abram, Jr., Dr. Martin Luther King, Jr., Randolph, John Lewis, and William T. Coleman (UPI photo)

At a White House meeting, May, 1966: (clockwise from bottom left) Clarence Mitchell, AFL-CIO official Andrew Biemiller, Dorothy Height, Randolph, Roy Wilkins, Joseph L. Rauh, Floyd McKissick, John Lewis, Vice President Hubert Humphrey, Attorney General Nicholas Katzenbach, President Lyndon Johnson, and Dr. Martin Luther King, Jr. (White House photo, A. Philip Randolph Institute)

Bayard Rustin and Randolph, 1971 (Irene B. Bayer photo, A. Philip Randolph Institute)

At the White House, May, 1969 (White House photo, A. Philip Randolph Institute)

At his testimonial dinner, New York, May, 1969 (Wallace Murphy photo, A. Philip Randolph Institute)

Council charging that although only one AFL-CIO union still retained the color clause in its constitution (the Brotherhood of Locomotive Firemen and Enginemen and the Brotherhood of Railroad Trainmen, which had sparked the Randolph-Meany exchange at San Francisco, had removed theirs in 1960), several others continued to segregate blacks into separate locals, or exclude them by tacit consent. Therefore, said the memorandum, reiterating one of Randolph's familiar demands, the AFL-CIO should abolish the remaining forms of discrimination within six months. Once again, Randolph had not acted like a member of "the team." And in October, the Executive Council—at its quarterly meeting, held at the Commodore Hotel, in New York City—not only denied his charges, but also, in a twenty-page report, censured him for causing "the gap that has developed between organized labor and the Negro community."

Expelling unions, the censure report said, reaffirming the AFL-CIO's position, "does not cure the offending practices. Put outside the ranks of the federation, the offending organization is left free to carry on its discriminatory practices—probably more stubbornly than ever." Moreover, the report continued, the membership would be "no longer accessible to corrective influences from the parent body through education and persuasion." When a reporter from the *New York Times* asked George Meany why such a reasoning did not also apply to the Teamsters and other unions that had been expelled for corruption, Meany replied, "It does not. I do not equate the problem of racial discrimination with the problem of corruption any more than I equate Hungary with Little Rock." Meany had not only voted to censure Randolph; he also had criticized him publicly. Randolph should stop making it necessary for the AFL-CIO to defend itself against baseless charges, Meany said, adding, "We can only get moving on civil rights, if he comes over to our side and stops throwing bricks at us. I think we could do a lot with his cooperation. But it seems in the last two or three years, he's gotten close to these militant groups and he's given up cooperation for propaganda."

Public reaction was again strongly in Randolph's favor. Noting that the only member of the AFL-CIO leadership to vote against censure was Randolph himself, Richard Parrish—treasurer of the Negro American Labor Council, and a member of that organization's pro-Randolph faction—said that the silence of Randolph's liberal colleagues on the Executive Council was an "outrage." "Where was Walter Reuther, where was Joe Curran, where was Jim Carey? Where were all these liberals when the vote was taken?" (According to the *New York Times*, Reuther, of the United Automobile Workers, was not at the meeting. David Dubinsky, of the ILGWU, was there, as were Curran, of the National Maritime Union, and Carey, of the International Union of Electrical Workers.)

Roy Wilkins, of the NAACP, said the AFL-CIO's censure of Randolph reflected the labor federation's "moral bankruptcy." Dr. Martin Luther King, Jr., called it "shocking and deplorable." Daniel Schulder, president of the New York chapter of the Association of Catholic Trade Unionists, said it would "gladden the hearts of labor racketeers, who can now be assured their position, together with the racists', is secure in the amoral vision of the AFL-CIO." Jimmy Hoffa and John F. English—of the expelled Teamsters—described the censure as "a gross injustice to a labor leader who has done more than anyone in the labor movement to maintain its integrity and unity in the fight for the complete integration of Negro and white workers in the house of labor. . . . No measure of equal force has ever been adopted by the AFL-CIO Executive Council against any leaders of . . . affiliates which continue to maintain Jim Crowism in their organizations." And a Chicago longshoreman told a meeting of the Negro American Labor Council, "I think we should go in force to Florida [where the AFL-CIO would soon be holding its convention] to let George Meany know that the Negro masses are behind Randolph."

Randolph's own response lacked the anger displayed by some of his supporters. On leaving the session at which the Executive Council had voted to censure him, he had merely deplored the tendency of the AFL-CIO's leaders "to equate opposition to trade union policies with opposition to the trade union movement." And when he next met his colleagues on the Executive Council—at the AFL-CIO convention, in Bal Harbour, Florida, in December, 1961—he reminded them that though they had "condemned and denounced" him at the Commodore meeting, in New York, "anyone who is in the labor movement and has gone through some 40 years of struggle . . . is not thin skinned. Consequently, I am willing to go through the fires in order to abolish second-class status for black people in this country. It must be done, and it must be done now—not tomorrow. We cannot wait for tomorrow. In a nuclear age, tomorrow may never come."

The Bal Harbour convention ended on a pleasant note. Felicitating Randolph, George Meany said, "As believers in democracy, we of the trade union movement welcome and understand the determination of those in our country who seek to give real meaning to the rights guaranteed by the Fourteenth Amendment. And perhaps we can even understand their impatience." Before the convention adjourned, it adopted a civil rights resolution calling upon the AFL-CIO to "intensify its drive to make fully secure equal rights for all Americans in every field of life and to assure for all workers, without regard to race, color, creed, national origin or ancestry the full benefits of union membership." It was the first time since Randolph entered the AFL, in 1929, that a civil rights resolution had been passed unanimously. It may not have been strong enough, as he said, but it was "the best resolution on civil rights the AFL-CIO has yet adopted."

All of this helped to unfreeze Meany's attitude toward the Negro American Labor Council; and, in 1962, he accepted Randolph's invitation—over the protests of the NALC militants—to address the Council's annual convention, in New York. This change of attitude also indicated that Meany had finally recognized that Randolph's determination to remain as the critical but loyal ally of the AFL-CIO had placed him in an extremely difficult and sensitive position with the anti-AFL-CIO militants in the NALC. As the *New York Times* put it, Randolph was involved in "a two-front battle of enormous complexity." He was fighting to restrain elements within the NALC from transforming it into a go-it-alone black labor federation, hostile to the AFL-CIO. And he was obliged, on the other hand, to maintain his pressure against discrimination in the organized labor movement, of whose leadership he was a part. "The Federation should be especially sensitive to the difficulty of Mr. Randolph's role," said the *Times*, "because it is caught in a similar squeeze between those who want more done against race bias and those who want nothing done."

Randolph's critics and opponents within the NALC did not, of course, share the *Times*'s compassionate assessment of his complex role. One of them, James Houghton, who was later expelled from the NALC for his alleged far-left leanings, was to say that Randolph's double role, as a spokesman for the cause of black labor and as one of the leaders of the AFL-CIO, made him "the greatest Uncle Tom in the American labor movement. It is impossible to fight discrimination from within the councils of organized labor."

By 1964, sentiments such as Houghton's had become so strong among the young NALC militants that Randolph resigned the presidency, claiming that the organization was coming increasingly under the influence of separatists and Communists. The Negro American Labor Council, under the new name of the Afro-American Labor Council, continues to exist today, in the words of an ex-member, as "a paper organization." James Houghton says of the failure of the NALC:

It failed as a functioning organization because the serious rank-and-file workers in branches around the country were kicked out. When their organizational pressure on the AFL-CIO became a threat to the labor bureaucrats, Meany had Randolph get rid of them. The pressure was against the racial practices in the AFL-CIO. When these elements were removed, Meany, who had first opposed the NALC, embraced it and said it had a role to play in the house of labor. Randolph regarded the serious rank-and-file elements as Communist-inspired and as a Communist threat. At the 1963–64 convention he made the following statement: "Rather than see the NALC become a dupe of the Communist conspiracy I would move to disestablish the NALC." Subsequently, a number of chapters around the country were put under trusteeship. All the solid brothers moved out of the NALC. That was the beginning of the end for it. The Randolph Institute has since replaced the NALC as the functioning organization in black labor affairs. Had there been a more serious rank-and-file upsurge the NALC could have generated enough stress to keep Randolph on the right track. He represented the Brotherhood of Sleeping Car Porters in the large councils of the AFL-CIO. As representative of this small union—with a failing membership—he was merely a titular head of black labor. He had to look across the table at leaders like McDonald of the Steelworkers, who had hundreds of thousands of members. Thus he was forced to capitulate. The NALC once put out a newspaper charging that the Steelworkers contract was "a sell-out contract." This embarrassed Randolph before the international presidents. McDonald asked him what's this about your paper saying my contract is a sell-out contract? This kind of thing was embarrassing for Randolph. The NALC had great potential for organizing black workers under a person of national stature. But it failed because of the pressure of the AFL-CIO and the weakness of Randolph.

By 1963, at the height of the civil rights protest movement, the AFL-CIO—though it refused to endorse the March on Washington—had become one of the strongest lobbyists for civil rights legislation in Washington. Thus, at its convention that year, at the Americana Hotel, in New York City, the federation adopted a resolution that, in Randolph's words, was "the strongest statement of labor's position on civil rights ever to come before a convention." Selected by Meany to lead the discussion on the resolution, Randolph had argued:

The labor movement cannot afford to measure its achievements in the field of racial justice by standards of other institutions. As a force for social progress, we have always prided ourselves on being in the forefront. Similarly, in assessing labor's contribution to civil rights, it is not enough to measure how far we have come; it is not enough to compare ourselves favorably with government or management. We must measure our achievements against the needs of our time, the demands of our democratic creed, the imperatives of the Judaeo-Christian traditions. . . . Social and political freedom cannot be sustained in the midst of economic insecurity and exploitation. . . . Freedom requires a material foundation. . . . Social justice and economic reform have become inextricably intertwined in our time. If we are to speak to the needs of these workers, the labor movement will have to tap its wellsprings of social idealism. It will have to renew its crusading spirit. It must move forward toward a new evangelical spirit to reach down and lift up the poor workers, the disinherited, those in poverty and despair. . . . The Negro looks to the labor movement to lead the struggle for full employment now. We cannot accept economic policies which envision 4½ percent chronic unemployment by 1980, when current trends indicate that most of that 4½ percent may be black. . . . The Negro will become more critical of labor precisely because he has learned to expect more from labor. These expectations are just and must be fulfilled. Let each of us individually and unequivocally embrace the Negro's struggle for freedom, and the labor movement will rise to its full moral stature. Let us do this, and when labor's rights are threatened, you will see an outpouring of black Americans into the streets in defense of their own rights.

No speech had better summed up his moral conception of the labor movement and its role in the social life of the country. Even George Meany conceded that it was "a moving speech." Yet, despite the strength of the AFL-CIO's commitment to civil rights legislation in the 1960's, it was unable or unwilling to fully translate that commitment into an uncompromising campaign against discrimination in its unions, particularly those in the building trades, which—though they, too, had scrapped their color clauses—still maintained a policy of either total black exclusion or, at the most, token inclusion.

Nor was it just in the 1960's that Meany started pulling the AFL-CIO into a closer co-operation with the civil rights struggle. In 1954—while he was still reluctant to take direct action against racially exclusionist unions—he had led the AFL into endorsing the Supreme Court's decision outlawing school segregation. Among the letters of protest that flowed in to Meany's Washington office from trade unionists in the South was one that said, "If I have to decide between being a Southerner and a trade unionist, I am going to be a Southerner." Meany's reply to them all was that they were welcome to leave the AFL if they found it difficult to live with its support of the Supreme Court's decision.

Randolph recalls that Meany took a similar position during the 1960's, when Southern members of Congress objected to the AFL-CIO's endorsement of President Kennedy's and President Johnson's civil rights programs. "If we lose a vote in Congress because of our stand on civil rights," Meany is said to have replied, "then that is the price we are prepared to pay." Randolph also says that "without the support of the AFL-CIO, most civil rights legislation would not have passed."

"There are four outstanding things about Randolph's career," says Ernest Rice McKinney, a colleague who has observed him since the 1920's. "The first is his understanding that capitalist society should not be the final form of human, social, political, and economic organization. The second is his understanding that the most potent force effecting a necessary social, political, and economic transformation is the working class and the organized labor movement. The third is his understanding that the Negro worker, as an oppressed individual in the country, has to be integrated in the labor movement. And the fourth is his tenacity in clinging to these ideas and ideals—his perseverance, courage, and high moral integrity."

An example of Randolph's consistent, almost inflexible, trade union morality was his role in the United Federation of Teachers strike in New York City, in the fall of 1968, after thirteen teachers—twelve white and one black—had been summarily dismissed or transferred by Brooklyn's black-controlled Ocean Hill-Brownsville school district. In 1964, Randolph, with Bayard Rustin as the executive director, had founded the A. Philip Randolph Institute, to represent "the Negro-Labor alliance" and to "strengthen the political coalition needed to assure democratic social change." Randolph, Rustin, and the Institute firmly supported the UFT's decision to strike in defense of the dismissed teachers. Inevitably, this left them in a most complex, paradoxical, and controversial position. No strike in recent memory had evoked so much hostility in New York's black community. A large number of blacks connected with the New York educational system saw the UFT's action not only as hostile to their interests—the control of their own neighborhood schools—but also as an expression of labor union racism.

According to one observer, "The impact on the city was enormous. The attack by aroused blacks on the UFT, a conspicuously liberal union with a superior record on racial questions, was intense. Questions of professionalism, of co-optation of aggrieved blacks by radicals to the left of the UFT, of black racist power politics (with the consequent eruption of anti-Semitism), of the correctness of the UFT's insistence on normal trade union values in a situation where to insist on them was to undercut the emergence of heightened black consciousness—all these combined to create an explosive situation."

Nevertheless, Randolph—president of a union that had once narrowly escaped being destroyed by the Pullman Company's contempt for the rights of black workers, and a vice president of the organized labor movement—felt obliged to insist upon normal trade union values, to support the strike as a basic labor-versus-management issue. And yet, in doing so, he was—as titular head of the A. Philip Randolph Institute, dedicated to welding a coalition between blacks and the labor movement —supporting a strike that, at least in New York, had the effect of under-mining that very coalition. Pilloried mercilessly, Randolph and Rustin were called traitors to the black community, not because their action had a destructive effect upon the political coalition they were trying to build between blacks and labor, but because, in supporting the UFT and its president, Albert Shanker, they were considered to have entered into a "racist" coalition against the political and educational interests of their own people.

One of the letters of protest Randolph received came from a black couple in Queens Village, New York: "My wife and I have long been admirers of yours. We are vastly dismayed. . . . The teachers union is demanding a degree of security which few other unionists enjoy, and that demand is being made at the expense of my children. This issue should not be settled with closed schools if due process is to be central." Randolph replied, in the clearest statement he made of his position:

Teachers do not possess job security if they can be arbitrarily fired or trans-ferred without a hearing. Every worker, whether skilled, unskilled, technical or professional, is entitled to be confronted by his accuser when he is pun-ished for an alleged failure to perform his duties, with a right to answer the charges and, finally, to refer same to an impartial arbitrator. I think it is generally conceded that the teachers have not been accorded due process and, as workers, they had to resort to the means which other workers resort to, namely, the strike, in order to get their case properly handled. Now, I am head of a union. . . . Before the Brotherhood started in 1925, a porter could be fired or taken off his job as a result of a complaint by any official of the Pullman Company, or even a passenger on a train. He had to go and look for another job for there was nothing he could do about it. . . . I am sure you are aware of the fact that black workers, until they began to organize in the unions, were the first fired and the last hired. They had no rights anyone was bound to respect. . . . I could not very well refuse to support the teachers' right to due process and job security since it is not only a basic part of our democratic life, but is indispensable for the ability of workers to hold jobs.

Though Randolph plays no organizational role in the Institute that bears his name—functioning mainly as its inspirational force—the organization symbolizes his economic approach to the racial problem, his support of a liberal coalition for social change, and his long campaign for a democratic and integrated labor movement. And though the Institute's chief mode of operation—political action—differs somewhat from the one—political agitation—that has characterized Randolph's public career, he strongly endorses its activities and purposes. Equally important, the AFL-CIO—which has borne the brunt of Randolph's agitation since the late 1920's—regards the Institute as an extension of his work in the trade union movement, and contributes both to its upkeep and to the execution of its programs.

In 1968, for instance, when the Randolph Institute began a campaign —led by its associate director, Norman Hill—to organize black trade unionists around the country to conduct voter registration drives, COPE (Committee on Political Education), the political arm of the AFL-CIO, collaborated closely with the Institute. And by 1971, the Institute, with COPE's help, had organized some seventy such groups of black trade unionists.

The Institute also works closely with the AFL-CIO Civil Rights Department in rooting out what George Meany calls "the last vestiges of discrimination in the labor movement." This is a reference to the building construction unions, still the most discriminatory segment of organized labor. Along with the Workers' Defense League, the educational arm of the Randolph Institute sponsors the Joint Apprenticeship Program, to recruit, tutor, and place blacks and Puerto Ricans in the predominantly white building trades apprenticeship training schemes. Headed by Ernest Green—the first black student to graduate from Little Rock's Central High School—the Joint Apprenticeship Program has, since 1965, brought more than 4,000 minority group trainees into the building trades.

In recognition of the Institute's work, the AFL-CIO Executive Council passed a unanimous resolution in May, 1971, calling upon all its affiliates to support the Institute's efforts to integrate the building trades industry and set up politically active trade union groups around the country. Explaining the Executive Council's action, George Meany told union presidents that the Randolph Institute was "one of the best investments" the AFL-CIO had ever made.

In the March, 1970, issue of *Harper's Magazine,* John Corry reported on a luncheon at the White House, to which the seventy-six-year-old George Meany had brought the entire Executive Council of the AFL-CIO. "Meany takes Nixon's arm," wrote Corry, "guides him around the luncheon table, and introduces him to the assembled vice presidents, all of them masters of their own labor dukedoms. 'Ah,' says President Nixon, when they reach A. Philip Randolph . . . 'the grand old man of American labor.' 'Ah,' says Meany, 'that makes two grand old men—him and me.' "

VII / Civil Rights: Doyen

It is hard to make anyone who has never met him believe that A. Philip Randolph must be the greatest man who has lived in the U.S. in this century. But it is harder yet to make anyone who has ever known him believe anything else. —MURRAY KEMPTON

21 / "The Meaning of Our Numbers"

The early 1950's marked the end of Randolph's pre-eminence as a black political figure in America, a status he had enjoyed since the late 1930's, when he and the Brotherhood of Sleeping Car Porters won their long struggle against the Pullman Company. This is not to say, of course, that he ceased to be a source of any influence in black affairs. With the rise of the modern civil rights movement, he no longer dominated the broad arena of the freedom struggle, but he remained the principal black spokesman for political and trade union democracy and for an economic solution to the American race problem. And since, as Jorge Luis Borges says, the essential dates of history remain, for a long time, secret, we cannot say when the mass energies he had helped to mobilize and release during the 1940's ceased, if they did, to actuate the civil rights protest movement of the 1950's and 1960's.

But he was simply never again to be the number-one black political figure in the country. There was, to be sure, nothing premature in his passage from the center of the black stage. For one thing, he was aging, having turned sixty-one in 1950. Times were changing. The political consciousness he once helped to raise, to which he was once able to appeal with consummate ease—at times, with telling effect—had grown beyond his control. And if he could not be dismissed as a useless anachronism, it was nevertheless true that the generous and graceful style of his spirit, his social conscience, and even his address—shaped in an old-world morality and fired in the radical enthusiasms of the first two decades of the century—were slowly receding before the more furious, abrasive, and staccato sensibilities of a new day.

By the late 1940's, his March on Washington movement, which had established the principle of fair employment in government policy, was practically dead. His successful movement to integrate the armed forces had served its purpose. The struggle for a permanent Fair Employment Practices Commission—which had kept the March on Washington movement breathing in its later years—collapsed in 1950, when a bill designed to achieve a permanent commission was emasculated by a coalition of Republicans and Southern Democrats. Once again, Randolph's only organization was the Brotherhood of Sleeping Car Porters—itself beginning to fade away, with the profound decline in railroad passenger service.

Outside of the AFL-CIO, where his prestige as a black labor leader was probably at its peak in the 1950's, Randolph had come to be regarded—among the younger fighters who had seized the reins of the freedom struggle—as something of an ancient father figure, or, as some of his admirers preferred to describe him, an elder statesman. But though the younger men, with fresh passions, felt the time had come for Randolph to withdraw to the wings—and though the sheer pace of events left him little or no choice—he continued to speak, however remote the accents may have sounded sometimes, upon all the questions that had engaged his public career.

The modern stage of the civil rights struggle had signaled its approach in 1947, when the Congress of Racial Equality, led by men like James Farmer, Bayard Rustin, and A. J. Muste, embarked upon the first Freedom Rides through the upper South. It emerged fully after 1954, when, as a result of litigation by the NAACP, the Supreme Court handed down its historic desegregation decision, overturning the old doctrine of separate-but-equal public facilities.

There followed, in the wake of this decision, an unprecedented florescence of black protest activity in the South, one of the earliest and most spectacular of which was the Montgomery bus boycott of 1955–56, led by the young Dr. Martin Luther King, Jr. In 1957, nine black children in Little Rock, Arkansas, reattracted world-wide attention to the American race problem when, despite the defiance of Governor Orval Faubus, they integrated Central High School. In 1960, after black college students in Greensboro, North Carolina, had launched the sit-in movement, the Student Nonviolent Coordinating Committee was formed. In 1961, a revitalized CORE again set out on daring and dangerous Freedom Rides, this time through the deep South. Dr. King's Southern Christian Leadership Conference, organized after the Montgomery bus boycott, became the spearhead of the massive direct-action street demonstrations against segregated public facilities that swept the South. The NAACP—the oldest and most prestigious of the freedom organizations, which had excelled at silent but indispensable court ligitation—and the National Urban League—which had devoted itself essentially to friendly persuasion—were both swept into aggressive mass motion. Quite often, possibly against their better wishes, they found themselves in the streets shouting, along with everybody else, "Freedom now!"

The country had never before been confronted by such an urgent, angry, broadly based, and eclectic (churches, labor unions, intellectuals, political liberals, students, militant activists) black protest movement. Moreover, it had never been required to lend its ear to such a cacophony of black chieftains, all driven by a common theme and engaged in a common cause, but still jealous enough of each other to want to preserve the distinctive tones of their different voices and the special character of their different activities. The major personalities were Dr. King, Ralph Abernathy, and Fred Shuttlesworth, of SCLC; Roy Wilkins, of the NAACP; James Farmer and Floyd McKissick, of CORE; Lester Granger and, later, Whitney Young, of the Urban League; John Lewis, Marion Barry, Stokely Carmichael, Diane Nash, James Forman, and Robert Moses, of SNCC; Dorothy Height, of the National Council of Negro Women, and Bayard Rustin, roving theoretician and strategist to the different organizations, and a moral conscience in his own right. Of course, among the authentically militant voices of the early sixties were also those of men like Elijah Muhammad and Malcolm X. But theirs was a different, more strident music, several beats away from the ecumenical rhythms of the civil rights protest movement.

With no protest organization of his own, Randolph, from the Brotherhood's office, at 217 West 125th Street, hovered like a presence emeritus over the struggle, neither wholly welcome nor wholly unwanted. Many of the younger leaders, especially when his ideas or opinions got in their way, regarded him, with whispered annoyance, as the old man. He cast too tall and imposing a shadow out of the past; his prestige interfered too much with their own freedom. Hadn't he already had his inning? If Rustin also referred to him as the old man, it was with more reverence and veneration, and because he himself now functioned quite frequently as Randolph's younger representative and ambassador among the different groups, promoting some of the projects around which the old man would like to see the movement unify.

But despite the coolness toward him, Randolph, as much by his presence as by his intrusions, was playing an absolutely vital role in the life of the civil rights movement. He was providing it with something it sorely needed, or, at any rate, lacked: a center of unity. The different leaderships were frequently a splintering of jealousies. Who had prior claims to what areas of activity? Who deserved credit for what programs and what successes? Whose tactics were more relevant to the nature of the struggle? Who was too militant and who was too conservative?

Murray Kempton has recalled that after the death of Medgar Evers, "Martin Luther King called an NAACP official to suggest that together they proclaim a day of national mourning and self-examination and was told that he was always rushing into cases where he had no place or business. The alliance between King and the NAACP has always been uneasy. They have moved by different roads in the same direction, King mainly in the streets, the NAACP in the courts." David L. Lewis, in his recent biography of Dr. King, tells of a heated public exchange between King and Whitney Young: " 'Whitney,' Martin shouted, 'what you are saying may get you a foundation grant . . . but it won't get you into the kingdom of truth.' Young angrily dismissed Martin's recent preoccupation with urban poverty as a sham. He, Young, had the key to viable urban programs, not Martin. Looking at King's expensive suit and burnished alligator shoes, he shot out, 'You're eating well!' Friends separated the eminent leaders before more damaging quotable words could be exchanged."

It was not always easy, therefore, to get the different leaders to sit together in the same room, unless they were representing their organizations at the White House, or unless Randolph had called them together to enlist their common support for one of his programs. He was the only figure, Kempton has said, who could reconcile "the painful personal differences" that befell "the Negro protest movement at the height of its sweep and fashion. . . . Randolph is alone among the leaders because he neither feels hostility for nor excites it in any other of them."

But, though he was always careful not to show it, Randolph had his favorites. He was closest in political outlook to Rustin, and relied heavily on the younger man's talents as an organizer. And he was closest in ethical temper to Dr. King, whom he regarded as the moral leader of the civil rights struggle. Nor was he above exploiting their jealousies, when it was expedient to the purpose of bringing them together. His "genius," says Bayard Rustin, "was to use Dr. King as his left leverage. Whenever he wanted all the leaders to support a program or demonstration, he always got King's co-operation first, for he knew that once King agreed to come in, none of the others would want to stay out." It was by the use of such tactics that he got the majority of the leaders to support the Prayer Pilgrimage to Washington, D.C., in May, 1957, the 1958–59 Youth Marches for Integrated Schools, and the monument to his interest in a civil rights coalition—the 1963 March on Washington.

One afternoon in December, 1962, Randolph and Rustin were sitting in the former's office, at the Brotherhood's headquarters, in Harlem, discussing the course of the protest movement, particularly the mass demonstrations Dr. King was leading in the South. Rustin, then executive secretary of the War Resisters League, often dropped in for such chats, as Randolph calls his informal discussions. Except for Rustin's deference to seniority, the two now got along like old friends, bore a certain resemblance in their physical stature, and had a deep respect for each other's political history and accomplishments.

In 1962, both Randolph, seventy-three, and Rustin, fifty-two, looked a good ten years younger than their ages. And, standing over six feet tall, with physiques that suggested an early debt to athletics, there was in their appearance "a strange mixture of strength and sensitivity," as Robert Penn Warren has written of Rustin.

For all his veneration of Randolph, Rustin's own credentials as a veteran activist were unchallengeable; and, in his career as a radical, he had sustained wounds of spirit and body that Randolph had never known. In 1942, he had been savagely beaten by police in Tennessee when he refused to ride in the back of a bus. During World War II, he had spent three years in the Lewisburg Penitentiary, as a conscientious objector. Arrested on CORE's first Freedom Ride, in 1947, he had spent twenty-two days on a North Carolina chain gang; and during the years of his civil rights activities he had logged a record of twenty-four arrests. As to Rustin's other credentials, his talents as an organizer had taken him, in the early 1950's, to India, where he served as chairman of the Free India Committee; to Ghana, Nigeria, and Tanganyika, where he worked with Kwame Nkrumah, Dr. Nnamdi Azikiwe, and Julius Nyerere; and to England, where he helped organize the Aldermaston peace marches. He had also helped Dr. King organize the Montgomery bus boycott in 1955, and later had drawn up the blueprint for the Southern Christian Leadership Conference. And, as Randolph could hardly forget, he had been an activist in the March on Washington movement, in 1941, and the League for Nonviolent Civil Disobedience, in 1948.

During their chat in the Brotherhood office, Randolph said to Rustin that while Dr. King's street demonstrations in the South were imperative, a complementary demonstration was needed, in order to embody in one gesture civil rights as well as national economic demands. Rustin, a Socialist, shared Randolph's economic approach to the race problem, and said he could not agree more. Did he have any ideas, Randolph asked. Rustin said he had none except, perhaps, a massive march on the nation's capital, calling for jobs, a higher minimum wage, and a guaranteed income. Randolph said that was a splendid idea, and he would be glad to receive a memorandum from Rustin outlining it in greater detail.

Two months later, after conferring with Norman Hill, then an assistant program director of CORE, and Tom Kahn, a white Socialist, Rustin returned with the blueprint of a march that would include all the civil rights organizations. Noting that Rustin's blueprint contained only economic demands, Randolph said it would have to be extended to contain, as well, the broad demand for freedom. Rustin said, "Fine. We'll call it a march for jobs and freedom."

As he had done with the Prayer Pilgrimage and the Youth Marches for Integrated Schools, Randolph approached King before seeking the support of the other civil rights leaders. According to Rustin, one of the other leaders, when approached, remarked under his breath, "Damn that Phil Randolph! If only he'd talk with us first before putting us in the position where we can't say we aren't going along with these damn things he wants."

It is not surprising, therefore, that feelings were somewhat ruffled when the leaders got together with Randolph to discuss the march. As one of the participants recalls, Roy Wilkins wanted to know who was going to be the organizer. There had never been any question in Randolph's mind: it would be Rustin. Wilkins, calm, urbane, and gifted in the acerbic understatement, indicated that the choice did not leave him with as much enthusiasm as he would like. Wilkins, it is believed, felt that Rustin's radical background would be no great asset to an enterprise that required the broadest possible base of national support. "Gentlemen," Randolph interjected, making it clear that his choice of Rustin was irrevocable, "we're either going to have this march or we're not." Wilkins replied that he might not be unwilling to go along, if Randolph himself became the national director. Randolph said it was fine with him, but that as national director he would need to select his own organizer, "and I want you to understand that I'm going to select Bayard." After Dr. King intervened to say that he himself could see no sensible objection to that, the decision was accepted unanimously. Despite Wilkins's early reservations, however, he and the NAACP were to give Rustin and the march the strongest organizational and financial support the effort received. "Whatever Roy's objections to me were then," Rustin now says, "I don't think he has them now."

Rustin's instructions—to organize a demonstration of 100,000 people in Washington, D.C., on August 28, 1963—were carried out from a small, ramshackle headquarters on West 130th Street. Visitors found it hard to believe that an enterprise of such proportions was being planned amid such humble appointments, in an office furnished with nothing more than a water cooler, a few scabrous and creaky old desks and chairs, and a small bank of temporary telephones. Assisted by a handful of black and white volunteers, Rustin prepared thousands of letters, instruction manuals, and newsletters; called upon hundreds of different organizations to participate; co-ordinated, across the country, the chartering of busses, trains, and airplanes; and designed the master plan of how to get 100,000 marchers in and out of Washington on the same day. It seemed to M. S. Handler, of the *New York Times,* that Rustin's skeleton staff was "bent on demonstrating that big things can be accomplished with small numbers and a small outlay of money."

The accomplishments would be far in excess of what could reasonably have been expected of such a modest outfit. Rustin and his helpers not only would bring more than 200,000 people into Washington; they would also display an astonishing mastery of the logistics involved in staging such a huge public event. They would mount and discipline what was, up to then, the greatest civilian invasion of the nation's capital. Above all, they would assemble in one place the broadest coalition of racial, political, religious, and conscience groups the country had ever seen.

But there were some serious political obstacles on the way to August 28. In June, his civil rights message having gone to Congress, President John F. Kennedy was expressing fears about "demonstrations which can lead to violence," and, consequently, damage or destroy the prospects for the passage of civil rights legislation. His fears, whether or not they would be allowed to affect the plans already laid, could not be lightly dismissed, for no president in this century—until Lyndon Johnson—had displayed a greater concern for the problems of black Americans. In any event, on June 22, Kennedy invited the march leaders to a meeting in the Cabinet Room of the White House.

The delegation included John Lewis, of SNCC; Dr. King, of SCLC; Whitney Young, of the Urban League; James Farmer, of CORE; Roy Wilkins, of the NAACP; and Randolph. According to Arthur Schlesinger, Jr., then one of Kennedy's aides, they were "as gifted and impressive a group as one could find in the country." After sharing with the visitors the special problems he faced in getting his civil rights legislation through Congress, the President turned his attention to the demonstration they were planning to mount, practically on the doorstep of the Congress. "We want success in Congress," he told the group, "not just a big show at the Capitol. Some of these people are looking for an excuse to be against us. I don't want to give any of them a chance to say 'Yes, I'm for the bill, but I'm damned if I will vote for it at the point of a gun.' It seemed to me a great mistake to announce a march on Washington before the bill was even in committee. The only effect is to create an atmosphere of intimidation, and this may give some members of the Congress an out." Without quite saying so, Kennedy was clearly suggesting that the march be called off.

The visitors expressed sympathy with the President's parliamentary problems, but said that they considered such problems no greater than the ones that had urged them to take to the streets. James Farmer made a telling point: "We would be in a difficult if not untenable position if we called the street demonstrations off and then were defeated in the legislative battle. The result would be that frustration would grow into violence and would demand new leadership."

Then Randolph, a veteran of such White House confrontations (and speaking, Schlesinger recalls, "with the quiet dignity which touched Kennedy as it had touched Roosevelt before him"), summed up the inevitability of an event that had swelled beyond its conception as political tactic into a welling tide of the popular will: "Mr. President, the Negroes are already in the streets. It is very likely impossible to get them off. If they are bound to be in the streets in any case, is it not better that they be led by organizations dedicated to civil rights and disciplined by struggle rather than to leave them to other leaders who care neither about civil rights nor about nonviolence? If the civil rights leadership were to call the Negroes off the streets, it is problematic whether they would come." The President did not get his wish—would even end up endorsing the march—but, to Schlesinger, "it was the best meeting I attended in my years in the White House."

The majority of Randolph's colleagues on the AFL-CIO's Executive Council also opposed the march. At a meeting in Unity House, in Pennsylvania, on August 13, the council issued a statement supporting the goals of the march but withholding endorsement of the event itself. The council said, however, that individual unions were free to make their own decisions. Walter Reuther, one of the dissenters from the Executive Council's statement, called it "anemic," while Randolph described it as "a masterpiece of noncommittal noncommitment."

The AFL-CIO's fears were similar to those of President Kennedy. "The civil rights legislation had not yet been enacted," George Meany explains today, "and while we did not object to any of our affiliates participating, we were worried that the march might touch off a situation which might set us back legislatively. I was fearful that there would be disorder, that people would get hurt, and that it would build up resentment in Congress."

But, as Randolph had indicated to President Kennedy, nothing, at that point, could stop the march—not Strom Thurmond's vicious personal attack upon Bayard Rustin, from the floor of the Senate, or Washington's annoyance that for an entire day, as James Reston said, "inhabitants of this privileged sanctuary" would be unable to buy a drink at a bar, get a taxi downtown, "or count on the colored cook coming in for dinner." Finally, everyone was resigned to the inevitable. President Kennedy even informed the leaders that he would be glad to receive them at the White House when the march was over.

When Randolph arrived in Washington, a few days before the march, he was feted by a group of senators. Called together by Paul Douglas, of Illinois, the senators and their wives and friends received Randolph in what one observer described as "the walnut-paneled opulence" of the Capitol's east front conference room. Against a background of good talk and fellowship, the hosts served tea, cakes, and dainty little sandwiches. Randolph, motivated by interests different from those of the gathering, had come not to make or cement friendships, but to influence important government people. Waiting for a chance to deliver his message, he moved with well-concealed impatience among the teacups, the polite conversation, and the dainties. A genteel part of him usually delighted in the fine flavors of such an afternoon. Today, however, the flavors were too soft and languid a counterpoint to the urgency of the mission that had brought him to Washington. It all moved Mary McGrory to observe, in the *Washington Evening Star,* that "in the long annals of human protest there has seldom been a buffet. None is recorded on the eve of Bastille Day or Easter Rising."

Randolph's reception at the National Press Club the following day, August 26, was more appropriate. After dining him briefly on stuffed peppers, the journalists allowed him an oration in defense of the coming march. He told them:

Demonstrations are the hallmark of every revolution since the birth of civilization. . . . These are the outbursts . . . the manifestations of deep convictions about the evils that people suffer. While they sometimes take the form of some irrational upsurge of emotionalism, they come from the fact that the people are the victims of long-accumulated wrongs and deprivations. Therefore, these are an outcry for justice, for freedom. And there is no way . . . to stem these demonstrations until the cause is removed; and the cause is racial bias, the cause is exploitation and oppression, the cause is second-class citizenship in a first-class nation. This is the cause for the march on Washington. This is the reason for the civil rights revolution. . . . The civil rights revolution is not trying to tear down a democratic government, it is not trying to overthrow a government, because a civil rights revolution is a bourgeois revolution. It is concerned with what it says—civil rights—and civil rights certainly will not upset our economic structure. . . . Therefore, we are seeking to implement our human rights. . . . No individual and no State has the right to take from me my life, my liberty, and my right to the pursuit of happiness. These are natural rights.

Two days later, on August 28, Randolph was the first to address the gathering of more than 200,000 at the Lincoln Memorial. It would be the last major speech of his public life. He said:

. . . Let the nation and the world know the meaning of our numbers. We are not a pressure group, we are not an organization or a group of organizations, we are not a mob. We are the advance guard of a massive moral revolution for jobs and freedom. . . . But this civil rights revolution is not confined to the Negro, nor is it confined to civil rights, for our white allies know that they cannot be free while we are not, and we know we have no future in a society in which six million black and white people are unemployed and millions live in poverty. . . . We want a free democratic society dedicated to the political, economic and social advancement of man along moral lines. . . . We know that real freedom will require many changes in the nation's political and social philosophies and institutions. For one thing, we must destroy notion that Mrs. Murphy's property rights include the right to humiliate because of the color of my skin.* The sanctity of private property take second place to the sanctity of the human personality. It falls to the Negro to reassert this priority of values, because our ancestors were transformed from human personalities into private property. It falls to us to demand full employment and to put automation at the service of human needs, not at the service of profits. . . . All who deplore our militancy, who exhort patience in the name of false peace, are in fact supporting segregation and exploitation. They would have social peace at the expense of social and racial justice. They are more concerned with easing racial tensions than enforcing racial democracy.

Then, after introducing the other speakers, Randolph presented Martin Luther King, "the man who personifies the moral leadership of the civil rights revolution"; and before the day was over, King, in his celebrated address, broadcast to the nation by radio and television, would not only justify Randolph's claim, but would also stamp himself as one of the most inspiring witnesses to the long dream of freedom.

August 28, 1963, expired upon the hauntingly beautiful strains of "We Shall Overcome," the black vesper hymn of that period. It was one of the last times it would sound so sweetly or with its peculiar admixture of melancholy, yearning, and stubborn faith. Today, if one tries to recover that music, across the gap of a decade, the words come with none of their old magic. Their melody clings, it seems, to the monumental face of that August evening, like optimism imprisoned in a memory. Many who try to reanimate the words today feel no answering spring in the soul.

What happened to the promise that once gave such life to "We Shall Overcome" is, at least in part, what tends to happen to a good deal of the American sense of social obligation. In such matters, a large number of Americans, uneasy at having to remain in daily touch with what they suspect to be their better impulses, spend it all in one big spree, one sweeping declaration, one contribution of conscience money, or one large burst of public feeling. It appears, in retrospect, that there was a

---

* During the debate over civil rights legislation in the early 1960's, Southern opponents arbitrarily gave the name "Mrs. Murphy" to any owner of public facilities whose "property rights" would allegedly be infringed by federal statutes against segregation.

large enough number of such people at the Lincoln Memorial on August 28, 1963, who were unable or unwilling to give consistent support to the sustained political action necessary to fulfill their sense of the country's social obligation, or keep steady faith with the insistent demands of justice.

Before the March on Washington was two days old, there were sounds of doubt, hinting at what would become of it. James Baldwin, wary and perceptive of his country and countrymen, had remarked, "The day was important in itself, and what we do with this day is even more important." The following day, James Reston, in the *New York Times,* said in greater detail what may have been going through Baldwin's mind: "This whole movement for equality in American life will have to return to first principles before it will 'overcome' anything. And as moral principles preceded and inspired political principles in this country, as the church preceded the Congress, so there will have to be a moral revulsion to the humiliation of the Negro before there can be significant relief."

Expressions of uncertainty when they were first made, both remarks contain, a decade later, the ring of prophecy. Few people seem to have gone back to first principles, for the moral energy that swept more than 200,000 marchers into Washington has—if we judge by the withdrawals, the polarizations, and the hardened strain of meanness in the contemporary spirit—left no enduring political legacy, with the possible exception of legislation to integrate public facilities and to extend the franchise in the South.

But the people's failure to return to first principles was not the entire reason. As the *New York Times* had also observed, the day after the march, the demonstration "appeared to have left much of Congress untouched—physically, emotionally, and politically." Three months later, the spirit of the March on Washington suffered another stunning blow when President Kennedy was murdered in Dallas. And, a year or two later, what was left of it may well have been swallowed up by Vietnam.

By the mid-sixties, the Vietnam war had not only reared up as one of the distractions from social concerns at home; it had also created a crisis of sorts within the civil rights movement. Randolph's Freedom Budget for All Americans, a $180-billion economic program that was supported with varying degrees of commitment by all civil rights organizations, failed to win the support of the federal government or the nation, which were preoccupied with Vietnam as an economic and moral priority. And the unity of the civil rights leadership—fragile in the best of times—did not survive Dr. Martin Luther King's decision to broaden his civil rights activities into an attack upon the war. In the debate surrounding King's action, some organizations argued that the civil rights movement could scarcely avoid taking an open stand against a war that was draining away the very resources that were required for the enactment of broad social programs. Others submitted that while individual leaders were free to play a role in antiwar activities, it would be a mistake to divert the civil rights movement from its primary and historic task—the struggle to achieve change within the social and economic institutions at home.

It is not clear what Randolph's position on this question was, since one is able to find no statement of his in the record. In the absence of that, what he has to say today must suffice: "I have always been opposed to wars in principle—though, as in the case of World War II, I am able to support those that are vital to the survival of our democratic institutions. Vietnam does not seem to me to be such a war. It represents, as far as I can see, no defense of our vital national interests. The moral commitment of the American government went beyond the reaches of liberal concern for our own problems in the sense that it committed an enormous and costly amount of the nation's resources to Vietnam—in terms of both money and human life. This, as I see it, is a great moral loss and a weakening of the country's moral fiber. As for Dr. King's decision to oppose the war, I cannot say I regarded it as any great contradiction. He was, after all, one of the moral leaders of the country. Opposing wars and fighting for civil rights have natural and complementary motivations. And long before Dr. King came along, the *Messenger*, which I edited in World War I, was fighting for civil rights and opposing the war at the same time."

In any event, Roy Wilkins's speech at the Lincoln Memorial now seems like a fitting epitaph to the March on Washington. "You got religion here today," he said. "Don't backslide tomorrow." Then he recited from the Scriptures: " 'No man having put his hand to the plough and looking back is fit for the Kingdom of Heaven.' "

For all that, it had been "the most beautiful and glorious" day of Randolph's life. As the thousands walked away from the Memorial, singing, he had stood at a deserted end of the platform, looking out over the grounds that were slowly emptying. Seeing him standing alone, Bayard Rustin broke away from a group of friends, went over, and put his arm around the old man's shoulders. "I could see he was tired," Rustin recalled. "I said to him, 'Mr. Randolph, it looks like your dream has come true.' And when I looked into his eyes, tears were streaming down his cheeks. It is the one time I can recall that he could not hold back his feelings."

VIII / Epilogue

It takes fortitude to be a man and no less to be an artist.

—RALPH ELLISON

22 / Plaudits

The old two-story frame house where the young Asa Randolph grew up, on Jesse Street, in Jacksonville, was torn down sometime during the 1940's. In its place today is a sprawling red-brick bungalow, which, as late as 1970, was still the most modern building on the block, though, arguably, not the most attractive. It looks, in fact, like a brash intruder among the older structures with their antique plastered front porches and wooden verandas. These are more charming for their age, and have set the tone of the block since the turn of the century. Intruders from the other architectural extreme—looking more like dead barnacles than defiant representatives of their time—are the oldest buildings on the block, standing a couple of doors from where Randolph once lived.

They are two dank and decaying wooden cabins, shouldering each other, and cannot have been built any later than during Reconstruction. Each has a low gabled roof and an old brick chimney jutting above the shingles. Though uninhabited, the larger seems to have been evacuated not too long ago—perhaps with haste, or total renunciation. Faded curtains still hang behind the dusty windowpanes, and an old rocking chair sits deserted on the decrepit porch. Both houses have large rotted holes in their floors and roofs; both are littered with broken furniture and the water-soaked leavings of those who lived there; and both are rimmed with encroachments of high grass and wild shrubs.

They are also the last immediate connections to Randolph's upbringing on Jesse Street. The smaller is the house in which Fanny Hansberry —one of the Randolphs' young neighbors—was born in the mid-1870's. The other is the one in which she grew up, and where she helped teach the Randolph boys to read and write. Now in her mid-nineties, Fanny Hansberry has not lived there since 1967, when, growing feeble, and having no remaining family, she was taken away by friends and neighbors and placed in a nursing home, on Van Buren Street—a small, old house of no special distinction, except that it is crammed with a few beds, and gives off the mixed odors of the aged and the sick.

Fanny's father, Theodore Hansberry, may not have been as refined as those black Jacksonvillians who, before and after the turn of the century, used to ride around the city in nice carriages. But, as a steamboat pilot, he was a man of some substance and, certainly among his neighbors, considerable prestige. He was as likely as any among the black elite to send his daughter to a select girls' school in New England, which he did. But that kind of education was sometimes fatal to the marital futures of Southern black girls. When they came back, they were often unable to find mates who were "suitable" to their acquired tastes and backgrounds. Young men who had themselves been sent to prestigious and expensive black colleges in the South were in short supply. Fanny had not found a suitable mate, and had never married. She had spent most of her life in Jacksonville as a schoolteacher, an enthusiastic church worker, and a beautiful and widely admired spinster.

Today, in the shabby-looking nursing home on Van Buren Street, among those who have little or no knowledge of her background—and in circumstances that are spectacularly inferior to those in which she was raised—she looks like a wizened, disinherited heiress, languishing anonymously in a poorhouse. Despite all of this, and a mind that seems incapable of all but occasional moments of coherence, she enlivens her corner of the nursing home with bursts of gratuitous observations, disconnected recollections, and smiles that are meant for no one and everyone. Much of this falls upon silence, partly because to the occupants of the neighboring beds she is an unfamiliar experience—they do not know how to appropriately engage her cultivated manners and speech—and partly because most of what Fanny says bears no relation to her present reality. Perhaps her neighbors—looking at her blankly or ignoring her entirely—are really thinking that she is no longer in her right mind.

There are probably only two surviving connections to Miss Hansberry's youth whom she steadily cherishes. One is Eartha White, a ninety-six-year-old humanitarian and social worker—also a spinster—who is perhaps the most widely known and highly esteemed black woman in Jacksonville. The other is A. Philip Randolph, whom she refers to, proudly, as "my Asa," not unlike an old, retired headmistress implying her decisive influence upon a student who went on to become famous.

Several years after Randolph had become famous—and she was beginning to fail in strength and memory—Miss Hansberry wrote him an undated letter ("March or April, I do not know which"): "Just think, you were a small boy, wearing dresses and curly hair and me teaching you ABC's from a card board with letters all over."

But perhaps "my Asa" suggested something more—a softer possibility that they, or she, may have sensed between themselves, long ago, when he had grown into a smart, handsome, and popular young man in Jacksonville. Recalling, possibly, a farewell party for Randolph, before he sailed for New York in 1911, she continued, in the same letter: "I did not see you as much as I wanted to, the others had you, and gone with the wind. Sorry I could not muster up courage to attend the party. I had a pretty dress to wear. You could have loved me more if you had seen me dressed." Perhaps. Yet the dress might have brought out nothing he had not already noticed. In March, 1966, after a visit to Jacksonville, during which he went to see her in their old neighborhood, he wrote her from New York: "Anyone can see that you were one of the most beautiful women in Jacksonville. You still are."

By the early 1960's, some forty years after he left Randolph and the *Messenger* to seek his fortune in Chicago, Chandler Owen still had not found it. But he had not given up. He still had big plans.

Throughout his rise to national prominence, Randolph had remained friendly with Owen, who spent most of his life in Chicago, working in a variety of public relations jobs. They corresponded regularly, and whenever Randolph visited Chicago, he and Owen greeted each other—in the language of their old comradeship in Harlem—as "Boy." Referring to the old times in Harlem, Owen once wrote to Randolph: "Those of us who became friends in those days were more enduring in our friendships."

After 1960, when Randolph's health began to decline, he went to Chicago less frequently. Owen now wrote more often, mostly with news of the several things he had going, but, though nothing ever seemed to mature, his announcements never waned in enthusiasm or optimism. Many of them arrived on letterheads marked "Chandler Owen Associates, Public Relations Specialists."

I have several things to take up with you—all of vital interest and good. . . . The GOP County Central Committee has just asked me to prepare a brochure for distribution—200,000 for Chicago alone . . . at a fee of $3000. I should complete it in 3 weeks.

This week I have an engagement with Gov. Stratton and 2 men from a Swiss Bank and an English investment concern with $200 million to go for fighting Negro slums.

Everything will probably come at once. . . . If I knew where you would be I'd send this letter showing how nearly I am to completion of my business and how large it is—over $200,000.

The big matter is in process and I was called down to go over it 4 days ago. When it is consummated we'll take a trip, if you can get off. . . . I think we can get from $500,000 to a million for the A. Philip Randolph Institute. Follow me!

I'm almost out of the woods forever. . . . The other big Internal Revenue Service check will be for between $150,000 and $200,000—tax free— which is equivalent to inheriting a million and a half dollars on which one would have to pay income tax.

Perhaps knowing his old friend only too well, Randolph usually refrained, in his replies, from commenting upon such pleasing prospects. There were times when he could not contain himself, however, such as when Owen wanted to use him as an occasion for fund raising. Owen once wrote him:

Andrew Carnegie once set up a $600,000 trust at 5 percent from which Booker T. Washington received $30,000 a year for the rest of his life. . . . Dinners were given over the country for Du Bois, one of which was held here, and a sum of approximately $20,000 was raised for Du Bois. Clarence K. Streit, a Cecil Rhodes scholar and for twelve years foreign correspondent of the New York Times, authored a book, "Union Now," which sold 600,000 copies at $5 each, giving him a gross of $3,000,000; and was given a testimonial dinner in Pittsburgh, cochairmaned by Claire Luce and Paul Mellon, from which they gave Streit $200,000 for himself. A group of us want to do something similar for you. We want you to take some of your time off for your Memoirs. Having completed them we can probably get "The Randolph Story" put in moving pictures. I have already asked Mr. Jerome Saxe, vice president and general manager of the Exchange National Bank on LaSalle and Adams Streets in Chicago to permit his bank to be used as the depository. All money would be made out directly to you and deposited in that bank subject only to your withdrawal or by anybody whom you may direct to act for you. . . . So soon as we shall have heard from you I will go in to see

John Johnson, publisher and editor of Ebony, Jet, and Tan, and ask him to be national chairman of the group. Along with him we will ask such people as Harry Belafonte, Lorraine Hansberry, T. K. Gibson, Sr., Julian Black, Dr. Theodore K. Lawless, and similar people throughout the country. . . . Randolph, this matter strikes me as being extremely important, and time is of the essence. While we will show the Randolph story and the tremendous leadership you have given over these last 25 or 30 years, at the same time I have back in my head the fact that you have a sick wife unable to walk . . . which must cost you around $1500 a month. I also realize we are not getting any younger, and working as hard as you do you could have a breakdown, in which event your entire house would be a hospital. This is all I need to say now, with a closing admonition which Marc Antony gave in "Julius Caesar," "There's a tide in the affairs of men which, taken at the flood, leads on to fortune. Omitted, all the voyage of their life is bound in shallows and in miseries. Upon such a full sea are we now afloat and we must take the current when it serves, or lose our venture."

Randolph replied immediately:

I am sure you know that I have no money and, at the same time, don't expect to get any. However, I would not think of having a movement started to raise money for me and my family. It is the lot of some people to be poor and it is my lot, which I do not have any remorse about. Besides, I am not in need of any bread, but even if I were, I would not wish a movement to help me get any. I note your reference to the movements for Booker T. Washington and Du Bois. I am in a little different position from them since I do have a job even though I can't get rich on it. I think both Washington and Du Bois deserved the support they received.

In 1964, a year after the March on Washington, Owen had an even more daring idea:

A group of my friends—white and colored—have agreed to help me get you the Nobel Prize. It is worth $40,000 with no income tax. You are the world's greatest peace producer. As head of the march on Washington you preserved peace in the world's greatest nation. We don't need any one's consent to boost them for the Nobel Prize.

Randolph withheld his consent, anyway:

I don't wish to have any campaign carried on for the Nobel Prize in my behalf. I have done nothing in the field of peace which justifies my getting the prize and I don't wish for any propaganda campaign to be carried on to create the idea that I am eligible for such a prize.

In September, 1967, Owen suffered a recurrence of an old kidney ailment. He reported to his friend in New York that the pain was almost unbearable. Still suffering, he wrote again in mid-October: "Our long friendship, never soiled, is nearing its close. . . . I've been in pain. If you were not living I would commit suicide today. . . . Our relationship through the years was great. How on earth can I go on? You keep on as usual." Early in November, Owen died.

At the December, 1967, meeting of the Brotherhood of Sleeping Car Porters Executive Council, William Bowe, the union's secretary-treasurer, moved that Randolph be reimbursed for personal expenses incurred in Owen's burial. The motion was carried unanimously, in recognition of the role Owen had played in the founding of the *Messenger,* and of the magazine's role in the struggle to organize the Brotherhood.

In 1964, a group of Harlem citizens petitioned Mayor Robert Wagner to rename Admiral George Dewey Square, at the intersection of St. Nicholas Avenue and 116th Street, in Harlem, as A. Philip Randolph Square. Mayor Wagner, son of the former United States Senator, whom Randolph had greatly admired, agreed. But, though the Mayor's approval would not be withdrawn, it stirred criticism among Dewey's admirers.

The Naval Academy Association of New York demanded that if Dewey's name was removed from the square in Harlem, another prominent landmark in the city be named for him. The *New York Times* said the proposal was "in line with a deplorable trend—changing of old established and historic place names to conform to some enthusiasm or personality of the moment. Mr. Randolph is a good labor leader; a fighter for civil rights and an estimable citizen; but before streets and Squares are named after him or any other distinguished contemporary, a little time should be allowed to pass by. History should be given a chance to make an assessment." At a City Hall rally, the Spanish American War Veterans, a doughty and determined band of octogenarians, raged against the proposed transgression of Dewey's memory. But at least one Randolph supporter, the Brotherhood's William Bowe, showed up in the middle of hostile territory. "Randolph," he told a reporter, "is as great a hero in peace as Admiral Dewey was in war."

No further protests were heard. By the time the square was officially renamed, however, it was a relatively small tribute, compared to that of

President Lyndon Johnson, who, in September, 1964, had awarded Randolph the Medal of Freedom, the country's highest civilian honor.

In 1929, Roy Lancaster, the first secretary-treasurer of the Brotherhood of Sleeping Car Porters, had not been renominated for the office. And in 1933, when the union felt its list of seven vice presidents was too long, it had dropped three of them. Since then, however, there had been no breaks in the original chain of the Brotherhood's top leadership, unless caused by death or retirement.

For most of the union's life, therefore, its leading officers were Randolph, president; Milton Webster, first vice president; Bennie Smith, second vice president; E. J. Bradley, third vice president; C. L. Dellums, fourth vice president; Ashley Totten, secretary-treasurer; and T. T. Patterson, Eastern Zone supervisor. Most of them were returned unopposed at every convention. They were the leaders of the revolution against Pullman, and had suffered to bring the Brotherhood to power; remembering that, few dared challenge their right to remain in the leadership. If, occasionally, a small revolt brewed on the convention floor, Milton Webster simply pulled out the old script of the Brotherhood's epic struggle—the moral of which was that if those leaders of the 1920's and '30's had not sacrificed against great odds, there would have been no Brotherhood. After Webster's recital, all rebellions usually collapsed.

On September 2, 1968, at the union's convention in New Orleans, Randolph made his last appearance as president of the Brotherhood. As he rose to make his farewell speech, only two of his original lieutenants remained: Bennie Smith and C. L. Dellums. Bradley had died in St. Louis in 1955; Patterson had died in Jamaica, West Indies, in 1959; Ashley Totten had passed away in 1963, in Frederiksted, St. Croix; and in 1965 Milton Webster had suffered a fatal heart attack at the Americana Hotel, Bal Harbour, Florida, while he and Randolph were attending an AFL-CIO convention. Patterson had been succeeded by Benjamin McLaurin, and Totten by William Bowe. Bradley's third vice presidency had been filled by his protégé, T. D. McNeil; Bennie Smith had been elevated from the second to Webster's first vice presidency; and, his fourth vice presidency having been abolished, C. L. Dellums had taken Bennie Smith's old position of second vice president. But several years before, when the founding fathers of the union held a secret meeting to discuss the line of succession in the event of Randolph's departure from office, it had been agreed that Webster would inherit the leadership, and that if Webster were not available the heir apparent should be Dellums. Thus, at New Orleans, Dellums took over the presidency from Randolph.

Randolph devoted almost all of his farewell speech to a discussion of national and international affairs. It was only toward the end that he remarked upon his going: "As I take my leave, I want to thank every Pullman, train and mail porter . . . for having given me the opportunity to play a humble role in building this mighty movement."

But, by then, the Brotherhood had long ceased to be a "mighty" movement. The virtual collapse of the railroad travel industry had reduced its membership to a mere 2,000 or so. And even while Randolph was taking leave of the presidency the union received news that the Pullman Company had been abolished and that its remaining sleeping cars had been sold to other companies. So Dellums had taken over the union not only in "trying times," as he said, but also amid fears that the organization would not long survive. What made him most unhappy, however, was having to bid farewell to the Brotherhood's founder:

To have worked for and with and under the guidance and supervision of a man like Randolph for more than 43 years, it hurts too much to see him go to be happy in succeeding him. There is a saying that no man is indispensable. . . . But there are men who are irreplaceable, and Randolph is. I can't fill his shoes. . . . Learning at the feet of this man was a great privilege. . . . I think he and I had the nearest philosophies, because even though I was never a member of the Socialist Party, I have always been socialistically inclined, and after knowing and hearing him, I've been a Socialist ever since. But the hardest philosophy for me to adopt was to have no desire for worldly goods.

On September 27, Willard Wirtz, Secretary of Labor in President Johnson's cabinet, wrote Randolph:

. . . my best hope for a long and fruitful retirement. . . . Our century has seen a growing recognition of the social needs of man, of his hopes, of his ambitions, and of his rights. You have unselfishly made the fulfillment of these needs the major struggle of your life. A great labor leader, our nation's elder statesman in the fight to grant every American his civil rights, a humanitarian, you stand as an example of the dedicated leader, as one of those few Americans who has given so much of his life for the betterment of mankind. . . . You have left your mark upon our nation and upon the world.

Though he had not been active in its affairs since the mid-1920's, and at times had not been a member at all, Randolph had remained close to the Socialist party. Most important, he had always considered himself a Socialist in the tradition of Eugene Debs, whom—as he wrote when Debs died in 1926—he had "learned to love with an undying love."

In 1944, accepting the Clendenin Award from the Workers' Defense League, Randolph referred to four "fundamental forces" that had shaped his life. The first three were a "rigid Christian parental guidance"; his wife, who "inspired me with confidence, faith in, and the will to hold fast to my ideals and principles without any hope of material reward or gain"; and trade unionism, which "made me understand the need for the practical implementation of ideals and principles with a sound organizational structure."

The fourth, he said, was his "early study of Socialist philosophy," his "extensive reading of Socialist literature," and his activity in the Socialist movement, along with "such fine spirits" as Debs, Morris Hillquit, Algernon Lee, Julius Gerber, Abraham Shiplacoff, August Claessens, Frank Crosswaith, B. Charney Vladeck, James O'Neal, Layle Lane, and Norman Thomas. The Socialist movement had "armed" him with an "understanding of the nature and significance and trend of the social forces and the historical evolution and mission of the working class," taught him "to look to the economic foundation of the question of race and color," and provided him with "a world perspective and the basis of the concept of the indivisibility of democracy, freedom and peace." The Socialist movement, he said, in conclusion, "invested me with the tools and techniques to spot the multiform, illusive, protective colorations of totalitarian movements and fronts, in the pattern of Nazism, Fascism or Communism," and helped him "to discern and evaluate the political opportunism of the two major capitalist parties, Republican and Democratic."

While Randolph spent the greater part of his public life trying to wrest from the existing political and economic order as much as he thought it was capable of yielding, he had never cast a vote for a regular-party candidate in a presidential election—until 1964, when, alarmed at the prospect of a Barry Goldwater presidency, he voted for Lyndon Johnson. In every election, he had supported the Socialist party candidate for president, either Eugene Debs or Norman Thomas.

In December, 1969, after being off the rolls for a number of years, Randolph rejoined the Socialist party, now led by Norman Thomas's successor, Michael Harrington. "I have always considered myself part of the democratic Socialist movement," he said, in a message accompanying his reapplication for membership. "I have shared its commitment to the exalted principles of liberty and equality for all men. So once again, it is time for me to pay my dues and to work with my comrades . . . for a just society and a peaceful world." At the national convention in New York City, in June, 1970, Harrington proposed Randolph as one of the party's honorary chairmen. "From the very beginning of his career as a public figure and leader of the freedom movement," Harrington said, "A. Philip Randolph has stood for the unity of blacks and whites, and especially black and white workers. And one of the remarkable facts of his career is that until this day—even when he was not active in the SP—he has consistently declared and described himself as a Socialist." The delegates greeted Harrington's proposal with acclamation.

One aspect of Randolph's commitment to a racial struggle within the context of an indigenous movement for social and economic change was reflected in the Freedom Budget for All Americans, announced in 1966 by the A. Philip Randolph Institute. Drawn up by a team of black and white economists and intellectuals, including Leon Keyserling, Vivian Henderson, Tom Kahn, Nathaniel Goldfinger, and Michael Harrington, the Freedom Budget advocated a ten-year expenditure of $180 billion on public programs. Among its demands were full employment; an adequate minimum wage; a guaranteed income to all those unable to work; the abolition of poverty and the eradication of slums; decent homes and modern health services for all; development of agricultural and natural resources; upgraded social security and welfare programs; and a massive program of building construction. These demands, according to the budget,

are essential to the Negro and minority groups striving for dignity and economic security in our society. But their legitimate aspirations cannot be fulfilled in isolation. The abolition of poverty (almost three-quarters of whose U.S. victims are white) can be accomplished only through action which embraces the totality of the victims of poverty, neglect, and injustice. Nor can the goals be won by segmental or ad hoc programs alone; there is a need for welding such programs into a unified and consistent program.

And, in a more recent statement, Randolph has written:

The problem of racial discrimination is not the reason why our society tolerates a high degree of unemployment and is willing to increase unemployment to combat inflation. Nor is it the reason why we do not build enough decent housing for everybody. If our schools are starved for funds, or if our health care system is primitive by West European standards, or if automation and cybernation are making millions of jobs obsolete, these problems will not be solved simply by changing the racial attitudes of whites. They are fundamentally economic problems which are caused by the nature of the system in which we live. This system is a market economy in which investment and production are determined more by the anticipation of profits than by the desire to achieve social justice.

Randolph's sense of the racial struggle, and of its relationship to a broader social movement, has not, in recent years, been as widely accepted as it once was. It certainly has not endeared him to those wings of the black movement that, since the mid-1960's, have been focusing upon exclusively black modes of struggle and political action—and who represent, in one sense or another, the re-emergence of black nationalism and particularism, as well as the effort to redefine black consciousness and reappraise its relationship to the things and processes of the country. Randolph's belief in a racial, political, and moral coalition—as the most desirable means of fighting for social justice in America—is troubling enough to those who presently uphold exclusively black priorities. But his criticism, since the mid-1960's, of urban rioters, the tactics and rhetoric of violence, and varying expressions of black power, black capitalism, and even black anti-Semitism has earned him their outright contempt and, in some instances, hostility.

The *New York Times* of Sunday, June 28, 1970, carried a full-page advertisement, "An Appeal by Black Americans for United States Support of Israel," sponsored by the A. Philip Randolph Institute. Militant and, possibly, third-world sentiments in the black community were outraged. Hoyt Fuller, editor of the monthly magazine *Black World*—whose publisher, John Johnson, was one of the prominent black Americans who had signed the advertisement—may have been raising one of the milder objections when, responding to the ad, he wrote in the October, 1970, issue of his magazine: "A. Philip Randolph is a grand old battler for Black liberation, but a man in his eighties now, and he deserves to be honored for his past contributions. In recent years, he has indicated very clearly in some of his public utterances that the times have begun to pass him by. He is out of step, and perhaps it would be wise if he retired into discreet silence before he is out of regard."

But Randolph's utterances had not been uniformly critical of the young black *avant-garde*. For instance, during his farewell speech to the porters, in New Orleans, in 1968, he had said, after reiterating his disagreement with the new militant tactics:

I am persuaded to agree that black militants have been responsible for deepening the American consciousness of the immediacy, magnitude and danger of the racial crisis in the cities. They have challenged and stirred the American mind and conscience about the exclusion of the cultural achievements of black Americans from the historiography of our American society. They have vigorously stressed the need for the Negro's interest in self-help. They have accented the search for identity and the Africans' contribution of an ancient glorious historical cultural heritage and endowment to world civilization.

And he had told a CBS interviewer in 1969:

I think they [the militants] have been instrumental in turning America around and giving it a sense of the danger of the grave crisis in the cities. They deserve that credit. I don't agree with their methods, but they have a romance in their heart for freedom. Victims of great oppression, youngsters who have dreams for a better future, they remind me of my own self in the '20's.

An article in the May, 1969, issue of *Ebony* magazine—which reported that archmilitants had "dubbed him 'Uncle Tom No. 2,' ranking him in dishonor just behind the NAACP's Roy Wilkins"—also quoted Randolph as saying:

The forces of advancing technology are not limited by national boundaries and they are sweeping the world. . . . Somehow we must find a way to become a part of this phenomenon that is sweeping the world and changing the world. The youngsters of today must direct their attention not only to the matter of racial identity and racial realization through African studies, but they must make certain they are not left behind in the scientific and technological revolution, because if they are, they will be in a hopeless state. There will be absolutely no way in the world whereby they can become an effective force. If the young Negro cannot become a part of this advancing technology his whole revolution will have been in vain.

The following month's issue of the magazine carried four letters, in response to the article on Randolph, indicating the polarities of esteem in which he is held by blacks. Said the first:

Your article on A. Philip Randolph was interesting; but if he is to be accurately described as a "black messiah," all I can say is no wonder we never got anywhere. It is amazing to see a man of his age with such erect bearing, after such a long time on his knees. How can it be rationalized that his was a "militant" attitude in 1925, when in the '60's the men who were really for black people either were "dusted" or on the run. A. Philip Randolph's past rights crusades can't convince me he was that effective in 1925, when in 1968, Martin Luther King was killed for trying to get two lousy dollars an hour in wages for sanitary workers. I hope that if Randolph ever has to explain why he was crying in front of the Lincoln Memorial, he just says that it was because his feet hurt.

The second said:

I am a 30-year-old black woman who is not non-violent. I may even be considered in-between the generation gap. I am an advocate of "black power," but . . . I think it is quite unfortunate that a man of the stature of A. Philip Randolph is considered an "Uncle Tom." Without men like Mr. Randolph, there would be no black militants today. Those who consider him an "Uncle Tom" do not know their black history. He was a radical at a time when it meant loss of life—without hesitation. He has given us the opportunity to shout out loud: "I'm black and I'm proud." Mr. Randolph has the courage of 100 black militants. I thank God that He has given us such a man.

Said the third:

It is appropriate that A. Philip Randolph was head of the Sleeping Car Porters. I'd say he's been asleep for some time. It's time now he woke up. Socialism is not the answer for the laboring man, black or white.

And the fourth said:

I fail to understand how even the most "militant" of our communities can call A. Philip Randolph a "Tom." I'm so proud of him and all that he's done not only for blacks but for America as well. He was out working for the cause of justice in an even more wicked time than ours.

The evening of May 6, 1969, less than a month after his eightieth birthday, Randolph was honored at a black-tie dinner in the Grand Ballroom of the Waldorf Astoria. There were more than 1,200 people on the ballroom floor and another 80—each a birthday "candle"—on the dais with Randolph. As he entered the ballroom, followed by his "candles," a six-piece band—led by Eubie Blake and Noble Sissle, his old friends and contemporaries—struck up "Happy Birthday" and "Hey, Look Me Over."

Standing to acknowledge the musical tributes, he seemed well worth looking over. He cut a remarkably distinguished figure in his evening clothes, with his fragile features and white hair. And though he bowed and gestured elegantly to those around him, like a man in consummate command of his accumulated graces, it was all formality, with not an ounce of familiarity. He managed, even with his cordial smiles, to look aloof from his company, as if he was quite happy to share with the occasion the ceremonial of his presence but nothing of his inner life. One was never more curious than then about what really went on behind his face.

The evening was filled with praise. Bayard Rustin disclosed that with the exception of his grandparents "no one has stood beside me in times of trial the way Mr. Randolph has. He is the only man I know who has never said an unkind word about anyone, or who refuses to listen to an unkind word about anyone, even though it may be true. I've known him all these years, and I still can't bring myself to address him in any other way but as 'Mr. Randolph.' " Mayor John Lindsay remarked upon his "sense of integrity and humanity, fused with humility and dignity." Governor Nelson Rockefeller said that Randolph's was a "name for America to conjure with, to learn from, to discover the best that's in our country."

Roy Wilkins thanked him for his example: "When I came along as a young man, you were my hero, my inspiration. You caught me at a time when every young college boy should be caught—when he is full of idealism and when he believes that the world can be changed. And here was a man changing it, who was confident it could be changed, who never faltered, who never gave his followers anything but the hope of victory. He is a man who has gained nothing out of the labor movement or the workers but the satisfaction of having been their savior, their advisor, their counsellor, and their inspiration. Celebrating his 80th birthday, he has no worldly goods, secret or non-secret." Mrs. Coretta King, widow of Dr. Martin Luther King, said that Randolph had been "a great inspiration" to her husband during his lifetime, that King had looked to him "for advice and counsel when he was a young man and a young leader. I want to thank you publicly."

And, speaking for himself and the organized labor movement, George Meany praised Randolph's "distinguished career as an active humanitarian." Referring to Randolph's struggle against discrimination in the AFL-CIO, Meany said: "There is ample evidence that the American labor movement responded, oft times too slowly. . . . Yet there is no question that the trade union movement played a role in the discrimination and exploitation that marked the industrial life of our country in years gone by. And let me state here and now that the trade union movement still has a job to do if it is to completely remove the spectre of race discrimination from its ranks. I salute Phil Randolph as a great trade unionist and a courageous fighter for justice and human decency." Commenting, a few days later, in the *New York Post,* James Wechsler wrote that Meany's remarks reflected not only his "largeness of spirit," but also "Randolph's remarkable gift for evoking the best impulses in those whom his life has touched."

Beaman Hearn, the young friend who came with Randolph to New York in 1911, is now a wealthy retired businessman, in Pensacola, Florida. The small fruit-and-vegetable business he opened on Davis Street, when he left Randolph in Harlem to return to his parents in Jacksonville, grew into one of the most thriving black-owned general stores in the city. The store was practically wiped out during the Depression, and, in the mid-1930's, Hearn and his wife, a graduate of Wilberforce University, took what remained of their savings and left for New York, where they built up another successful grocery business, at the corner of Manhattan Avenue and 116th Street. They did this by catering almost exclusively to the down-home tastes of the Southern migrants who flowed into Harlem after the Great Depression. In 1948, tiring of the grocery business, the Hearns sold the store, went to live in Pensacola, and started investing their savings in real estate. By 1960, when his wife died, Hearn, the owner of several houses, had become one of the wealthiest men in the city.

Today, in his early eighties, he is in poor health and lives alone in one of the finer residences on North Sixth Avenue. Like Randolph, he is childless and has no immediate family remaining. But, unlike Randolph, he is his own housekeeper, despite a heart ailment that has weakened him considerably. Now and then, a few of his distant relatives come over from Jacksonville to cook and clean for a few days, or, as they prefer to say, to look after him. He would probably like them to come more often, but, knowing that his age, health, and wealth are no secret, he cannot be sure whose interests they are really looking after when they lavish attention upon him.

He moves through his tastefully and expensively furnished house—the walls hung with faded family photographs and diplomas, and the fine old pieces of furniture layered with dust—with a look of renunciation and resignation. Most of his pleasure these days seems to come from his cigars. He draws on them with a vigor and blows out the smoke with a delectation that belies his frail, hunched body and the boredom in his weak voice. When he clenches a cigar, drawing back his lips occasionally to show his teeth, or stylishly removes it with his thumb and forefinger to gesture home a point of conversation, he announces the style of someone who has been used for a long time to acting like a man of substance. He once delighted in wheeling his impressive Cadillacs around the city—there have been five of them over the past fifteen years—but today he looks upon the well-kept 1967 model parked in his garage as simply a means of taking him to the supermarket and back. And, unable to effectively supervise his holdings of more than twenty homes and tenements in Pensacola, he has been steadily disposing of them for some time now.

Besides his cigars, Beaman Hearn enjoys one other enthusiasm: it is talking proudly of "the famous A. Philip Randolph," his old boyhood friend from Jesse Street, Jacksonville, with whom—"think of it"—he used to play marbles and baseball, preach back-yard funeral orations over dead cats, and shoot birds to bake them into pies.

Though Randolph remains unimpressed with his fame, and feels no passion for possessions such as Beaman Hearn's, he himself seems to enjoy telling friends and visitors of this old boyhood playmate from Jacksonville, who is now "one of the persons of great wealth in the South."

Of course, he, too, is widowed, is nursing a heart ailment, and lives by himself, in his Ninth Avenue apartment. He appears anything but bored with his situation, however. If there is a natural melancholy attached to being old, ill, and by oneself, he seems to endure it with the same aplomb that marked his active life. He even manages to appear contented, taking the few liberties his present condition allows him, and not at all querulous about the limits.

He spends most of his time at home, resting, receiving visitors, or reading. He welcomes an occasional social call on the phone, but he himself seldom picks up the phone to call anyone. Visitors usually find him sitting erect in a high-backed easy chair, his legs crossed, and a book on his lap. Scattered on the floor around him are several old volumes, mostly books on political theory and religious history, and a selection of current magazines.

Because of his heart ailment, Randolph collapses occasionally from dizziness. His physician recommends mild and regular physical activity to strengthen his heart, and at seven-thirty every morning he exercises in his bedroom and jogs a few laps through his apartment. Short outdoor walks are also recommended, but he is seldom able to take these. Because he might suffer a fainting spell in the street, he must always be accompanied, and there is not always someone available. Though, unlike Beaman Hearn, he has a housekeeper, who comes in from nine to five, he does not consider it a part of her contract to escort him outdoors; besides, with women, he is old-fashioned enough to feel that men ought, always, to be the escorts. Thus, he is able to take his occasional walks only when Bayard Rustin or William Bowe, of the Brotherhood, come around, or when they send one of their co-workers. It is also they who find young people to accompany him on his visits to the doctor and the barber in Harlem; and on his occasional trips out of town, to AFL-CIO conventions and Executive Council meetings, political affairs in his honor, or college campuses, to accept honorary degrees.

On his occasional public outings, Randolph still manages—perhaps with more ease than ever before—to treat unpleasantness or racial slights as if they did not exist. One afternoon in 1970, a young man took Randolph to the ANTA Theater, on West Fifty-second Street, to see Moses Gunn in a matinee performance of *Othello*. When it was over, the two of them walked to the corner of Fifty-third Street and Broadway, and stood there for more than twenty minutes as the young man tried to hail one of the several empty taxicabs that passed them on the way downtown—all the drivers just happening, at that moment, to be looking the other way.

It was an experience to which the young man was quite accustomed, but today it was not an indignity he wished to share with someone as venerable as Randolph. He hoped for the miracle: that one of the cabs would pull up, as they were doing for white people only a block down the street. But he hoped in vain. Acutely embarrassed on Randolph's account, he avoided the older man's eyes, for fear of what he might find there. Nor did he want to express his anger, for fear of involving Randolph in his own emotions, or, worse, having to share with *him* an acknowledgment of their common situation. There was no certainty, of course, that the situation had registered one way or another upon Randolph, for he kept talking animatedly about other matters. But how could he not have felt anything? Their situation, the young man concluded, was not so common after all. It was shared by two quite different sensibilities: by a young black man, still in the power of his rage and his pride; and by an older, wiser, stronger one, who not only had conquered rage, but also, like an artist, had raised and distilled pride into a fine statement of self-mastery.

Whatever Randolph may have been thinking about the passing taxicabs he kept to himself. What he had been talking animatedly about all along was the acting of Moses Gunn—whose voice had impressed him as a remarkably powerful instrument, grained and edged with pain and sensitivity; and whose performance he had no doubt found far more absorbing than the cab drivers' conduct, one of the more vulgar racial side shows of the national culture.

The two finally got back to Randolph's apartment by taking a bus down Seventh Avenue, the older man still declining to volunteer any response to what they had undergone at Fifty-third and Broadway. Riding down Seventh, the young man sought consolations: Randolph would probably prefer the bus, anyway. It is the way he had traveled throughout his life in Harlem, and he probably enjoyed reacquainting himself with the traveling masses. Then, too, he had a reputation for tipping cab drivers rather heavily, so it was also a considerable saving all around.

One Sunday afternoon in January, 1970, having heard that Randolph had moved into the ILGWU houses, on Ninth Avenue, a group of residents in the Chelsea area held a reception in P.S. 33, at Ninth Avenue and Twenty-sixth Street, to welcome him into the neighborhood. One runs a certain risk in welcoming Randolph into anything, for, liking to rock boats, he does not always reward his hosts with what they wish to hear. Replying to the speeches of welcome, Randolph observed upon the importance of building the brotherhood of man. That, apparently, was good, for there were loud cheers. He then wandered into one of the political controversies of the time—not really wandering, since there was a connection in his mind to what he had said earlier: "I congratulate Leonard Bernstein for calling a meeting in his home to raise funds for the legal defense of the Panthers. While I do not share the Panther philosophy, I will defend their right to exist as a political group and to propagandize their beliefs. Because if one Panther loses his right, then each of us is threatened." No cheers. Then he wound up—not really having broken the thread of his theme—by thanking the Chelsea residents for welcoming him into their community, "because it is hard to be a stranger and because no man can live alone." The cheers returned.

Notes

Of the numerous sources used, this portrait is indebted most of all to A. Philip Randolph himself. He graciously obliged the author with several hours of personal interviews, suggested a number of other useful personal sources, and provided access to a large portion of his files at the A. Philip Randolph Institute, New York City. He was an invaluable source for general background material, but none more so than the material on his parents, his boyhood in Florida, and his first years in New York.

The files of the Chicago division of the Brotherhood of Sleeping Car Porters (at the Chicago Historical Society) were also a rich source of material not only on some of the major aspects of Randolph's life, but also on the Brotherhood itself and its officers. The *Messenger*, which Randolph edited between 1917 and 1928, is the most important source for his early career as a radical journalist and propagandist. These files are now to be found at the Schomburg Collection of the New York Public Library (in bound volumes) and in the library's regular collections (on microfilm). Convention proceedings of the Brotherhood, the AFL, and the AFL-CIO are the chief source of material on Randolph's activities in the councils of organized labor. The files of the New York division of the Brotherhood (now at the Library of Congress) became available only after this manuscript was completed, and therefore were not consulted.

Unfortunately, the majority of the important personal sources for Randolph's life were not available, all having died before this work began. They are his parents, James and Elizabeth Randolph; his brother, James; his wife, Lucille; and his closest friends and colleagues, Chandler Owen and Milton Webster. According to Randolph, a large portion of his papers, dealing with his early life, was destroyed by a fire in the New York office of the Brotherhood in the 1930's.

The Acknowledgments supplies a complete list of archives and personal sources used. All interviews were conducted between April, 1969, and June, 1971.

Chapter 1

Claude Brown quoted: *Manchild in the Promised Land* (New York: New American Library, Signet, 1965), p. vii.

The first modern wave of black migration to the North: Carter G. Woodson, *A Century of Negro Migration* (Washington, D.C.: Associated Publishers, 1918), pp. 159–166; cited by Gilbert Osofsky, *Harlem: The Making of a Ghetto* (New York: Harper Torchbooks, 1968), p. 20. This migration is referred to in chapter 4 of this text as "the migration of the Talented Tenth." Early twentieth-century migrants, politicians, realtors, etc., in Harlem: Osofsky, chapters 2, 3, 7, 11; James Weldon Johnson, *Black Manhattan* (New York: Atheneum, 1968 [orig. pub. 1930]), chapter 13; and Seth M. Scheiner, *Negro Mecca* (New York: New York University Press, 1965), pp. 30–38. Marcus Garvey's influence on Kwame Nkrumah ("I think that of all the literature that I studied, the book that did more than any other to fire my enthusiasm was the *Philosophy and Opinions* of Marcus Garvey . . ."): quoted by E. U. Essien-Udom in his Introduction to *Philosophy and Opinions of Marcus Garvey,* 2nd ed., Amy Jacques Garvey, comp., (London: Frank Cass & Co., 1967), p. xxv, from *Ghana: Autobiography of Kwame Nkrumah* (New York: Thomas Nelson & Sons, 1957), p. 45. Jamaica's People's National Party, founded in 1938, received its earliest impetus from the Jamaica Progressive League, formed earlier in Harlem; among the league's founders were Jamaicans W. A. Domingo and W. Adolphe Roberts.

Membership of the Brotherhood of Sleeping Car Porters in 1968: figures supplied by Benjamin McLaurin, in interview. Randolph as spokesman for civil rights leaders at the 1958 White House meeting with President Eisenhower: Allan Morrison, "Dean of Negro Leaders," *Ebony,* November 1958. Arthur H. Schlesinger, Jr.'s description of Andrew Mellon: *The Crisis of the Old Order* (Boston: Houghton Mifflin, 1957), p. 61. C. L. Dellums and Rachelle Horowitz quoted on Randolph's bearing and dignity: interviews. Joseph L. Rauh on Randolph's dignity: interview. Jean-Paul Sartre ("The men Faulkner likes . . .") quoted: "William Faulkner's Sartoris," in his *Literary and Philosophical Essays* (New York: Collier Books, 1962), p. 83. Gertrude Elise Ayer ("He is full of lovely greeting . . .") is quoted from an interview. Randolph's and Milton Webster's meeting with Willard Townsend and James Carey in Chicago's Palm Café: George McCray, "Labor Front,"

Chicago Defender, June 26, 1943. Randolph's Christmas greetings to his neighbors: copies in his files. His apology to President Truman over mimeographed letter: interview with James T. Farrell.

"His only vanity is his manners . . ." and the Black Muslims' trust of Randolph: Murray Kempton, "A. Philip Randolph," *The New Republic,* July 6, 1963. Randolph's defense of Malcolm X's right to attend Harlem community meeting: Kempton, and interview with Randolph. In the same interview, Randolph expressed his personal admiration of Malcolm X. His view of Adam Clayton Powell's importance to the black community: interview. The account of the pro-Powell protest meeting, called by Randolph: David Halberstam's report to the *New York Times,* December 30, 1966; Kempton in the *New York Post,* December 30, 1966.

Origins and description of the Dunbar Apartments: Osofsky, *Harlem,* pp. 155–158. Some prominent Dunbar residents: interviews with Randolph and Leigh Whipper. Randolph's mugging at the Dunbar: interviews with Randolph, Whipper, Bayard Rustin, and Corrie Jones. Lucille Randolph's last years and life with her husband: interviews with Randolph, Mrs. Jones, Mr. and Mrs. Benjamin McLaurin, Vincie Kendrick; material in Randolph's files.

Chapter 2

The biographical material on Randolph and his family is derived mainly from interviews with Randolph. Lester Volie sees Randolph as an example of the labor leader who could be "superbly cultured . . .": see his *Labor USA* (New York: Harper, 1958), p. xiv. The New York *Amsterdam News* called Randolph "the number one Negro leader in America" in its issue of July 12, 1941, after Randolph's threat of a march on Washington had forced President Roosevelt to issue Executive Order 8802.

Randolph's attitude toward the church as a religious and social institution and his relationship to the Bethel AME Chapel in Harlem: interviews with Randolph, his correspondence with the Reverend Richard Allen Hildebrand (in his files), and an interview with the Reverend Henderson Randolph Hughes. W. E. B. Du Bois in his *The Autobiography of W. E. B. Du Bois* (New York: International Publishers, 1968), p. 187, also describes the African Methodist Episcopal church as having been "the greatest social institution of American Negroes."

The discussion of the origins, development, and expansion of the AME church is developed from the following readings: Lerone Bennett, Jr., *Pioneers in Protest* (Baltimore: Penguin, 1969); W. E. B. Du Bois, *The Philadelphia Negro* (Philadelphia: University of Pennsylvania Press, 1899); *Encyclopaedia of the AME Church* (Philadelphia, n.p., 1916); E. Franklin Frazier, *The Negro Church in America* (New York: Schocken, 1963), and *The Negro in the United States* (New York: Macmillan, 1957); J. Wesley Gaines, *African Methodism in the South* (Atlanta: Franklin Publishing House, 1890); Daniel A. Payne, *History of the AME Church* (Nashville: AME Sunday School Union, 1891); Christopher Rush, *A Short Account of the Rise and Progress of the AME Church in America* (New York: n.p., 1843); George A. Singleton, *The Romance of African Methodism* (New York: Exposition Press, 1952); Charles Spencer Smith, *A History of the African Methodist Episcopal Church* (Philadelphia: AME Book Concern, 1922); Benjamin Tanner, *An Apology for African Methodism* (Baltimore: n.p., 1867); Carter G. Woodson, *The History of the Negro Church*, 2nd ed. (Washington, D.C.: Associated Publishers, 1921).

Richard Allen's account of his break with St. George's Church is quoted by Payne from Allen's *The Life Experience and Gospel Labors of the Rt. Rev. Richard Allen* (Philadelphia: AME Book Concern, n.d.). The African Free Society as an "ethical and beneficial brotherhood" and as the "first wavering step of a people": Du Bois, *The Philadelphia Negro*, p. 19. The AME church enters Florida after the Civil War, and freedmen in Tallahassee cry with joy: Tanner, p. 421.

Monticello described: U.S. Works Progress Administration, *Florida: A Guide to the Southernmost State* (New York: Oxford, 1944), pp. 438–439. Black political militancy in Monticello during Reconstruction ("We understand that the White People in this Place . . ."): William Watson Davis, *The Civil War and Reconstruction in Florida* (Gainesville: University of Florida Press, 1964), p. 607. The *Christian Recorder* as a "dangerous document": Du Bois, *Economic Cooperation Among Negro Americans*, Atlanta University Publications no. 12 (1907), p. 60.

AME church histories abound in biographical data about Henry M. Turner. But the following are especially useful for a story of his life, a discussion of his political activities, and an account of his relationship to black nationalist and back-to-Africa movements, from 1890 to 1910: J. Minton Batten, "Henry M. Turner: Negro Bishop Extraordinary," *Church History*, September 1938, pp. 231–246; W. E. B. Du Bois, *Black Reconstruction in America* (Cleveland and New York: World, Meridian, 1964 [orig. pub. by Harcourt, Brace, 1935]), pp. 367, 498–499, 502, 504, 506, 511; and Edwin S. Redkey, *Black Exodus: Black Nationalist and Back-to-Africa Movements, 1890–1910* (New Haven: Yale University Press, 1969). Turner's speech to the Georgia legislature in 1868 is excerpted from the full text in Singleton, *African Methodism*, appendix B, pp. 3–16. An abridged version is also to be found in Bradford Chambers, ed., *Chronicles of Black Protest* (New York: New American Library, Mentor, 1968), pp. 130–132.

Uneducated black ministers held up to ridicule by their "more haughty

. . . co-workers": Kelly Miller, *The Ministry, the Field for the Talented Tenth* (Washington, D.C.: Murray Bros., 1911), p. 13.

Chapter 3

The material in this chapter is based mainly on interviews with Randolph and the following residents or natives of Jacksonville, Florida: Deacon Argrett, Ethel Barnett, Arthur Garvin, Arthur Glass, Fanny Hansberry, Samuel Harper, Beaman Hearn, Vincie Kendrick, Ruth Lofton-Smith, Dr. James W. Parker, Joseph Preston, Annabelle Richardson, Chester Satterwhite, Charles Spears, and Eartha White.

The following were consulted for descriptions of Jacksonville around the turn of the century: *Jacksonville, Florida* (Jacksonville: Chamber of Commerce, 1916); Charles W. Smith, *Jacksonville and Florida Facts* (Jacksonville: H. & W. B. Drew Co., 1906); and Thomas Frederick Davis, *History of Jacksonville Florida and Vicinity, 1513–1924* (Gainesville: University of Florida Press, 1925). Jacksonville a good place for blacks: James Weldon Johnson, *Along This Way* (New York: Viking, 1968 [orig. pub. 1933]), p. 45; and interview with Annabelle Richardson.

Dollar Money Law. Du Bois, *Economic Cooperation Among Negro Americans*, p. 60. "Low salaries mean . . . the average rural minister . . .": Harry Roberts, "The Rural Negro Minister: His Work and Salary," *Rural Sociology*, vol. XII (1947), pp. 285–297.

Historical background of the Cookman Institute: Jay S. Stowell, *Methodist Adventures in Negro Education* (New York and Cincinnati: Methodist Book Concern, 1922), pp. 77–81.

Du Bois replied to Booker T. Washington's position—enunciated in the "Atlanta Compromise" address—in his "Of Mr. Booker T. Washington and Others," in *The Souls of Black Folk* (Chicago: A. C. McLurg, 1903). Two outstanding discussions of the Washington-Du Bois controversy are August Meier, "Radicals and Conservatives" and "The Paradox of W. E. B. Du Bois," in his *Negro Thought in America, 1880–1915* (Ann Arbor: University of Michigan Press, Ann Arbor Paper Books, 1966), pp. 171–206.

Chapter 4

The material in this chapter is based mainly on interviews with Randolph.

Early twentieth-century migration and black settlement of Harlem: see Woodson, *A Century of Negro Migration*, pp. 159–166; Osofsky, *Harlem*, chapters 2, 3, 7, 11; Johnson, *Black Manhattan*, chapter 13; and Scheiner, *Negro Mecca*, pp. 30–38. The figures on the black population of Manhattan in 1910 are from Osofsky, p. 18. John G. Taylor's complaints about "white renegades" assisting the black residential expansion in Harlem were published in the *Harlem Home News,* April 7, 1911. White residents fleeing Harlem: Johnson, *Black Manhattan,* p. 150.

W. E. B. Du Bois resigns from the Socialist party to escape discipline: see his *Dusk of Dawn* (New York: Schocken, 1968 [orig. pub. by Harcourt, Brace, 1940]), p. 235.

Morris R. Cohen describes himself as "philosophically a stray dog": Cohen, *Faith of a Liberal* (New York: Henry Holt & Co., 1946), p. 3.

For a discussion of Charles W. Anderson's influence in black Republican politics in New York, see Osofsky, *Harlem,* pp. 95–96, 161–168; and Meier, *Negro Thought in America,* pp. 254–255.

Chapter 5

This chapter is based mainly on interviews with Randolph, Theophilus Lewis, Reginald Johnson, James Vander Zee, Thelma Boozer, and Leigh Whipper—all of New York City.

The Reverend Reverdy C. Ransom, one of the distinguished black orators of his day, and one of the early members of the Niagara movement, also held moderate Socialist views; his opinion that the race problem would be solved by Socialists was expressed in 1897, and is quoted in Meier, *Negro Thought in America,* p. 185.

Chandler Owen as "a man of ready wit and agile tongue": George S. Schuyler, *Black and Conservative* (New Rochelle, N.Y.: Arlington House, 1966), p. 137.

The program of Randolph's Independent Political Council was later printed in the *Messenger,* November 1917.

Claude McKay's description of Hubert H. Harrison: McKay, *A Long Way From Home* (New York: Arno, 1969), pp. 41, 113. Harrison's praise of Randolph's and Owen's antiwar pamphlet, *Terms of Peace and the Darker Races,* was printed in the *Messenger,* November 1917.

William Dufty is quoted from his series of articles on Randolph in the *New York Post,* December 28, 1959, to January 3, 1960. For the Justice Department's judgment of the *Messenger,* see "Radicalism and Sedition Among Negroes as Reflected in Their Publications: The Investigating Activities of the Department of Justice, Exhibit 10," *Senate Documents,* 66th Congress, 1st session, 1919, vol. 12, p. 172.

Chapter 6

The material in this chapter is drawn chiefly from the files of the *Messenger* and from interviews with Randolph, Theophilus Lewis, and Ernest Rice McKinney.

The typical Harlem radical as "an over-educated West Indian without a job": Roi Ottley and J. William Weatherby, eds., *The Negro in New York* (New York: Praeger, 1969), p. 225, quoting a remark by Kelly Miller.

Horace Cayton and George Mitchell are quoted from their *Black Workers and the New Unions* (Chapel Hill: University of North Carolina Press, 1939), p. 378.

Du Bois's statement "Theoretically we are part of the world proletariat . . ." appeared in *Crisis,* December 1921. His "we do not believe that the methods of the IWW are today feasible" was quoted by the *Messenger,* July 1919, in an article titled "The Crisis of the Crisis."

John F. Hylan's and Morris Hillquit's vote in the 1917 mayoral election: James Weinstein, *The Decline of Socialism in America* (New York: Random House, Vintage, 1969), p. 154. Randolph's vote as candidate for comptroller: Weinstein, p. 73, quoted from the *New York Legislative Manual* (Albany, 1920), p. 786.

Chapter 7

The files of the *Messenger* are the main source for this chapter.

The quotation from President Woodrow Wilson's speech to Congress, asking a declaration of war, is from Alfred Fried, ed., *A Day of Dedication: The Essential Writings and Speeches of Woodrow Wilson* (New York: Macmillan, 1965), p. 308. The Socialist party's emergency convention in St. Louis: David A. Shannon, *The Socialist Party of America* (Chicago: Quadrangle, 1967), p. 95.

Figures on the black participation in the war effort: John Hope Franklin, *From Slavery to Freedom* (New York: Random House, Vintage, 1969), pp. 455–476; Edmund David Cronon, *Black Moses* (Madison: University of Wisconsin Press, 1964), p. 28. Cronon quotes from Emmett J. Scott, *Scott's Official History of the American Negro in the World War* (Chicago: Homewood Press, 1919), p. 32, and from Jerome Dowd, *The Negro in American Life* (London: Jonathan Cape, 1927), p. 189. "First your country, then your rights": a slogan Randolph recalls being used by Du Bois during the war.

The patriotism of the black press: see Frederick G. Detweiler, *The Negro Press in the United States* (Chicago: University of Chicago Press, 1922), pp. 67–68. Detweiler quotes from Robert Russa Moton, *Finding a Way Out:*

An Autobiography (Garden City, N.Y.: Doubleday, 1920), pp. 248 f.; and Scott, pp. 361 f., 116, passim. According to Detweiler, p. 68, the *Crisis*, May 1917, quoted the *Chicago Bee* as saying:

. . . the Negro is willing today to take up arms and defend the American flag; he stands ready to uphold the hands of the President; he stands ready to defend the country and his President against this cruel and unjust oppression.

Robert Russa Moton's letter to President Wilson was reprinted in the *New York Age,* March 22, 1917. Roscoe Conkling Simmons's statement "I am an American, proud of it . . ." is quoted in Detweiler, p. 70. For a full list of the more conservative black leadership, see Francis L. Broderick and August Meier, *Negro Protest Thought in the Twentieth Century* (New York: Bobbs-Merrill, 1965), p. 79.

Hubert Harrison's editorial, "The Descent of Du Bois," and his account of how he came to write it are reprinted in his *When Africa Awakes* (New York: Porro Press, 1920), p. 54. The editorial may also be found in Joanne Grant, ed., *Black Protest: History, Documents, and Analyses* (Greenwich, Conn.: Fawcett Premier Book, 1968), p. 185.

Du Bois's essay "The Talented Tenth" is, of course, widely reprinted. Here it is quoted from Harvey Wish, ed., *The Negro Since Emancipation* (Englewood Cliffs, N.J.: Prentice-Hall, 1964), pp. 62–73. Cayton's and Mitchell's comments on the Talented Tenth are quoted from their *Black Workers and the New Unions,* pp. 375–378. Henry Lee Moon's view of the leaders of the Niagara movement: see Wilson Record, *The Negro and the Communist Party* (Chapel Hill: University of North Carolina Press, 1951), p. 9, quoting from Moon, *Balance of Power: The Negro Vote* (Garden City, N.Y.: Doubleday, 1948), p. 100.

The statement "No intelligent Negro is willing to lay down his life for the United States . . ." was made by William L. Colson, a contributing editor to the *Messenger,* and quoted by Representative James F. Byrnes in a speech to the House of Representatives on August 25, 1919. Commenting on Colson's statement, the *Messenger,* in its issue of October 1919: "We find no fault with these quotations."

The Espionage Act and the prosecution of white antiwar Socialists in 1917–1918: Shannon, *The Socialist Party,* chapter 5.

The account of Randolph's and Owen's arrest, investigation, and arraignment in Cleveland: interview with Randolph, and material from the files of the United States Attorney, Northern District of Ohio, Cleveland.

Chapter 8

The files of the *Messenger* are the main source of this chapter.

Race riots and postwar black disillusionment: the figures on the hanging and imprisonment of black soldiers in Houston, Texas, are from Franklin, *From Slavery to Freedom,* p. 460. Franklin, p. 474, also gives the number of black casualties in the St. Louis race riots and the number of blacks lynched between 1917 and 1918. "The basic cause" of race riots during the "red summer" of 1919: August Meier and Elliot Rudwick, *From Plantation to Ghetto,* rev. ed. (New York: Hill and Wang, 1970), p. 220.

Kelly Miller quoted on "After the Negro has proved his value and worth . . .": see his *Kelly Miller's History of the Negro and the World War* (Washington, D.C.: Austin Jenkins Co., 1919), pp. 551, 554.

The postwar "crisis in American values": Arthur I. Waskow, *From Race Riot to Sit-In* (New York: Doubleday, Anchor, 1966), p. 1. (Waskow refers to 1919 as the year on which John Dos Passos chose to center *U.S.A.,* "his trilogy about intense conflict and a crisis in American values.") W. E. B. Du Bois's postwar disillusionment and prediction of race war: Meier and Rudwick, p. 222. Claude McKay on the origins of his poem "If We Must Die": see his *A Long Way From Home,* pp. 31–32. The *Messenger* ran Archibald Grimké's poem, "Her Thirteen Black Soldiers," in its issue of October 1919. Randolph and Owen as "wild-eyed Reds of the deepest dye": Abram L. Harris, "The Negro Problem as Viewed by Negro Leaders," *Current History,* vol. XVIII (1923), pp. 410–418.

Recognition of Randolph's "sound interpretation of the economic history of this country": editorial in the New York *Call,* June 27, 1919, reprinted in *Revolutionary Radicalism: A Report of the Joint Legislative Committee of the State of New York Investigating Seditious Activities,* 1920, vol. II, pp. 1464–1466. The letter from "A staunch American" to Archibald Stevenson: copy obtained from the files of the Lusk Committee (as the Joint Legislative Committee was also called) and supplied to the author by Professor Bernard John Poll.

The *New York World* commented on "the radical forces in New York City . . ." in its issue of June 4, 1919 (quoted in the *Messenger,* August 1919). Representative James Byrnes's House speech on black radicals was made on August 25, 1919 (reported in the *Messenger,* October 1919).

Chapter 9

The main sources for this chapter are the files of the *Messenger;* Cronon, *Black Moses;* Amy Jacques Garvey, *Garvey and Garveyism* (London:

Collier-Macmillan, Collier Books, 1963); Amy Jacques Garvey, comp., *Philosophy and Opinions of Marcus Garvey;* Theodore Vincent, *Black Power and the Garvey Movement* (Berkeley, Calif.: Ramparts Press, n.d. [probably 1971]); and interviews with Randolph.

Hubert Harrison as the intellectual progenitor of black nationalism in Harlem: in an article, "Patronize Your Own," reprinted in his *When Africa Awakes,* p. 87, Harrison writes:

The doctrine of "Race First" although utilized largely by the Negro businessmen of Harlem, has never received any large general support from them. If we remember rightly, it was the direct product of the out-door and indoor lecturers who flourished in Harlem between 1914 and 1916. Not all who were radical shared this sentiment. For instance, we remember the debate between Mr. Hubert Harrison, then president of the Liberty League, and Mr. Chandler Owen, at Palace Casino in December, 1918, in which the "radical" Owen fiercely maintained "that the doctrine of race first was an indefensible doctrine"; Mr. Harrison maintaining that it was the source of salvation for the race. Both these gentlemen have run true to form ever since.

Harrison also wrote, p. 8, of the inaugural meeting of his Liberty League:

That meeting at historic Bethel on June 12, 1917, and the labors of tongue and pen out of which that meeting emerged were the foundation for the mighty structures of racial propaganda which have been raised since then. This is a fact not generally known because I have not hankered after newspaper publicity.

Harrison's exchange with Mary White Ovington, his views on class consciousness versus race consciousness, his opinions of, remarks to, and resignation from the Socialist party: *When Africa Awakes,* pp. 57, 76–89. See also his *The Negro and the Nation* (New York: Cosmo-Advocate Press, 1917), pp. 21–29, 48–58, for his earlier advocacy of socialism. The Socialist party's *Bulletin* recommends pushing the sale of the *Messenger* and the *Emancipator:* see *Revolutionary Radicalism,* p. 2007.

Garvey on the origins of the UNIA, his arrival in the United States, and his decision to organize in New York: see *Philosophy and Opinions,* pt. II, pp. 124–134 (reprinted from *Current History,* September 1923). See also *Philosophy and Opinions,* pt. II, p. 57, for his first impressions of the NAACP office. Garvey described as "a little sawed-off, hammered down black man . . .": Vincent, *Black Power and the Garvey Movement,* p. 99, quoting John Bruce, who said he was "among the first American Negroes" Garvey called on after arriving in the U.S.

Randolph's recollection of his first meeting with Garvey: interview, and the recording of a talk Randolph gave at a fund-raising affair for the Young People's Socialist League, in New York City, in 1967; tape now in the possession of the A. Philip Randolph Institute. James Weldon Johnson's account of

"Harlem's first real sight of Garvey": *Black Manhattan,* p. 253. (According to some observers, Harrison's Liberty League was swallowed up by Garvey's UNIA soon after the latter was founded in New York. And Claude McKay remarks in his autobiography, *A Long Way From Home,* p. 42, that Harrison claimed he had an idea for a pan-African movement, "but Garvey, being more spectacular, had run away with it.")

Garvey claims a membership of 2 million by June, 1919: *Philosophy and Opinions,* pt. II, p. 129. Launching of the Black Star Line "to own, charter . . . and navigate ships of various types . . .": Cronon, *Black Moses,* p. 50. Negro Factories Corporation founded: Cronon, p. 60. Garvey on UNIA membership of 4 million by August, 1920, and on his status as "a leader of his race": *Philosophy and Opinions,* pt. II, p. 130. Herbert J. Seligman's article in the *New York World Sunday Magazine,* December 4, 1921, was reprinted in the *New York Age,* December 10, 1921.

Randolph's claim that he and Owen "were the theoretical exponents of achieving the goal of 'Africa for the Africans' ": *Messenger,* August 1922. In the same article, Randolph wrote:

It is well known that Garvey began his propaganda in harmony with the *Messenger*'s principles in order to get a hearing. He shifted his propaganda after he got a foothold. It is a verifiable fact that Brother Marcus got his first knowledge of the African problem from a program drawn up by the writer and presented at a conference, held at the late Madam C. J. Walker's home, Irvington-on-the-Hudson, out of which grew the "International League of Darker Peoples." Mr. Garvey was there and participated in the conference.

Garvey on "Capitalism is necessary to the progress of the world . . .": *Philosophy and Opinions,* pt. II, p. 72. Garvey on "If the Negro takes my advice . . ." and "It is a vicious and dangerous doctrine of social equality . . .": pt. II, pp. 69, 132.

Though the *Messenger* had been somewhat critical of Garvey since 1920, it became harshly so only in 1922. Its anti-Garvey articles are too numerous to mention. Among those not cited in this chapter, special note might be taken of the following: "The Garvey Movement: A Promise or a Menace," December 1920; "Garveyism," by Randolph, September 1921; "Black Zionism," by Randolph, January 1922; "Reply to Marcus Garvey," by Randolph, August 1922; "The Only Way to Redeem Africa," by Randolph, a three-part series running from December 1922 to February 1923.

William Pickens's letter refusing a Garvey honor was reprinted in the *Messenger,* August 1922. Du Bois calls Garvey "the most dangerous enemy of the Negro race . . .": Cronon, p. 190, quoting the *Crisis,* vol. XXVIII, pp. 8–9. Garvey on "I regard the Klan, the Anglo-Saxon clubs . . . as better friends of the race . . .": *Philosophy and Opinions,* pt. II, p. 71. Garvey on

"Before Owen and Randolph can speak of the failure . . .": quoted by Randolph in his "Reply to Marcus Garvey," *Messenger,* August 1922, from the *Negro World,* July 8, 1922. Account of the arrival of the human-hand package: see Randolph's story in the *Messenger,* October 1922.

For information on the African Blood Brotherhood, its politics and leadership: see Theodore Draper, *American Communism and Soviet Russia* (New York: Viking, 1960), chapter 15. See also Schuyler, *Black and Conservative,* pp. 123, 145; and Harold Cruse, *The Crisis of the Negro Intellectual* (New York: Morrow, 1967), pp. 115–146. Cruse also has a critical discussion of black radical and black nationalist politics in Harlem in the 1920's. W. A. Domingo on Garvey's "execrable exaggerations, staggering stupidities . . .": see his open letter to the *Messenger,* March 1923.

Garvey calls letter to the Attorney General "the greatest bit of treachery . . .": *Philosophy and Opinions,* pt. II, p. 294.

Domingo's pleasure in Garvey's downfall may well, as he suggests, have exceeded Owen's—at least equaled it. After Garvey's conviction, Domingo telegraphed the Attorney General congratulating him on having caged the "Tiger": Claude McKay, *Harlem: Negro Metropolis* (New York: Dutton, 1940), p. 170.

Chapter 10

Main sources: *Messenger;* Schuyler, *Black and Conservative;* "The Reminiscences of George S. Schuyler," in the Oral History Collection of Columbia University; interviews with Randolph, Schuyler, Theophilus Lewis, Lucille B. Wolfe, Ernest Rice McKinney, Noble Sissle, Gertrude Elise Ayer, and Leigh Whipper.

Langston Hughes describes the *Messenger:* see his *The Big Sea* (New York: Knopf, 1940), p. 233. Origins of the Friends of Negro Freedom: see the *Messenger,* April-May 1920. Schuyler describes meetings of the Friends of Negro Freedom, experiences with Randolph and the *Messenger,* cultural scenes and activities in Harlem, and Chandler Owen's renouncement of socialism: *Black and Conservative,* pp. 124–140, 144, and in interview. See also his "Reminiscences," pp. 69–82. Some of the prominent speakers at Friends of Negro Freedom lectures are listed in the *Messenger,* February and March 1923. James Weldon Johnson describes strolling in Harlem: *Black Manhattan,* pp. 162–163. Owen said by the *New York Age* to have become president of the California Development Company: reported by Schuyler in his *Messenger* column, "Shafts and Darts," October 1923.

The *Messenger*'s impact: Meier and Rudwick, *From Plantation to Ghetto,* p. 199. The New York *Call* praised the *Messenger* in the *Call*'s issue of June 27, 1919 (reprinted in *Revolutionary Radicalism,* p. 1464). Some of the complimentary letters from liberal and leftist intellectuals were reprinted in the *Messenger* of March and May-June 1919, October 1920, May, August, and September 1923.

Failure of socialism among blacks: "Despite all the talk about . . . unite and fight . . .": Schuyler, in interview. Sterling Spero and Abram L. Harris discuss the "instability" of Harlem Socialists and the reasons for their failure in their *The Black Worker* (New York: Atheneum, 1968 [orig. pub. 1931]), pp. 398–401. For discussions of the early history of blacks in the Socialist party, see Spero and Harris, pp. 402–414; Weinstein, *Decline of Socialism*, pp. 63–74; Shannon, *The Socialist Party*, pp. 50–53; and Record, *The Negro and the Communist Party*, pp. 15–20. Kelly Miller advises blacks that their interests lie with capitalism: "The Negro as a Workingman," *American Mercury*, November 1925. Eugene Debs's statements on the St. Louis race riot and the Socialist party's policy toward blacks: Spero and Harris, pp. 405–406. (His statement on Socialist party policy is quoted from I. M. Rubinow, "The Negro and Socialism," New York *Call*, May 19, 1912.)

George Schuyler recalls Stuart Chase's visits to the *Messenger*'s office in his *Black and Conservative*, p. 147.

Chapter 11

The main sources for this chapter and for chapters 12–14 are the voluminous correspondence among officers of the Brotherhood of Sleeping Car Porters—as well as among the Brotherhood, the Pullman Company, and government agencies—in the files of the Chicago division of the Brotherhood (now at the Chicago Historical Society); Randolph's files; the records of the United States Mediation Board (at the National Archives and Records Service, Washington, D.C.); files of the *Messenger* and its successor, the *Black Worker*; Brailsford Brazeal, *The Brotherhood of Sleeping Car Porters* (New York: Harper, 1946); Spero and Harris, *The Black Worker*, pp. 430–460; Murray Kempton, *Part of Our Time* (New York: Dell, Delta Book, 1955), chapter 8; "The Reminiscences of Benjamin McLaurin," in the Oral History Collection of Columbia University; interviews and correspondence with Randolph, C. L. Dellums, Ulas Crowder, Benjamin McLaurin, O. W. Bynum, Samuel Harper, Joseph Preston, Jessie Martin, William Bowe, Chester Satterwhite, Nat Evans, Ernest Rice McKinney, Rogers Whitaker, and Arthur Dubin. Dubin's files on Pullman memorabilia were also consulted.

The account of efforts to enlist Randolph as organizer of the Brotherhood is based on interviews with Randolph, William Bowe, Ulas Crowder, and O. W. Bynum; material in Randolph's files; and *Story of the Porter—a Saga in Trade Unionism: BSCP Silver Jubilee Anniversary and 7th Biennial Convention*, September 1950. In the "Report of the Proceedings of the Biennial

Convention and Fifteenth Anniversary Celebration of the Brotherhood of Sleeping Car Porters," September 1940, p. 110, Ashley Totten reports:

. . . it would be necessary to employ the services of a man who was independent of the Pullman Company, who had the ability and the courage, the stamina and the guts, the manhood and the determination of purpose to lead the porters on. The task of finding such a man fell upon your humble servant. . . . I went to Brother Randolph.

For background information on the Brotherhood's origins, the Pullman Company's Plan of Employee Representation, the porters' wages and working conditions, and the union's struggle against Pullman, see, e.g., the following articles by Randolph—all, except where indicated otherwise, in the *Messenger:* "Case of the Pullman Porter," July 1925; "Pullman Porters Need Their Own Union," August 1925; "The Pullman Company and the Pullman Porter," September 1925; "Randolph's Reply to Perry Howard," October-November 1925; "The Truth About the Brotherhood of Sleeping Car Porters," February 1926; "An Open Letter to Mr. E. G. Carry," September 1926; "Notes of the Brotherhood of Sleeping Car Porters," October 1926; "Pullman Porters Fight Paternalism," *American Federationist,* June 1930. These articles in the *Messenger* are also valuable background sources: Ashley Totten, "Pullman's Soothing Salve," January 1926; Totten, "An Expose of the Employee Representation Plan," April 1926; Frank Crosswaith, "Crusading for the Brotherhood," June 1926; Totten, "Robbing the Porter," June 1926; F. Boyd, "Previous Struggles of the Pullman Porters to Organize," September 1926. See also *The Pullman Porters' Grievances,* a pamphlet published by the BSCP; and *The Pullman Porters Attempt to Organize,* Federal Council of Churches of Christ in America Information Service bulletin, February 9, 1929 (both at the Chicago Historical Society).

The travel route from the West Coast to New York, before transcontinental railroads: based on Justin Kaplan, *Mr. Clemens and Mark Twain* (New York: Pocket Books, 1968), p. 1; and interview with Arthur Dubin.

George Pullman's early interest in improving sleeping cars, and the origins and development of the Pullman sleeping car enterprise: Carrol R. Harding, *George M. Pullman (1831–1897) and the Pullman Company* (New York: Newcomen Society, 1951), pp. 1–19; Stanley Buder, *Pullman: An Experiment in Industrial Order and Community Planning, 1880–1930* (New York: Oxford, 1968), chapters 1–2; Joseph Husband, *The Story of the Pullman Car* (Chicago: A. C. McLurg, 1917); and Arthur Dubin, "A Pullman Postscript," *Trains,* November 1969.

Pullman's preference for the emancipated slave as porter, and the company as the largest employer of black labor: Husband, p. 155, and an internal office memorandum in the files of Arthur Dubin. The porter as "a higher grade of Negro": a popular estimate by sleeping car travelers, recalled by Rogers Whitaker. E. D. Nixon's account of how the traveling porter was regarded: see his interview with Studs Terkel, *Hard Times* (New York: Pantheon, 1970), p. 117. Murray Kempton on "The Pullman porter rode his car . . .": *Part of Our Time*, pp. 240–242.

History of porters' wage rates, including comment of L. S. Hungerford that "you can get all the men you require to do the work": Brazeal, *The Brotherhood*, pp. 208–213; and miscellaneous material in the BSCP's files. The account of the porters' working conditions is based on interviews with old porters, the BSCP's and Randolph's files, articles in the *Messenger* (especially from July 1925 through the end of 1926); Brazeal, p. 15; and material in the files of Arthur Dubin. For general background, see Robert E. Turner, *Memories of a Retired Pullman Porter* (New York: Exposition Press, 1954). Information on the Society for the Prevention of Calling Sleeping Car Porters George was obtained from Arthur Dubin's files.

Milton Webster's account of the history of the porters' efforts to organize: the BSCP's *Black Worker*, August 1936. Ashley Totten's account of the 1924 wage conference in Chicago: see his four-part series, "Why the Plan Is a Fraud," in the *Black Worker*, February 15–April 1, 1930.

Chapter 12

Randolph agrees to organize the Brotherhood: interview. Benjamin Stolberg, in an article in the *New York Times*, July 11, 1926, quotes Randolph as saying that the porter was "made to order to carry the gospel of unionism. . . ." The New York *Amsterdam News* reported the founding of the Brotherhood in its issue of September 2, 1925. Randolph's account of the inaugural meeting: interview.

The account of Randolph's organizational tour of the West and Midwest: interviews with Randolph, Benjamin McLaurin, Ulas Crowder, C. L. Dellums, and Samuel Harper; and material in Randolph's and the Chicago BSCP files. Comparison of Randolph and Webster: Kempton, *Part of Our Time*, chapter 8.

Recruitment and organizational activities of E. J. Bradley, in St. Louis, and Dad Moore, in Oakland: interviews with Randolph, Crowder, and Dellums; also extensive Moore-Webster correspondence in the Chicago BSCP files. E. D. Nixon's first impressions of Randolph: Terkel, *Hard Times*, p. 119.

Stool pigeons: Totten's definition of a stool pigeon appeared in the *Black Worker*, August 1930. Nat Evans's experiences with stool pigeons in St. Paul, Minnesota: letter to the author. McLaurin's account of stool pigeon activities and of Pullman's attempt to have Randolph arrested: "The Reminiscences of Benjamin McLaurin," pp. 163, 253, 257–258.

Loyal company porters attend 1926 wage conference in Chicago: minutes of the "Joint Conference Held in Chicago, January 27 to February 5, 1926, Between Elected Representatives of the Porters and Representatives of the Pullman Company," Pullman Company, Chicago, 1926 (copy at the New York Public Library). Bennie Smith's undercover activities for the Brotherhood during 1926 wage conference, his discharge by Pullman, and his subsequent arrest in Jacksonville: interviews with Randolph, Dellums, and Crowder; correspondence in Randolph's and the Chicago BSCP files. See also Smith's account of his experience in Jacksonville, in the "Report of Business Transacted by the Sixth Triennial Convention upon the Forty-third Anniversary of the Brotherhood . . . ," September 1968, pp. 89–91, and Randolph's letter to the *New York Times,* June 17, 1927.

Prominent blacks oppose labor unionism: see, e.g., Kelly Miller, "The Negro as a Workingman"; and T. Arnold Hill (quoting Miller), "The Dilemma of Negro Workers," *Opportunity,* February 1926. See also Perry Howard, "Open Letter to Pullman Porters," *Spokesman,* November 1925.

Opposition of black churches: interviews with Randolph and Crowder; "The Reminiscences of Benjamin McLaurin," pp. 129–130, 132, 183, 186; Milton Webster's speech in "Report of Proceedings: First Triennial Convention and Twenty-eighth Anniversary of the Brotherhood . . . ," October 1953, p. 38. (The BSCP's convention proceedings contain valuable information on all aspects of the union's struggle to organize. They are also a rich source for Milton Webster's spicy and hard-hitting oratorical style.) See also Brazeal, *The Brotherhood,* pp. 44–47; *Story of the Porter;* Randolph-Webster correspondence in the Chicago BSCP files. A later discussion of the attitude of the black church to labor unions is Horace A. White, "Who Owns the Negro Church?" *Christian Century,* February 9, 1938.

Opposition of the black press: interviews with Randolph et al.; various BSCP convention proceedings; Webster-Randolph correspondence in the Chicago BSCP files; files of the *Messenger;* Brazeal, pp. 50–56; Spero and Harris, *The Black Worker,* pp. 435–437. Cayton and Mitchell, *Black Workers and the New Unions,* pp. 397–398, provide a general discussion of the attitudes of the black church and the black press toward labor unions. At the Brotherhood's First Triennial Convention, in Los Angeles, October, 1953 (see p. 47 of the "Proceedings"), Milton Webster summed up the opposition the union received from the black press:

. . . money is a mysterious thing that moves a lot of people in a lot of different ways. . . . When the history of this organization is written . . . one of the darkest pages will be the treachery of those who betrayed this organization. As one man told me . . . he made fourteen thousand dollars writing articles against the Brotherhood.

Still, opposition from large sections of the black press could not have been too surprising to the Brotherhood's leaders. As early as May, 1924, more than a year before the BSCP was founded, the *Messenger* had commented upon the National Negro Press Association:

It is not only worthless, but it is a menace and a disgrace. It adopts a resolution in its annual convention endorsing unionism. It also repudiates the eight-hour day, more wages, and better working conditions for black workers.

Though the white New York metropolitan press was largely favorable to the Brotherhood, one of the exceptions, hardly surprising, was the *Wall Street Journal*. The *Messenger* of September, 1927, reported the *Journal* as accusing Randolph of "advocating doctrines that are a menace to race relations."

Prominent civil rights, liberal, and Socialist figures in New York strongly supported the Brotherhood. A New York Citizens Committee of One Hundred in Behalf of Pullman Porters included: Robert Bagnall, A. A. Berle, Franz Boas, Heywood Broun, John Dewey, W. E. B. Du Bois, Harry Fosdick, Morris Hillquit, Fannie Hurst, James Weldon Johnson, William M. Kelly, Freda Kirchwey, Harry Laidler, Eugene O'Neill, the Reverend Adam Clayton Powell, Sr., Paul Robeson, Joseph Schlossberg, Helen Phelps Stokes, Benjamin Stolberg, Norman Thomas, B. Charney Vladeck, and Walter White.

Randolph's response to the storm of criticism ("When I enlisted in the cause . . ."), and also an emotional appeal to the porters, appeared in the *Messenger*, March 1926.

For the Brotherhood's attitude toward the Watson-Parker bill (which became the Railway Labor Act of 1926), see Brazeal, p. 64; and Spero and Harris, pp. 449–451.

Chapter 13

Provisions of the Railway Labor Act of 1926: *Reports of the United States Board of Mediation*, Washington, D.C., 1929.

The account of the Brotherhood's long legal struggle and the privations of its membership and leadership is based mainly on the following: voluminous correspondence, newspaper clippings, and union documents in the Chicago BSCP files; files of the *Messenger* and the *Black Worker;* interviews and correspondence with Randolph, C. L. Dellums, Ulas Crowder, Samuel Harper, O. W. Bynum, and Jessie Martin; "The Reminiscences of Benjamin McLaurin"; and correspondence in the files of the Mediation Board (at the National Archives and Records Service, Washington, D.C.).

The figures on the Brotherhood's fluctuating membership: Brazeal, *The*

Brotherhood, pp. 221–222 (these figures, particularly in the early years, include financial as well as nonfinancial members).

Chapter 14

The mood of organized labor, the inception of the NIRA, and the amendments to railroad legislation: this discussion relies on Irving Bernstein, *Turbulent Years: A History of the American Worker, 1933–1941* (Boston: Houghton Mifflin, 1970), pp. 205–215. See p. 206 for the Railway Labor Act "as full of holes . . . as Swiss cheese" and for the number of railroad unions represented by company union plans in 1932; p. 34 for the excerpt from Section 7a of the NIRA and for how the *New York Times,* William Green, and John L. Lewis described the new NIRA.

Joseph B. Eastman co-operated behind the scenes with efforts to amend the railroad legislation, mainly by prodding Roosevelt and liberal senators: on May 19, 1934, Louis Howe, secretary to the President, appended the following note to his copy of a reply he had sent to one of Randolph's letters: "Mr. Eastman wants bill S. 2411 which will amend the Emerg. R.R. Trans. Act of 1933, so as to put Pullman Co. under jurisdiction of this Act, to be passed" (from the Franklin D. Roosevelt Library, Hyde Park, N.Y.).

Testimony and submissions (including positions taken by Randolph and Senator Clarence C. Dill) leading to the amendment of the Railway Labor Act and the Emergency Railroad Transportation Act: U.S. Senate, 73rd Congress, 2nd session, *Hearings Before the Committee on Interstate Commerce,* S. 3266, April-May, 1934; *A Bill to Amend the Railway Labor Act,* H.R. 9861, June 21, 1934; *A Bill to Amend the Emergency Railroad Transportation Act of 1933,* S. 2411, February 26 and 27, 1934 (all published by the Government Printing Office, Washington, D.C.). See also House of Representatives, *Hearings Before the Committee on Rules,* H.R. 9861, June 12 and 13, 1934 (Government Printing Office, Washington, D.C.).

Randolph's correspondence with Walter White (re "exclusion legislation"): NAACP papers, in the Library of Congress.

The Mediation Board's certification vote, intervening events, and the Brotherhood's victory: Chicago BSCP files; Randolph's files; Randolph-White correspondence in the NAACP papers (Library of Congress); Brazeal, *The Brotherhood,* pp. 100–114; A. Philip Randolph, "Pullman Porters Win," *Opportunity,* October 1937; A. Philip Randolph, "Pullman Porters Vote for Organization They Want," *American Federationist,* July 1935; interviews with Randolph, C. L. Dellums, William Bowe, and O. W. Bynum; *Report of Proceedings of the Seventh Biennial Convention and Silver Jubilee Celebration of the Brotherhood . . . ,* September 1950, pp. 138–139. Webster's

anecdote of his "rough stuff" speech in Cincinnati, in 1928: *Proceedings,*
September 1950, p. 128.

Chapter 15

The main sources for the origins, development, and decline of the National
Negro Congress (including Randolph's role as president): Ralph Bunche,
"The Programs, Ideologies, Tactics, and Achievements of Negro Betterment
and Interracial Organizations," unpublished research memorandum prepared
for the Carnegie Foundation-Gunnar Myrdal Study, June 1940, pp. 319–323,
350–371; files and microfilm records containing the papers and copies of the
official proceedings of the National Negro Congress (at the Schomburg Collection of the New York Public Library); Cayton and Mitchell, *Black Workers and the New Unions,* pp. 415–424; Record, *The Negro and the Communist Party,* pp. 153–165, 191–200. Meier and Rudwick, *From Plantation to
Ghetto,* pp. 245–246; Irving Howe and Lewis Coser, *The American Communist Party,* 2nd ed. (New York: Praeger, 1962), pp. 356–358; Cruse, *The
Crisis of the Negro Intellectual,* pp. 171–178; material on the NNC in Randolph's files; interviews with Randolph.

Aims and objectives of the NNC and the number of delegates and organizations at the first meeting, in Chicago: John P. Davis's Introduction, *The
Official Proceedings of the National Negro Congress,* February 14–16, 1936,
pp. 3–4.

Randolph's health when invited to take the presidency of the NNC: report
from the Mt. Sinai Consultation Service, April 21, 1936 (copy in Randolph's
files). George S. Schuyler sees Randolph "panting for leadership": *Black
and Conservative,* p. 242. Claude McKay on Randolph's qualifications for
the NNC presidency: see his *Harlem: Negro Metropolis,* pp. 229–230. Randolph's first presidential address is reprinted in the NNC's *Proceedings,*
February 14–16, 1936, pp. 7–12.

Communist infiltration and control: Record, p. 153; Howe and Coser,
p. 356. Randolph defends the NNC against Communist-front charges, after
first meeting in Chicago: McKay, *Harlem,* p. 230, quoting a public statement by Randolph. On June 22, 1937, Randolph wrote Walter White, of the
NAACP, stressing "the general policy of the NNC to cooperate with and
support the recognized existing Negro organizations engaged in the struggle
for the liberation and advancement of the Negro people" (NAACP papers,
Library of Congress). Ralph Bunche's detailed account of Randolph's resignation from the presidency: "The Programs, Ideologies, Tactics," pp. 357–
371.

Randolph on the need to oppose Nazism and Fascism ("What does the

Battle for Britain mean . . .") : "The Battle for Britain," an editorial by him published by the New York Chapter of the Committee to Defend America by Aiding the Allies, August 1940 (clipping in Randolph's files).

Randolph explains his opposition to NNC's dependence on Communists or the CIO for financial help: "Why I Would Not Stand for Re-Election for President of the National Negro Congress," a public statement appended to *The World Crisis and the Negro People Today,* reprint of his last presidential address to the NNC (copy in Randolph's files). The *New York Times,* April 28, 1940, quoted Randolph:

The Communist Party is not primarily, or fundamentally, concerned about the Negro or labor in America, but with fulfilling and carrying out the needs and demands of the consolidation of the foreign position of the Soviet Union in world politics.

On May 10, 1940, he wrote Arthur G. McDowell, labor secretary of the Socialist party, in Chicago:

I could not go any further with an organization which was receiving its dictation and orders from the Communist Party. I, at one time, thought that we would be able to prevent the Communists from assuming control of the organization, but I found it was hopeless. [From Socialist party papers, in Perkins Library, Duke University.]

And Earl Browder, in "The Reminiscences of Earl Browder," Oral History Collection of Columbia University, has recalled: "I think it was Randolph who took the initiative in the breaking of the United Front that kept it from becoming a general one."

For another contemporary speculation upon the future of the NNC, see Lester Granger, "The Negro Congress—Its Future," *Opportunity,* June 1940.

Chapter 16

The definitive study of the March on Washington movement of the 1940's is Herbert Garfinkel, *When Negroes March* (New York: Atheneum, 1969). It is one of the main sources for this chapter—which deals only with some of the highlights of the march movement. Other major sources are Randolph's files; the Franklin D. Roosevelt Library, Hyde Park, N.Y., for correspondence surrounding the threatened march (in mid-1941), the issuance of Executive Order 8802, and the events preceding it; Walter White, *A Man Called White* (New York: Viking, 1948), pp. 186–193; Lerone Bennett, Jr., *Confrontation: Black and White* (Baltimore: Penguin, 1966), pp. 143–168; Joseph P. Lash, *Eleanor and Franklin* (New York: Norton, 1971), pp. 528–535; "The Reminiscences of Benjamin McLaurin"; interviews with Randolph, Bayard Rustin, and C. L. Dellums.

President Roosevelt assures the European democracies ("We Americans are vitally concerned in your defense of freedom . . ."): State of the Union Message, January 6, 1941, quoted in Garfinkel, p. 17. Will Winton Alexander blames Sidney Hillman for failing to write antidiscrimination clauses into defense contracts: "The Reminiscences of Will Winton Alexander," Oral History Collection of Columbia University, p. 675. Milton Webster calls federal government "the greatest culprit in the discriminating practices . . .": BSCP *Proceedings,* September 1950, p 131.

Joseph P. Lash quoted ("Early in July, Mrs. Bethune . . ."): *Eleanor and Franklin,* pp. 528–529. Mrs. Roosevelt addresses BSCP's convention dinner: BSCP "Proceedings," September 1940, pp. 88–91.

Mrs. Roosevelt telephones Stephen Early to suggest White House meeting for Randolph, Walter White, and T. Arnold Hill: Early's "Memorandum for General Watson," 9/19/40 (FDR Library). White House press conference misrepresents position of civil rights leaders, and subsequent controversy: Early's "Memorandum for the President," 10/14/40; Early to White, 10/-18/40; Citizens Nonpartisan Committee for Equal Rights in Defense (telegram) to Roosevelt, 10/20/40; White to Early, 10/21/40 and 10/25/40; Roosevelt to Randolph, White, and Hill, 10/25/40; NAACP press release ("FDR Regrets That Army Policy Was 'Misinterpreted' "), 10/26/40; Hill and Randolph to Roosevelt, 10/31/40 and 11/1/40, respectively (all in FDR Library). See also White, *A Man Called White,* pp. 186–188, for his account of the controversy, including Early's kicking of a black New York policeman in the groin and White's call for Early's dismissal from the White House staff. The kicking incident is also reported in Lash, pp. 531–532. White thanks the President for insuring "a square deal for Negroes in the defense of our country . . .": Lash, p. 532.

Randolph on Monroe Trotter's audience with President Coolidge: interview. Randolph conceives March on Washington Idea, on southbound railroad trip with Milton Webster: see Webster's account in BSCP *Proceedings,* September 1950, p. 129, and September 1956, p. 13.

Randolph issues first statement calling for a march: press release, "How to Blast the Bottlenecks of Race Prejudice in National Defense," by A. Philip Randolph, issued by the BSCP, January 15, 1941 (copy in Randolph's files). Garfinkel quoted on the response of the more conservative civil rights organizations ("This was not the kind of action . . ." and "The reluctance of the NAACP and Urban League leadership . . ."): *When Negroes March,* pp. 39–40. Membership of the March Committee: listed on letterhead of the March on Washington Committee.

Randolph issues the official call to march: Garfinkel, pp. 56–57. See also Randolph's article, "Let the Negro Masses Speak," *Black Worker,* March 1941. William Dufty quoted on preparations for the march: "A. Philip Randolph," *New York Post,* January 3, 1960. Randolph calls for 100,000 march-ers ("When 100,000 Negroes march on Washington . . ."): press release, "Negroes Out to Shame America for Jobs and Justice," by A. Philip Ran-dolph, issued by the BSCP, May 29, 1941. The *Pittsburgh Courier* calls the march "a crackpot proposal": clipping of an undated editorial in Randolph's files.

Randolph writes to invite administration officials to the march: two exam-ples are Randolph to Mrs. Roosevelt and to William Knudsen, 6/3/41. He seems also to have written to Henry Stimson on the same date, for on June 23 he wrote Stimson "to renew my invitation" (letters in FDR Library).

Washington's response: Mrs. Roosevelt replies to Randolph on June 10 (quoted from an undated *New York Times* clipping in Randolph's files). Stephen Early to Wayne Coy on 6/6/41 "enclosing herewith a copy of a letter from A. Philip Randolph . . . to Mr. William S. Knudsen" and won-dering if "it would not be possible . . . for you to appeal to Mayor La Guardia . . ." (FDR Library). Wayne Coy, in "Memorandum for the Presi-dent," 6/16/41, suggests that Roosevelt support S.R. 75, introduced by Sena-tor W. Warren Barbour, of New Jersey (FDR Library).

Communist opposition to Randolph and the march: Howe and Coser ("Those Negro leaders who felt . . .") quoted: *The American Commu-nist Party,* p. 415. See also Record, *The Negro and the Communist Party,* pp. 203–205, 219–222; and Garfinkel, pp. 42–53. C. L. Dellums quoted ("We told our white friends . . ."): interview.

The City Hall meeting with Mrs. Roosevelt and La Guardia, and the White House meeting with the President: Lash, pp. 534–535; White, pp. 189–192; interviews with Randolph. The reconstruction of the exchanges be-tween Randolph and the President during the White House meeting is based partly on various accounts Randolph has given—to the author, among others —and partly on a verbatim account (possibly written from an interview with Randolph) in Bennett, *Confrontation,* pp. 150–151. La Guardia suggests that Roosevelt call in Randolph and White "and thresh it out right then and there": "Memorandum for the President," from Edwin M. Watson, 6/14/41 (FDR Library). Randolph rejects the President's request to call off the march, pending the White House meeting: telegram to Roosevelt, 6/16/41 (FDR Library).

Randolph balks at several drafts of the executive order: interview with Jo-seph L. Rauh. Mrs. Roosevelt's hope that "from this first step, we may go on to others": letter, 6/26/41, in Randolph's files.

Youth arm of the March on Washington Committee denounces Randolph for canceling the march: Garfinkel, p. 67; interviews with Randolph and Bayard Rustin; press release in Randolph's files. See also Garfinkel, p. 68, for excerpts of Randolph's long letter stating his reasons for calling off the march.

Benjamin McLaurin assesses the Roosevelts: "The Reminiscences of Benjamin McLaurin," p. 320. Roy Wilkins's assessment of the executive order and of the Roosevelts: column in the New York *Amsterdam News,* July 5, 1941. Lerone Bennett's appraisal of the significance of the executive order: *Confrontation,* p. 152. An anonymous respondent to a questionnaire in Randolph's files also makes the following appraisal of the March on Washington movement:

MOWM was a response to the intolerable conditions Negro citizens suffered in the early years of the war effort of the 1940's. It came into being at a time when Negro citizens were excluded from all phases of national defense, were segregated in the Armed Forces, were frozen to ghettos by poverty and the existence of restrictive covenants, were severely handicapped in training and education because of the segregation in public schools and institutions of higher learning in the South, and were effectively excluded from almost all aspects of American life. . . . It was the most radical and drastic of the movements heretofore developed within the Negro community. It attempted to use the techniques of struggle which were part of organized labor's struggle for recognition. It challenged the existing Negro organizations and radicalized their methods of attack on the problem of discrimination to some extent. It provided considerable experiences for the emerging body of leaders within the Negro community. It gave hope to Negroes everywhere, whether or not they participated directly in the movement. . . . There is no question but that MOWM set in motion forces which helped to revolutionize race relations in the United States. It served notice on the United States government that Negro citizens would no longer tolerate the conditions they then suffered. It concretized the feeling which was widespread among Negroes, "That if we have to die for democracy, we might as well die right here at home." It forecast the coming social explosions

Chapter 17

Randolph acclaimed for his role in the issuance of Executive Order 8802; the New York *Amsterdam News* ranks him "along with the great Frederick Douglass . . ." in its issue of July 12, 1941. Du Bois describes his action as "the most astonishing in our later leadership": "As the Crow Flies," April 1943 (a Du Bois column, from an unidentified publication, in Randolph's files). Murray Kempton on the BSCP as "a kind of cathedral" and Randolph as "a paladin": *Part of Our Time,* p. 248.

Randolph recommends Gandhian tactics to the March on Washington movement: Bennett, *Confrontation: Black and White,* pp. 157–158; Garfinkel, *When Negroes March,* pp. 135–136. An unidentified and undated newspaper clipping in Randolph's files, "Randolph Urges Negroes to Try Non-Violence," says in part: "The program of non-violent civil disobedience and non-cooperation should include refusal of Negroes to obey any law which violates their basic citizenship rights, such as Jim Crow cars and all forms of discrimination." See also "Randolph Tells Technique of Civil Disobedience," *Chicago Tribune,* June 26, 1943. In August, 1942, Randolph instructed T. D. McNeal, chairman of the St. Louis division of the march movement, to send the following cablegram to Gandhi, in the Poona jail:

The March on Washington Movement hails the struggle of India for independence. We pledge you our moral support for freedom and the victory of the United Nations. Negro people of America are also fighting for their democratic rights. Winning democracy for India and the Negro is winning the war for democracy.

MOWM criticized: the *Pittsburgh Courier* calls Randolph's nonviolent civil disobedience campaign "the most dangerous demagoguery on record," in its issue of January 23, 1943. Randolph dismisses the *Courier*'s criticism as the whinings of the "petty black bourgeoisie": Bennett, *Confrontation,* p. 159. In the *Chicago Defender,* June 12, 1943 ("Randolph Blasts Courier as 'Bitter Voice of Defeatism'"), Randolph wrote: ". . . the March . . . Movement is certain to survive the ravings of this commercial champion of comfort and conservatism." See also the *Defender,* July 17, 1943 ("A Reply to My Critics"), in which Randolph stated:

. . . the black petit bourgeoisie and intelligentsia are scared. They write about a struggle in which they have never participated. . . . They want to abolish it [Jim Crow] with words; that is, some of them do and some of them want to keep Jim Crow to continue to shoot at it. They advise the use of the type of technique which involves no risks and requires nothing more than ink and paper.

MOWM lacks formal organizational structure ("The power of the new movement is mysterious . . .") and Randolph dangles march threat: see Edwin Embree, *13 Against the Odds* (New York: Viking, 1944), pp. 211–230 (Embree also quoted in Bennett, p. 158). Impatience with a march movement that doesn't march: see, e.g., the *Pittsburgh Courier*'s editorial, "To March or Not to March," January 2, 1943.

Large MOWM rallies in the summer of 1942: interviews with Randolph, Theophilus Lewis, Benjamin McLaurin, Dr. Laurence Ervin, Max Delson, Bob Delson; Randolph-Webster correspondence in Randolph's files; Garfinkel, pp. 77–96. For an account of Randolph's reception at Madison Square Garden, see also Theophilus Lewis, "Plays and a Point of View," *Interracial Review,* July 1942. MOWM "had reached a peak" in 1942: Ellen Tarry, *The Third Door: The Autobiography of an American Negro Woman* (New York: McKay, 1955), p. 193 (quoted in Garfinkel, p. 97).

Randolph attacked by Carlotta Bass: see the *Los Angeles Tribune,* July

20, 1940. The *Pittsburgh Courier* in its editorial of January 2, 1943, also called upon Randolph to disband his movement in favor of the NAACP.

Dissension within the MOWM: unsigned letter ("My Dear Philip Lord Randolph . . ."), dated 8/24/42; officer in New York complains of "getting fed up . . . ," letter to Randolph, 2/9/43; the series of letters from Webster to Randolph, concerning differences with the Chicago march organization, dated 4/10/42, 8/25/42, 8/27/42, and 8/29/42 (all in Randolph's files). Chicago organization complains to Randolph of Webster's attitude: Garfinkel, p. 116.

Randolph sought for public office: the account of Randolph's appointment by Mayor La Guardia to the New York Housing Authority and of his refusal is based on Randolph's letter to La Guardia, 5/19/42 (in the Municipal Archives and Records Center, New York City), and on a story in the *New York Times,* June 17, 1942, announcing Frank Crosswaith's appointment.

Bipartisan support to run for Congress and Randolph's refusal: New York *Call* ("Why I Can't Run for Congress on the Old Party Tickets," by A. Philip Randolph), April 28, 1944. The *Times,* April 13, 1944, reported Herbert D. Bruce, a Harlem Tammany leader, as saying that, while he was ready to support Randolph, he would not support the Reverend Mr. Powell "under any circumstances." See Tarry, *The Third Door,* p. 193 (quoted in Garfinkel, p. 94), for another reference to Powell's announcement of his candidacy during the Madison Square Garden rally, 1942. According to Miss Tarry, "with thousands of Negroes listening, there is strong suspicion that the stage of Madison Square Garden became a sounding board for personal ambitions." Dorothy Norman sees Congress as "a fitting climax" to Randolph's career: *New York Post,* May 1, 1944. Randolph telegraphed Bradley on April 12, 1944, to ask his advice on running, and Bradley telegraphed his reply the following day; Bennie Smith wrote Randolph his opinion of Randolph's possible candidacy on April 18, 1944 (all in Randolph's files). The *New York Times,* April 19, 1944, also reported Randolph's refusal to run. In an interview with this author, Randolph has added:

I probably would have beaten Powell, but I couldn't leave the porters. The Brotherhood was the first significant black trade union organization. Besides, it would have appeared as if I was simply using the porters as a steppingstone to power.

The Socialist party nominates Randolph to run with Norman Thomas on the Socialist ticket for president, and Randolph's refusal: Randolph's telegram to Harry Fleischman (national secretary of the Socialist party), 5/13/-44; also Randolph's letter to Fleischman, 5/24/44 (both in Perkins Library, Duke University). See also the *New York Times,* June 5, 1944. In June, 1950, Roscoe Conkling Bruce, Sr., again tried to obtain support for a Randolph candidacy from the Twenty-second Congressional District. Bruce wrote Carmine De Sapio, the Tammany leader, on June 16, "urging you and your organization to support" Randolph, and, on the same day, wrote to inform Randolph of his letter to De Sapio. Randolph replied to Bruce on June 22, 1950, saying ". . . I have no desire to run for Congress. . . . I want to be free to carry on whatever efforts I can in the interest of various economic, social and political changes that may require the support of both major parties." (This correspondence is in Randolph's files; the copies of Bruce's letters are marked "Publicity.")

The account of the Boss Crump affair in Memphis is based on interviews with Randolph, numerous press releases issued by the Brotherhood, and newspaper clippings from the Memphis *Press-Scimitar* and *Commercial Appeal;* also "A. Philip Randolph Defies Boss Crump," his speech at the First Baptist Church, Memphis (all in Randolph's files).

C. L. Dellums quoted on Randolph and female admirers: interview.

Chapter 18

The chief sources for this chapter are the files of the *New York Times;* interviews with Randolph and Bayard Rustin; and material in the Harry S Truman Library, Independence, Missouri, and the National Urban League papers (at the Library of Congress).

Randolph on the 1947 draft bill: his statement that the bill was "pregnant with indecency" was also made in a letter to President Truman, 6/21/48 (Truman Library).

The Committee Against Jim Crow in Military Service and Training, formed on November 22, 1947: reported in the *New York Times,* November 23, 1947. Among the 118 members, according to the report, were: Joe Louis, Dr. Channing Tobias, J. Raymond Jones, George S. Schuyler, L. D. Reddick, Dr. Horace Mann Bond, Horace Cayton, Rufus E. Clement, and Dr. W. H. Jernigan.

Rustin refuses conscription: letter to Local Board No. 63, November 16, 1943 (copy in Randolph's files). In the letter, Rustin also stated: "I was compelled to resist war by registering as a Conscientious Objector in October, 1940. However, a year later, September, 1941, I became convinced that conscription as well as war equally is inconsistent with the teachings of Jesus. I must resist conscription also." Randolph, after reading Rustin's statement "with great interest and feeling," wrote to "applaud" him on April 17, 1944.

Account of the White House meeting with Truman: interview with Randolph. See also the *Times,* March 23, 1948.

Randolph's testimony before the Armed Services Committee and his clash with Senator Wayne Morse: *Congressional Record,* 80th Congress, 2nd session, Senate, April 12, 1948, pp. 4416–4418 (Armed Services Committee testimony inserted in the *Record* by Senator Morse). See also report of the hearings in the *Times,* April 1, 1948.

Randolph counsels against the draft in public meetings: one such meeting was reported by the *Times,* July 18, 1948. The previous day, the *Times* had quoted Bayard Rustin as saying that the League for Nonviolent Civil Disobedience "would not encourage evasion of the new draft law by fraudulent means such as feigning illness, fake dependents and other subterfuges. . . . The strength of the movement lies in truth and in those men who openly inform government that they are violating an unjust law." Earlier, on May 8, the *Times* had reported that Randolph and nine marchers paraded in front of the White House for an hour, handing out buttons inscribed "Don't Join a Jim Crow Army." Randolph was quoted in the news item as saying, "If we must die for our country, let us die as free men—not as Jim Crow slaves."

The black community's reaction: the *Amsterdam News* opposes Randolph in a signed editorial. The editor mailed a clipping of the editorial to President Truman, with a covering letter, dated July 23, 1948, saying, "We are desirous of receiving your views and condensed comments on this mailed editorial" (Truman Library). A prominent Washington stockbroker assures Truman that Randolph speaks only for himself: letter, dated 4/9/48 (Truman Library). The *Pittsburgh Courier*'s attack (April 10, 1948), Walter White's objection to Senator Morse's criticism of Randolph, the Reverend Adam Clayton Powell's support of Randolph's position, and Earl Brown's article (April 10) in the *Amsterdam News* were all inserted in the *Congressional Record,* Senate, July 12, 1948, pp. 4418–4422. The National Urban League's statement and Lester Granger's *Amsterdam News* column: the Urban League papers (Library of Congress). See also (Urban League papers) Roger Baldwin to Granger, 6/24/48; Granger to Baldwin, 7/29/48; Max Malmquist to Granger, 4/19/48; and Granger to Malmquist, 4/27/48. One Urban League board member wrote Granger, while the league's statement was being drafted: "Though we can't officially advocate civil disobedience, I'm glad Randolph and his buddies are. It may speed up action more than our temperate approach" (Urban League papers, Library of Congress).

Seventy-one per cent of draft-age blacks favor civil disobedience campaign: *Times,* June 5, 1948. Max Lerner's comment ("Randolph and Reynolds come closer to the true feelings of the masses . . ."): quoted in Garfinkel, *When Negroes March,* p. 216, from the reprint of a *PM* editorial in *Crisis,* May 1948.

Truman issues executive order against bias in federal employment: see the *Times,* July 27, 1948. Randolph queries Truman on the wording of the order: telegram to the President, 7/30/48 (Truman Library). Truman replies through senator: in the *New York Herald Tribune* of August 19, 1948, Randolph was quoted as saying: "Through Senator J. Howard McGrath, chief spokesman for the President, we have been given assurance that segregation in the armed services is unequivocally banned under the Executive Order of July 26." Randolph congratulates Truman: telegram to the President, 7/30/48 (Truman Library).

Bayard Rustin opposes Randolph's decision to disband the civil disobedience campaign: for the Winfred Lynn case, see *The War's Greatest Scandal! The Story of Jim Crow in Uniform,* a pamphlet by Nancy and Dwight Mac-Donald, published by the March on Washington movement (Xerox copy in BSCP papers, Chicago Historical Society). Randolph calls press conference to disband the League for Nonviolent Civil Disobedience: interviews with Randolph and Rustin; see also report in the *New York Herald Tribune,* August 19, 1948. According to the report:

> Bayard Rustin . . . made it clear that the movement will continue without Mr. Randolph. In a statement issued here, nineteen officials of the League rejected Mr. Randolph's stand and promised to carry on the civil disobedience campaign until "there is an unconditional order or law stating that non-segregation in military service is the national policy."

Randolph calls rebel group "a pacifist nucleus": statement by Randolph and Grant Reynolds, October 11, 1948 (Urban League papers, Library of Congress).

Randolph comments today (interview) on why it was easy to forgive Rustin: "I couldn't entertain any ill will toward Bayard for what he did, because I knew of his service in behalf of freedom."

Chapter 19

The main sources for this chapter are the following reports of convention proceedings of the American Federation of Labor: 49th Annual, October 8–18, 1929; 53rd Annual, October 2–13, 1933; 54th Annual, October 1–12, 1934; 55th Annual, October 7–19, 1935; 56th Annual, November 16–27, 1936; 57th Annual, October 4–15, 1937; 61st Annual, October 6–16, 1941; 63rd Annual, October 4–14, 1943; 64th Annual, November 20–30, 1944; 66th Annual, October 7–17, 1946. For more detailed discussions of Randolph's annual confrontations with the AFL convention, see Marc Karson and Ronald Radosh, "The American Federation of Labor and the Negro Worker, 1894–1949," in *The Negro and the American Labor Movement,* Julius Jacobson, ed. (New York: Doubleday, Anchor, 1968), pp. 155–187; and Brazeal, *The Brotherhood of Sleeping Car Porters,* pp. 151–170.

The AFL looks with "disfavor upon trade unions . . . which exclude . . . persons on account of race or color": Karson and Radosh, p. 155.

Randolph's opinion that "the dissolution of the American Federation of Labor would inure to the benefit of the labor movement . . .": *Messenger,* May-June 1919.

Thomas R. Brooks's description of William Green: see his *Toil and Trouble* (New York: Dell, Delta Book, 1964), pp. 150–151. Randolph's first impressions of an AFL convention: *Messenger,* November 1926. John Brophy on Randolph ("a thorn in the side of prejudice . . ."): "The Reminiscences of John Brophy," Oral History Collection of Columbia University, p. 542.

The attitudes toward Randolph at various AFL conventions: Milton Webster recalls that "nobody spoke to him . . .": *Report of Proceedings of the Second Triennial and Thirty-first Anniversary of the Brotherhood . . . ,* September 10–14, 1956, p. 11. Randolph, Julius Hochman, and A. H. Raskin are quoted from interviews. Jacob Potofsky is quoted from "The Reminiscences of Jacob Potofsky," Oral History Collection of Columbia University, p. 673. James Wechsler's comment appeared in the *New York Post,* October 26, 1961.

Randolph "profoundly influenced" the "evolution of AFL racial policies": Walter Galenson, *The CIO Challenge to the AFL* (Cambridge: Harvard University Press, 1960), p. 626.

Chapter 20

Main sources are these reports of AFL-CIO convention proceedings: 1st Constitutional, December 5–8, 1955; 2nd Constitutional, December 5–12, 1957; 3rd Constitutional, September 17–23, 1959; 4th Constitutional, December 7–13, 1961; 5th Constitutional, November 14–26, 1963. Also the files of the *New York Times* and interviews with Randolph.

John L. Lewis invites Randolph to join with CIO unions: interview with Randolph. Thomas R. Brooks describes George Meany: *Toil and Trouble,* pp. 232–233.

Randolph explains the objective of his resolution at the 1959 convention in San Francisco (". . . to destroy the old principle of local trade union autonomy . . ."): interview.

General response to Meany's outburst at the 1959 convention: the *New York Post* commented editorially on September 25, 1959. The *Baltimore Afro-American*'s comments, the Trade Union Leadership Council's letter, and the NAACP's wire to Meany: from undated newspaper clipping in Randolph's files. Meany explains his remarks at off-the-record luncheon in Washington, D.C.: Drew Pearson, "Washington Merry-Go-Round," *New York Mirror,* October 11, 1959; *New York Times,* October 6, 1959; and an article by Ted Poston in the *New York Post,* October 5, 1959. Poston also wrote:

The Post learned that the official record of the AFL-CIO convention has been "amended" to drop Meany's vitriolic attack on Randolph when the latter insisted upon pushing for stronger anti-discrimination action. . . . A spokesman in Meany's Washington headquarters refused to deny or affirm the report, but said: "Surely, Mr. Meany would have the same right to amend the remarks as a Congressman has to amend his remarks in the Congressional Record."

Meany recalls the San Francisco convention incident twelve years later: interview. A. H. Raskin reports Randolph's reaction: interview. See also Raskin's story of the convention in the *Times,* September 24, 1959. Randolph says Meany's language was "the way of life in the trade union movement . . .": quoted in Drew Pearson's "Washington Merry-Go-Round," October 11, 1959. Raskin reviews the controversy ("the unhappiest aspect of the bitter exchange . . .") in the *Times,* January 21, 1960.

Founding of the Negro American Labor Council: see the *New York Times,* May 28, 1960. A speech by Randolph to the steering committee of the new organization, on November 14, 1959, states the council's philosophy and objectives (copy in his files).

The AFL-CIO Executive Council censures Randolph: see the *New York Times,* October 13, 1961. Public reaction: Richard Parrish asks where the AFL-CIO liberals were: *Times,* November 12, 1961. Roy Wilkins, Dr. Martin Luther King, Jr., and Daniel Schulder denounce the AFL-CIO: quoted in the *Times,* October 14, 1961. Jimmy Hoffa and John English back Randolph against the censure report: resolution passed by the General Executive Board of the Teamsters, December, 1961 (copy in Randolph's files). Randolph's remarks went further than those quoted in the text; he also accused his colleagues on the Executive Council of "moral paralysis, pessimism, defeatism, and cynicism" (*New York Times,* November 12, 1961).

The *Times* comments editorially on the "enormous complexity" of Randolph's "two-front battle" in its issue of October 14, 1961. James Houghton's remarks on Randolph: interview.

Meany defies Southern labor unionists' criticism of the AFL's support of the Supreme Court's 1954 desegregation decision: *American Labor,* August 1968.

Ernest Rice McKinney appraises Randolph's public career: interview. Queens Village couple criticizes Randolph's support of the UFT strike, and Randolph's reply: correspondence in Randolph's files. The activities and programs of the A. Philip Randolph Institute: interview with Rachelle Horowitz.

Chapter 21

Much of this chapter relies on interviews with Randolph and Bayard Rustin.

The emasculation of the FEPC bill by Republicans and Dixiecrats in 1950: Garfinkel, *When Negroes March,* pp. 162–170.

Murray Kempton quoted on Dr. King's rebuff by the NAACP and on Randolph being the only figure to reconcile "the painful personal differences" among civil rights leaders: see his "A. Philip Randolph," *The New Republic,* July 6, 1963. David L. Lewis on the verbal clash between Dr. King and Whitney Young: see his *King: A Critical Biography* (New York: Praeger, 1970), p. 358.

The description of the Harlem office from which Rustin organized the march is based on M. S. Handler's report to the *New York Times,* August 21, 1963.

The march opposed: the account of President Kennedy's meeting with the civil rights leaders is based on Arthur M. Schlesinger, Jr., *A Thousand Days* (Boston: Houghton Mifflin, 1965), pp. 968–973. The AFL-CIO Executive Council fails to endorse the march: *New York Times,* August 13 and 14, 1963. George Meany explains the reasons: interview. Senator Strom Thurmond's attack on Bayard Rustin: *New York Times,* August 16, 1963. According to this report, Thurmond stated that Rustin "had been sentenced on a morals charge in 1953 and that he had subsequently been arrested for vagrancy and lewdness." Rustin, as quoted in the same report, replied:

An individual involved in a character charge cannot deal with it himself. This must be done by my peers who, as you know, are the Christian ministers of the Negro communities and the civil rights leaders. . . . Character is a matter of judgment within the context of a whole life. It is for my peers to judge me and my life.

The report also quoted a public statement by Randolph, in defense of Rustin:

I am sure I speak for the combined Negro leadership in voicing my complete confidence in Bayard Rustin's character, integrity, and extraordinary ability. Twenty-two arrests in the fight for civil rights attest, in my mind, to Mr. Rustin's dedication to human ideals. That Mr. Rustin was on one occasion arrested in another connection has long been a matter of public record, and not an object of concealment. There are those who contend that this incident, which took place many years ago, voids or overwhelms Mr. Rustin's ongoing contribution to the struggle for human rights. I hold otherwise.

Randolph's address to the National Press Club: text in *U.S. News and World Report,* September 9, 1963.

Randolph on Vietnam: interview.

Chapter 22

The sections on Fanny Hansberry and Beaman Hearn are based on visits to Jacksonville and Pensacola and interviews with Randolph, Hearn, Miss Hansberry, Arthur Glass, Samuel Harper, and Eartha White.

Chandler Owen's letters: in Randolph's files.

Randolph's farewell address to the Brotherhood of Sleeping Car Porters and C. L. Dellums's accession to the presidency: "Report of Business Transacted by the Sixth Triennial Convention," September 2–4, 1968, pp. 1–18, 93–96.

Randolph's speech accepting the Clendenin Award: copy in his files.

Randolph rejoins the Socialist party: material supplied the author by the party's national office, New York City. Named at Socialist convention as honorary chairman of the party: notes of the convention, made by the author.

For Randolph's Freedom Budget program: see *The Freedom Budget for All Americans,* published by the A. Philip Randolph Institute, 1966. His more recent statement ("The problem of racial discrimination is not the reason why our society tolerates a high degree of unemployment . . ."): quoted from his epilogue, "A Policy for the Seventies," in Harold G. Vatter and Thomas Palm, eds., *The Economics of Black America* (New York: Harcourt Brace Jovanovich, 1972), pp. 291–292. Randolph to CBS interviewer on black militants: transcript of a recorded interview (in the files of the A. Philip Randolph Institute).

Account of Randolph's eightieth birthday dinner at the Waldorf: from notes by the author; and *A. Philip Randolph at 80: Tributes and Recollections,* a brochure published by the A. Philip Randolph Institute.

Welcome to Chelsea-Penn Station South: notes by the author.

Acknowledgments

I am deeply indebted to the following:

A. Philip Randolph, for his co-operation.

For interviews and recollective letters: Deacon Argrett, Gertrude Elise Ayer, Roger Baldwin, Ethel Barnett, Eubie Blake, Thelma Boozer, William Bowe, O. W. Bynum, Ulas Crowder, C. L. Dellums, Bob Delson, Max Delson, Arthur Dubin, Dr. Laurence Ervin, Nat Evans, James T. Farrell, Amy Jacques Garvey, Arthur Garvin, Arthur Glass, Fanny Hansberry, Samuel Harper, Beaman Hearn, Julius Hochman, Dr. Clarence F. Holmes, Rachelle Horowitz, James Houghton, the Reverend Henderson R. Hughes, President Lyndon B. Johnson, Reginald Johnson, Corrie Jones, Vincie Kendrick, Harry Laidler, Layle Lane, Theophilus Lewis, Ruth Lofton-Smith, Jessie Martin, Ernest Rice McKinney, Mr. and Mrs. Benjamin McLaurin, George Meany, Dr. James W. Parker, Joseph Preston, A. H. Raskin, Joseph L. Rauh, Annabelle Richardson, Oscar Rosner, Bayard Rustin, Chester Satterwhite, George S. Schuyler, Noble Sissle, Charles Spears, Judge Harold Stevens, President Harry S Truman, Liza Tutson, James Vander Zee, Mrs. Milton P. Webster, Sr., Milton P. Webster, Jr., Leigh Whipper, Eartha White, Rogers Whitaker, Lucille D. Wolfe.

The officers and staff of the following libraries, archives, and collections: Manuscript Division, Library of Congress; Chicago Historical Society; Hall Branch, Chicago Public Library; Hayden Burns Library, Jacksonville; Moorland Collection, Howard University; National Archives and Records Service (Social and Economic Records Division and Legislative, Judicial and Diplomatic Records Division); New York Public Library; Municipal Archives and Records Center, New York City; *New York Times* library (for clippings on Randolph); Oral History Collection of Columbia University; Peace Collection, Swarthmore College; William R. Perkins Library, Duke University; Franklin D. Roosevelt Library; Schomburg Collections, New York Public

Library; Tamiment Institute, New York City; Harry S Truman Library; and the Archives of Wayne State University.

Earl Browder and Jacob Potofsky, for permission to consult their "Reminiscences" at the Oral History Collection of Columbia University.

For special help in obtaining material: Frederick Coleman, U.S. Attorney, Cleveland; Olga Corey (permission to consult the Lewis Corey papers at the Columbia University Special Collections); Carl Cowl; Rachelle Horowitz and Bernice Wilds, the A. Philip Randolph Institute; Ernest Kaiser, the Schomburg Collection; I. E. Levine, Director of Public Relations, City College of New York; Archie Motley, the Chicago Historical Society; Professor Bernard John Poll, State University of New York, Albany; Dave Potter, the *Chicago Defender;* Dr. C. B. Powell, editor-publisher emeritus, the New York *Amsterdam News;* A. H. Raskin; Bayard Rustin; L. J. Shackleford, president of the Chicago division of the Brotherhood of Sleeping Car Porters; Donald Slaiman, Civil Rights Department, AFL-CIO; Evan Thomas (permission to consult the Norman Thomas papers at the New York Public Library); Poppy Cannon White.

Leslie Dunbar and the Field Foundation, for a grant to assist with the research.

Maxine Greene, Irene Sachs, Dr. Marvin Goldstein, Alfred and Syslin Small, and Irwin Suall, for indispensable help.

Daisy Grandison and Kathy Flanders, for their work on the manuscript.

Theophilus Lewis, Irving Howe, and Bayard Rustin, for reading the manuscript in whole or in part and for their helpful criticisms.

Robert Lescher, my agent, who guided me over some of the strange terrain of book publishing.

William B. Goodman, my editor at Harcourt Brace Jovanovich, who understanding quite well what he asked nevertheless asked me to write this book.

William Shawn, editor of *The New Yorker,* without whose patience, understanding, and generosity I could not have done it.

And my wife, Eugenia, who suffered me through some trying times and was unfailing in her encouragement and support.

Index